ROUSSEAU AND THE SPIRIT OF REVOLT

Rousseau
and the Spirit of Revolt

A PSYCHOLOGICAL STUDY

William H. Blanchard

Ann Arbor
The University of Michigan Press

TO MY SON,
GREG

Permissions

I wish to acknowledge the kind permission of the following publishers for authorization to reproduce some of the quoted material in this study.

Basil Blackwell & Mott, Ltd., for the material from *The Political Writings of Jean-Jacques Rousseau*, edited by C. E. Vaughan (1962).

Clarendon Press for the material from *The Letters of David Hume*, edited by J. Y. T. Greig (1932).

Librairie Armand Colin for the material from the *Correspondance générale de Jean-Jacques Rousseau*, edited by T. Dufour and P.-P. Plan (1924-34).

Editions Gallimard for the material from the first three volumes of the *Oeuvres complètes de Jean-Jacques Rousseau* in the Pléiade edition. The Bibliothèque de la Pléiade is published under the editorial direction of B. Gagnebin and M. Raymond. Additional editing and commentary are by the following:

Volume I: R. Osmont

Volume II: B. Guyon, J. Scherer and C. Guyot

Volume III: R. Derathé, F. Bouchardy, J. Starobinski, S. Stelling-Michaud, J.-D. Candaux and J. Farbre.

Editions Garnier Frères for the material from *Du Contrat social* (1962), which also contains Rousseau's first two discourses, the *Considerations on the Government of Poland*, and the letters to D'Alembert and Christopher de Beaumont. Garnier has also given permission for the quotations from *Émile ou de l'Éducation*, edited by F. and P. Richard (1961).

Chez A. Jullien, for the material from the *Annales de la Societe Jean-Jacques Rousseau*. (1905-).

McGraw-Hill and Yale University for the material from *Boswell on the Grand Tour: Germany and Switzerland 1764,* edited by F. A. Pottle (1955).

William Morrow & Co., Inc. for the material from *The Splendid Century: Life in the France of Louis XIV* by W. H. Lewis (1957).

Thomas Nelson & Sons, Ltd. for the material from *The Life of David Hume* by E. C. Mossner (1954).

Cambridge University Press for the material from *Jean-Jacques Rousseau, A Critical Study of His Life and Writings* by F. C. Green (1955).

Preface

Many creatures and natural phenomena are threatening to man. But they have a certain aspect of menace or give a warning which can serve as a signal for avoidance. Only man has learned to disguise his malevolent intentions with an amiable gesture. From this capacity we derive our sense of the diabolical. No story of genuine evil is complete without it, from the grinning wolf of Little Red Riding Hood to Hamlet's discovery that a man can smile and smile and be a villain. Even murder, performed in a moment of hot anger, seems at times less evil than hypocrisy.

Thus, Rousseau discovered the meaning of evil when he encountered the society of eighteenth-century Paris. His first discourse, which was addressed to the question of the effect of science and the arts on morals, did not really come to grips with the influence of science and the arts. With Rousseau it was never a question of science and philosophy per se, but the genuine desire for truth versus the pompous display of erudition. It was the polite urbanity of civilization versus the honesty of man's natural inclinations that he wished to portray. A society which had prescribed forms of behavior for every occasion not only masked the true nature of man, but opened the door to evil. For here a devil could masquerade as a gentleman.

> Before art had fashioned our manners and taught our passions to speak an affected language, our morals were primitive but natural; and the differences in conduct proclaimed at first glance the varieties of character. Human nature was not basically any better, but men found their security in the ease with which they could see through each other; and this advantage, of which we no longer understand the value, spared them many vices.[1]

It was, then, the origin of evil that he sought to investigate in his first discourse. Here, also, while condemning science and art, he raised the icon of truth and made it synonymous with virtue. We cannot believe that he had never met a false person before he came to Paris or that he had never been false to anyone himself. What is remarkable in Rousseau, in spite of his failure to achieve the complete candor he sought for himself, was the intensity of his desire. That a man can love virtue and seek personal honesty, that he can determine to cast aside his defenses and show himself just as he is—and fail in the attempt—is one of the intriguing mysteries of psychology.

Jean-Jacques Rousseau was one of the first explorers of the world of veracity, a world which appears quite different when one is swimming over the surface. In the plunge into the depths one faces strange ambiguities not previously visible. It is a landscape of the absurd, with sharp contradictions. Not surprisingly, therefore, a man accustomed to the commonplace mendacity of our society finds himself, in such surroundings, beyond the reach of his own thought, drifting into a paradox from which there is no escape. In these depths Rousseau suffered a lonely and terrifying death of the spirit, but he was able to record his experience for mankind, to leave a warning of the dangers and a challenge for others to understand his ordeal.

The problem encountered by Rousseau seems to have become one of the great dilemmas of modern man. While scientists discover daily more facts than we can assimilate, truth, in the sense of veracity, recedes ever farther from our reach. Camus has said that there are truths but no truth;[2] yet each nation, each faction, each human creature clings with a certain fatal resolve to its own particular verity. In recent years, while the deft theoretician turns truth into doctrine with surprising alacrity, we have seen these doctrines become vehicles for aggrandizement. The urge to make men free has become an exportable commodity, and it now spills more blood than the ancient desire for conquest. The discovery of the importance of sexual satisfaction has called forth a knowing smile of fulfillment to advertise everything from perfume to pills.

We have ample cause to seek a society which encourages candor in its policies and pronouncements as well as in its human relationships. But the sick citizen faces a severe test when he encounters the plague. That difficult and dangerous frontier in the relationship between man and his society is littered with the discarded utopias and the broken promises of past civilizations. Yet it is from this very region that we must gain the understanding to solve the most challenging social problems of our day.

Jean-Jacques Rousseau sought to discover the relationship between personal candor and good government, opening the door to a new field of study. Recognizing that this task required an unusual moral courage, he declared himself ready and set out upon his venture. From a modern vantage point, with the insights into human nature recently acquired, it is clear that he was not fully aware of the risks he faced. In his effort to shape the structure of the good society he came face to face with his own weakness. But his failure was never a complete rout. In his bold approach he overturned some of the sacred falsehoods of his age. In his effort to tell the "truth" about himself and his society, he has brought us face to face with the relative nature of truth. By his honesty he has exposed the limitations of a simple, unreflective honesty. In his attempt at frankness he questions the sincerity of us all.

This book can best be decribed as a psychological study of Rousseau and his political ideas. However, I have tried, whenever possible, to avoid psychoanalytic terminology. Rousseau has proved a fascinating subject for psychological study from the time of Janet, and previous writers have scrutinized him thoroughly. Proal[3] has summarized the results of a number of these studies, Heidenhain[4] has examined Rousseau from a psychiatric point of view, Starobinski[5] has completed a very sensitive and penetrating study of Rousseau's ideas and the concept of transparency, and Guéhenno,[6] while writing a biographical study, has illuminated many aspects of Rousseau's character. Despite the many studies available on Rousseau, there is a particular facet of his psychology which has been incompletely explored and which, I believe, has a unique importance for our time. This is his work in the political field, particularly in the politics of revolution. By the term, "political," I have in mind a concept much broader than the one Vaughan employed in his study of Rousseau's *Political Writings.*[7] With Rousseau almost every idea was colored by political implications. In *Emile*, his book on education, and one of his most profoundly political works, one finds the very basis for the idea of thought control, a concept applied with greater force in his *Considerations on the Government of Poland.* Because of the broad sense in which I have interpreted the field of politics the scope of my study of Rousseau's political writings is both more extensive and less complete than Vaughan's. For example, I have examined the first *Discourse*, the *Letter to d'Alembert*, and *Emile*[8]—all disregarded by Vaughan—whereas I have not discussed in detail such works as the *Letters from the Mountain* and many of Rousseau's minor political fragments. Space limitations and the necessity of dealing with Rousseau's life experiences have precluded more detailed discussion. It has seemed more important to show the relationship between his life and his politics than to give further examples of his political ideas. I have attempted to trace the evolution of Rousseau's childhood sado-masochism to the moral foundation for his adult personality. I have taken this particular facet of his rich and varied psychological life as a basis for demonstrating the relationship between personality and political belief. Of necessity many aspects of his psychodynamics which might tempt the depth psychologist and which have been discussed more fully by other writers have been omitted. I have also, for the most part, passed over the work of such writers as Cassirer,[9] Choulguine,[10] Cobban,[11] Derathé,[12] Durkheim,[13] and Hendel,[14] who have effectively demonstrated the many influences besides the psychological which were important in the evolution of Rousseau's political ideas, namely, the Calvinist religion, the city of Geneva, and writers such as Montesquieu and Grotius, some of whom he refuted and others whose ideas he incorporated.

My object is not to present a complete critique of Rousseau's political writings. This has been done before. But many of Rousseau's most ardent followers behaved as though they had never read his political works. Rousseau talked about ideas, but there was a feeling behind his ideas which was expressed with even greater eloquence. It was as though he were saying to his readers, "Don't do what I say; do what I feel!" Some of his ideas were directly contrary to those of the leaders of the French Revolution. In many respects he was a conservative—even for his time. Yet the revolutionists hailed him as a hero, and his works had considerable importance in shaping both the direction and emotional climate of the French Revolution. It is my contention that the revolutionists knew their man. In calling on the name of Rousseau they were responding to something that cannot be found in his works if one reads them for their intellectual content alone. Perhaps this is why he has been such an enigma for so many years. Scholars have studied his works and neatly lined up the ideas. Removed from their context, these ideas no longer stir the hair at the back of a man's neck. In like manner the heart is impotent when it lies on the dissecting table.

I would like to carry the reader back into the time of Rousseau to enable him to feel as did Rousseau. I want him to feel the heat of Rousseau's anger at his enemies and the agony of his conflict between pride and self-loathing. I wish to give the reader the sense of Rousseau's peculiar groveling arrogance—from inside, not just as an observer, for I am convinced that the men of the Revolution felt as Rousseau did; they identified with him.

But I do not want to end merely with an appreciation of Rousseau's feelings. There is much to be learned about both him and ourselves if we can discover how he failed in his search for truth. It is important to understand him with the intellect as well as with the heart.

It was characteristic of him that an air of sweetness masked his strong hostile impulses. He loved mankind, particularly the weak. But out of his sweetness there flowered a destructive force that would have laid waste the world if it could have been harnessed to one of our modern weapons. I think it is important to penetrate Rousseau's mask of sweetness because I see much of his spirit in the United States today. There is something very nice and very virtuous about us in America. Like Rousseau, we want to save the world. We pity the unfortunate peoples of the earth. But there is something about this pity that frightens me. I am afraid of where it may take us if we do not look deep into its source and examine, with a critical eye, our need for righteousness.

ACKNOWLEDGMENTS

The primary sources consulted for this study have been the Pléiade edition of Rousseau's collected works, especially the *Confessions*, Dufour's voluminous *Correspondance générale*, and Vaughan's *Political Writings of Jean-Jacques Rousseau*. After this study was well underway I came upon Alexander and Juliet George's psychological study of Woodrow Wilson, which impressed me by its readability and freedom from technical jargon. I have attempted to produce a book which will have a similar clarity of expression.

I am indebted to the authorities of the Bibliothèque de l'Institut de France for permission to study some of Rousseau's letters, to M. Eric Berthoud, director of the Bibliothèque de Neuchâtel, for permission to examine the collection of Rousseau's original manuscripts, and, in particular, to Mlle Claire Rosselet, former director of the Bibliothèque de Neuchâtel for assisting me in many ways, both with manuscript material and in deciphering Rousseau's handwriting. An attempt to study the rough changes in Rousseau's manuscripts in relation to the alteration of his personality was abandoned as it appeared to be unproductive.

The easy informality which prevails in many university libraries has made it possible for me to make use of several Rousseau collections and related material without fee or formal application. In this connection I would like to thank the Widener Library at Harvard, the Sorbonne in Paris, and the University Research Library at the University of California, Los Angeles.

I have translated into English quotations from sources in which the text is in French. Whenever I have made a rather free translation (or where the meaning is particularly important), I have followed the translation with the original French in parentheses. I have not found any of the current translations completely satisfactory for my purposes, but I have often been influenced by reading the following:

Rousseau, J.-J., *The Social Contract and Discourses*, translated, with an introduction, by G. D. H. Cole (New York: Dutton, 1950).

Rousseau, J.-J., *A Lasting Peace Through the Federation of Europe and the State of War*, translated by C. E. Vaughan (London: Constable, 1917).

Rousseau, J.-J., *Political Writings*, translated and edited by F. Watkins (London: Nelson, 1953).

Rousseau, J.-J., *Émile*, translated by Barbara Foxley, with an introduction by A. B. de Monvel (London: Dent, 1955).

Rousseau, J.-J., *The Confessions of Jean-Jacques Rousseau*, translated by J. M. Cohen (London: Penguin, 1954).

Unfortunately, space does not permit a detailed description of the assistance I have received from friends and colleagues in the fields of history, political science, French literature, and psychoanalytic theory. For the correction of many errors, repair of oversights, and the slow and painful pruning of cherished but unnecessary paragraphs I am indebted to Crane Brinton, Guy Endore, Alexander George, George Havens, Harold Lasswell, Ernest Lawrence, Nathan Leites, Benjamin Nelson, Elias Porter, Arnold Rogow, Ralph Ross, Harry Silberman, George Wilbur, and Victor Wolfenstein. I would also like to express my thanks to Carol Talpers and Aryline Strobel, who have given their time to work on editorial problems in the preparation of the manuscript, and Catherine Lambert, who has checked some of my French translation.

Contents

"The first man to attack, not this or that idea or philosophy, but the very foundations of traditional civilization, had to be someone who was not a part of it: Jean-Jacques Rousseau."

—William Ebenstein, *Great Political Thinkers*

"It is a question, indeed, whether Jean-Jacques ever thought at all—whether he ever realized the difference between assertion and demonstration, or between prejudice and conviction—whether his arguments ever amounted to more than the rhetorical expression of a personality—whether it was not because he gave philosophic speciousness to random declamation that the men of the revolution hailed him as a prophet."

—Francis Gribble, *Rousseau and the Women He Loved*

"His reasonings always proceeded from principles, which were, it is true, the offspring of a distempered imagination that disqualified him from cool enquiry, but the consequences he deduced from them were so strictly logical, that it was impossible to view, without astonishment, a display of so much sagacity and so much folly upon the same topic."

—Olivier de Corancez, *Anecdotes of the Last Twelve Years of the Life of J. J. Rousseau*

". . . it may be doubted whether even professed students of the subject have yet grasped either the vast range of thought which Rousseau opened up, or the goal to which it pointed."

—C. E. Vaughan, *The Political Writings of Jean-Jacques Rousseau*

On Stage

I

THE GENEVA OF ROUSSEAU'S CHILDHOOD was a city dominated by the Reformation and, above all, by the spirit of Calvin. In 1712 when Rousseau was born, Calvin had been dead for more than a century and a half, but his influence still shaped the laws and customs of his city. The Consistory (a body of elders and clergymen) watched over the morals of Geneva and regulated the minute details of the citizen's life. Sumptuary laws forbade luxury in dress, such as silk gowns or gold trim, limited the amount of jewelry that could be worn, the number of servants, the number of guests at various types of celebrations and parties, and prescribed the dishes that could be served (with special prohibitions in regard to dessert) and the cost of wedding presents and other gifts. The elders of the city were permitted to enter any home to ensure that the laws of the community were followed. The good citizens were themselves derelict in their duty if they did not notify the Consistory when a neighbor violated these solemn regulations. Even the hours of rising and retiring were specified by law, for sleep itself, if carried beyond the minimum requirements for health, was considered to be a self indulgence offensive in the sight of God. In many respects the atmosphere of Geneva was similar to that of the early Puritan settlements in America,[1] in which hard-working, sober, serious people kept a sharp eye on their neighbors and did not allow dancing, public amusements, or professional entertainers. There were, however, some striking differences. The city was a self-contained unit with an esteemed tradition and certain major institutions which dominated the countryside. The university was one of the institutions which, from the days of Calvin, had been an influential and highly respected force in the community. Geneva was a city of intellect as well as industry, and while the ideas that circulated among the citizens were hinged and fenced by an overriding caution about sinful suggestions, there were, nevertheless, many influences which tended to broaden their perspective and reopen closed issues. Geneva was an international city. Many foreigners lived within the protection of its walls. Some had business there, and others had come to escape persecution at home.

Among the latter group was an ancestor of Jean-Jacques, Didier Rousseau.

While many of the refugees, on becoming citizens, found a more severe tyranny in the Genevan government than they had escaped at home, they bore their new chains without complaint, proud that, as responsible voters, they had fashioned each link themselves. There was a certain innocence in this republican pride, since the Council of Two Hundred selected the candidates for public office and determined beforehand that the citizens chosen would be those above reproach.[2] The Genevans were protected from many of the abuses of a democracy and retained unsullied their naive faith in "popular" choice. Since they believed in the benevolence of their elected magistrates they did not hesitate to deliver into the hands of the officials those neighbors who failed to observe the laws of the city.

To an outsider such a dour and watchful community might well seem intolerable. To Voltaire it was an envious beehive distilling gall instead of honey. Ritter has given us a graphic picture of the sad, serious aspect of Geneva. He reports, for example, that David Rousseau, another of Jean-Jacques' forefathers, was chastised for playing the violin and permitting dancing in his home[3] and that Rousseau's own mother, Suzanne Bernard, caused a scandal by leaving the city, unescorted and disguised as a peasant, to visit a theater in the vicinity.[4] There was, however, another quality to Geneva not to be found in public records and legal documents. Rousseau tells us of societies for discussion and debate, of public dinners in the parks, of improvised wrestling and boxing matches, and of dancing in the streets with the wine flowing freely.[5] He remarks on the occasional drunkenness and profanity accompanying these gatherings and on the general feeling of community acceptance of such behavior. The sober citizens did not like to advertise this aspect of their community, and Jean-Jacques was severely censured for his efforts to show that the Genevans were capable of enjoying themselves. Yet his description serves as an interesting contrast to the dry and stiff Geneva seen by most visitors.

Geneva was, in short, a city of many conflicting influences. Set in the heart of European intrigue, its political life retained a certain innocent simplicity. Devoted to God, its citizens developed, nevertheless, a sound business sense and a phenomenal capacity to prosper in this world. While they lived under one of the most severe and detailed codes of moral restraint in the West, the people were capable of a spontaneous and almost childlike gaiety. Although candidates for public office were selected by the local aristocracy, the inhabitants retained a sense of being their own masters and a conviction that a righteous man among them need fear no one but God. This was the city of Jean-Jacques Rousseau.

II

Rousseau's mother died about eight days after his birth, but her presence was to haunt his entire childhood. By the time he was old enough to understand the meaning of "mother," she had already become a family legend. She had become, for him, a kind of goddess: charming, wise, cultured, a distillation of all the mystery, sensitivity and intuition which have been attributed to womankind. From Ritter's search of the early records of Geneva we learn that in the eyes of the Consistory Suzanne Bernard was less goddess and more woman—perhaps more of a compliment to her than the elders of Geneva would concede. Her beauty and charm as a young woman are evidenced by the apparently irresistible attraction she exerted on a M. Vincent Sarasin, a thirty-six year old married man and father of two children who was warned several times by the Consistory that he must cease his attempts to see Mlle Bernard. M. Sarasin, for his part, expressed some surprise when called by the Consistory, since he had already discussed this troublesome attraction with Pastor Gaudy and agreed to try to discontinue the relationship.[6]

Apparently, his attempt was unsuccessful, for soon he was tearing down the hedge in the rear of the Bernard home in order to see the fascinating Suzanne, only to be met by the watchful Pastor Bernard. After returning to knock on the front door and again being intercepted by the alert father, M. Sarasin gave it up as a bad day and left for home. When called before the Consistory for this incident, the distraught lover invented the wild tale that he was considering the purchase of the property next door and was examining it "inside and out," that he knew Mlle Bernard was not home and had already explained to her skeptical father that he was not trying to see her. The members of the Consistory, finding this story rather difficult to believe, censured him severely. Nor did Suzanne escape without damage to her reputation. Despite the protestations of her parents and other relatives, the Consistory assumed that such a devout admirer must have had at least mild encouragement.[7]

Suzanne, however, had other qualities besides her charm. We have already noted her defiance of the laws regarding attendance at theaters. The Consistory also records that when she was called before them to explain her behavior, she refused to come and had to be sent for.[8] It was perhaps as much her spirit as her beauty which brought her to the attention of Isaac Rousseau, Jean-Jacques's father.

Isaac was highly erratic and unpredictable. He worked for a while as a watchmaker's apprentice. Then, impatient with the long period of preparation, he gave up this work to become a dancing master. In Geneva such an occupation placed him on the lower fringes of society, and since he was able to teach only foreigners (no respectable Genevese would study dancing) he was not very successful. He traveled a great deal, apparently to see the world outside Geneva, and finally resumed his apprenticeship and became a master watchmaker.

Rousseau does not mention how his father met Suzanne, but he reports their marriage as a "triumph of love." They were, he says, passionately devoted to each other, but fate blocked their marriage. Finally, Gabriel Bernard, Suzanne's brother, fell in love with Theodora Rousseau, the sister of Isaac. Theodora, he tells us, refused to marry Gabriel unless her brother could marry Suzanne. "Love arranged everything and the two marriages took place on the same day."[9] Unfortunately for this romantic tale, Ritter discovered in the records of the Consistory that Gabriel and Theodora "scandalously anticipated" their marriage and that a son was born October 19, 1699, eight days after the ceremony.[10] It was probably through this first marriage between the families that Suzanne and Isaac met. They were married five years later.

Marriage, however, did not dampen the wanderlust of the impetuous Isaac. After the birth of his first son, François, he was off on a long trip to Constantinople, probably as a result of difficulties with his mother-in-law, who lived in the same house with him. He returned six years later in 1711, shortly after the death of his wife's mother.[11] Jean-Jacques was born June 28, 1712—"the sad fruit of this return"[12] and the herald of his mother's death. Isaac was thrown into a fit of grief at the loss of his wife whom he had so recently rediscovered, and he was unconsolable for years to come. The agony of this loss was the source of a peculiarly intense and ambivalent feeling between the young Rousseau and his father. Isaac's love for Jean-Jacques was always accompanied by tears and the child sensed "by his sighs and his convulsive embrace that there was a bitter regret mingled with his caresses."[13] There was in this relationship not only the mixture of pain and love, but the older Rousseau's attempt to recapture his wife in his son, who resembled her. He constantly told the young man that he was more to him than a son and as the older man embraced him, Jean-Jacques got the strong impression that the emotional excitement of his grief actually intensified his feeling of love. "Give her back to me," the older Rousseau would cry, "console me for her"[14] as though he were demanding of the young man that he repay him for the loss of his wife by assuming her identity. Thus, there developed in the young Rousseau a strong sense of guilt about the death of his mother, a guilt reinforced by his father's constantly describing the beauty, talent, and moral worth of the mother and reminding the son, amid tears of affection, of the terrible loss he had inflicted on the world.[15]

Rousseau's guilt must have been all the more painful since he was unable to feel genuinely the loss of his mother. She was someone he had never known, but he was expected to weep for her as though he remembered her affection with the same warmth and directness as did his father. When Isaac would suggest that they talk of her, Jean-Jacques would reply, "Very well, father, but we are going to cry."[16] Yet it was this very agony of tears and reminiscences that seemed to stimulate the older man to his greatest affection toward young Jean-Jacques. Here, in his early childhood we find the first signs of that strong association between pleasure and suffering that was to dominate his life.

While Isaac was a hot-tempered and severe father, he was capable of a spontaneous indulgence toward his younger son. Rousseau recalls that his older brother, François, was often neglected and abused, but he asserts that he had only the most tender affection for him, even though the fellow began to acquire low habits and was seldom seen around the house. François, he says, returned his love—to the extent that a profligate is capable of loving.[17] Obviously, there was some reservation about this fraternal tenderness. The situation was one which would be likely to arouse the most severe rivalry between the two boys.[18] Rousseau, however, remembered only feelings of love and pity. In his *Confessions* he describes a beating of François by his father and his own attempt to intervene by throwing his arms around his brother and receiving the blows intended for him.[19] This feeling of communality in suffering was soon to be repeated with his cousin Abraham.

The frequent absence of François and his eventual fall from parental grace produced in the elder Rousseau an even greater attachment to his second son. Isaac and Jean-Jacques became close companions, and the two of them spent hours together reading the romantic novels left by the mother, as though to capture her presence again through her favorite books. Sometimes they would read until dawn, and when Isaac heard the morning larks he would declare with sudden shame that he was more of a child than Jean-Jacques.[20]

After they had finished the novels of Suzanne, they turned to the books of the maternal grandfather, which were apparently of a sturdier sort—Plutarch and Ovid, for example. The young Rousseau was enthralled by Plutarch and the lives of heroes. The romantic novels of his mother had prepared him to see all history as a grand romantic adventure, and he readily imagined himself in the leading role. The weeping and remorse indulged in from time to time with his father had already developed in him a special predilection for the hero who suffers. Thus, it is not surprising that, while he read many novels and histories, there is only one hero whom he remembers having imitated as a child. This was Scaevola, the Roman warrior who held his hand in the flame of a burning brazier to show his indifference to pain when Porsena threatened to have him burned alive. Rousseau was reading the story of Scaevola to the family during a meal when he suddenly grasped a hot chafing dish in imitation of his hero. He mentions that the family was quite startled by his behavior, but there is no indication that he was punished or reprimanded in any way.[21]

Another particularly striking incident from his childhood demonstrates his capacity to gain favorable attention and even to profit from his ability to convey a sense of pathos. His father had ordered him to go to bed without supper for some piece of mischief. Rousseau passed through the kitchen where he had to say goodnight to the various members of the family. Then, standing before a joint of beef with his poor slice of bread in his hand, he said in a pitiful voice, "goodnight roast."[22] This little performance earned him a full supper. His father's anger was apparently easily managed by a pathetic demonstration from his favored son.

His Aunt Susan took the place of his mother in the home, and being a gentle woman she made little attempt to discipline the young Jean-Jacques. Apparently, her indulgent and tender care evoked some of the inexpressible and painful longing he felt toward his lost mother. In his attitude toward his aunt were the beginnings of that strange tender-tearful feeling which was to play such a prominent part in his relationships with the other women in his life. Rousseau recalled a song of his aunt's which was one of the few he could remember from his childhood; a song which he could never finish humming without a flood of tears—even in his old age.

Looking back at these childhood experiences of Rousseau, one gets a feeling of something theatrical, something that does not quite ring true about his early life. One sees a little boy on stage, always performing for the applause of his family, always overacting in his tearful scenes, as though he must keep up his performance in order to be loved. In spite of his insistence that he was the darling of his father and his aunt, one senses a strong anxiety about his performances. It is as though he was always conscious of the terrible calamity which his birth brought to the family, and he had to distract them with his histrionics to keep them from remembering his guilt. No doubt the romances he read with his father helped to teach him the method, but an acute sense of guilt was certainly the driving force behind his behavior. "Rousseau the actor" reappears several times in this book. Like many another actor he frequently lived his part so well that he believed it himself.

III

It was not long before Rousseau's excitable father became involved in a dispute with a French captain and determined to leave town and break up his family rather than suffer the indignity of arrest. Jean-Jacques was placed in the care of his Uncle Bernard, who sent him to board with Pastor Lambercier "to learn, along with Latin, that petty rubbish that goes by the name of education."[23] His cousin, Abraham Bernard, was sent with him to the pastor's home and became his close companion. It was here, at the hands of the pastor's sister, that Rousseau experienced the first awareness of his awakening sensuality and of the masochistic nature of his sexual feelings. Mlle Lambercier was an affectionate woman who permitted the two boys to sleep with her, but she was also the disciplinarian.

> As Mlle Lambercier had a mother's affection for us, she also exercised a mother's authority, which she sometimes carried to the point of inflicting some children's punishment on us when we deserved it. For a long time she was content to threaten, and the threat of a punishment which I had never experienced appeared very frightening.[24] But when it came I found the reality less terrible than the anticipation; and the strange thing is that this punishment increased my affection for the one who inflicted it. It required all the strength of my affection and all my natural gentleness to prevent me from seeking the return of this same treatment by further disobedience, for I had found in the suffering, in the very shame of the beating, an element of sensuality which left me with more desire than fear of receiving another punishment by the same hand. . . . Who would have believed that this childish punishment, received at the age of eight by the hand of a woman of thirty,[25] should decide my tastes, my desires, my passions, my very self for the rest of my life, and in a direction quite opposite from the one in which they should have developed naturally. Once my feelings were inflamed my desires went so far astray that, limited as they were to this early experience, they never sought any other kind. In spite of the sensuality which seethed in my blood I preserved myself pure and unsullied up to the age when the

coldest and most phlegmatic temperaments have developed. Tormented for a long time without knowing why, I devoured beautiful women with my feverish eyes, my imagination recalled them incessantly, only to make use of them in my fashion as so many Mlle Lamberciers.[26]

This spanking scene, mentioned by numerous writers, was certainly a factor in the development of Rousseau's adult attitude.[27] Yet many children are spanked by women. We not only note the spanking but also the thorough preparation he had already received in the art of deriving pleasure from suffering. The convulsive embraces of his father, the Scaevola episode, the whole tenor of his childhood points to a developing tendency toward masochism long before this incident.[28] The spanking by Mlle Lambercier, who permitted him to sleep with her and who probably aroused his sexual feeling, merely served to localize a general and diffuse libidinal excitement which he had already experienced in connection with suffering for his father.

The sexual pleasure derived from the spanking of Mlle Lambercier might have continued for some time had she not begun to suspect that Rousseau was enjoying his punishment. Under the pretext that she found it exhausting, she discontinued this form of discipline and gave the two boys a room of their own, instead of permitting them to sleep in her bed. However, another opportunity for Rousseau to suffer a masochistic satisfaction soon came his way. This second situation would probably have meant no more to him than the frequent childhood experience of injustice if it had not been preceded by his physical pleasure in suffering. He was accused of breaking some teeth from a comb belonging to Mlle Lambercier. Questioned and threatened, he continued to protest his innocence. His cousin was also accused of "another crime no less grave,"[29] and both continued to maintain their innocence. This stubborn denial in the face of what seemed to be good evidence against the boys called for more severe punishment, and Rousseau's Uncle Bernard was sent for. He administered the punishment instead of Mlle Lambercier, and this time it was severe and painful.

Now a new element enters the picture. The physical punishment was administered by a man, and the intense pain diminished the sensual gratification formerly obtained from it. Instead, he found rising in him the proud, fierce exhilaration of righteous indignation. This time the real satisfaction came from his thrill of injured innocence—the glorious feeling of the martyr who suffers nobly for his cause.

The bodily pain, although severe, I hardly sensed; I felt only indignation, rage, despair. My cousin, in a case very much like my own, had been punished for an involuntary fault as though it were a premeditated action. He became infuriated after my example and, so to speak, raised himself to a level of excitement in keeping with my own. Together in the same bed we embraced each other with convulsive transports, suffocating ourselves, and when our young hearts were relieved enough to express our anger, we sat up and cried a hundred times with all our might: Carnifex![30] Carnifex! Carnifex!

I feel, in writing this, my pulse beating faster; these moments will always be with me even if I should live a hundred thousand years. That first sense of violence and injustice has remained so deeply engraved on my soul that every idea related to it brings back my first emotion, and this feeling, related only to myself in its origin, has developed such a consistency in itself and has become so detached from personal interest, that my heart is inflamed at the spectacle or the tale of every act of injustice whoever may be the object and wherever it is committed, as though the effect of it were to fall upon myself.[31]

While Rousseau suffered a great deal as a result of this beating, it is clear that he also derived from it a certain pleasure, a feeling of outraged innocence, that raised him in his imagination far above his "torturers." This experience represented the beginning of a striking change in his masochistic impulse, the change from sexual masochism to moral masochism. It provided him with a father he could hate, thus releasing, to some degree, the strong aggressive impulses which he had restrained in the presence of his real father. Further, his hatred helped him to mask the sexual aspect of his masochistic feelings. Formerly, he felt guilty when he was aroused by punishment, but now the joy in suffering gave him a pure feeling of virtue. Physical pleasure in suffering was minimized, and he developed a feeling of being socially uplifted, fine and noble. He was able to remain unaware of his aggressive and hostile feelings toward others when he played the role of martyr. As long as he could believe that others were persecuting him through no fault of his own, he could keep his conscience at rest. Thus, he constantly arranged situations so that people would abuse him.

But this picture of the suffering Rousseau gives only one side of his complex character. Rousseau had strong aggressive impulses which were held back in early childhood. The normal boyhood impulses to fight, to conquer, and to hate one's enemies had been thwarted in him. He was petted and protected by his father and aunt and was never allowed to run into the street and play with other children. He was raised as a hothouse plant and schooled in the suppression of anger.

However, once his guilt was assuaged the anger could come out. Not long after the second spanking incident Rousseau was engaged in street fights in defense of his cousin Abraham. He was crusading for the underdog, and aggression never troubled his conscience in such situations. He found that once he could recapture his feeling of injured innocence, he could permit himself to be thoroughly vindictive. He was normally a timid fellow, but when he began to burn with righteous indignation he became bold. While he often boasted of his kind and gentle disposition, he secretly disliked his timidity and longed to overcome it. His passion for justice gave him the opportunity. In describing his feelings after the beating from Uncle Bernard, he tells how his blood boiled at any tale of injustice and how he always put himself in the place of the victim, hating the persecutor. It is only a step from this point to the turning of the victim on his persecutor. The underdog now becomes the tyrant and the masochist becomes a sadist. In fact, Rousseau's next words are:

> When I read of the cruelties of a fierce tyrant, or the subtle atrocities of a rascally priest, I would willingly go and stab these wretches, even if I should perish a hundred times in the act. I have often worked up a sweat chasing or throwing stones at a cock, a cow, a dog, any animal that I saw tormenting another merely because it felt itself stronger.[32]

If one observes a little boy charging down the street after a frightened cock, flinging stones at it as he runs, one thinks only of the cruelty of children. One has to look into the mind of the child to discover that he has identified with the cock's victim and is really chasing a tyrant. However, it is never difficult to find a justification for cruelty if the desire is there. Freud's observation that masochism and sadism are but two sides of the same coin, two expressions of the same basic impulse, is nowhere better illustrated than in the personality of Jean-Jacques Rousseau.[33]

This sadistic quality in sweet and gentle creatures makes the age-old problem of good and evil complex. Our rejected side often comes back to take us unaware when we are most secure in our righteousness. Such was the case with Jean-Jacques. His struggle for virtue against the malevolent adversary within himself represents one of the most difficult battles of the human mind. And it is all the more remarkable when we remember that it was a battle in darkness against an unknown assailant—for Rousseau never accepted nor understood his sadistic impulses. He looked everywhere for his mysterious enemy except the one place where he dared not inquire.

IV

There are two other experiences from the childhood of Rousseau which seem to serve as models for many of his adult relationships. These were his simultaneous "affairs" with Mlle Goton and Mlle Vulson, which took place when he was about twelve. He introduces the story of these two women in the *Confessions*, describing how he tyrannized and monopolized Mlle Vulson and how he was completely submissive with Mlle Goton. The relationship with Mlle Vulson appears to have been the rather typical attraction of an older girl for a young boy who adores her. She enjoyed being with him and making a show of kindness toward him in order to attract older admirers. But for Rousseau, it was a very serious affair, and he was brokenhearted when he discovered that she was to be married. His friendship with Mlle Vulson had about it a certain platonic quality, a calmness which distinguishes it clearly from his other affair. He said of Mlle Vulson, "I loved her as a brother, but I was as jealous as a lover."[34]

With Mlle Goton, however, the relationship was decidedly sexual. Rousseau does not tell her age, but she appears to have been younger than Mlle Vulson. It is probably the only time in his life that he met a girl who sensed his masochistic needs and who complemented them with certain desires of her own. He describes her as a rather proud, overbearing little person who enjoyed giving orders. The two of them played a game in which he was a schoolboy and she was the schoolmistress. The relationship that developed was rather similar to his encounter with Mlle Lambercier except that in this case the girl was apparently deliberately exciting him.

> . . . the strangest thing about her was a mixture of boldness and reserve difficult to imagine. She took the greatest liberties with me, but never allowed me to take any with her; she treated me exactly like a child: which makes me think that she had either ceased to be one or that, on the contrary, she was enough of a child to see nothing but play in the danger to which she exposed herself.[35]

His reference to the exact nature of these "liberties" is always vague. He mentions only that the favors she granted were those to be "asked for on my knees"[36] and that he was completely submissive to her. However, the favor that he desired from her is unmistakable: He would have liked to have her spank him on the buttocks. He was much too ashamed of this desire to ask for it openly, yet he tells us in his *Confessions* that this was for him the ultimate sexual experience.

My old childish taste, instead of passing away, became so closely associated with the other (sexual attraction) that I could never separate it from any of the desires kindled by my senses; and this madness, added to my natural timidity, has left me with very little initiative in the presence of women. I have never dared to ask and have not been able to take what I wanted since the type of pleasure I required—to which the other is only the culmination—can neither be taken by him who wants it nor guessed by her who could grant it. Thus I have passed my life in silent yearning among those I loved most. Never daring to mention my peculiar taste, I achieved at least some satisfaction from relationships which retained a suggestion of it.[37]

Clearly, a relationship which suggested his secret desires was the one with his haughty little "schoolmistress." She would browbeat him, give him orders, perhaps even spank him from time to time. At least she kept him in a fever of anticipation of such a spanking, for he trembled with expectation whenever he was in her presence. The pleasure from this experience with Mlle Goton was so intense that it frightened him. He was aware that if she had commanded him to perform a dangerous act, he would do it instantly, and he mentions his fear that he could not have survived his experience with her much longer. "My own heart beats would have choked me."[38] Rousseau's elders soon discovered that there was more than childish play in his experience with Mlle Goton, and the two were separated. But this experience with a commanding woman had been firmly imprinted on his character, and he was to be particularly receptive to a woman who would pretend to dominate him.

The word "pretend" is here extremely significant and it was to have important implications for his later relationships with women.[39] Rousseau wanted only to play games with the girls. As long as both parties understood that it was just a game, he would go to any lengths to carry out his part of the performance, but if a woman of noble birth tried to command him because of her position in society or remind him of his obligations to her, the relationship changed immediately. It became a kind of moral sado-masochism with Rousseau goading and provoking his victim, watching for the slightest sign of her impatience, and then accusing her of tyranny. Once a woman had presumed to take seriously her power to command him, he was on the attack.

There were few women in his life who both sensed his need and had the ability to strike the right note in their relationship with him. It was always a woman with a certain childlike, playful quality about her who was able to charm him and obtain his devotion without rousing his anger. He was extremely sensitive and vulnerable when he was reminded of his obligations to others, but he responded by going to great lengths to show that he had no obligations to anyone. He could be completely natural and friendly with children and dogs because they demanded nothing of him, but the expectation that he show a kindness when he did not feel it would rouse him to fury.

[2]

The Wanderer

I

THE GUILT-RIDDEN FANTASIES OF HIS CHILDHOOD as well as his protected environment had developed in the young Jean-Jacques a timid and somewhat furtive personality. At the same time he was a physically attractive young man, capable of a certain open and natural friendliness. He was quick to forgive an injury if he believed that it was not intended, and he could be quite demonstrative with others when he felt secure. He already showed some signs of intelligence, but a youth without a father or mother could not be offered the luxury of an extensive education, and his uncle soon began to seek a trade for his young charge. Jean-Jacques was first sent to the office of the city registrar to learn accounting, which he found unbearably tedious. He was discharged as unfit after a short period of trial, and his uncle decided he should be apprenticed to an engraver. Thus, two months before his thirteenth birthday, he was bound to a young master, Abel Ducommun, for a five-year period. The freedom of his childhood came to an abrupt end. He found Ducommun to be a crude and rough character with a short temper who needed little excuse to beat him. Out of his contempt for his master, Rousseau lost interest in his trade. A sensitive child, easily hurt by criticism, he felt crushed and humiliated in his new environment. He forgot his interest in history and learning and sought only for some device to cheat his master. He began to steal both food and time, hiding away to engrave something for his own amusement so long as it would be of no use to Ducommun. The latter beat him for his thefts, for his idleness, and for any other cause that seemed appropriate. Soon the young Rousseau developed a certain callousness about his beatings. He accepted them as an inevitable accompaniment of his way of life, as the humiliated private soldier accepts the guardhouse. While he was not attracted to the rough companions he found in his new occupation, he accepted them with the same resignation, joining in their activities and developing a coarse and indolent disposition. However, while he adopted the behavior of his fellow workers, he could not really enjoy this new life.

14

He was bored by the activities of these friends and soon escaped to a world of his own where he could read and imagine himself the hero of a great romance. He read everything from cheap novels to philosophical essays with the same voracious avidity. The more he was beaten for surreptitiously reading when he was expected to be working, the more passionate became his devotion to reading. He spent all his money on books, even exchanging his shirts, ties, and other clothes for a few precious volumes. It would seem that, in this escape to the world of books, he was seeking to recapture the lost relationship with his father. The long hours in which he and his father had read to each other, and in which he had felt a certain exclusive paternal love, were revived in his hours of loneliness and oppression.

During this period Rousseau often escaped the tedium of his employment by wandering with his companions in the environs of Geneva outside the city gates. One evening as he was approaching the city, he saw the gates closing before him. He had been in this situation before, and he knew his master would beat him severely for not returning by sundown. He resolved not to return at all, but to roam the world seeking a life of adventure. Just sixteen at the time, he accepted his new decision with lightness of spirit. As he traveled along, he felt convinced that some fine lady would soon come upon him and offer him her favors. With this idea in mind he rambled at a leisurely pace, singing and often stopping under castle windows in the hope that the lovely maiden would be attracted by the sound of his voice. When a certain priest of Confignon suggested that he seek the protection of Mme de Warens, a convert at Annecy, he accepted the older man's advice and began his journey.

Rousseau's vivid imagination, his capacity to find delight in anticipating an imaginary future, was always an outstanding feature of his personality. It explains his feeling of happiness and his sense of adventure as he left his only employment with no prospect of finding any other to travel down the highway, singing. He had many travels during this period of his life, in which originated his love of nature; however, the striking feature of all his adventures was his capacity to project his own fantasies on the world around him, to see more than was really there.

> . . . young desires, enchanting hopes, brilliant prospects filled my soul. Every object I saw seemed a guarantee of happiness that was just around the corner. In the houses I imagined rustic feasts, in the meadows playful scampering, beside the streams bathing, strolling, fishing; delicious fruit on every tree and voluptuous in-

timacies in its shade; on the mountains vats full of milk and cream, the charms of leisure, peace, simplicity; the joy of going I knew not where.[1]

Unfortunately, it was the same capacity for vivid imagination which, in later years, resulted in his discovering plots and conspiracies against him. But we are moving ahead of our story. We have yet to meet Mme de Warens, the woman who was to exert the greatest influence on his life.

From the priest's description of Mme de Warens and from the religious tone which he had given to his suggestions, Rousseau had pictured a pious old lady. He was delighted to find, instead, an attractive young woman of twenty-eight. She also had a certain childlike irresponsibility and impulsive warmth which made her seem even younger. She lived with her "servant," Claude Anet, who was also her lover, although the reserved Anet presented such a calm and matter-of-fact manner in her presence that not until much later did Rousseau suspect the relationship.

It was clear from the beginning that a great deal of Mme de Waren's attraction for Rousseau lay in her resemblance to him.[2] She also had lost her mother at birth and, like himself, she had impulsively left her unhappy surroundings (in this case her husband and her religion) to throw herself on the mercy of King Victor-Amadeus. The king settled a pension on her because of her zeal for Catholicism. In his description of his first meeting with her, Rousseau constantly remarked on the similarity between her life, her personality, and his own. He even mentioned that she had a mouth "like mine."[3] This tendency to choose a love object because of a resemblance to himself was characteristic. All of his significant and enduring love relationships with women represented this type of attraction.

But another equally important element in the character of Mme de Warens was a certain sense of play with which she approached life. As Rousseau remarked, "She enlarged her plan in her head and viewed her objective on a grand scale."[4] Life was for her a kind of play-acting in which she was to have the center of the stage, planning great schemes and surrounded by admirers. That none of her many business ventures succeeded did not deter her from beginning others. In the same spirit she undertook the education and development of Rousseau, serving as his teacher and mother at the same time. In reality the experience was more like that of two children playing house.

The quality of fantasy pervaded their relationship to such a marked degree that it is not clear whether Mme de Warens imagined the early

girlhood and womanhood which she described to Rousseau or whether
he distorted the little she told him in accord with his own fantasies.
In any event, his version of her early life in his *Confessions* is
quite untrustworthy. Rousseau describes her as a sensitive woman whose
husband did not understand her. He says she was seduced by a M. de
Tavel, her mentor in philosophy, who taught her only those principles
necessary to achieve his ends. According to Rousseau "he attacked her
by means of sophistries and succeeded in showing her that the duties
to which she was so attached were like the prattle of the catechism,
intended only to amuse children."[5] Actually, this story fits so well with
Rousseau's own beliefs regarding the dangers of overintellectualizing
that we might well suspect the tale on that basis alone. Further, Montet
points to several circumstances in the relationship of M. de Tavel and
Mme de Warens which would seem to contradict Rousseau's assertion.[6]

Montet has shown that she left Pays de Vaud (Vevey) not because
of "domestic troubles" with her husband, with whom she was generally
on good terms, but because she had induced him to sink his money into
one of her business ventures—a silk-stocking factory (which she began
with M. Laffon). She could not admit that the venture was a failure,
that creditors were clamoring for their money, and that she had been
appropriating money from the factory for her own private use. Instead, she chose to flee the unpleasant situation and leave her husband to
face the collectors.[7] She left with a full load of baggage, which included
her husband's gold watch, his gold-headed cane, the best books in the
family library, and many of the joint possessions of herself and her
husband,[8] to take a health cure in the baths at Amphion in Savoy. She
departed with her husband's blessings and his expectation that she
would return. Once in Savoy she threw herself on the mercy of King
Victor and declared herself a refugee from Protestantism.

When Rousseau met her she was living on a modest pension from
the king, which she earned by occasional care of prospective converts.
She undertook to educate him as she had educated herself—by a light-
hearted search for knowledge of all kinds: botanizing in the woods,
conversation with the learned men of the town, and reading. Rousseau
had always been an ardent reader since his early experience with his
father. Mme de Warens encouraged him in this pursuit and may even
have improved his taste. She also had an influence on his religious views
—although perhaps not in the direction that her Catholic advisers would
have approved. The origin and nature of her religious opinions are not
clear. She seems to have received some instruction from Magny, the
leader of the pietistic movement in Pays de Vaud, and her husband was
of the opinion that this influence was decisive,[9] but the extent of her

indoctrination[10] now seems doubtful.[11] Certainly, her Catholicism was more of an expediency than a conviction. It was perhaps her idea of following her "natural" inclinations and her refusal to accept any religious authority which had the greatest influence on Rousseau. She had a simple conviction that God was good and that he would understand her if she acted in good faith.

Not only were her religious views unorthodox, but in other respects as well she was a likely mentor for an incipient rebel. As a child she had not been content with a girl's education, but had studied the medical and natural history books of her father. She was always regarded as independent and headstrong and resented the domination of any man. Nor was she satisfied, as were most women of her time, to play the role of the submissive female while she ruled behind the scenes. She preferred to engage in business ventures and other pursuits which were, particularly in her day, reserved for men. Apparently, she could let a man manage her affairs only when she felt herself to be above him. The three men known to have been her lovers (Rousseau, Anet, and Wintzinried) were all younger than she was and were her social inferiors.[12] Claude Anet had been her servant for some time before he became her lover.[13]

But again it is important to emphasize the element of fantasy in the affairs of Mme de Warens. She was not a masculine woman who wanted to destroy men and usurp their position. She was actually incapable of such a thing. The illusion of commanding was important to her, not actual domination; and it was this spirit of play that made her such an attractive figure for Rousseau. He could see himself as the poor wanderer who had come under the protection of a kind and powerful mistress, and he felt he could obey her always.

II

Despite their attraction for each other, Rousseau's first stay with Mme de Warens was brief. She showed considerable sympathy for him when he related the tale of his wanderings and the conditions under which he had left Geneva, and she offered him her help and suggestions. He felt that she would have liked to urge him to return home to Geneva and to his own religion, but was fearful of saying this openly lest the word of her heresy reach the ears of the Church and deprive her of her pension. Instead, he was sent to a hostel at Turin, which had been established for the instruction of converts to Catholicism. Here he experienced his first homosexual advance from a young convert who called himself a Moor. Rousseau was repelled by this experience and thought the youth was completely out of his mind. He tried to tell others of his encounter, but he was told that one does not discuss these things. This adventure, combined with his feeling that most of the converts were not sincere and that the priests were rather callous about their mission, gave him a profound distaste for Catholicism. However, he felt trapped by a situation in which he could never see Mme de Warens again and could get nowhere in a Catholic country unless he simulated a conversion. This he did and finally left the hostel saddened and guilt-ridden about the whole affair. He had hoped to obtain some minor post for his "conversion," but he was turned out with a collection of twenty francs and sent on his way.

Once released from his dreary surroundings, he was again filled with the euphoria of adventure which he had felt on first leaving Geneva—a feeling of being completely free with no responsibilites or obligations and a conviction that fortune would soon come his way. This sense of freedom was a frequent experience in his youth. He was always restive when faced with any kind of task which kept him inside and occupied with monotonous activities. As soon as he could toss aside his responsibilities, he felt as though a burden were lifted from his shoulders. That he seldom had enough money to last him for a week did not seem to bother him. He had a tremendous sense of the magnificence of life, the wide variety of possible experiences, and the beauty of nature. He felt it an unjust imposition to be forced to occupy his mind with lowly and trivial things for most of the day, when he had only one life to live and there was so much to see and do.

After his release from the hostel, he walked about the city of Turin, saw the posting of the guard, visited the palace, and, when he became hungry, walked into a dairy where he was given some cream cheese and two sticks of bread. He was delighted with this simple meal and his own informal way of obtaining it. He continued for several days to inspect the city, always eating simply and spending his few francs slowly. His taste had not been cultivated by fine sauces and his expectations were few.

However, Rousseau did not live by his simplicity alone. He was a handsome young man, and, although he was very shy with women, he was easily encouraged by a small kindness. Even his shyness proved to be an advantage in his encounters with married women or women older than he was. Such women were often attracted to him because his lost and forlorn air presented a perfect object for mothering. Once he had their attention, they sensed his silent but passionate adoration, for he fell in love with almost every woman who was kind to him. Soon the motherly feelings were mingled in a kind of amorous haze which added a special tenderness to the attraction they felt for him. Some, sensing his reserve, made the sexual advances themselves. Others waited for his silent adoration to manifest itself. The latter were generally disappointed, as happened in his encounter with a young matron of Turin. He was running out of funds and began to go from one establishment to another to try to pick up some small engraving job. Mme Basile, the wife of a small shop owner, invited him to do some work for her and fed him breakfast. Her husband was away on business and Rousseau, once having been fed, found her irresistible. He followed her about heaving long sighs to the consternation of the clerk, who had been left to watch over her in the absence of her husband. Finally, Rousseau found her alone with her embroidery and threw himself at her feet. While he was trembling with desire, his intense fear of displeasing prevented him from doing more than kiss her hand, and Mme Basile, while apparently aroused by his obvious passion, was herself too inexperienced to give him the instruction and encouragement he required. Thus, the affair came to nothing, except that the clerk conveyed his suspicions to the husband when he returned and Rousseau was told to go on his way. However, he gained a certain feeling of moral worth from his failure as a lover. He sums up the affair in his *Confessions* with the comment:

> Never were passions as lively and, at the same time, as pure as mine. Never was love more tender, true, and disinterested. I would have sacrificed my passion a thousand times for that of a person I loved. Her reputation was more dear to me than my life and never, for all the pleasures of gratification, would I wish to endanger her repose for a single moment. As a result I have brought so much care, so much secrecy, and so many precautions to my undertakings that none of them has ever been successful. My lack of success with women has always come from loving them too much.[14]

In general Rousseau has accounted for his extreme hesitation in making advances to women by the strict environment in which he was raised. Certainly, Protestant Geneva was a severely controlled moral climate; but it was even more important in Geneva that the man take the initiative. Further, the Rousseau, Bernard, and Lambercier homes were, if anything, less restrictive than the majority of Genevan households. The older Rousseau was an impetuous fellow with a passionate temperament, and Jean-Jacques's Uncle Gabriel Bernard and his Aunt Theodora had been called before the Consistory for "anticipating" their marriage. Pastor Lambercier had been admonished for his levity and because of a rumor, started by Pontverre,[15] a neighboring priest of

Confignon, that he came into his sister's room and helped her dress in the morning. He was also accused of excessive drinking in the taverns and of chasing peasant women. While none of these charges was substantiated by the Consistory, that body evidently felt that Pastor Lambercier was lacking in the type and degree of gravity expected from the clergy.

Thus, we must look further than the general moral climate created by Rousseau's mentors if we wish to discover the cause for his reluctance to take the initiative with women. When we reflect that Mme Basile was probably furious with him for his failure to follow through on his silent but passionate declarations, it becomes increasingly obvious that Rousseau was restrained, not by love, but by his fear of hurting. This fear of hurting women was indeed pathological. He had to be, not just fairly confident that they wanted him, but absolutely certain. He had to be completely free of doubt and cleared of any guilt before he could proceed. At such times we are again reminded of his father's implied accusation that he was responsible for the death of his mother and of the anguish which this thought had caused him as a child. A woman had for him the connotation of a delicate and fragile flower, beautiful to look at but easily destroyed. Yet we find again and again in Rousseau's own story of his life that he is always protesting his softness, his gentleness, and his love of women, while at the same time he cannot resist the impulse to hurt them and to make them suffer. We shall have further occasion to examine the nature of these two attitudes toward women.

It was not long after his encounter with Mme Basile that he obtained a position as a valet to the Countess de Vercellis, a widow who was dying of cancer. His service with this woman was rather uneventful, but on the breaking up of her household after her death, a small ribbon belonging to one of her lady's maids was found missing. Rousseau had taken this trifling item and, as he tells us, he hardly troubled to conceal it. Soon it was discovered in his things, and when he was questioned about it he claimed that Marion, one of the servant girls, had given it to him. She was called with Rousseau before the Count de la Roque, nephew of the deceased woman, who was determined to find out who was guilty. Rousseau accused her again, in front of the count, and she was so surprised and confused by his accusation that she could only glance at him with what he calls "a look that would have disarmed the demons," but he adds, "my barbarous heart resisted."[16] She begged him to tell the truth, but he became all the firmer in his accusation. She began to cry, saying she had always believed he was good, and again pleaded for justice, but Rousseau remained adamant. Finally, the count dismissed them both, saying the guilty one would be punished by his conscience. He was certainly correct, for the memory of this incident disturbed Rousseau for the remainder of his life. He tells us that the girl returned to haunt him in his dreams, and he imagined all sorts of calamities having befallen her as a result of her disgrace and her inability to get a good reference.

Rousseau explains his behavior on the grounds that he was afraid of being punished. He says that he accused Marion merely because she was the first person who occurred to him when he wanted to direct suspicion away from himself. On the surface this would seem a rational explanation for the behavior of a timid and rather characterless youth. But we have already learned to look beneath the surface of Rousseau's explanations. He claims that his timidity was the cause of his accusation, yet his bold persistence is more suggestive of a prosecuting attorney. He can recall no pleasure in connection with this incident, but such pleasure, if it existed, could easily be masked by the horror and guilt which followed Marion's disgrace.

From his description of Marion it is clear that he found her quite attractive. She had, he says, a fresh complexion and "an air of such modesty and sweetness that one could not see her without loving her."[17] From his extensive description of Marion's feeling of injured innocence it would seem that Rousseau derived a certain satisfaction from his ability to identify with her and picture her feelings in his imagination. He held this sweet, innocent girl at his mercy. When he told his story he was not aware of modern psychological investigations which indicate that the sadist is sexually attracted to his victim. He was unable to understand his behavior, but he reported all the feeling he could recall in his fervent desire to convey a true image of himself to posterity. His introspective report is so thorough that the mere description is almost sufficient in itself for an explanation. "When I accused that poor girl," he says, "it is strange but it is true that my friendship for her was the cause."[18] It was only after the case was closed that he was left with a strong sense of guilt at the enormity of his crime.

The Marion incident, like the spanking episode, has been profoundly disturbing to Rousseau's biographers. Some state that Rousseau must have exaggerated his perversity. Jules Lemaître[19] cannot believe that it happened.[20] Those who accept it tell us it was a transient, unhealthy experience which one should forget, since Rousseau was not cruel as an adult. However, there is good reason to believe that this incident, while extremely painful and disillusioning for Marion, may have had a decided positive influence on him. He places the time of his moral reform at a later period of his life, but it may be that his later zeal for virtue was prompted by this sudden recognition of the devil in himself. It was clearly disturbing to him, perhaps because for the first time he had an unmistakable glimpse of his own diabolic potentiality. It may well have served as a stimulus to his soul-searching.

III

After his departure from the household of Countess de Vercellis, Rousseau experienced an increased masochistic tension. The stimulation of the experience with Marion, combined, no doubt, with his desire for punishment, produced a restless upsurge of his sexual fantasies. He was tormented by desire, but was afraid to tell anyone the kind of satisfaction he required. Soon he was haunting the dark alleys and streets of Turin, taking down his trousers and exposing his buttocks to passing women in the hope that one of them would walk up to him and give him the smack on the rump which he so fervently desired. After the shocked screams of a group of girls had summoned a man who chased him, caught him, and ridiculed him, he abandoned this activity.

He soon found another employment in the house of the Count de Gouvon, where his intelligence was recognized and the count began grooming him for a role of importance in the household. However, when his advances to the count's granddaughter were rebuffed, Rousseau lost interest in his new assignment. Bright as were the prospects, he could see before him a long period of inferiority which he could not tolerate. He dreamed of greater conquests and adventures and was soon joined in his fantasies by a fellow Genevese called Bâcle. The two of them began to talk of travel, and Rousseau pictured the meadows, mountains, and streams he had known before. Also, he began to see in the distance the chance of a further relationship with Mme de Warens. Suddenly, his occupation seemed slow and tedious, even his bright prospects seemed inconsequential beside the pleasures of youthful freedom. Thus, he left with his friend Bâcle on a tour of the Alps and finally to Chambéry, where he arrived again at the door of Mme de Warens. In a fit of passion and tears, he threw himself at her feet and kissed her hand. "Poor little one,"[21] she said, and welcomed him into her home. From this point on, the mother-son relationship between Rousseau and Mme de Warens seems to have become settled. She continued to call him "little one," and he called her "mamma." She took it upon herself to care for him and to find him an occupation. In consultation with friends she obtained one job after another for him, but Rousseau, though he tried them all for a while, was soon back at her door. In the meantime he dined and lodged with her, reading the books in her library and talking with her. Frequently, he would find some reason to travel (an imagined illness that needed the baths, an errand for his beloved "mamma"), but he always returned.

It was not long before "mamma," with her usual frankness, admitted to him that she and Claude Anet, her supposed servant, were lovers. The grave Anet served as a fitting complement to her extravagance. Where she was excitable and spontaneous, he was sober and cautious. While he was with her he served as a check on some of her fancies, for she respected his judgment. She was an ardent botanist and frequently tramped through the hills looking for plants. Rousseau accompanied her, sometimes with and sometimes without Anet. On occasion they would take a picnic lunch and eat in the hills. Mme de Warens continued to find positions for her new charge, but her advisers told her he had little talent and Rousseau's unsteady employment seemed to confirm their opinions. Finally he pleaded illness, a strange and intolerable malady that began with a roaring in his ears and involved palpitations of the heart, constrictions of the chest, and spitting blood. The nature of the illness varied from time to time.[22] He ascribed it to his passions, his burning with love for no object, that was so exhausting; yet this illness seemed to vanish whenever there was a pretty face nearby or the road for adventure was open. Mme de Warens took pity on him. She soon ceased to find jobs for him and encouraged him to follow his own interests.

Music had always held a great fascination for him, and she loaned him a book on the subject and encouraged him to learn. With the help of the local choirmaster, he developed his musical ability. Soon his life became a pleasant round of little adventures, traveling from time to time, reading and learning, but most of all enjoying the company of his "mamma" to whom he could talk for hours. He was jealous of any interruption of this conversation by visitors, and he could not wait to be alone with her again after the visitor had left. With such persistence on Rousseau's part it was impossible for Mme de Warens to make any private plans which were not known to him and which did not excite his curiosity, for he wanted to know everything about her—to share her entire life. When she was sent on a secret mission to Paris for the king of Sardinia, she found it necessary to get her "little one" out of the way. He was to accompany "M. le Maitre," the choirmaster,[23] on a journey as far as Lyons. He obeyed her reluctantly, but found himself longing to return to her as soon as he had left. When Le Maitre fell helpless in an epileptic seizure on the streets of Lyons, Rousseau called for help, gave the name of the inn at which they were staying, and returned home.

When he arrived at Annecy he found only her maid, Merceret, for

Mme de Warens had taken Anet with her to Paris. Left without the presence of his beloved "mamma," he was struck with a pang of remorse for his hasty departure from Lyons. He felt acutely the agony which poor Le Maitre must be suffering on recovering from his seizure to find himself alone in a strange city. In his *Confessions* he pauses over this desertion as his second major crime. Like the incident of Marion and the ribbon, it apparently returned to plague him when his virtue was being celebrated throughout Europe.

But it was June in Annecy and the palpable presence of summer was everywhere. The song of the nightingale filled the air, and the earth was covered with grasses and flowers. Soon he was filled with the urge to wander. Toward the end of June (1730) he met Mlle Graffenried and Mlle Galley as he was walking in a valley near the town. This meeting, while it occupies a relatively small part of his *Confessions*, seems to have made a profound impression on him. Rousseau conveys, in his account of this little adventure, a sense of impressionable, full, and unexplored youth, of limitless romantic possibilities. This encounter was to serve him over and over again in his fantasy as a source for his romantic tales.

He was walking beside a small stream when he heard the two girls having trouble making their horses cross to the other side. He had known Mlle Graffenried from her visits to Mme de Warens, and the young lady called him by name and asked for help. Rousseau led the horses through the water and was about to take leave when he heard the young ladies whispering. "No. No!" said Mlle Graffenried, "You can't escape us like that. You must come with us. You are our prisoner, under arrest."[24] Here was one of those situations which delighted Rousseau—being commanded by a beautiful girl. Soon Mlle Galley joined in the game. "Yes, yes. Prisoner of war. Get up on the horse behind her. We will render an account of you." Rousseau hastened to obey, and soon the three of them were galloping across the countryside, he with his arms locked tightly around Mlle Graffenried to maintain his position on the horse. They rode to Mlle Galley's estate at Toune, which was deserted except for the tenant farmer and his family. The girls prepared a meal for him, and they spent the day cavorting in the woods. They teased him and flirted with him, but they were almost always together, and Rousseau was too shy to make advances, yet the intimacy and excitement of this encounter and the natural environment gave him a feeling of simple happiness of which he seldom found the equal in his later life.

We dined in the farmer's kitchen, the two friends sitting on benches on either side of the long table and their guest between them on a three-legged stool. What a dinner! What a charming memory! Why, when man can taste such pure and genuine pleasures at so little cost, should he look for others? Never could a supper at one of the little spots in Paris approach that repast. I am speaking not only of the gaiety and innocent happiness, but of the sensual pleasure as well.

After dinner we practiced a small economy. Instead of taking the coffee which remained after lunch we kept it in order to better enjoy the cream and cakes which they brought with them; and to keep our appetites in good condition we went into the orchard to complete our dessert with cherries. I climbed a tree and threw down bunches of fruit, and they gave me back the stones, tossing them through the branches. Once Mlle Galley, holding out her apron and throwing back her head, presented such a perfect target and I aimed so well that I threw a bunch right into her bosom. How we laughed! I said to myself, 'Oh if my lips were only cherries, how gladly would I throw them there!'[25]

It was the atmosphere of his experience with the two young ladies that Rousseau sought to recapture all his life. It was a feeling which he tried to convey in both the *New Eloise* and *Emile*, a sense of the innocent attractions of youth, a kind of eternal puppy love which would not become sullied by carnal knowledge. To him the desire for a woman was always more than possession. It was a kind of exquisite torment which he loved to prolong and mull over in his mind and describe for others. He liked to imagine that his beloved was just about ready to yield to him, but something prevented her at the last minute. This fantasy is, no doubt, related to his masochistic character, and the satisfaction which he always gained from thinking of himself as the underdog, the deprived one.[26] Another factor was certainly his strong guilt about any active approach to a fine lady, his feeling that to have sexual relations with a woman was inherently brutal and sadistic. In any event the innocent, youthful type of love which he idealized was to become the central concept of the romantic movement. This feeling is best typified by his description of his one moment alone with Mlle Galley.

We passed the day in this manner frolicking about with the greatest freedom and always within the bounds of decency. Not a single questionable word, not a single shady joke. We did not impose this restraint on ourselves; it came of its own accord. We only followed the prompting of our hearts. In short, my modesty—some will say my stupidity—was such that the greatest liberty which escaped me was once to kiss the hand of Mlle Galley. It is true that the circumstances gave a special value to this slight favor. We were alone, I found it difficult to breath, she had lowered her eyes. My mouth, instead of finding words, took the notion of fastening on her hand, which she gently withdrew after it had been kissed, regarding me at the same time with a glance which betrayed no annoyance. I do not know what I might have said to her, but her friend came in and seemed to me at that moment quite ugly.

. . . Those who read this will not fail to laugh at my gallant adventures and note that after many preliminaries the most advanced of them ended with a kiss on the hand. Oh my readers, do not deceive yourselves! I have perhaps had more pleasure from my affairs which ended with a kiss of the hand than you will ever have in yours which only begin at that point.[27]

Soon, however, they noticed the day was coming to an end and felt obliged to return to the town before nightfall. The three of them parted with regret and planned to meet in the future, but though Rousseau walked the street in front of Mlle Galley's house from time to time, he failed to see either of the two young ladies again.

IV

During this period of his youth Rousseau also became passionately attached to certain young men who entered his life. They were generally men like his lost father: the impetuous madcap, the carefree, irresponsible young wanderer. Bâcle was one of these. Another was the traveling French musician who called himself Venture de Villeneuve and who charmed him by the ease with which he sang without any apparent musical study. Venture was always witty, seductive in conversation, and unusually daring with women. As Rousseau remarked, "Even the most modest women were amazed at what they endured from him.[28] Soon he found himself infatuated with Venture, who carried off every conquest in such an effortless manner that it seemed anyone could do the same if he merely cast aside his doubts. Rousseau tried to imitate his wit, and on one occasion attempted to pass himself off as a traveling musician named Vaussore de Villeneuve. But when he composed a piece of music for a M. de Treytorens, a professor of law in Lausanne who gave concerts in his home, the rendition proved such a horrible concatenation of sounds that he recognized it was not sufficient to act like a musician in order to achieve success.[29]

Always in hope that he would soon find his "mamma," he journeyed to Vevey, her birthplace, back to Lausanne and on to Neuchâtel, where he spent the winter learning music by teaching it. He continued to wander about the country in his free time, and one day at Boudry he had an encounter with Father Athanasius Paulus, a Greek Archimandrite collecting funds for the restoration of the Holy Sepulcher. As the priest could speak only Italian, he sought an interpreter who could help him through the French-speaking countries. Since Rousseau had nothing better to do, he agreed to accompany Paulus on his mission. But Paulus often found difficulty in getting a permit to solicit funds, and he was occasionally ordered out of districts they entered. At Soleure the French ambassador, De Bonac, who spoke Italian, interviewed Paulus himself and, apparently deciding his mission was a fraud, sent him packing. Then he turned his attention to Jean-Jacques, who had announced himself as a Parisian interpreter. Throwing himself at the ambassador's feet, Rousseau confessed his true identity and his role in the affair, which was indeed a minor one. He was forgiven and placed under the protection of M. de Bonac's secretary for a time. From Soleure he returned to Neuchâtel where he found it very difficult to get pupils who would tolerate his instruction. Remembering that Mme de Warens was in Paris, he applied to M. de Bonac for help and was offered a position in that city as companion to the nephew of a Swiss colonel. But when he arrived in Paris in June 1731 the appointment turned out to be that of servant to the young cadet, and Rousseau declined the opportunity. His journey, however, was not without some success for he received news that Mme de Warens had left Paris and had gone to Savoy or perhaps to Switzerland.

Off he went once more toward the country of Savoy, traveling on foot, sleeping where he could, and delighting in the scenery. Considering his fresh youthful appearance, his friendly and open manner, and the ease with which he took up with strangers it is not surprising to find him in the midst of another homosexual encounter[30] similar to the one he experienced in the hospice at Turin. One evening in Bellecour he was approached by a man who wanted to "have fun" with him and suggested that the two of them masturbate together. Rousseau was filled with terror and dashed away imagining the man was pursuing him. We do not know what encouragement he may have given to his would-be seducer, but the incident left him with a strong sense of guilt and he was so upset by it that he stopped his own practice of masturbation for a long time.

On this same journey to Savoy he fell into the hands of a designing abbé who found him sleeping on a bench and offered to share his bed with him. Rousseau shuddered when the abbé tried to excite him during the night and, pretending not to understand what the man was about, he excused his uneasiness on the grounds that he had recently been approached by a homosexual. He described the encounter with such obvious disgust that the abbé abandoned his attempt and they parted the next day on friendly terms. Thus, pure and unsullied, despite the designs of male and female, he returned to Savoy and the bosom of Mme de Warens.

V

When he finally located his beloved "mamma," he discovered she had moved to another home in Chambéry, and he resolved to return to her there. She welcomed him with her usual warmth and indulgence, noticing, no doubt, that he was becoming quite an attractive young man and an experienced traveler. He was now twenty-one and still had found no permanent occupation. He had made a few perfunctory attempts at teaching music, but had spent most of his time wandering over the countryside. Mme de Warens found employment for him as a clerk-surveyor, but he could not accept the idea of performing a meaningless task merely to make a living. He began to spend more and more of his time reading and studying music. Soon he proposed to her that he become a music teacher once again. His indulgent "mamma" was finally won over, more by his persistence and caresses than by his arguments.

At last he was free to go from house to house, teaching the ladies and flattering the mothers. As he told Mme de Warens of his adventures she became concerned for him. She determined to save him from the scheming young women, with whom he was coming in contact, by giving herself to him. It is not surprising that the shy young Rousseau should have his first sexual experience with a woman older than himself. However, the mother-son relationship which had existed between the two of them for so long made it difficult for Mme de Warens to accomplish her goal. All intimacy between them was quickly transformed into a kind of cuddly mothering, but Rousseau, while passionately devoted to her, had never, except perhaps in fantasy, regarded her as a sexual object. Further, her own nature was not that of the coquette. Although an excitable, emotional person, she was not sensual. Since she fancied herself as something of a philosopher, she resolved to seduce Rousseau, if we can call it seduction, with logic. She explained to him that he was a man now and should begin to know women as a man knows them. She used many circumlocutions and elaborate explanations, but she finally made clear what she was proposing. With a certain deadly seriousness, as though discussing a business proposition, she gave him eight days to think it over.

Rousseau was terrified by the whole idea. It was an adventure which he had not sought and did not understand. Finally, he determined to go ahead with it since he did not want to offend "mamma." The experience, when it came, proved to be an anticlimax. Even in the sexual embrace, Mme de Warens was more tender and mothering than passionate. He felt as though he were committing incest. The experience brought him closer to Mme de Warens and even to Claude Anet—for she did not trouble to conceal this relationship from her other lover—but this seduction by logic left Rousseau with a profound skepticism about the uses of reason. He maintained a great respect for reason rightly used, but he was one of the first to see the perverse uses to which it may be turned by those who would hide from their true feelings. He attempted to excuse Mme de Warens for her behavior by placing the responsibility on her early seduction by M. de Tavel, but his resentment of her misuse of reason is unmistakable.

> I repeat, all her faults came from her errors, never from her passions. She was wellborn, her heart was pure, she loved honest behavior, her inclinations were straight and virtuous, her taste refined, she was made for the elegance of manners which she always admired but never followed, because instead of listening to her heart which guided her well, she listened to her reason which misled her. When false principles led her astray, her true feelings always contradicted them; but, unfortunately, she had pretensions to philosophy and the morality she conceived for herself corrupted what her heart dictated.[31]

It was not long after his new relationship with Mme de Warens that Claude Anet died and Rousseau became the master of the household. It may be that his strong sense of guilt contributed to his feeling of impotence in this new position.[32] Regardless of his changed relationship with Mme de Warens, he was still "little one" to her, and she could not take his admonitions about thrift seriously. As "little one" he did not have the same authority as Anet, and he felt his efforts to control her were fruitless. She would joke with him, call him her "little mentor,"[33] and continue her extravagance. He attempted to save some of her money by hiding it from her, but she would soon uncover his little hoard and replace it with a larger amount. This caused him such embarrassment that he soon abandoned his efforts.

It was, of course, not part of the dependent nature of Rousseau to assume responsibility for the finances of Mme de Warens. He had many desires himself, particularly for travel, which required the outlay of funds over and above those needed for mere sustenance. His letters to her during his travels are filled with requests for money and hints that his purse is empty. One reads in them the attitude of a boy who is not genuinely willing to accept the role of man of the house. Rousseau finally reasoned that since she would spend her money on strangers anyway and since he was unable to control her, she might as well spend it on someone who loved her. In his own wild fantasies he conceived the idea that, by becoming a musician and composer, he would soon achieve such success that he would be able to support her. Thus assured, he had little hesitation in spending her money on his little schemes and little difficulty in persuading the imaginative Mme de Warens that his adventures would soon be profitable.

As a woman who loved to take charge of men, she was attracted by the timidity and sensitivity which might have repelled another. Here was a creature whose very being she could absorb. She indulged him as she would an infant; she invited his desires and swathed him in a protective felicity; she educated him with her books, her own ideas. She awakened his burgeoning sensuality and cooled it in the folds of her flesh. She occupied his thoughts and his sensations day and night until she had soaked into his skin and he could not subsist without her. No amusement would give him joy without the exhilaration of her presence. Without a sense of himself, he was a man devoured.

It was in this period of his absolute possession of "mamma" that Rousseau achieved his greatest happiness. He was entirely hers, her son and her lover as well. This was a period of picnicking in the country and botanizing in the hills, when he would come to her room to kiss her awake in the morning and sip coffee with her for hours. This was the time he prolonged in his imagination far beyond the point at which it had actually ceased.

Owing to his poor health Mme de Warens rented a country home, which they called Les Charmettes, where the two of them continued their idyllic existence. He describes the date of this move as the summer of 1736.[34] Then we hear of a journey to Montpellier for a cure, an affair with a woman along the way, a sudden attack of guilt over his unfaithfulness to "mamma" and a return to Les Charmettes, only to discover that his place has been taken by a burly young blond hairdresser named Wintzinried. This is the story Rousseau tells in the *Confessions*.

Actually, the lease and some of Mme de Warens' private papers indicate that Les Charmettes was not taken until July 6, 1738,[35] and Rousseau's romantic utopia was ended some time earlier by the arrival of Wintzinried, who completely replaced him in Mme de Warens' affections. He had none of his letters with him at the time of writing the *Confessions*, and he had, it appears, spent previous summers in the valley of Charmettes with Mme de Warens. His transposition of the scenes of his greatest happiness was, therefore, quite natural. As a further explanation of his error, the ascendancy of Wintzinried was a gradual process and was delayed even further in Rousseau's imagination. He was already expert at creating in his own mind the world he preferred, and he had some justification for believing he could survive this newcomer. There were several callers and many had received largess at Mme de Warens' door; yet he had outlasted them all. The casual visits of this barber were merely a source of annoyance at first. To elucidate these events more fully, it is necessary to examine not only the *Confessions* but Rousseau's letters to Mme de Warens as well. The letters indicate an awareness on his part that he was being replaced by the newcomer. In the following pages, as we recount the story of this period, it becomes apparent that his return from his travels to Mme de Warens was motivated primarily by fear of losing her and by a sudden realization that Wintzinried had become her lover.

VI

It was not long after the arrival of Wintzinried that Rousseau imagined he was desperately ill with a heart ailment. Perhaps he vaguely sensed this threat to his happiness and hoped the role of an invalid would awaken the waning interest of Mme de Warens. But she was familiar with this tactic and encouraged him to travel and seek a cure for his condition. Thus, he set out for the baths and doctors of Montpellier.

At Moirans, on his way to the Rhone Valley, he met the woman with whom he was to have his first truly sensual love affair. Mme de Larnage, a woman in her forties[36] who had recently separated from her husband, found Rousseau charming, and since they were traveling in the same direction, they soon became well acquainted. To cover his provincial origin Rousseau pretended to be an Englishman by the name of Dudding. His behavior with Mme de Larnage was in many respects a curious foretaste of his future behavior with ladies of quality. He persisted in believing that she was not really attracted to him, but was only leading him on in order to tease him. In spite of his vanity and his protestations of his own merit, he had a distinctly low opinion of himself. He identified himself with the working classes, the underdogs, and felt that no fashionable French lady could look on him with anything but contempt. When he was in the presence of Mme de Larnage he trembled as much from his feeling of her superior social status as he did from being sexually attracted to her.

Mme de Larnage was not one to be easily discouraged. She continued to flirt with him and to try to make it clear that she was not just teasing; she meant business. Rousseau found that the longer he was with her the less he felt any of his old symptoms. The grave malady which appeared about the time Wintzinried first began to play court to Mme de Warens was now vanishing and a new kind of palpitation was taking its place. Finally, at Valence Mme de Larnage determined to seduce him. She managed to escape the Marquis de Torignan, her elderly traveling companion, by suggesting a stroll. As they were walking beside the town moat, she became so passionately tender and suggestive that her intent was unmistakable. Surely she was still teasing, he thought. What if he were mistaken in his estimate of her feelings? What if his passion induced him to take unwarranted liberties: then, horror of horrors, she would be offended.

The resolute Mme de Larnage would not be dissuaded by his silence. She pushed on, clasping his hand and placing it to her breast in an expression of tender regard. This was too much for Rousseau. He was now convinced that she was exciting him only so that she could ridicule him and scorn him later. His sexual excitement turned to anger and he began to sulk. His many masochistic experiences with women had not prepared him for this type of encounter. Unconsciously, he was still seeking the old tormenting, guilt-ridden relationship.

But the heroic lady was an accomplished professional in the art of love. She knew nothing of his masochistic desires, but she did know what she wanted. Soon her arms were around his neck and her lips pressed against his. For the remainder of their journey together they were lovers. Once he was sure of her, Rousseau lost his bashfulness. She had never established a motherly relationship with him, and this enabled him to enjoy her with an uninhibited pleasure that was lacking in his experience with Mme de Warens. "I owe it to Mme de Larnage," he says, "that I shall not die without having known sensual pleasure."[37] She soon moved her lady's maid into Rousseau's carriage and asked him to join her. "I can assure you," he says, "that in this manner we did not find the journey tedious, and I would find it very difficult to describe the country through which we passed."[38] It was one of the few times in his life that his attention had been taken from the glories of nature.

This experience, if it had continued, might well have had a marked change in his masochistic sexual orientation. The "little boy" attitude which had succeeded so well with Mme de Warens had involved him in perpetually guilty, incestuous feelings. His relations with her were clouded by "a secret oppression of the heart,"[39] and he was always reproaching himself for harming her. The striking difference in his experience with Mme de Larnage he described as follows:

> With Mme de Larnage on the other hand I was proud of my manhood and my happiness and abandoned myself with joy and confidence. I shared the sensations that I roused in her and was sufficiently master of myself to contemplate my triumph with as much vanity as voluptuousness and thus to derive from it the means of increasing it.[40]

Mme de Larnage, for her part, was quite content to continue the relationship indefinitely. She urged him to join her in Bourg-Saint-Andeol and spend the winter there. Perhaps if he had been more certain of Mme de Waren's affection, he could have left her with greater confidence, but already her letters had become infrequent and rather cold, and Rousseau, who could face any uncertainty in his environment or his finances, could not bear a loss of affection. In spite of his adventurous spirit and his novel ideas, he was, in love, a decided conservative. He had a strong tendency to stick to the old and familiar as long as he could and to return—even to the guilt-ridden relationship with Mme de Warens—when he felt it might be withdrawn from him. He sensed the exclusive and exotic nature of his relationship with her, and he knew he could never find another "mamma" like her. He had searched for her too long before he found her. In order to build a more mature relationship with Mme de Larnage, he would have required complete assurance that he could always return to the old symbiosis if he wished.

Mme de Larnage parted from him at Montpellier with the understanding that he would join her at Bourg-Saint-Andeol as soon as she had prepared the way. But once he was left alone with his thoughts, his concern about the affection of Mme de Warens overwhelmed him. He sent her several anxious letters and received infrequent replies. She was cold and rather critical. She had begun to tire of his role of the cute little boy, and she suggested it was time he began to grow up. Rousseau, who remembered the days when she encouraged him to be her "little one," was deeply hurt. Throughout his childhood he had yearned for the ideal mother he had never known. Mme de Warens had seemed to fill all his needs. She was mother, lover, educator, and friend. She was his whole life, and she was slipping away from him. He was torn with the impatient desperation of a child. His physical complaints returned in all their force, and he tried to arouse her protective, maternal feelings. This was the only way he had learned to relate to her, and in his moment of panic it was the only tactic he could use. On October 23, 1737, he wrote to her from Montpellier:

> It is a month since I arrived in Montpellier without having received any news from you, although I have written several times and by different routes. You must know I am not very much at ease about this, and that my situation is not the most pleasant. However, I protest to you, Madame, with the greatest sincerity that my very great worry comes from the fear that some accident might have happened to you.

There follows a detailed description of the routes by which she might send mail and the days on which she should post it, followed by his signature. Then, by way of a postscript:

> If you want to send me something by way of the merchants of Lyon, and if you write, for example, to Ms. Vepres by the same post as to me, I should actually receive their letter at the same time as yours.
>
> I was going to close my letter when I received yours, Madame, of the 12th of this month. I do not believe I deserve your reproaches on my lack of exactness. Since my departure from Chambéry, I have not passed a week without writing to you. As for the rest, I want to be honest with myself, and, although it seems to me rather hard that the first letter I have the honor of receiving from you is filled only with reproaches, I agree that I deserve all of them. What, Madame, would you have me say? When I act, I think I am doing the most beautiful things in the world, and then it turns out that they are only stupidities: I recognize that very well myself. It will be necessary to resist this silliness in the future and pay more attention to conduct. . . .
>
> As to the letter of M. Arnauld, you know, Madame, better than I what suits me as a recommendation. I see that you imagine because I am in Montpellier I can see things more directly and judge what there is to do, but, Madame, I ask you to realize that outside my rooming house and landlord, it is impossible for me to make any liaison nor know the surroundings beyond the world of Montpellier. . . . You depict such a pleasant situation for me in Montpellier that, in truth, I do not know any better way of correcting that which cannot be confirmed than to plead with you to take the opposite view. . . . I do not dare to hope for the return of my health because it is in worse condition than when I left Chambéry; but, Madame, if God deigns to give it back to me, I would make no

other use of it than to try to ease you of your care, and to support you as a good and tender son and thankful pupil. You exhort me, Madame, to remain here until St. John's Day (June 21). I would not do it if they should cover me with gold. In my whole life I have not known a country more antipathetic to my taste than this, nor a life more boring, more dull than at Montpellier.

Since Mme de Larnage had left him at Montpellier, he was no doubt telling the truth, but a pang of guilt pricked him, and he added:

I know you don't believe me. You are still full of the beautiful scenes that those who have been here describe for others. . . . As to my health, it is not surprising that it is not improving. First, my food is worth nothing, but nothing. I say nothing and I am not joking. The wine here is too strong and always upsetting. The bread is passable, in truth, but there is neither beef, nor cow (milk), nor butter. One eats only bad mutton and an abundance of fish, everything always prepared in a stinking oil.[41] It would be impossible to taste the soup or stew which is served us at my rooming house without vomiting.

I don't want to say any more about it because if I told you things exactly as they are you would be full of more pity for me than I deserve. In the second place the air does not suit me; another paradox even more unbelievable than the preceding ones, however, it is true. One could not deny that the air of Montpellier is very pure and balmy in the winter. However, the proximity of the sea makes one fear for those who have chest trouble, thus one sees many tuberculars here. A certain wind that they here call the marine brings from time to time dense and cold fog, full of salty and acrid particles which are very dangerous. Therefore, I catch cold here, sore throat, and quinsy more often than at Chambéry. Let's not say any more about that now because if I told you any more, you would not believe a word of it. I can insist, however, that I have only told the truth.[42]

Rousseau was twenty-five at the time the above lines were written, but he was obviously a very young twenty-five. These letters to Mme de Warens, almost all of which contain requests for money or for other assurances of love, display a side of him which is much more disguised in the *Confessions:* his complete and naked dependency. When we look on Rousseau, the adult, the fiercely independent philosopher, the man who would accept gifts from no one and who declined the pensions of kings, we understand better the secret craving against which he was fighting.

Mme de Warens' response to his plea was apparently without warmth, and she must have given him a suggestion of the relationship which was developing between herself and Wintzinried, for he was soon crying out to her (December 4):

> . . . For God's sake, don't let me die of despair (Au nom de Dieu, rangés les choses de sorte que je meure pas au désespoir). I approve of everything; I will submit to everything except one situation, to which I feel unable to consent, even if I should be a victim of the greatest misery. Ah, my dear Mamma, are you still my dear Mamma? Have I lived a few months too long?
>
> You know there is one case where I would accept this matter in all the joy of my heart. But that case is unique. You know what I mean.[43]

The "one case" to which he refers was probably the *ménage-à-trois* established between himself, Anet, and Mme de Warens, a situation made all the more acceptable by the fact that it was buried in the irretrievable past. He resolved to return at once and recover whatever was left to him of his former position.

If he had not allowed himself to suspect the full intimacy established between his "mamma" and Wintzinried, his fears were confirmed on his return. Mme de Warens, with her casual, direct manner, took him aside to explain the status of the newcomer. "I will die of it,"[44] he cried, but she assured him that no one dies of such things and that he should learn to share with his brother as Claude Anet had done with him. But Anet was a quiet, reserved man who concealed his injured feelings behind a composed mask. Rousseau was young, passionate, excitable, and intensely possessive. His struggle to adopt a philosophical attitude was bound to end in failure. He made an attempt to abide by the wishes of his "mamma," resolving to like his adopted brother in spite of the latter's loud blustering ways. After the move to Les Charmettes, he even succeeded in convincing himself that he had no animosity for Wintzinried and would teach him a few useful things as Anet had taught him. But the new pupil did not show much eagerness for instruction. No doubt he sensed the hostility behind his tutor's tender words of advice and resolved to have as little to do with him as possible. Rousseau tells us that this intruder was a loud, pale, silly youth "with a face as dull as his mind," who traveled about dressing the hair of ladies of quality and boasted that he seduced them all. "Vain, silly, ignorant, and insolent he was in other respects the best fellow in the world."[45] These words were written almost thirty years after the event, but even then it is clear that he could not face the enormity of his hatred of Wintzinried.

Rousseau remarked, when speaking of his earlier days with Mme de Warens, that he would sometimes leave her in order to enjoy the pleasure of thinking about her. No doubt in his lonely existence at Les Charmettes, he spent much of his time conjuring up his "mamma" as he would have her—always devoted, always true, always solicitous of his welfare and sharing his personal thoughts. While he wandered about by himself, reading his books, taming the pigeons and bees, and devising philosophical critiques, he could have her just as he wanted her in his imagination. When she and Wintzinried returned to town in the winter of 1738-39, Rousseau remained at Les Charmettes alone with his dreams.

While he continued to address her as "mamma," he gradually began to resign himself to his new position. He saw the time approaching when he could no longer ask her to care for him, and during the cold winter evenings he prepared a letter to the governor of Savoy requesting a pension. He sent the draft to her for correction and improvement. The letter is of little consequence, but one finds in his comments about it—in his striving to strike the right tone between pride and humility—the beginning of a struggle with his concept of himself which he was never quite able to resolve. Even in these early years he regarded himself as a man with great potentiality, a man who was superior to those from whom he had to ask favors. Yet he recognized that he must show a certain humility if he were to gain anything from them. In commenting about his efforts to Mme de Warens he says:

> . . . If I am capable of producing a masterpiece, this document, to my taste, is it. Not that it was created with such great art, but because it is written with the feeling which suits a man whom you honor with the name of son. Surely a ridiculous pride would scarcely suit me in my present state, but I have always believed that one could, *with arrogance* and, however, without debasing one's self, preserve a certain dignity in misfortune and in supplications, which is more suitable to obtain the graces of an honest man than the most abject cowardice.[46]

The expression "with arrogance" instead of "without arrogance"[47] (an obvious slip) indicates that other thoughts were crowding in upon the young Jean-Jacques as he composed his humble plea for aid. With Rousseau, even in his most subservient moments, a fierce pride was simmering just beneath the surface. It was not the pride of self-confidence, but the burning resentment of a man who felt rejected, unloved, and misunderstood. The wound left in his heart by the loss of Mme de Warens was festering, and he sensed within himself a great talent, a beautiful soul which he could not convey to others and which he felt was doomed to perish unrecognized.

We have no evidence that his letter to the governor was ever sent. In any event, he did not receive a pension for his efforts, and Mme de Warens was finding it more difficult to support him. The new master, Wintzinried, was now obviously the favorite, and when Rousseau would get angry with him, he was made to apologize. Rather than lose his "mamma" completely, he forced himself to do this, but it soon became apparent to him that he was actually the intruder in the affair of two people who would be much happier without him. He determined to leave, and Mme de Warens encouraged him by finding him a position as tutor with M. de Mably, chief provost of Lyons.

Rousseau felt that he had enough knowledge for his new task, but he reckoned without the vigor and ingenuity of the Mably boys. They seemed to him a strange species of wild animal. All of his resolutions to be gentle and sweet with them were fruitless, for they soon reduced him to a raving demon. He was always devising techniques to ferret out their tricks, but no sooner had he uncovered one scheme than he was the victim of another. Finally, he formed the habit of creeping away from them to his room to drink wine stolen from M. de Mably's cellar. Soon his petty thefts were discovered, but the kind M. de Mably merely removed supervision of the wine cellar from him without mentioning the reason.

In his *Emile* Rousseau exercised the writer's gift—the capacity to turn every defeat of life into an advantage by writing it out of his system. In that tale he had only one child to manage, and his quick wits were far ahead of those of the youngster. Always in control, always level-headed, the masterful tutor of Emile, with a sort of effortless logic, arranged the life of his young charge in such a way that the youth was educated in spite of himself.

Reality, however, was not so kind, and he soon concluded that he was not temperamentally suited to be a tutor. In the loneliness of his room he grieved over the Eden he had left and the state into which he had fallen. Perhaps, he thought, he had exaggerated Mme de Warens' coolness. Wintzinried was not really the favorite. She would be delighted to see him again, and the welcome home would be sweetened by his long absence. He resolved to leave his wretched quarters and seek his true home again. But when he returned to Les Charmettes, he discovered that things had not changed since his departure. He was a stranger, an outsider, and although Mme de Warens welcomed him with her usual kindness, he found no place in her heart. He stayed in his room most of the time reading, studying music, and devising a sys-

tem of musical notation which consisted of marking the scale by num-
bers instead of drawing lines. The more he worked on this system, the
more he became convinced that it would make his fortune. Some day
he would return, the scorned but ever-faithful lover, to rescue her
from poverty. With this fantasy as a source of inspiration, he left for
Paris in 1741.

Thus it was that Rousseau left home for the last time. He was now
truly on his own and responsible for his own survival. Having finally
admitted to himself that Mme de Warens no longer cared for him, he
could no longer remain dependent on her. His youth had ended with
a sudden jolt, and his *Confessions* record this period as one might describe the departure from paradise.

> I was still young but the sweet feeling of joy and hope that en-
> livens youth left me forever . . . and if sometimes afterward an
> image of happiness suggested itself in my desires, it was no longer
> the same. I felt that if I obtained it I would not really be happy.[48]

VII

Many details are missing from these highlights of Rousseau's childhood and youth, such as his passing affair with Suzanne Serre in Lyons
on the way to Paris, another instance in which he placed himself in
the role of the noble, self-sacrificing lover. Yet even if every incident
in these early years was catalogued, it is doubtful that there is enough
data to account for his unique character. So many forgotten experiences have formed him that it is perhaps best to stop here to take note
of his intense need to be loved—a need which dominated his life and
which breathes in every line of his letters. The collection of his correspondence can be opened almost at random to find him pleading with
a friend not to forget him, expressing his fear that he has not been
understood, grasping always for some greater intimacy, some deeper
contact with the very soul of another. His early relationship with his
father and his years with Mme de Warens had fostered this need, and
his final loss of his "mamma" left him with the conviction he could
never hold a friend—that others would soon lose interest in him and
gradually slip away. This fear was at the root of his intensely possessive and personal relationships, his desire that his friends know all his
faults and accept him without reservation. It was at the base of his
desire to be completely frank and open with others and his inability
to achieve such candor.

The Paris of the 1740's, which he was approaching, was a city
molded by another hand. It was the product of a personality so differ-

ent from his that he could scarcely have chosen a more hostile environment. All his life he had been terribly afraid of ridicule or teasing of any kind, and in Paris persiflage and raillery were the chief pastimes of polite society. Yet with his rustic background and his desire for sincerity and honesty, he was perhaps uniquely suited to be the critic of Parisian manners and morals. Plunging into the literary life of the times, he was both charmed and repelled. His passionate attachments and his experience with injustice produced a fermentation of his untried eloquence, a cry of revolt that awakened the Western World.

[3]

Rise to Fame

I

IN THE CONTEXT of the popular psychology of our day with its emphasis on "adjustment," Rousseau's search for the natural man and his description of society as "unnatural" may seem like the protestations of a social misfit. Certainly, Rousseau was not "adjusted" and never became adjusted to the French society in which he found himself. However, from the viewpoint of human relations, the society created by Louis XIV and perpetuated by the regent and by Louis XV and Louis XVI was profoundly unnatural. The peculiar and perverse artificiality of this society reached from the courtier at Versailles to the peasant in the countryside. Each was forced by the circumstances of his time to become an actor on the stage of history, cast in a part in which he did not believe.

The country noble left his spacious estate and his servants to occupy, as a courtier, a dismal little compartment in the palace. He adopted elaborate and superficial manners to please the king, while pretending that he was delighted with the royal accommodations. The peasant, who lived in a rich and abundant countryside was forced to hide any semblance of wealth and present a face of abject misery and squalor for fear that the tax farmer would extort a few more sous from his dwindling supply.

Louis XIV had created the social life which Rousseau discovered on his arrival in Paris, and though the Sun King was dead, his influence still dominated France. The manners, the customs, and the attitudes he created continued until they were swept away in a violent upheaval —a sudden bursting forth of suppressed hatred.

Perhaps no other king has inspired such extensive imitation, not only in his own people but even in the societies of his enemies. However, it is important to distinguish between imitation and identification. The son who identifies with his father through his close personal association absorbs some of his father's self-confidence as well as his mannerisms. He resembles his father not only in taste and speech, but in character as well. It is significant that with the glittering personality of Louis XIV, it was only the glitter that rubbed off on his society.

42

His mannerisms, his speech, his walk, and his attitudes were slavishly copied, but his genius for personal government and his power to inspire what Toynbee[1] has called "mimesis" were bequeathed to no one.

Louis XIV's regard for form was supported by the classical tradition of his time, but he gave it a special emphasis and precision which marked classicism for the succeeding generations. Under his influence court etiquette came to dominate Paris. The manners were so intricate that they involved a life study.

> Who for instance could guess that at Versailles it was the height of bad manners to knock at a door? You must scratch it with the little finger of the left hand, growing the finger nail long for that purpose. . . . That if the lackey of a social superior brought you a message, you had to receive him standing and bareheaded? You have mastered the fact that you must not knock on a door, so when you go to make your first round of calls on the great houses in the town, you scratch: wrong again, you should have knocked. Next time you rattle the knocker, and a passing exquisite asks you contempuously if you are so ignorant as not to know that you give one blow on the knocker at the door of a lady of quality. . . .
>
> Who could sit down in the presence of whom, and on what, was perhaps the most fruitful source of bickering, the unending Battle of the Three Chairs: the armchair, the chair without arms, and the *tabouret*, or three-legged stool. So important was this matter considered that two prominent people could not meet without a preliminary skirmishing by messenger as to the type of chairs they were to sit upon. Madame, wife of a *Child of France*, proposes to visit her daughter, the Duchess of Lorraine; the Duke of Lorraine claims to sit in an armchair in her presence, and the matter at once becomes an affair of state. Long negotiations are conducted by the French and Lorraine Foreign Office, a deadlock is reached, and the visit is cancelled.[2]

How did such a society come into being? What was the origin of the king's desire to surround himself with precedent and protocol, and why did he take such a personal interest in the social life of his times?

It was the policy of Louis XIV to destroy the power of the nobility. Both he and his father, Louis XIII, had come under the pressure of powerful nobles, and both nearly lost their throne because of the power of rebellious dukes and barons. Louis was determined to crush these gentlemen once and for all. However, he sought to achieve his aims primarily through his influence on the structure of the society of his times. In the days of feudalism the noble was a power. He raised troops who fought for the king, but they were responsible to their noble commander and might be turned against the king if he threatened their interests. By the time of Louis XIV this system had long been crumbling and soldiering had become a profession. But Louis still feared the nobles—particularly those who remained in the provinces, tending their estates and retaining popular support. Consequently, under Louis society regarded the country noble as a provincial booby.[3] The rustic gentleman was scorned because his clothes were out of fashion; he did not know the latest news of the court and—worst of all —he made countless mistakes in manners. He was regarded as a ridiculous fool if he allowed someone beneath him in the hierarchy to sit in an armchair in his presence, and he was a boor if he slighted his betters in some inconsequential matter of protocol. Thus, attendance at court became the only way of maintaining one's position in French society.

Louis fostered this situation by choosing favorites from those who lived at the palace in little closet-like quarters with one window. The ultimate mark of royal disapproval was expressed in his phrase, "He is a man I never see." As a result, nobles attended him everywhere, crowding into the closely packed anteroom outside his chamber in the hope of being one of the chosen few to watch him dress, following him about the palace, cocking their heads to catch his words so they could be repeated later to lesser mortals not privileged to be in the royal presence.

Such was the personal magnetism of Louis that soon dramatists and comedians were making sport of the foolish provincial who was confused by the courtly manners of Versailles or swindled in Paris. The move to the cities of France was greatly intensified during his reign, and the neglect and ruin of provincial estates was an inevitable consequence.

Louis completed the destruction of the country noble by replacing him with the intendant.[4] This officer, responsible directly to the court, administered the collection of taxes for the king and ruled in cases of law. On occasion the noble seigneur even found himself taken to court by one of his peasants. Tocqueville[5] has shown that many phenomena associated with the postrevolutionary era—administrative centralization, the destruction of the power of the noble, the rise of the public servant —were actually characteristic of the old régime. In one sense serfdom had been abolished; the peasant was free to quit his lord's estate, to sell his own goods; his physical, social, and economic mobility was greatly increased. As the noble lost power, he also lost his sense of responsibility for the welfare of his peasants. He no longer felt obligated to see that they were taught useful occupations or that their living conditions were satisfactory. Each year the Royal Council alloted a certain amount of money to the provinces for relief of the poor. It was distributed by the intendants. Such a situation of long-range welfare and the collection of taxes for a distant benefactor removed much of the personal element from provincial administration and increased the tendency of public officials to shift responsibility for their failure to provide help in cases of crop failure or other states of adversity. The peasant developed pride in being his own master, but also felt anxiety in having no one on whom to depend except himself and his own efforts.[6]

Perhaps the greatest single cause of anxiety and revolt was the endless series of taxes placed on the peasant. Nobles were exempt from most taxes, but the peasant was squeezed for money because he was the least able to defend himself. He was squeezed and squeezed until his incentive to produce declined, and his energies were devoted to presenting an appearance of complete poverty to the tax assessor. Tax collectors in the reigns of Louis XIV, Louis XV, and Louis XVI attempted to spy out the secret sources of peasant wealth, but crafty peasants became so skilled at hiding their produce and minor comforts that the tax farmers sent to collect the taxes would return with an amount far below that assessed for a community. The tax collector was forced to make up the difference from his own pocket or go to jail. Any compassion or sympathetic understanding on his part was fatal. As a result, the job became very unpopular and fell into the hands of the most ruthless and unscrupulous members of the community. Methods used were little short of extortion and blackmail, and the men who collected taxes differed little from brigands and highwaymen. Such a state of affairs naturally made tax dodging respectable.

Rousseau had a direct and intimate knowledge of the effect of the taxes on the personality of the French peasant. He tells of a walk in the woods and his decision to stop at a farmer's house and ask for food and drink, for which he offered to pay. The farmer, who kept his buildings in poor repair, welcomed him suspiciously at first and gave him skimmed milk and coarse barley bread, saying that was all he had. Rousseau consumed the food with such obvious relish that the watchful peasant became convinced that he was not a spy sent to ferret out the wealth of the land. He then delved into his secret hoard, bringing out fine bread, a ham, and a bottle of wine, and refused his guest's offer of payment. The incident made a profound impression on Rousseau. As he says in his *Confessions:*

> It was the germ of that inextinguishable hatred which afterward sprang up in my heart against the vexations which these unhappy

people must suffer, and against their oppressors. That man, although in easy circumstances, did not dare to eat the bread he had earned by the sweat of his brow and could only avoid ruin by displaying the same misery wich prevailed all around him. I left his house equally touched and indignant, deploring the fate of these beautiful lands on which nature had lavished her gifts only to make them the prey of barbarous tax farmers.[7]

In the literary world France was still living on the reputation of its great classical writers: Corneille, Racine, Molière, Bossuet, La Fontaine, Saint-Simon. But the classicist of the seventeenth century had been replaced by the neoclassicist of the eighteenth. Form and discipline, which formerly shaped and molded taste, had now usurped it altogether. Science was the rage and analysis was in high fashion. Ladies of quality were performing scientific experiments to entertain their friends. Little explosions and chemical bubblings were occurring in the salons of Paris. Men and women of society had become amateur philosophers. In science, literature, and the arts, the dilettantes far outnumbered the professionals. There was much intellectualizing on the value of friendship and the grandeur of virtue. Behavior was carefully studied, and men and women achieved reputations for being "a noble friend" or "a man of virtue."

This was the atmosphere which greeted Rousseau on his arrival in Paris. The impression which Parisian society made on this country boy from Savoy is perhaps best expressed by the hero of his *New Eloise*:

It is not that people have failed to welcome me cordially, with friendship, kindness, and that they have not bestowed upon me a thousand courtesies. But that is exactly why I am complaining. How can you become immediately the friend of a man you have never seen? The honest human interest, the simple and moving effusion of a frank soul, speak in a language very different from the false demonstrations of politeness and the deceptive appearances which the customs of the world demand. I am very much afraid that a person who, on first sight, treats me as a friend of twenty years standing could treat me after twenty years as though I were a stranger if I had some important service to ask of him. When I see these dissipated gentlemen take such a tender interest in so many people I can easily believe that they are not genuinely interested in anyone.[8]

II

Rousseau's system of musical notation earned him a hearing by the French Academy of Sciences, but his work was found wanting. The system was, they said, difficult to learn, and besides, a certain Father Souhaitti had already brought forth a similar idea. However, his encounter with the French Academy and his frequent visits and examinations introduced him to many of the distinguished literary men and scientists of Paris. He formed a close friendship with Diderot, and the two of them often discussed their plans for the future together.

Father Castel, a priest whom Rousseau occasionally visited, advised him to try his hand with the ladies, and here a success of sorts finally came his way. He was introduced to Mme de Broglie and other ladies of Paris society including the famous Mme Dupin, with whom he promptly fell in love. But his love letter to her was returned with a few frigid words, and M. de Francueil, her stepson suggested he visit the home less often. Here again, he had failed to find that happy mean between arrogance and "base cowardice" which he had sought in his letter to the governor of Savoy. Having presumed too much he now felt obliged to apologize, and his furious pride, which would not yield to mere control, had to be subdued altogether. He wrote two letters to Mme Dupin and her husband on April 9 and 10, 1743, in which he poured out his regrets.[9] In his first letter he asked pardon of Mme Dupin for his effrontery in writing to her and begged forgiveness for his advances. His letter to M. Dupin was composed as a second and more indirect appeal to that gentleman's wife. He assured M. Dupin that he was not blind or vain enough to imagine he could ever be of any use to him. He insisted he had no talent or merit beyond his desire to please. He mentioned Mme Dupin's visible distaste for him and hoped that she could be brought to endure his presence. He passed, in short, from a casual assumption of equality with the Dupins to the attitude and approach of a family servant. This unsteady and erratic vacillation between pride and subservience was a critical element in his character. Sensing his own capacity for greatness, but unaware of how to proceed, convinced in advance of his unworthiness, he was ready to confess and own his guilt, even before he was accused.

With Mme de Broglie his approach was both more reserved and more successful. She secured a position for him as secretary to the Count de Montaigu, the French ambassador to Venice. Soon after his arrival in Venice, M. de Montaigu recognized Rousseau's quick intelligence and delegated considerable responsibility to him. Rousseau, for his part, had little respect for the ambassador and gradually came to regard himself as the center of the French embassy. He quarreled with his employer over protocol and constantly devised schemes to show his own tact and efficiency and highlight the ineffectiveness of M. de Montaigu. It is not surprising, therefore, that the two of them had a final heated argument in which Rousseau stalked out without his wages. The entire affair lasted about a year, and he was again without funds.

During his stay in Venice he had allowed some friends to talk him into visiting prostitutes, but he was so terrified of infection and so disturbed by the slightest physical defect in his partner that his experiences were not very enjoyable to him. Ever since childhood he had obtained his primary sexual satisfaction from masturbation and the masochistic fantasies which he associated with his act. His dreams were so much more pleasant than real women that he found little appeal in prostitutes. While one of the girls was able to work him into a fury of excitement, a slight malformation of her nipple was sufficient to discourage his attentions. The girl ended the affair by advising him to give up women and study mathematics.

Rousseau returned to Paris from Venice in the hope of presenting his own side of his quarrel with M. de Montaigu and obtaining some portion of his salary which the ambassador had detained after his departure. He finally recovered enough to pay his debts in Venice, but not enough to support him for any time in Paris. He determined, therefore, to seek his success in music and settled down at the Hotel Saint-Quentin to write and study. He was in the process of composing an opera in the French style, which he called *The Gallant Muses*. At this little hotel he met Thérèse Levasseur, the chambermaid who later became his mistress. A shy illiterate creature, she has been described by some writers as mentally defective. Rousseau's long relationship with Thérèse has been of much concern to his biographers. Scorn has been heaped on her. Rousseau has been criticized for the vulgarity of his taste in selecting Thérèse as a lifelong companion, and some writers consider his choice one of the many mysteries of his character. Vulliamy explains the matter by remarking that Rousseau needed her as a sexual object and as someone to cook for him. He sees no great mystery in the choice.

> In speaking of Rousseau's alliance with Thérèse, we cannot share the horror of those righteous, priggish, or sentimental persons who have been so much distressed by what they regard as the incongruity of his alliance. No one is fool enough to suppose that intellectual parity is what men really seek in women.[10]

Yet, Rousseau, in many of his previous contacts with women, had been charmed by their intelligence. Further, he remarks in his *Confessions* that chambermaids and shop girls seldom attracted him and that he was more stimulated by the fine complexion, elegance, and refinement of a lady of quality.[11] One must look further, therefore, for an explanation of his attraction to Thérèse.

In his identification with the weak and helpless, Rousseau showed great affection for all creatures who reminded him of his own condition. He was fond of children and could talk to them for hours provided he was not responsible for them. He also loved dogs and was, in later life, so solicitous of the happiness of his dog that he almost refused an audience with the king of England on the grounds that his dog might grow lonely, waiting for him to return, and run away. The weak creatures of the earth meant much to him, for they were the source of his strength. In relations with women Rousseau exhibited this same mixture of emotions. He loved to tremble with desire and supplication at the feet of great ladies, but he also enjoyed the righteous feeling of defending the underdog. Since a great lady could hardly be considered an underdog, she could satisfy only one side of his nature. She enabled him to revel in his masochism, but she failed to inspire the protective fury of the crusader.

The circumstances of his meeting with Thérèse placed her in the role of a defenseless creature who brought forth his sympathy. Protecting her, Rousseau sensed once again that proud feeling of the champion of the weak, the fighter against injustice.

> The first time I saw this girl appear at table I was struck by her modest bearing and still more by her lively and gentle glances, of which I had never seen the like before. The company at table . . . teased the little one; I defended her. Immediately the gibes were turned against me. Even if I had not felt a natural liking for that poor girl, compassion and defiance would have given me one. I have always admired decency in words and demeanor, particularly in the opposite sex. I became her avowed champion. I saw that she was touched by my protection and her looks, animated by a gratitude she dared not express in words, became all the more eloquent. She was very timid and so was I. Yet the intimacy which our common reserve would seem to preclude was very soon established.[12]

Rousseau remarked that he sought in Thérèse "the simplicity and docile heart," which Mme de Warens had found in him.[13] Here the identification is complete. Thérèse was but a reflection of Rousseau's estimate of himself, a helpless creature who needed to be cuddled and protected. While he was never able to teach her to read or write with any facility, she could cook and sew, and she proved capable of caring for his general physical needs. There were some arguments, as there are in all relationships, but Thérèse remained with him through all his difficulties and persecutions and—considering his painful urethral condition, a long-standing malady, which prevented any sexual intimacy in his later years—was a remarkably constant companion. Unfortunately, however, Rousseau acquired Thérèse's mother along with the daughter, and the old lady proved a veritable harridan. She sent for various relatives to share his meager earnings. She was constantly reminding him of unpaid bills and accepting money from his friends behind his back, never missing an opportunity to humiliate him in one way or another and describing him to his friends as a cruel tyrant. Diderot, who loved to give advice on virtue, would listen to the old woman's complaints and make recommendations for her care. This inquisitive concern on Diderot's part caused the first estrangement between him and Rousseau.

For his basic livelihood Rousseau was employed as a secretary to Mme Dupin, who had forgiven him his impudence, and to her stepson M. de Francueil. He earned enough for his subsistence and had sufficient free time to continue work in the musical field. He revised a work of Voltaire's for opera at the request of M. de Richelieu. His *Gallant Muses* was finally presented in 1745, much to the consternation of Rameau, who considered it an unworthy piece of work. Diderot introduced Rousseau to many of his literary friends and to the famous Holbach circle where atheism and virtue were the favorite topics of discussion. Rousseau was impressed by these learned conversations on the improvement of character and determined to reform his own impetuous nature. A test of his resolve occurred when he received an inheritance after the death of his father. Rousseau found himself waiting for news of the money with the greatest impatience. When the bill of exchange finally arrived, he grasped the envelope with feverish haste and began to tear it open. All at once he stopped himself and determined that he would not be such a slave to self-interest. He put the letter aside and did not open it until morning, after which he sent some of the money to Mme de Warens. This was his first serious effort to form a new character for himself, more in keeping with the ideals of Parisian society.

But with Rousseau the reform had to be more than a mere appreciation of virtue. He saw with the clear eye of a stranger the superficiality of salon morality: the double meanings, the sallies, the wit in place of wisdom. He had brushed against these fine "philosophical" people and had been profoundly influenced by them, but he was unable to accept their light-hearted approach to liberal reform. Timid and vacillating though he was, he determined to go beyond the mere mouthing of virtuous sentiments. His Genevan boyhood and his early religious experiences, which taught him to root out the sin within himself, his desire to please, and his provocative, masochistic temperament combined to provide a unique and original twist to the general idea of the perfectability of man and the reform of society.

It was M. de Franceuil who introduced Rousseau to Mme d'Epinay, the lady who was to play such an important role in his future life. She was Francueil's mistress and, while dining at her home with his employer, he was exposed to further conversations on love, character, and personal merit. So moved was the impressionable Jean-Jacques by this Parisian passion for virtue that he refused to deliver a secret letter from Mme d'Epinay to M. de Francueil out of his loyalty to the latter's wife. Further, he informed Mme d'Epinay that he would not visit her again if she made any more efforts of the same kind through him. Instead of being offended by his behavior, Mme d'Epinay praised his loyalty, and her friendship for him increased.

Through such incidents as these Rousseau began to gain stature among his new companions. His circle expanded beyond Diderot and Francueil to include the Abbé de Condillac, D'Alembert, and other habitues of the Holbach circle. He composed his first successful opera, *The Village Soothsayer*, and completed an article on music for the *Encyclopedic Dictionary* of Diderot and D'Alembert. But his forward-looking friends were frequently in trouble with the law, and it was not long before Diderot was imprisoned in the keep of Vincennes for his *Letter on the Blind*. Rousseau was touched by his plight and frequently visited him. On one of these occasions he was reading the *Mercure de France* as he walked along the road toward the keep. His eye chanced on the offer of a prize by the Dijon Academy for an answer to the question: Has the progress of the sciences and arts done more to corrupt morals or improve them? This simple offer served as a catalyst for one of his great moments of inspiration which he described in one of his letters to Malesherbes:

If ever anything resembled a sudden inspiration it was the change that took place in me as I read this. All at once I felt my mind dazzled by a thousand illuminations, a crowd of vivid ideas came upon me, all at the same moment, with a force and confusion which threw me into an unexpressible turmoil. I felt my head caught up in a giddiness like intoxication. A violent palpitation oppressed me, my chest heaving, no longer able to breathe while walking, I dropped under one of the trees on the avenue and passed half an hour there in such agitation that, on arising, I saw that the front of my vest was wet with my tears and I was unaware of having shed them. Oh Monsieur, if I could only have written a quarter of what I saw and felt under that tree, with what clarity I would have made men see the contradictions of our social system, with what force I would have exposed all the abuses of our institutions, with what simplicity I would have demonstrated that man is naturally good and that it is only through institutions that he becomes bad.[14]

Rousseau immediately composed a first draft of a reply to the question posed by the Academy and showed it to Diderot, who suggested some changes and urged him to compete for the prize.[15] The product of his efforts was his *Discourse on the Effect of the Arts and Sciences on Morals*, which won the prize of the Academy. This first *Discourse* set the basic tone for his future literary style. In many respects it is unfortunate that the Academy posed its question in regard to the arts and sciences, for Rousseau's major quarrel was not with culture, as such, but with the social conventions of his day.

It would be difficult to reconstruct completely the psychological background of his inspirational experience, but perhaps some elements of it may be described. Rousseau's early identification with the underdog and the pleasurable thrill of righteous indignation he obtained from opposing any form of oppression have already been mentioned. His identification with Thérèse in his desire to protect her from her tormentors and his sympathy with the French peasant who could not enjoy the fruits of his own labor are examples of this strong tendency. Yet he did not find in these experiences the ecstasy he discovered on the way to the keep of Vincennes. To find a comparable experience, one must return to that early beating by his Uncle Bernard and the ecstasy of his union with his cousin Abraham. This experience had the same passionate, emotional quality that he felt under the tree on the road to the keep. It seems evident from his description of his fervent embrace with his cousin that the two boys felt very close to each other because of their mutual suffering. Rousseau longed for a similar attachment, another passionate friendship with a man; yet he was terrified of overt homosexuality. The idea of falling in love with a man was extremely repulsive to him. He needed another basis for emotional involvement. In his *Confessions* one does not sense the degree of his attachment to Diderot until the latter is imprisoned, when Rousseau remarks, "Nothing could ever express the anguish I felt at my friend's misfortune." He believed he might go mad with concern for Diderot, and he felt a "pang of my heart" when he passed the keep. When he finally had an opportunity to see Diderot he "made one leap, uttered one cry; I pressed my face to his; I embraced him tightly, speaking to him only with my tears and my sobbing; I was choked with tenderness and joy."[16] He strove desperately to identify himself with Diderot, to feel his feelings, to console him in his misery, and he visited him every other day. Clearly, he was working himself up to a state of ecstasy similar to that experienced with his cousin.[17] He required only another beating or persecution to fuse himself completely with his beloved Diderot. Diderot had been imprisoned for his philosophy, his provocative ideas. Why could not Rousseau suffer the same experience? But where could he find a vehicle for his final act of faith and love? At this point he read the question posed by the Academy of Dijon.

Rousseau had no particular grievance against the arts and sciences. He had never had a formal education, but he was studying chemistry at the time and striving to become a successful composer, and he had a deep respect for the literature and history of the French. However, he had closely identified himself with the injured virtue of Diderot, and he felt within him the old fury against injustice—a feeling that inspired him to the attack. As he remarked in his *Discourse*, "It is not science . . . I am abusing; it is virtue I am defending."[18] In playing the role of defender of virtue, he described the arts and sciences as corrupting morals, since they "throw garlands of flowers over the chains of iron" which weigh man down.[19] By distracting him from the struggle for human liberty, they make a slave of man. Rousseau had clearly been trapped by his own subject matter. What he wanted to say was that society was wrong, social manners were hypocritical and stupid, social morals corrupt, evil men in power, and injustice everywhere. Since he felt society had degenerated morally and since his subject was the arts and sciences and their effect on morals, he could not very well say that morals had been improved! Thus, his peculiar and distorted attack led to his condemnation by the intellectuals as well as by the influential authorities of his time.

The theme of the *Discourse* was essentially that, despite the phenomenal development of the arts and sciences, morals had not been improved. If anything, he contended, man had been distracted from true moral attainment by the refinement of manners and the excessive sociability introduced through the arts. As a result men spent their energies learning how to please one another instead of striving toward genuine virtue.

Rousseau's attack on the arts and sciences did not have the same antiliberal implications that such an approach would have today. In eighteenth-century France, it was fashionable to be an intellectual. The term "intellectual," with the derogatory implication of "egg-head," was not used. Translations of Rousseau's first *Discourse* refer to his statement that he would be at no pains to please the "intellectuals"[20] and that all "intellectuals" save one (Montaigne) were forever making a parade of their talents.[21] Yet the actual expression in both these instances is "beaux esprits," a satirical term as used in his essay, but a term which predates the condemnation of intellectuals as a group.[22] In short, Rousseau was not attempting to curry favor with those in power by an attack on intellectuals. He was attacking intellectuals for their failure to inspire revolt, for hiding behind quips and witticisms, for failure to reform society. Rousseau said many times in later works that he was not opposed to education or learned men as such, but only to the false, showy display of learning as a form of entertainment and a distraction from the great social problems of the day.

There was another reason why Rousseau cut himself adrift from all support. A martyr is not a true martyr if he has the whole intellectual community behind him. His negative answer to the question posed by the Academy came in part from his desire to stand as the lonely and defiant one—the one who, like his friend Diderot, had struck out against established authority and accepted beliefs.[23] The punishment which he anticipated for his heresy is evident in the preface, in which he remarks:

> I foresee that I will not easily be forgiven for the position I have taken. Setting myself against that which is admired by the man of today I can only expect universal condemnation.[24]

The desire to suffer as a martyr explains only the provocative nature of Rousseau's first *Discourse*. It does not tell why he was so profoundly stimulated by a question dealing with the arts and sciences nor does it reveal the psychological sources for his argument.

The experience that brought forth his first *Discourse* was not unique in the annals of literature. His description is similar to reports of mystical ecstasies of saints or the strong communion Bucke[25] and others have reported as an indication of a "cosmic consciousness." In Rousseau's case, however, one has the impression that he added nothing to what he actually felt. For such an imaginative person this is remarkable. To him it was a wonderful emotional experience, but he heard no voices and claimed no contact with the supernatural. He felt it as something entirely within himself. Somehow the ideas suggested by the item in the *Mercure de France* brought forth such a rush of exhilarating emotion that he achieved a kind of spiritual ecstasy. What was there about this "discovery" that the arts and sciences had enslaved man that brought him such overwhelming pleasure?

F. C. Green[26] has indicated one of these factors in the "sour grapes" mechanism. Rousseau was struggling for success in the world of arts and letters at the time, and he had met with a great wall of discouragement. His scheme of musical notation had been ignored, his opera achieved very limited recognition. It seemed he would be a minor scribbler and music copyist for the remainder of his career. If he was destined for failure in the artistic world, did this really mean he was unworthy? Certainly not! The mere outward show of success was no indication of the virtue of a man. He would convince himself and others that the success he had failed to achieve was not really worth having. Gran[27] makes a similar point, but stresses the sudden emergence of Rousseau's half-forgotten memories of Geneva and its austere moral climate at a time when he was a failure in Paris.

Starobinski[28] compares the fall of man, as illustrated in the first *Discourse*, with Rousseau's own fall from grace over the incident of the broken comb. Here for the first time the young Jean-Jacques discovered that one's personal knowledge of innocence is not a sufficient defense against the apparent proof of guilt, that each man's conscience is a separate entity and cannot be made transparent to another human being. Thus came the rude exit from the paradise of his childhood simplicity, his naive trust in the godlike wisdom of adults, into the world of uncertainty and shifting appearances. "How sweet would it be to live among us," he cries out in the first effusion of his tearful discovery, "if our external appearance were always the image of our heart's inclination."[29] This was the message that came to him in that moment of rapture on the way to the keep. If only one could return to that forthright and open world—that time before deception and ambivalence! The innocence of these childhood years symbolized for Rousseau the time of natural sweetness and docility, before an oppressive sense of external authority brought a feeling of personal slavery.

But what was there about literature and the arts and sciences which aroused these dormant feelings? To phrase the question of the Academy in another way, what had been the effect of literature, the arts, and sciences on morality? Literature had a profound association with Rousseau's past. Connected with the period of innocence when his father read to him, it was also associated with a state of slavery. It might be hypothesized at this point that, in the question posed by the Academy, he reacted only to the word "literature" and worked the arts and sciences into his essay after his emotional experience.

As a child actor, playing the part of his mother, he read to his father and learned to be docile and passive in dealing with this tempestuous and erratic character. In this relationship he sacrificed the more active, striving, masculine side of himself for peace and security. Only in adulthood did he realize half-consciously that he had been a willing slave. Not fully understanding his own experience, he recognized that his feelings had a certain universal quality. When he happened on the question posed by the Academy of Dijon, it acted as a sudden trigger, releasing the pent-up and confused feeling about asceticism and freedom, learning and slavery. Projecting his own childhood experience on all of mankind, he remarked:

> (The arts, literature, and the sciences) stifle in men that feeling of original liberty, for which they seem to have been born; cause them to love their own slavery, and so make of them what is called a civilized people.[30]

More than any of his other works his first *Discourse* was a truly personal document. In almost every reference to the subject he mentions that, for him, civilization, the arts, and sciences, represented a feminine subservience.

> Richness of costume may proclaim the man of opulence, and elegance the man of taste: the healthy and robust man is known by other signs; it is under the rustic habit of a laborer, and not under the gilt of the courtier that one finds strength and vigor of body. Fancy dress is no less a stranger to virtue, which is the strength and vigor of the spirit. The honest man is an athlete who is glad to wrestle naked; he scorns all those vile ornaments which prevent the use of his forces and for the most part have been invented only to *conceal some deformity* (italics mine)....[31] What fatal splendor has succeeded the Roman simplicity? What is this foreign language? What are these effeminate manners? ...[32] One sex dare not approve anything which is not proper to the pusillanimity of the other.... Tell us, celebrated Voltaire, how many strong and masculine productions you have sacrificed to our false delicacy....[33] Study of the sciences is more likely to make man soft and effeminate than firm and courageous.[34]

This sudden attack on slavery after a moment of inspiration, this assertion of a heretofore unsuspected masculine side of himself, would certainly indicate, if we had not already suspected it, that the docility and sweetness of his childhood were not altogether a product of his father's indulgence. We know that the older Rousseau had a quick temper, was often in public disputes, and beat his elder son until the boy left home. Jean-Jacques must have been terrified by the scenes of violence and may often have heard the screams of his brother from an adjacent room. In such a situation an imaginative child was free to elaborate in his own mind the terrible image of what might be happening to his brother. He no doubt adopted the submissive role as a response to terror and learned to love his new-found position only when he had forgotten its cause.

Once having accepted this passive role, he was safe. He was loved and accepted by his father. He was indulged as a child who could do no harm. This state of innocence persisted for a time at Bossey, but with the incident of the broken comb his childhood paradise came to an end. To paraphrase Starobinski once more, the period of transparence was over, and Rousseau was faced with the obstacle, the opacity of his own soul, the inability to communicate his innocence, the terrible sense of injustice. But by a peculiar twist of character this very obstacle gave him a more intense and violent pleasure than the transparence had ever afforded. He clasped his cousin in his arms, and the two of them cried out in a rage, filled with a sense of their own virtue.

It happened that at the time of his revelation he was on his way to visit another friend who was unjustly imprisoned, a friend whom he had clasped in his arms with a cry of anguish as he had his cousin Abraham, deriving a certain pleasure from his identification with his friend. On the way to the keep he chanced on the question which set him reflecting on the role of literature in the development of virtue, and he experienced once again some of his old feelings of outraged innocence. This time, however, there was an assertion of a certain distinctly provocative element. He was no longer content to suffer and take consolation in his sense of virtue. One might even suspect that for the first time he began to recall some of his feelings toward his father before he had adopted the role of the docile pet. An anger, a rebellion against unjust authority surged up within him. Did he experience a frightening return to consciousness of his competitive and hostile feelings toward his father which had been so deeply repressed for so many years? If these feelings did recur, they must certainly have overwhelmed him. But apparently there was also a certain catharsis, a relief that his anger had at last emerged.

The memory of the incident was soon shrouded, and Rousseau forgot most of his thoughts under the tree. But he did recall the feelings and gave vent to them in his *Discourse*. Critics of the time were struck by the boldness, the fire, the "masculinity" of his expression.[35]

However, concurrent with this note of rebellion the *Discourse* also portrays his longing for the lost transparence of his childhood. Outrage and nostalgia were both a part of it, giving the entire essay a strong sense of irony. These two contrary feelings were to persist in

Rousseau's life and his future writings, giving rise to strange and seemingly inexplicable twists in his meaning and his style. He had accepted the role of the rebel, the man of virtue who protests against injustices, but he could never forget that early period of his life when goodness came easily, without protest and struggle, when he felt loved and understood by an all-seeing and all-powerful parent.

III

Rousseau recognized that his first *Discourse* was a hasty, poorly thought out work, and he regarded it as the least worthy of his writings.[36] He showed it only to Diderot. This was his way of drawing close to his friend and making his essay a part of their private experience together. He had forgotten the work when the Academy informed him that he had won the prize.

One might well ask how Rousseau could have achieved such recognition if his essay was so illogical and inconsistent. Actually, Dijon was one of several provincial cities which possessed local academies in imitation of the famous French Academy in Paris. French society at the time was one of active intellectual curiosity which reached to all levels of the people. In many instances the search for the unique and original dominated the minds of minor academicians and respect for logic took second place.

But Rousseau's essay was more than merely unique. He had that gift of style which few writers possess—a capacity for teasing out and portraying in graphic detail the weakness of manners and customs. Here, for example, is a quotation from the first *Discourse:*

> How sweet would it be to live among us if our external appearances were always the image of our heart's inclination; if decency were only virtue, if our maxims served to guide our conduct, if true philosophy were inseparable from the title of philosopher! But so many good qualities too rarely go together; and virtue is seldom seen amid such grand ceremony. . . .
>
> Today, now that more subtle research and more refined taste have reduced the art of pleasing to formalities, there prevails in our manners a cheap and deceptive uniformity, and all minds seem fashioned in the same mold: without ceasing politeness demands one thing, propriety ordains another, and thus must we always follow them, never our own inclinations.[37]

Obviously, the art to which Rousseau refers is the art of social graces. While he makes a few jabs at art and science as such, these arguments are by far the weakest in the essay. Science, he says, being the effect of idleness, generates idleness and causes a loss of time to society. But it was the social insight in his first *Discourse* which aroused his readers against the moral laxity of his time. Even this early work had the epigrammatic style, that quotable quality which gave his sentences the ring of truth.

> Civilized peoples cultivate them (the arts and sciences): happy slaves, you owe to them that fine and delicate taste on which you pride yourselves, that sweetness of character and urbanity of manners which makes commerce among you so smooth and easy; in a word the appearance of all the virtues without having any.[38]

The French society of his time was, as a matter of fact, too exquisite. People had laughed at the overrefinement of manners and had made sport of the French nobility, but Rousseau was angry. He was not content with a bright quip. He was leading the charge, and though his followers were still at quite a distance, he was a primary figure in the destruction of the way of life of the old régime.

IV

It is sometimes difficult for us to remember that Jean-Jacques Rousseau, who had such a profound influence on French history, was actually a Genevan with the traditional Genevan gravity where moral issues were concerned. While he loved a good time and visited the theater twice a week, he firmly believed that the most valuable aspect of a society was the virtue of the people. Like his Calvinist forefathers, he found little merit in a religion which preached a doctrine of virtue but practiced a broad tolerance and a facile indulgence toward all forms of vice. Nor was he content (as was his patron, Mme Dupin) to present a tidy little essay on friendship and its role in uplifting one's moral character. He was not intrigued by remedies; he demanded total reform. He was not interested in poking fun at society and amusing his contemporaries with little rapier thrusts of wit. He stepped forth with a broad bladed axe and struck at the roots of French manners and morals.

Rousseau's contemporaries often remarked that he lacked a sense of humor; yet his writings conveyed more than a mere lack of this quality. A certain direct sincerity about his style gave his readers the feeling he was pouring out his heart to them. His pose as one honest man amid a pack of liars and knaves was actually quite convincing. The injection of humor into his works would have detracted from his effectiveness. It was this quality of directness, this humorless honesty which produced so much more resentment against Rousseau than against the other writers of his time. There are many examples in which Rousseau was attacked for saying, with all seriousness, something that had been said in jest many times before. Perhaps the most striking illustration of this is the contrasting reaction of the public to Rousseau and Grimm when they were both attacking French music.

Rousseau had long been charmed by Italian music. His *Village Soothsayer*, an opera which gained him considerable recognition, was a departure from the classic French style of Rameau in the direction of the more lively Italian music. Shortly before the *Soothsayer*'s performance in Paris, an Italian opera company visited the city and made a profound impression. Many prominent people in the literary and artistic world expressed their enthusiasm for Italian music and proclaimed its superiority to French music. The way was thus prepared for Rousseau's *Village Soothsayer* and its success was assured. However, the controversy between the French and Italian partisans had now become heated. Rousseau, in typical fashion, described the supporters of French music as the more powerful and more numerous party, made up of the great, the rich, and the ladies, while opponents were a "little group" of the really talented people, the men of genius, the true lovers of music; in short, the underdogs.[39] The champions of Italian music gathered under the queen's box at the opera, and their opponents used as their headquarters the area under the king's box. Soon pamphlets were flying back and forth, and Grimm and Rousseau both joined the fray. But while Grimm's pamphlet, *The Little Prophet*, was an amusing and witty piece, written with tongue in cheek, Rousseau's *Letter on French Music* was a deadly serious, point by point attack that struck at the heart of the slow, unmelodious French style and the French language. His attack stunned Paris and raised so many cries against him that he felt sure he was about to be assassinated. Grimm observed that the French would forgive anyone who made them laugh, but could find no pleasure in this coarse brute who tried to demonstrate that the French language is inept and unsuitable for musical composition and that the French had never had music and never would have.[40]

It is quite ironic that Rousseau, in his own perverse way, loved passionately the very people whose music, manners, and culture he so vigorously attacked. In contrast to Voltaire, the Frenchman who admired English freedom, Rousseau, the Genevan, adored the French. He was profoundly impressed by French literature and the French theater. But his peculiar and complex nature was such that he could not love anyone or anything without a contrary provocative tendency. This conflict of love and hate, this tender fury, produced much apparent inconsistency in his works. At one point in his *Confessions* he expressed his feelings quite openly:

> My heart beat with joy at its (France's) least success and its reverses afflicted me as though I had suffered them myself. If this folly had only been a passing one I would not bother to mention it, but it became so deeply rooted in my heart without any reason that when later at Paris I was playing the antidespot and proud republican, I felt, in spite of myself, a secret predeliction for this very nation I found to be servile and for the government I affected to condemn. The ridiculous part of it was that, being ashamed of an inclination so contrary to my maxims, I never dared confess it to anyone, and I jeered the French on their defeats while my heart bled for them more than did their own. I am surely the only man who, living in the midst of a people who treated him well and whom he adored, has put on among them, a pretense of scorn. In short, I have found this partiality so strong, so constant, so invincible, and so disinterested on my part that even after I have left the kingdom, since its government, magistrates, and writers have vied with one another in unleashing their invective against me, and since it has become fashionable to overwhelm me with injustices and outrages I have been unable to cure myself of my folly. I love them in spite of myself, although they maltreat me.[41]

While this quotation shows a certain insight, on Rousseau's part, into his perverse nature, he did not really accept the fact that the abuse he received was a response to his provocation. He always felt others should read his heart, see through to his true feelings, and ignore his outward behavior. Since he was conscious only of his love for his fellowmen, he expected them to love him in return, and he never really understood the anger he aroused.

v

The prize for his first essay brought Rousseau's name into great prominence. It was about this same time that his only really successful musical work, *The Village Soothsayer*, began to achieve popular recognition. These twin victories brought him to the attention of the literary men of his time. While his circle of friends gradually widened, he regarded Diderot and Grimm as his closest companions. When

Grimm had first come to Paris, he was alone and without friends. It was natural, therefore, that the sympathetic Rousseau should take him in hand and introduce him to the influential literary men in the city. When Grimm lapsed into a long depression as a result of an unsuccessful attempt to win the love of an actress, Rousseau stayed with him all day and the Abbé Reynal all night. The two friends finally succeeded in rousing Grimm from his depression. Once Grimm recovered, Rousseau found that they were no longer as close as they had been. Pity was for him the primary vehicle in the expression of his friendship. He had first been attracted to Grimm when the latter was a stranger, a German in Paris. When Grimm began to achieve social success, the two men began to see less of each other. Finally Rousseau said to him, "Grimm, you are neglecting me; I forgive you. When the first intoxication of your uproarious success has spent itself and you feel its emptiness, I hope that you will come back to me. You will always find me the same. As for the present don't strain yourself (ne vous gênez point). I leave you free of obligation and I will wait for you."[42] Grimm, no doubt, recognized the condescension and possessiveness behind Rousseau's magnanimous gesture, for their relationship seems to have deteriorated from this time. Another factor in the gradual estrangement from both Grimm and Diderot was the new personality which Rousseau acquired along with his success.

In 1752, in the early stages of his literary popularity, Rousseau had a serious attack of his old malady, a constriction of the urethra which caused him severe pain and made urination almost impossible. Mme Dupin sent for a doctor Morand who gave her some advice on his condition. When word of it got to Rousseau he took it to mean that he had only six months to live. He resolved to spend his remaining days living the life of virtue of which he had spoken in his first *Discourse*. He had proposed that men should be natural. He had professed to despise social convention. Therefore, he resolved to root out from his behavior all pretense and sham, to be completely honest and sincere in his relationship with others, to avoid the servile manner, the flowery speech, and the fancy clothing which he had criticized with such firmness in his *Discourse*. He gave up his best wig and wore a simple round one. He abandoned his sword, stripped the gold lace from his clothing, and refused to wear white stockings. When Thérèse's brother stole his white shirts, he replaced them with coarse linen. As a final gesture he sold his watch, saying that he no longer needed to know the time. Certainly, his intention to be "natural" and sincere was genuine, but in characteristic fashion, with a lack of awareness of his aggressive and hostile feelings toward others, he was often rude when he intended only to be honest.

He was basically a timid person with a strong desire to please, but he had long been frustrated by his inability to conform to the complex social customs of Parisian society. His success with the first *Discourse* gave him an opportunity for a frontal attack on the very customs which had been giving him so much trouble. He showed a certain insight into his own motives when he remarked in his *Confessions*, "My foolish and sullen silence, which I could not overcome, came from my fear of being unable to perform the social niceties. In order to give myself courage, I decided to trample them all underfoot. I became cynical and sarcastic out of shame; I affected to despise the politeness I did not know how to practice."[43] However, by discarding all the usual frills and courtesies of polite society, Rousseau, with the uncanny instinct of the public-relations man, was doing the very thing that would attract notice to himself. Underneath his shy exterior, he loved attention, and, while he did not recognize this side of his personality, his actions inevitably betrayed this trait to others. The mistake on the part of his literary enemies lies in their assumption that he was deliberately and consciously playing for attention. As in the incident in which he exposed his behind to the girls, he now was exposing his personality for a similar intention. Gone, however, was the sense of evil attached to his action. Through an alliance between his conscience and his exhibitionistic desires he was now exposing himself for high moral purposes.

The new character he had adopted was unsteady at best. He still had a horror of hurting the feelings of anyone, and his façade of boldness and abruptness was only a façade, nothing more. When he was having breakfast at a cafe, he heard a retired officer boasting of having been present at a rehearsal of *The Village Soothsayer* and describing the author in great detail. Rousseau became extremely embarrassed for he felt someone would recognize him and call to him, thus exposing the lies of the storyteller. He blushed, hurriedly finished his chocolate, and slunk away.

On the performance of *The Village Soothsayer* for the king, he gives us another indication of the malaise he felt in his role of social rebel. He had expected jeers for his outlandish behavior and dress and had prepared himself for social disapproval (a symbolic smack on the buttocks in more socially acceptable form), but when people were nice to him in spite of his conduct, he was completely disarmed.

On that day I was dressed in my usual careless manner; with a growth of beard and a poorly combed wig. Regarding this lack of propriety as an act of courage, I entered, in this fashion, the very hall where the King, the Queen, the royal family, and the whole court were soon due to arrive. I went from there to take the seat to which M. de Cury conducted me, which was his own. It was a large box seat opposite a smaller and higher one where the King sat with Mme de Pompadour. Surrounded by ladies and the only man in the front of the box I could not doubt that I had been placed there for the very purpose of being seen. When the house lights came on and I saw myself, dressed as I was, in the midst of people very elegantly attired, I began to be ill at ease. I asked myself whether I was in my proper place, if I was suitably dressed, and after some minutes of uneasiness I answered, 'yes,' with a firmness which perhaps came more from the impossibility of undoing what I had done than from the strength of my conviction. . . . But whether it was the effect of the presence of the King or the natural disposition of those around me, I saw nothing but civility and kindness in the curiosity of which I was the object. I was so touched by this that I commenced to be disquieted all over again about myself and the fate of my play, fearing that I might destroy the favorable impression of these people who seemed to wish only to applaud me. I was armed against their raillery, but their benevolent attitude, which I had not expected, overcame me so completely that I trembled like a child when the play began.[44]

In one sense Rousseau's naturalism was the most unnatural thing about him. Yet in another sense this proud republican, this bold conqueror of Paris, represented a suppressed side of his character which had been held in abeyance by his fear of hurting others and by his need to please. There were several instances in his past life when he had exhibited a bold, audacious, and even cruel side to his character. He defied his Uncle Bernard, rushed with his fists to the defense of his cousin Abraham, and tortured poor Marion until she was in despair. But in the incident of Marion and the stolen ribbon, Rousseau's boldness was not supported by a sense of virtue, and it left him with a terrible ache of guilt and anguish. He learned from this experience that he he could only take pleasure in hurting others when he could wound with the sword of justice. He was a complex character who loved to suffer and to hurt, to please and to offend, and he was evolving a style of life that would permit some satisfaction of his many passions.

Instead of meeting his new mode of life with abuse, as he might have expected, Parisian society, with its search for the unique and different, found him charming. He became a "character" and was much sought after at social functions. He was soon known as "the virtuous Jean-Jacques." Everyone wanted to meet him and dispute his ideas. He became so popular that he longed for his former privacy, and the time he spent answering his critics by letter distracted him from his plans for further literary work. Parisian booksellers were notoriously sharp in their dealings with new authors, and Rousseau had made almost nothing from his first literary effort. He was soon badly in need of money. However, when he was asked to present himself to the king after the performance of his *Village Soothsayer* and M. de Cury indicated his belief that Rousseau was about to receive a pension, he became upset. The mixture of his extreme shyness, his urethral difficulty which necessitated frequent trips from the room to relieve himself, and his republican principles against accepting money from those in power caused him to depart from Fontainebleau the next day. When Diderot heard of his behavior, he was outraged. He was already somewhat annoyed by his friend's title as a man of virtue, an appellation which had formerly been Diderot's alone. He pointed out that Rousseau had an obligation to support Thérèse and her family and should apply for the pension. But Rousseau, who could live for several years at the expense of Mme de Warens (who cared for him out of love) could not take a sou from the king. "How should I be able to speak again of independence and disinterestedness?" he told himself. "So long as I took that pension I should have to flatter or be silent."[45] Diderot accepted an extravagant financial reward from the empress of Russia, who "purchased" his library and then paid him to be its custodian, and Voltaire was enjoying pensions from Frederick the Great and Mme de Pompadour. Rousseau refused pensions all his life in spite of his own great need. The terrible, slow torture of his withdrawal from Les Charmettes had made him acutely conscious of the pain of being dependent on someone who did not love him.

But the new Jean-Jacques was not created overnight, nor could he always afford the luxury of virtue. When his union with Thérèse bore its first fruit he felt unable to support his child, and since he had heard others describe how they had left their illegitimate children at the local Foundling Hospital, he chose this method of avoiding what appeared an insupportable burden. He reports that a total of five of his progeny were disposed of in this fashion to the distress of Thérèse who wanted to keep them.[46] While he came to regret his act in later years and made efforts to find his lost children, they were beyond recovery and neither he nor Thérèse had kept any record of their distinguishing physical characteristics.

VI

In November 1753 the Academy at Dijon posed another question of interest to Rousseau: the origin of the inequality of mankind. In order to give the matter thought, he left with Thérèse for the wooded country of Saint-Germain, where he remained eight or ten days developing his ideas while wandering in the natural surroundings he loved. The country air seemed to improve his health as well as his inspiration, and he resolved to seek this type of environment for his future creative work.

His second *Discourse*, on the origin of inequality, gave him a more direct opportunity to expand on his favorite theme of the superficiality and injustice of society. Aside from the fanciful construction of early history and primitive man, its theme is similar to that of the first *Discourse*, although it is much better written. In the state of nature, said Rousseau, man was simple, rude, and natural. He took what he wanted by force if he was strong enough. With the advent of civilization, refined manners, and the temptations of luxury, man has been seduced into slavery through his greed and vanity. He has sold his natural liberty to rulers who promise him personal luxury, prestige, and the illusion of power.

In the *Discourse on Inequality* Rousseau showed himself capable of careful preparation. Having rid himself of the first burst of energy and indignation against society, he began to develop his ideas and buttress them with logic, while, at the same time, maintaining the full charge of his eloquence. In the second *Discourse* appears the statement of his new manifesto. Here he tried to do for society what he could never do for himself: to eradicate forever the slave in man, to free him from the yoke of custom and submission to his fellows.

With a deliberate evolutionary approach Rousseau illustrated the various differences between the savage and the civilized state; the excess food consumed by civilized man, the late hours, the countless artificial sources of excitation, exquisite foods, overheating, etc. The clothes, tools, and entertainments with which civilized man had surrounded himself had finally made him incapable of survival if he were once more placed in his natural habitat. In this sense he remarked, with his usual propensity for exaggeration, that if nature had intended man to be healthy, "a thinking man is a depraved animal."[47]

A gift for the grand flourish was Rousseau's strength as well as his greatest weakness. Exaggeration was an integral part of his eloquence, and, while attracting readers by its dash and boldness, it often carried him far beyond his meaning. The same tendency for exaggeration characterized his emphasis on the competitive (as opposed to the cooperative) aspects of society, portraying each man as ready to profit by the misfortune of his neighbor.

Shortly after completing his second *Discourse*, he decided to accompany Gauffecourt on a trip to Geneva. During the journey Gauffecourt's attempt on the virtue of Thérèse caused the friendship between the two men to cool decidedly, and Rousseau did not return with him. He traveled through Savoy on the way to Geneva and spent a few heart-breaking moments with Mme de Warens. He was pained to see her in worse financial straits than ever. He urged her to come and live with Thérèse and himself, but she refused, preferring to cling to her small pension, and offered Thérèse her only remaining jewel—a ring from her finger. This so touched Rousseau that he felt like a scoundrel leaving her alone without help. He left her a small sum of money, but he always felt as though he should have given up everything at that moment and devoted his life to making her last years happy.

His return to Geneva and to the religious environment of his childhood had a profound effect on him. He had always detested the irreverent Parisian chitchat about God, and he found that he more than ever admired the simple faith of the Genevans, who had, he felt, the good sense not to argue about things not subject to argument. He had taken to reading and studying his Bible and had been more impressed by the ethical message of Jesus than by all the ritual he had encountered. He soon concluded that the outward form of religious worship meant very little and was dependent on the laws and customs of a country. The only truly significant aspect of Christianity was in the words of Jesus Christ.[48] With these beliefs and with the example of the solid citizens of Geneva before him, he decided to return to the faith of his father and apply for the citizenship which he had abandoned as a youth. After some wrangling the Consistory, making an exception in his case, restored his citizenship and admitted him to communion.

Rousseau was so impressed by his native city that he dedicated his second *Discourse* to the Republic. He was charmed by his fellow citizens and the town of his birth and decided, in one of his impulsive, emotional flurries, to live there forever. However, aside from the few friends he made there, he soon found that his countrymen were not so captivated by his works as he was by Geneva. His second *Discourse* was received unfavorably by the Council, and it had little success with the Genevans. Such remarks as the following may well have shocked the solid property-conscious citizens:

> The first man who, having enclosed a piece of land, took it into his head to say *this is mine*, and found people simple enough to believe it, was the true founder of civil society. From what crimes, wars, murders, what miseries and horrors would not one have spared mankind who, pulling up the stakes or filling in the ditch,

had cried to his fellowman, 'Beware of listening to this imposter; you are lost if you forget that the fruits of the earth belong to everyone and the earth itself to no one.'[49]

Although the *Origins of Inequality* was a much more effective piece of writing than the first *Discourse*, it did not win the prize from the Academy. Nevertheless, it established Rousseau's reputation as an iconoclast and made a much deeper impression on his literary colleagues than the first *Discourse*. Rousseau was already famous before it was published. With its publication he became notorious. Many of his former friends in Geneva were cool toward him, and others attacked him openly. However, in both Paris and Geneva small groups of Rousseau partisans were beginning to form. His stature among the Holbach circle began to grow, and Diderot urged him to write an article for the *Encyclopedia*. In 1755 his *Discourse on Political Economy* appeared in that controversial work. With this new work there came a certain change in Rousseau's attitude toward the state. Still the rebel and champion of individual freedom, he demonstrated serious concern for the preservation of effective government.

This work showed the emergence of his attempt to reconcile the rights of the individual with the necessity of preserving a peaceful community. In his second *Discourse* he had shouted "Imposter!" at the first man to enclose a piece of ground. Now he described property as "the most sacred of all the rights of citizens."[50] In the earlier works he spoke of the natural propensities of man. Now he spoke of man the social animal, and he considered problems such as the basis for public justice and the derivation of authority. Such creatures as kings existed and exercised authority in the modern state. Further, since the desires of the individual in a state of nature might conflict with those of his neighbor, laws were necessary to keep the peace.

In this work he began to evolve in more detail his idea of a "general will" for the good of society and to distinguish it from the individual will to personal gain that characterized the members of the society. Rousseau's general will was a kind of ethical absolute which he did not expect to see arise from every deliberation of the people, for mortals can be deceived and misled. Even when a popular government —one based on the general will of the people—has been elected, there is no guarantee that those in authority will have the wisdom to distinguish between what is good for them and what is good for their people as a whole.[51]

How, then, could one restrain this desire for individual gain and self-glorification which upset the economy? Rousseau had several answers to this question. The first was good legislation: laws based on the general will. Since the power of a law is based more on its own inherent wisdom than on the severity of the magistrates, the lawgiver is all important. However, the people must also love the law, and this can only happen when the reign of virtue has been established. To accomplish this difficult feat Rousseau called forth all the forces of education, not only in the schools but in the very structure and conduct of the state, to instill the ardor of patriotism in the citizens.[52]

It is a significant and enduring aspect of Rousseau's political philosophy that the stability of a state and the contentment of its citizens were based on human emotion rather than on the logical organization of the governmental mechanism. Even the law, which he regarded as "the most sublime of all human institutions,"[53] was a matter of the integrity of the legislator, his capacity to listen to his heart and hear the beat of the general will. One cannot obtain obedience, he said, by mere punishment; and the more clever precautions one invents to counter cheating among public officials, the more ingenious will be the schemes devised to evade them.[54] While he despised despotism, he recognized that an even greater danger to the state lay in the political apathy of its citizens. When the state loses the ardor of its people, they engage in personal economic adventures and petty power struggles. The individual wills gradually assert themselves over the general will, and the dissolution of the state is already accomplished in the hearts of citizens before the armies are defeated and the buildings crumble.[55]

Rousseau did propose some measures which he felt might promote a sense of virtue in citizens without the prior existence of great patriots. In his third secton on public subsistence he recommended heavy taxes on all luxuries such as servants, rich furniture, and fine clothes. This would serve to discourage at least the more exaggerated excesses and, at the same time, reduce the burden of taxation on the poor.[56] In regard to agriculture he would reverse the tax policy of France (without mentioning that country by name). He pointed out that heavy taxes on crops amount to a tax on honest effort and that the example of several other nations demonstrates that, where the farmer is not so severely taxed, he will produce more.[57] Money, he felt, was the source of much of the evil in society. Farmers were forced to sell their produce cheap to get money for the heavy taxes. The emphasis on a money economy resulted from the aggressive national self-consciousness of one country in regard to another. Everyone wanted to impress foreigners instead of attempting to make the people happy. There should be, instead, scrupulous care in enabling each man to earn the basic necessities of life. Personal taxes and taxes on essentials "directly attack the right of property,"[58] which, as noted, he now regarded as sacred.

At this point it would seem that Rousseau's revised attitude toward property calls for some clarification, for he would severely restrain the use of luxury property even though he feels the first condition of the social compact is that "each person should be maintained in the peaceful possession of what belongs to him."[59] However, the apparent change from his earlier writings is more in appearance than in actuality. The cry of "Imposter!" toward the property owner is still in his heart. Now, however, he refines his attack and directs it toward the man who claims more property than he can cultivate, who seeks exclusive privileges through the accumulation of wealth, who subverts the law by his demand for special consideration—in short, that demon from the bowels of hell, the rich man.

> Are not all the advantages of society for the rich and powerful? Do they not hold all the lucrative positions? Are not all the favors and exemptions reserved for them alone? Is not the public authority always on their side? If an esteemed gentleman robs his creditors or performs other knaveries is it not always with impunity? Are not the beatings he delivers, the violence he commits, the very murders and assassinations of which he is guilty, matters to be hushed up and which at the end of six months no one questions any longer? But if the same man is robbed, the entire police force is immediately in operation and God help the innocent persons who come under suspicion! Does he pass through a dangerous region? He is accompanied by escorts from the country. Does the axle on his chaise break? Everyone flies to help him. Does someone make a noise at his door? He speaks a word and all is silence. Is he hampered by the crowd? He makes a gesture and everyone gets out of his way. Does a wagon driver bar his passage? His servants are prepared to beat the driver's brains out and fifty honest pedestrians, minding their own business, had better be crushed under the wheels than an idle blackguard be delayed in his coach.[60]

There is a special quality of venom in this description of the rights of the rich which transfers the problem from the sphere of an equitable economic adjustment to that of open class warfare. It is a foretaste of that frenzy which was to be brought to a climax during the French Revolution. Rousseau's own personal struggle with submission and domination was at the root of the problem. He pictured the rich and poor as separate beings. The rich man was not merely showing an excessive zeal for his own security, he was deliberately and consciously forcing the poor man under and taking a perverse delight in watching him suffer. For evidence on this point we need only return, for a moment, to the *Origin of Inequality* to find the statement:

> . . . if one sees a handful of the rich and powerful at the height of grandeur and fortune while the crowd grovels in misery and obscurity, this is because the former value the things they possess only to the extent that others are deprived of them, and that, without changing their condition, they would cease to be happy if the common people ceased to be miserable.[61]

Here, again, is one of those graphic instances in which Rousseau projected his internal dynamics onto the forces of social conflict. He magnified the deliberate cruelty of the rich man in order to justify the intensity of his own aggressive impulses. It was only through his identification with the poor and their suffering that he could release his rage against the rich—and other representatives of authority.

The first two discourses were written when Rousseau was "intoxicated with virtue," a period which lasted, in its highest intensity, from four to six years after his personal reform. With the departure from Paris his personality underwent a change. The *New Eloise*, which he began shortly after his arrival at the Hermitage—the cottage provided him by Mme d'Epinay—was a sharp break from the style and content of his previous political writings. From championing Spartan virtues he shifted to writing one of the "effeminate" novels which he had formerly decried. But the change was, according to Rousseau, merely a return to his former self, for he was naturally dreamy and sensual. Further, it was by no means a mere reversion but an oscillation between the two sides of himself, for his earlier sentiments were to return again and again. He describes the change as follows:

> Up to that time I had been good, thereafter I became virtuous, or at least intoxicated with virtue. This intoxication had begun in my head, but it passed into my heart. There the noblest pride sprang up from the ruins of uprooted vanity. I pretended nothing, I became in reality what I appeared, and during the four years at least that this inspiration lasted at its full strength there was nothing under the sun which can enter into the heart of man of which I was not capable. This was the origin of my sudden eloquence, and of the truly celestial fire which consumed me and spread to my first books, a fire which had not emitted the least spark in forty years because it was not yet kindled.
>
> I was truly transformed; my friends, my acquaintances no longer recognized me. I was no longer that timid, shame-faced rather

than modest man who dared not speak or show himself, who was disconcerted by a playful word and blushed at a woman's glance. Bold, proud, intrepid I carried with me everywhere an assurance the firmness of which was based on its simplicity and which resided in my soul rather than in my external behavior. The contempt which my profound meditations had inspired in me for the manners, principles, and prejudices of my age rendered me insensible to the railleries of those who had acquired them. I crushed their little witticisms with my remarks as I might crush an insect between my fingers. What a change! All Paris repeated the pungent and biting sarcasms of that man who, two years before and ten years afterwards, never knew how to find the right thing to say nor the word he should use.[62]

It is difficult to tell how much of this is fantasy. The above quotation is reminiscent of Thurber's celebrated *Secret Life of Walter Mitty*. Rousseau admits that during this period "my friends and acquaintances led this fierce bear around like a lamb and, limiting my sarcasms to unpleasant but general truths, I never could say an unkind word to anyone."[63] Yet there is no mistaking the vigor, exhilaration, and forcefulness of his writing. Regardless of how others were impressed by him during this period, the "natural man" was very real to his creator. He saw himself on the mountain top, thunder and lightning around him, shaking his fist at the universe. The feeling is unmistakably pleasant.[64]

The loss of this "celestial fire" began when he left Paris for the Hermitage. Here, he tells us, amid quiet rural surroundings, his hatred for the follies of society subsided. Actually, the retreat from Paris may have been occasioned as much by the difficulty of maintaining his aggressive façade as by his love of the country life. Rousseau had carved an iconoclastic character for himself. Any failure to keep up the attack would be immediately noted by his public if he remained always on display. His departure was an example of the showmanship of which he was a master, as well as a product of his need for escape. During the settlement in the Hermitage his relationship with Thérèse grew more strained. The little secrets her mother had induced her to keep from him produced a certain silence and distance between them. Rousseau's possessive nature, augmented as it was by the scars of his withdrawal from Mme de Warens, could neither tolerate nor overcome this estrangement. Soon it began to affect their sexual relationship. "When I possessed her," he said, "I felt that she was still not mine; and the single idea that I was not everything to her caused her to be almost nothing to me."[65] He gradually replaced the intimacy of their relationship by his own private autoerotic fantasies. The retreat from the world was complete.

For a long time Rousseau had been meditating on a proposed book which he called "Political Institutions," the larger work from which he finally extracted the *Social Contract*. During the stormy period in Paris he had worked intermittently on this project, but the frequent controversy, the public show, and the feeling that he should answer his critics left him little time for the logical study of social theory which should form the basis for this more important effort. The leisure he had expected at the Hermitage was interrupted, not only by the solicitations of Mme d'Epinay but by the more compelling demands of his own sexuality. Erotic daydreams crowded his life at the very moment when he had such great enterprises in view.[66] At last he determined to yield to them in order to write them out of his mind. During this period of erotic turmoil—the love affair with Sophie, the quarrel with Mme d'Epinay, and the provocative cat and mouse game with Mme de Luxembourg—*Emile* and the *Social Contract* were finally completed, a six-year effort in the course of which his faith in his own natural goodness was severely shaken. The man of virtue, who had been created from his inspiration on the road to the keep, proved a difficult and austere figure to maintain. With the change in personality came a change in political philosophy and style. The first two discourses, filled with enthusiasm for the natural and spontaneous in man, yielded to the tenor of the *Social Contract*, which outlined the need to preserve the structure of the state and to subdue the individual will, the selfish and personal desires, the human passions.

VII

Rousseau remarked that he was discouraged from settling in Geneva not only by the coolness of the citizens but by the news that Voltaire had rented a home near that city. In his early years his idol was Voltaire, as he was of all the young writers of Paris, but six months after Voltaire moved into the environs of Geneva he sent Rousseau a letter acknowledging the receipt of his second *Discourse*, "your new book against the human race," and remarked that on reading it "one is seized with a desire to walk on all fours." It was a letter full of the typical caustic wit of Voltaire, but it also contained a serious attempt to answer some of Rousseau's arguments. It was both a great compliment and a sharp thrust. It ended with "tender esteem" and an invitation to visit the author in Geneva to "drink the milk of our cows."[67]

Rousseau was apparently deeply touched and challenged by this letter. In his reply he acknowledged "the homage which we all owe you as our chief," but prepared a point by point answer to Voltaire's critique of his work.[68] He felt both a reverence for Voltaire's genius and a strong competitive feeling. Voltaire, although he attacked the tyranny of religion and bad government, was a member of the monied class, that new band of tyrants which Rousseau saw rising to threaten the freedom of man. Further, he was a representative of Parisian wit and clever conversation, the very ingredients of social corruption which he had now brought to the homeland of the self-styled citizen of Geneva. Rousseau saw Voltaire, with his great power and influence, corrupting the simplicity of Geneva with the frivolous conversation, the Parisian visitors, and the plays which were being performed at Les Délices (Voltaire's name for his new estate). While he had an impulse to contend with Voltaire for the soul of his beloved city, he remarked in his *Confessions* that he felt himself to be timid and a poor speaker, unable to battle "against an arrogant and wealthy man, supported by the prestige of the great, spouting a glittering eloquence, and already the idol of the women and the young people."[69]

It seems very probable that Rousseau, in reminiscing about his reasons for not settling in Geneva, was strongly influenced by his memory of his later quarrels with Voltaire and anticipated them in the story of his life. He actually continued to consider the idea of residence in Geneva for some time. It was a full year and a half after his interchange of letters with Voltaire that he rejected the post of librarian of Geneva which had been proffered through the efforts of Dr. Tronchin.[70] By this time the influence of Voltaire had grown to the point where he was to boast that every time he shook his wig he powdered that tiny republic. Further, there had been another interchange of letters between the two men; still amiable, but one which more sharply divided them in their philosophy of life. The feeling of their essential difference was growing, and Rousseau had come to resent bitterly Voltaire's prominence in Geneva, a status which contrasted sharply with such a mediocre one as librarian.

Meanwhile, Rousseau had received an offer of a small cottage on the estate of Mme d'Epinay. It was an old dilapidated building which she had completely rebuilt to suit Rousseau and his entourage. He had been hounded in Paris by a constant stream of visitors who wanted to meet him and talk with him, and in spite of an outward show of rudeness, his intense need for acceptance and approval from others made it impossible for him to turn them away. Mme d'Epinay had long been interested in him, and he had dined with her frequently since his introduction by M. de Francueil. She prided herself on breaking convention and on entertaining controversial figures. In her early years, she had the effrontery to marry for love and had expected her husband to remain faithful after marriage. When her husband informed her that he would follow the usual convention of taking a mistress after marriage, she defied society in other ways. It was the custom in her day to send children away from home to be nursed and raised by a peasant family. This left the mother free. Therefore, when Mme d'Epinay announced her decision to nurse her own son, she created a scandal. Both her own family and her husband's family protested her strange behavior, but she was adamant and insisted that her child remain at home.[71] It is not surprising that such an unusual woman should have taken an interest in the unconventional Jean-Jacques.

But Rousseau was not easily won. He wanted to make sure no strings were attached to the offer. When he had first seen the Hermitage and before it was remodeled for him, he had remarked to Mme d'Epinay—"Ah, Madame, what a delightful place to live in! Here is a refuge absolutely made for me."[72] But when the offer of the residence was actually made the decrepit old place had been considerably improved, and it no longer seemed so appropriate for a proud republican. Although he was charmed by her offer and covered her hand with tears of gratitude, he soon began to wonder about her remarks that she had certain "projects" with which she wanted help and that she could offer him some "compensation" for this assistance. Rousseau indignantly replied that he would be no one's valet and that he was not for sale. Mme d'Epinay apologized, and Rousseau apologized. He explained to her that she must learn to read his heart and not pay too much attention to the words he used. Mme d'Epinay, for her part, insisted that he would have complete freedom in his new home and sought the help of her friends in encouraging him to stay. She referred to him as "my bear"[73] and described the Hermitage as his retreat from the world. He was finally won over, and once the decision was made he became so eager for his new residence that he moved in before the snow was off the ground. His fear of being dependent and the sudden eagerness once his fears were assuaged was typical of him. He had reached a point in his life where he was playing the brusque cynic, yet he was terrified of his own submissive nature which lay just beneath the surface. He knew that if Mme d'Epinay made demands on his time, he would feel compelled to obey. He was trying to obtain complete assurance that she would never take advantage of his submissiveness.

There may well have been other grounds for Rousseau's hesitation in moving to the Hermitage. Mme d'Epinay had been discarded by her former lover and was now the mistress of Grimm, with whom Rousseau was not on the best of terms. Grimm advised Mme d'Epinay against taking Rousseau into the Hermitage. The nature of his objection is not clear. He may have been jealous of a man whose fame far eclipsed his own on the same estate with his mistress. And Rousseau had pointedly called attention to the cold and calculating way in which Grimm had used his friendship to secure introductions in French society. Further, the stern disciplinary character of the German did not mesh well with Rousseau's moody and changeable disposition. It is possible that they had both experienced a foretaste of the coming rift between them, and Grimm may have felt he had best warn Mme d'Epinay against Rousseau before Rousseau warned her against him.

Jealousy is the most probable motive for Grimm's warning and, in view of the aura of affectionate tenderness about many of the encounters between Rousseau and Mme d'Epinay, the jealousy may have had some foundation. Although it is unlikely that Rousseau ever became her lover, she certainly teased him outrageously, and he responded with his typical excitability. When he remarked in his *Confessions* that she was flat chested and completely devoid of sensuality,[74] he was writing with the venom of his later feelings.

It was clear from the beginning of their relationship that Mme d'Epinay was not the innocent, child-like type of woman that he favored. Although a rebel in many respects, she was also a society lady, a woman of the world. Regardless of her assurances to him, she considered it her right to show him off occasionally and to expect a certain amount of attention from him. This proved to be the deadly element in their relationship, for Rousseau, who would do anything for love, would do nothing out of social obligation. If he made an attempt to placate Mme d'Epinay's demands, it was only out of his fear of offending her and because, in the early part of his stay at the Hermitage, he had a genuine affection for her.

Meanwhile, Diderot, who detested Mme d'Epinay, resented his friend's departure from Paris. He was forever urging Rousseau to return, and while he was always gentle and pleading in his remonstrances, others in the Holbach circle ridiculed the "natural man," claiming that his vanity was such that he could not last a month away from the adoration of Paris. It was true that Rousseau was vain, that he loved flattery, and that his new character was in part a mere affectation, a product of his desire to be the center of attention. Nevertheless, his love of the country was quite genuine. He had had all he could take of terraced lawns and shaped bushes, of rouges and flounces, of holding onto the wool of some silly woman while he watched her knit and tried, in his own ineffectual way, to make conversation. He longed for the untrained foliage of nature, streams and woods, country wines, simple food, and the opportunity to eat and retire early. He welcomed this retreat as providing him an opportunity to work on the literary projects he had planned. But this man of nature discovered, once ensconced in his retreat, that he needed a friend to whom he could pour out his heart. Much as he admired self-sufficiency, he could not live on his own esteem. This enemy of society was, at heart, a most sociable person.

His domestic bliss and the solitude of nature were short-lived. Mme d'Epinay made more demands on his time than he had anticipated, and the shrewish Mme Levasseur proved to be a real barrier to his relationship with Thérèse. Rousseau was attracted to Thérèse more out of pity than love. He remarked in the *Confessions* that he had "no more desire to possess her than I had desired Mme. de Warens, and the needs I satisfied with her were for me purely sexual and had nothing to do with her as an individual."[75] His primary pleasure with Thérèse was in the protective feeling he felt for her and in their quiet walks together. When the family moved to the Hermitage this bond between them became exceedingly thin. Thérèse had always been the least accepted of Mme Levasseur's children. While secretly accepting gifts from Rousseau's friends and patrons the old woman gave much of her bounty to her other children, leaving Thérèse to depend on Rousseau for support. She felt intuitively that if Thérèse showed the slightest sign of luxury, her lover might cease to feel the pinch of financial pressure. She was always complaining privately to Diderot, Grimm, and others of the poverty in which they lived and insisted that Thérèse keep her machinations secret from Rousseau. The whisperings and secret conversations of mother and daughter might well have aroused doubts in a normal person, but for a sensitive, suspicious personality like Rousseau, they were positively threatening. He extracted a promise from Thérèse that none of her numerous relatives would be invited to the Hermitage, but when he was away they were invited without Thérèse's permission, and she was enjoined not to tell him of their visits and of the food they consumed. She consented out of family loyalty, but the burden of her secrets gradually came between her and her lover. Rousseau resented the many private intrigues, and the quiet walks in the woods with Thérèse were gradually crowded by many unspoken thoughts. Soon he ceased to suggest these woodland wanderings and noted with regret that she did not seem to miss them.[76]

His loneliness was further complicated by Diderot's angry letters from Paris accusing him of neglecting the welfare of Thérèse's mother, by Grimm's conspiring to set up Thérèse and Mme Levasseur with a tobacco shop in order to take them from the Hermitage, and by the knowledge that Grimm and Diderot were developing one of those close passionate friendships which he so fervently desired. He learned also, from the gossip of the Holbach literary circle, that his retreat to the countryside of Montmorency was regarded as a mere pose. At this juncture of his life, with both his mistress and his friends apparently turning against him, Rousseau felt very much alone.

[4]

The Worlds of Libel and Love

I

THE ACCOUNT OF ROUSSEAU'S QUARREL with his friends and his love affair with Sophie (Countess d'Houdetot) is one of the most complicated stories in his life. Neither the quarrels nor the love affair can be understood without reference to each other. They reverberate back and forth on each other like the notes of a great organ, setting up overtones contained in neither. And Rousseau appears in all this turmoil like a frightened musician who has lost his place in the score.

For this period I have relied primarily on the *Confessions* and *Correspondance* of Rousseau, making use of the *Mémoires* of Mme d'Epinay only in areas where Rousseau is silent. Suspicion has justifiably been cast on this latter work,[1] but parts of it present explanations of events which are found nowhere else. It is important, therefore, to examine the "other side" of the story, for each party may have perceived the events in such a way as to protect his own ego. As I have followed each quarrel to its conclusion before going on with the next, this chapter consists of a series of overlapping events occurring in the same general time period.

II

The seeds of Rousseau's rupture with the Holbach circle had been growing for a long time. The gossipy literary climate of this salon was permeated by an atmosphere of such arrogant atheism that D'Alembert and even Turgot were to find it a bit too overwhelming. Rousseau, while no defender of orthodoxy, had a strong conviction that there was some kind of god whom each man had a right to worship in his own way. He resented the ridicule directed toward religion by the Holbachians, and he never really felt at ease in the baron's salon. The baron regarded himself as the leader of a new cult, and, while he tolerated priests and other religious friends, he recognized no obligation to respect their beliefs. On one occasion the group decided to make sport of a country curé who had requested Diderot to give his opinion of the curé's play, *Bathsheba*. Diderot invited him to the den of the Holbachians, and the assemblage was instructed to simulate an ecstasy of enjoyment to flatter the vanity of the priest and encourage him to make

79

a fool of himself. Rousseau was profoundly put out by this cruel form of amusement. One account[2] shows him jumping to his feet, snatching the manuscript from the curé, proclaiming to the bewildered man that the company was attempting to make a fool of him and stalking out the door. He was not a man for the refined and delicate tortures of the Holbach circle. His resentment of their polite little sallies formed the basis for many if his attacks on sophisticated learning and for his differentiation between "natural reason" and the showy display of erudition which passed for great thinking in the society salons.

In his break with the Holbach circle he also began to draw away from Diderot. His intense pride and his possessive nature required a special kind of devotion and understanding from those close to him. Diderot, his principal friend at this time, was of such a different temperament and background that mutual understanding, let alone devotion, was seldom possible. A fiery, emotional, talkative extrovert, Diderot loved to be sociable and could not understand Rousseau's withdrawal to the Hermitage in order to write. Diderot had a reputation as a conversationalist and was well on the way to being hailed as the man of virtue until Rousseau upstaged him. Diderot, who expressed the greatest affection for his friend during the latter's stay in Paris and during the early part of his life at the Hermitage, could not forget that he had already achieved considerable recognition in the field of letters when Rousseau first came asking for advice. He had been generous with his opinion on matters of style and literary criticism, but he had also considered it his right—even his duty—to advise on matters of virtue as well. While Rousseau's concept of virtue was that of the independent, natural man, who ignored the conventions and vices of society, Diderot was more of a virtuous busybody. He hurried about helping his friends, advising them, cheering them with his wit, and, in general, doing his good deed for the day. His many protests to Rousseau on the immorality of his retreat to the Hermitage and his complaint that Rousseau was unfair to Thérèse's poor old mother in keeping her on the country estate through the cold winter months were examples of his efforts to do good deeds. For him inspiration came from conversation with his friends, and he regarded Rousseau's retreat as a personal affront to their friendship. Diderot was an extravagant creature of whims, who readily forgot an injustice or a slight, who spent his money freely, and who often kept a carriage waiting half a day, having forgotten instructing the driver to wait. Rousseau had the sober, Genevan sense of punctuality and severity in morals. He often brooded over injustices done him, and he spent his money carefully, for waste or extravagance disturbed him.

While at the Hermitage, Rousseau still relied on Diderot as his chief critic and yearned for the approval and suggestions of his friend. However, when they made appointments to meet, Diderot was almost always late. Sometimes he did not arrive at all, keeping Rousseau waiting at Saint-Denis for the remainder of the day. But Rousseau was so preoccupied with his own work that he often became impatient when Diderot suggested discussing his own plans or a phrase he had in mind. Diderot's account of Rousseau's thoughtlessness in this respect has become famous in literary history. From the *Mémoires* we learn that Rousseau had taken the manuscript of the *New Eloise* to Paris for Diderot's comments. After he had been at work on it for three days, Diderot asked his friend's help on a literary work of his own. "It is late," replied Rousseau, "and I am not used to sitting up."[3] Diderot's daughter also repeats this story in her *Mémoires*.[4]

Such was the relationship between these friends during the early days of Rousseau's stay at the Hermitage. The situation was further aggravated when Diderot finished his play *The Natural Son* and sent a copy to the Hermitage. Rousseau had already been deluged by Diderot's letters and criticism for withdrawing from society. Now, in this play, he discovered a remark by Constance directed to Dorval that seemed particularly appropriate to himself: "The good man lives in society, and only the wicked man is alone."[5]

Rousseau was deeply wounded by this remark.[6] It was much too similar to many of the things Diderot had said and written to him. Further, it was not tempered by any of the restraint and qualification used in conversation. "Only the wicked man is alone!" This was, to Rousseau, a blunt and cruel accusation. He wrote complaining of the unfairness, but "with a tenderness which made me moisten the paper with my tears."[7] No doubt the tears had dried by the time the message reached Diderot, for he persisted in asserting that hermits were a queer lot and left no doubt in Rousseau's mind that he was considered a hermit—in spite of the fact that he was only twelve miles from Paris and with a mistress, her mother, and a stream of visitors attracted by his fame and reputation.

Diderot insisted that his efforts to draw the hermit from his retreat were motivated only by his love and desire to have his friend always nearby, but there were many other subtle aspects to the story. Diderot, like Rousseau, was very possessive in his attitude to friends. He despised Mme d'Epinay, not only because he considered her disreputable but because she was closely attached to both Grimm and Rousseau. Duclos, who through his own rudeness had been turned away by Mme d'Epinay, rushed back to Paris to tell everyone what a tart she was and how Grimm was in love with her. Diderot, remembering his friend's prolonged depression after being rejected by a Parisian actress, feared for his peace of mind. The absence of Grimm drove him to tears, and he went into an ecstasy of delight whenever his Damon returned. He felt a similar possessiveness toward Rousseau and engaged in numerous outlandish schemes to bring him back to Paris. It was typical of Diderot that he thought he knew what was best for his friends, and to his mind Rousseau needed Paris as badly as Paris needed Rousseau.

In spite of the injustice of Diderot's position, Rousseau could not simply ignore him. He did not believe a difference of opinion could continue to exist between true friends. His letters are filled with elaborate justification of things that require no justification, explanations and dissections in the nature of "first you said this, and then I naturally had to say that." His remarks to Diderot during this period betray a litigious quality symptomatic of more serious disorders to come. Unable to accept that some questions of morality and justice cannot be resolved, he always believed that there was somewhere an unshakable and unquestionable judgment of what was right in every case. Since he acted in accord with his "conscience," he felt he could not be wrong. Nor was he content with the mere assertion of innocence. He wanted to prove it—even in the most inconsequential matters. The following is from one of his many letters to Diderot in early 1757 about Diderot's play and the phrase which offended him:

> I wish to sum up in a few words the history of our disputes. You sent me your book. I wrote you afterward the most tender and reasonable note I ever wrote in my life, in which I complained with all the gentleness of friendship of a very questionable maxim, which could be applied to me in a very injurious manner. I received in response a very dry letter. . . . My reply had all the vivacity of an honest man insulted by his friend; you retorted by an abominable letter. I still defended myself, and very firmly; but not trusting myself in the fury into which you had thrown me, and, in such a state, fearful of hurting a friend, I sent my letter to Mme d'Epinay, asking her to judge our differences. She returned me this same letter, urged me to suppress it and I did. Now you write me another letter in which you call me wicked, unjust, cruel, ferocious. That is the substance of what has passed between us.
>
> I wish to put to you two or three very simple questions. Who is the aggressor in this affair? If you will, relate all that has happened to a third person, show my first letter and I will show yours. Con-

ceding for the moment that I had taken your reproaches in bad grace and that I was wrong in this respect, who, of the two of us, was the most obligated to take a reasonable tone in order to bring the other around?[8]

The two warring philosophers were finally brought together when it was pointed out to Rousseau that Diderot was in difficult political circumstances with his *Encyclopedia* and that he had been accused of having plagiarized his *Natural Son* from Goldoni. Rousseau, touched by the plight of a friend in trouble, continued to visit Diderot in Paris and even went with him to the Holbach salon from time to time.

III

During his stay at the Hermitage Rousseau produced *The New Eloise*, a book different in style and technique from everything else he has written, except some of his personal letters. It set the tone for much of the romantic literature that was to follow, and it is his primary claim to fame as a romantic writer. In this book he attempted the moral reform of French society. *The New Eloise* represented a striking contrast to novels of seduction, intrigue, and casual infidelity so popular with the previous generation of readers. While the romantic novels of Richardson and Sterne had already attained considerable popularity in England, it was *Eloise* that was destined to replace *Manon* in France. In his novel Rousseau sought to recapture the devoted love relationship of Eloise and Abelard as a lesson in virtue for the jaded sophisticates of French society, to demonstrate that passion is intensified and sweetened by being prolonged and held in abeyance. He attempted to present to the French people the value of restraint based on moral principles.

It is curious that *The New Eloise* evolved in his mind out of his autoerotic fantasies and was first conceived only for his own satisfaction. In the early stages of his amorous fantasies, he had no intention of putting them on paper, but through his attempt at defense against his own erotic excitation he finally evolved the idea of teaching a new morality, using the vehicle of a romantic novel.

It is enlightening to trace these dreams from their beginning through their gradual evolution and, finally, their crystallization in the person of a living object, the Countess d'Houdetot, the "Sophie" who became Rousseau's one great romantic love, a beloved who seems expressly designed for his erotic peculiarities.

When Rousseau arrived at the Hermitage he had many projects in mind, and he saw it as an ideal place for contemplation. The tendency to reach the height of his productivity in rural woodland surroundings is a striking aspect of his character. He recorded his feelings as follows:

> Although it was cold and there was still some snow on the ground, the earth was beginning to sprout, there were violets and primroses to be seen, the buds were beginning to open on the trees, and the very night of my arrival was marked by the first song of the nightingale, which was heard almost at my window in a wood adjoining the house. . . .
>
> I set aside my mornings for copying, as I had always done, and my afternoons for walking, armed with my little notebook and pencil: for never having been able to write and think at my ease except *sub dio*, I was not tempted to change my method. I made up my mind that the forest of Montmorency, which was almost at my door, would henceforth be my study.[9]

In the early days of his stay and throughout much of the first summer, he carried through these plans with relatively little interference. The feeling of estrangement from Thérèse had not yet developed, and Mme d'Epinay was too busy with friends to pay him more than an occasional visit. His initial relationship with her was in some respects similar to that with Mme de Warens, yet there were subtle differences. Rousseau was no longer an unknown youth seeking a loving and protective "mamma." He was forty-four years old and a famous literary figure whose natural virtue was the talk of Paris. He earned his living by copying music, and he was determined not to be seduced from his way of life by any inducements, not even human kindness, the one to which he was most susceptible. His obdurate refusal to accept pensions and gratuities of any kind had irked his friends, many of whom were accepting the largess of wealthy patrons. This same fierce desire for independence had caused him to be cautious in accepting the Hermitage as a retreat and even to test Mme d'Epinay with a few insults to make sure she was really making the offer out of friendship. However, her eagerness to make him feel at home and free to do as he pleased soon convinced him that she wanted him near her out of a tender regard for his welfare.

In the history of Rousseau's relationship with women, gratitude and love were never far apart, and his passionate excitability was an open invitation for any woman to try her power to charm him. Mme d'Epinay already had a lover in Grimm, but he was a man of literary affairs, constantly on the move from one country to another. Rousseau was close at hand. She was forever inquiring about his comfort, bestowing tender kisses upon him, and providing in little ways for his happiness. When she could not visit him, she would write him from

Paris. She sent him her picture and asked that he send his. Finally, she sent him one of her underpetticoats which she informed him she had worn and suggested that he make himself a vest of it. This gift produced a great wave of sentiment in Rousseau. It was, he said, as he kissed the petticoat with tears in his eyes, "as though she had stripped herself to clothe me."[10] However, the cautious Mme d'Epinay took care to strip only by mail and never in front of the excitable Jean-Jacques.

After his early period at the Hermitage Rousseau began to feel the increasing distance between himself and Thérèse as well as the growing estrangement of his former friends in Paris. He felt very much alone and desperately wanted someone to whom he could pour out his heart. While Mme d'Epinay aroused him, he had certain reservations about her. She was the mistress of Grimm and in constant correspondence with him. The loyalty of Thérèse was divided between himself and her mother. Rousseau, with his passionate possessiveness, wanted someone who belonged to him alone. In the solitude of his walks he began to long for such a companion and he searched the early years of his youth for some memory of his idealized love relationship. "My blood took fire,"[11] he says of this period, in which he was absorbed in his fantasies for long intervals. He has described the evolution of these fantasies and the final decision to control them by imposing order and coherence on them:

> This intoxication, to whatever point it was carried, did not go so far as to make me forget my age and my situation, to flatter me that I could still inspire love, or induce me to try at last to communicate this devouring but futile fire by which I had felt my heart to be consumed in vain ever since my childhood. I did not hope for it, I did not even desire it. . . . What did I do on this occasion? My reader has already guessed if he has followed me with the least attention so far. The impossibility of attaining real persons precipitated me into the land of chimeras, and seeing nothing in existence worthy of my delirium, I nourished it in an ideal world which my creative imagination soon peopled with beings after my own heart. . . .[12] After many futile efforts to banish all these fictions from my mind, I was at last completely seduced by them and I was occupied only with trying to put them in some sort of order and sequence in order to construct a kind of novel.[13]

In a sense, he felt he could redeem himself for his long hours of autoerotic activity by using these fantasies to create a novel which would benefit morality.

IV

When Rousseau made up his mind to turn his fantasies into a novel, he had already elaborated the setting. The intensity of his "amorous delirium" had abated to some extent, and the characters had settled into three primary figures. Two of them were women with a child-like innocence reminiscent of the Mlle Galley and Mlle Graffenried of his early youth, who had apparently made a profound impression on him. He had identified himself with the third person, the hero—later to be called "Saint-Preux"—and gave him the same passionate temperament, as well as the desire to suffer morally, which he sensed in himself. The heroine he called "Julie".

In the process of writing his novel he received an unexpected visit from Countess d'Houdetot, whom he had already come to know as "Sophie" during her previous visits to Mme d'Epinay. She had visited him once before at the height of his erotic fantasies and had left an impression of light gaiety "making the air ring with her laughter."[14] She saw very little of her husband, but her lover, Saint-Lambert, Rousseau's close friend, had encouraged her to visit him. On her second visit she arrived dressed in man's clothes, and this masquerade heightened his feeling of romance and adventure.[15] She came into his life at a time when he was constantly glowing with a passion that had no object. She talked to him of her great love for Saint-Lambert, and as he listened he soon found himself identifying her with the Julie of his novel who loved Saint-Preux. But he himself was Saint-Preux, or was he Saint-Lambert? His romantic ardor had so confused his mind that the figures of his fantasy blended with those of reality, and he was not sure where one began and the other ended. Not until her departure, when he tried to think of Julie again and could think only of Sophie d'Houdetot, did he realize he was in love with her.

In his romance with Sophie, Rousseau has traditionally been regarded as the villain of the affair. Morley speaks of the Countess d'Houdetot as the "unwilling enchantress bearing in an unconscious hand the cup of defilement" and remarks that "through no fault of her own" she had been the cause of Rousseau's passion. For Rousseau he reserves what is perhaps the most eloquent condemnation in the history of biography:

> . . . we watch a being with a soul all blurred, body all shaken, unstrung, poisoned by erotic mania, rising in slow clouds of mephitic steam from suddenly heated stagnancies of the blood, and turning the reality of conduct and duty into distant unmeaning shadows. If such a disease were the furous mood of the brute in

spring time, it would be less dreadful, but shame and remorse in the ever struggling reason of man or woman in the grip of the foul thing, produces an aggravation of frenzy that makes the mental healer tremble . . . the whole offers a scene of moral humiliation that half sickens, half appalls, and we turn away with dismay as from a vision of the horrid loves of heavy-eyed and scaly shapes that haunted the warm primæval ooze.[16]

While Sophie was a good deal more provocative in the affair than Morley would have us believe, she was not exactly the type of enchantress to inspire even a lonely hermit with love at first sight. Her face was marked by smallpox scars and her color, as Rousseau mentions, was not very good.[17] Apparently her animation and her simplicity of manner attracted him. She was twenty-seven at the time of their meeting, and she had probably heard about Rousseau not only from Saint-Lambert but from her cousin and sister-in-law, Mme d'Epinay. The latter had no doubt described Rousseau's passionate excitability. Having met him several times at Mme d'Epinay's home and once at the Hermitage, it seems likely that she already had a good idea of his character by the time of her second visit.

It is doubtful that she deliberately set out to inflame his passion. From all accounts she seems to have been the type of woman who repressed all awareness of her sexual feelings. She regarded Saint-Lambert as though he were her husband, and sex for fun was as evil an idea to her as was hatred or anger toward anyone. Such women often have strong sexual feelings which appear only in dreams in which they are chased by a hairy brute of a man, but in waking life they are the picture of virtue. A woman of this type often retains much of the softness, simplicity, and spontaneous warmth of the child. She is quick to believe others, to see the good in everyone, and to feel an instinctive pity for those who suffer. It would not be difficult for such a woman to convince herself that she could carry on a strictly platonic relationship with a man indefinitely. Since she is not conscious of sexual feelings, she is unaware of their expression. When she clasps the hand of a male friend in both of hers, she does it only to demonstrate appreciation of what he has said. When she weeps on his shoulder, her only conscious desire is for protection and sympathetic understanding. If she arouses sexual feelings in a man, it is because he does not understand her. The point is, of course, that he understands a side of her she is not willing to acknowledge, a side which grows all the stronger when she gives it no satisfaction. As a result of the "demure little girl" image which she has created for herself and for others she can find sexual satisfaction only when she can quite literally "forget herself"—forget she is supposed to have nice platonic thoughts, imagine she is a harlot or a savage, and become for a moment another person.

Rousseau's description of his Sophie is remarkable in its representation of such a personality—even to her episodes of forgetfulness.

> She had a very natural and agreeable wit which was a fortunate combination of gaiety, carelessness, and naiveté. She overflowed with delightful sallies which were quite spontaneous and which often escaped her inadvertently. . . . As for her character it was angelic, gentleness of soul was its foundation, but aside from prudence and strength it contained all the virtues. . . . Her heart was incapable of hatred, and I believe that this similarity to myself contributed greatly to my passion for her. . . . Finally, that which proves unquestionably the purity and sincerity of her excellent disposition is that, being subject to phenomenal spells of absent mindedness, she committed ridiculous indiscretions with consequences quite damaging to herself but which were never offensive to others.[18]

These "indiscretions" which were damaging to herself suggest that the shadowy side of Sophie's character had already begun to assert itself in some ways, but she was going through a period when she had been deprived of male attention. Her husband and her lover were both away at war. She had a house full of servants and no responsibilities. Certainly, these factors were important determinants of her decision to pay a second visit to Rousseau.

This second visit proved fatal for Rousseau's passionate temperament. His need for tenderness, for a cuddly, innocent type of love, has already been noted. Sophie, in describing her feelings for Saint-Lambert, apparently displayed these feelings in abundance. Since she never gave vent to hostility, she must have appeared to him as an ideal lover, a woman able to give everything and ask for nothing. But perhaps the most important feature of her personality for Rousseau, was her capacity for pity. In the modern world, where the chronically ill have come to be regarded as "hypochondriacal" and the injured as "accident-prone," it is difficult to recapture the picture of Sophie with her unskeptical outpouring of sympathy for all the unfortunate creatures of the earth. With such a woman Rousseau could play the role of the poor lonely man whom no one loved—the misunderstood genius. That he had already cast himself in such a role is revealed by his comments about his activity before Sophie arrived, but at that time he had only himself for a sympathetic listener.

I believed I was approaching the end of my career without having tasted in full scarcely a single one of the pleasures for which my heart yearned, without having given expression to the intense feelings that I felt it had in reserve, without having savored, not even having come close to that intoxicating pleasure the power of which I felt in my soul, and which for want of an object was always suppressed and could not escape in any way except through my sighs. . . . Devoured by a need to love that I could never satisfy I saw myself approaching the gates of old age and dying without having lived.

These melancholy but touching reflections caused me to turn back on myself with a regret which was not without a certain pleasure. It seemed to me that destiny owed me something that it had never given me. For what purpose was I born with delicate faculties if they were to remain unused to the end? The sense of my own internal worth gave me a feeling of injustice which, in some degree, compensated for it, and caused me to shed tears which pleased me as they flowed.[19]

It is unlikely one could find such a frank and unashamed admission of a love of suffering anywhere except in the works of Rousseau. His letters to Sophie are filled with similar declarations. It is not surprising he was attracted by her capacity for pity.

When Rousseau first discovered his love for Sophie he was struck dumb in her presence, and the only way he could free his tongue was to tell her all his feelings. She expressed sorrow at his foolishness, but continued to visit him and tell him how much fun the three of them (Saint-Lambert, Sophie, and Rousseau) could have together once he got over his infatuation. Her conception of him as a kind of addition to her entourage (without including a woman for him) suggests that she rather enjoyed his possessive frenzy. She maintained the attitude of "affectionate friend" in the conviction that their relationship would soon settle into a platonic one. Her friendship was, according to Rousseau, "too strong to be true,"[20] and he began to suspect she was teasing him and leading him on—perhaps even with the encouragement of Saint-Lambert. She met him in the woods alone, leaving her servant behind on the road; she invited him to dine at her home, telling him that she was all alone; she even asked him to spend the night. They saw each other constantly, yet Rousseau could extract nothing from her except her friendship.

Here was a truly complicated situation. Rousseau, who took a woman's "no" to mean "no," could not understand Sophie's affectionate attentions to him. How could she be so kind and sympathetic if she did not love him? At times he began to believe she was really wavering, and he pressed his attentions on her, but then the prudent young lady reminded him of his great friendship for Saint-Lambert and he was instantly crestfallen. At times he would get angry with her, but, "her compassionate sweetness was invincible. She reproached me in a way that pierced my heart."[21]

It would seem that in Sophie, Rousseau had at last discovered the perfect vehicle for his masochistic needs, a woman who would lead him on forever, make him suffer and yet sympathize with his suffering, but never disappoint him by yielding to his passionate declarations of love. This suffering was inexpressably more delightful to Rousseau than any overt sexual relationship would have been. He once admitted that he did not "truly desire" her to yield to him,[22] but there is serious question as to how much real insight he had into his motives. Sophie was what nowadays would be called a tease, but unlike most women who tease she had found an ideal victim—a man who loved to suffer.

v

But what of Thérèse during this idyllic romance? Was she, too, content to suffer? Quite the contrary. Thérèse's feeling for Rousseau seems to have been the rather direct, uncomplicated feeling of the mistress who had grown weary of her lover, but who does not enjoy seeing another woman take him away. Further, Mme d'Epinay, at whose cottage Rousseau was staying, was concerned that Rousseau no longer paid her his former attentions. While it is unlikely that she ever carried on more than a teasing and flirtatious relationship with him, she must have noticed that he no longer went into ecstacies over her old petticoats.

Mme d'Epinay was, in fact, disturbed by the woodland wanderings of her "bear" and his new-found enchantress. She had long regarded herself as a close friend of Mme d'Houdetot, yet the two women were basically so different that it was difficult for them to understand each other. Mme d'Epinay had suffered through the agonies of her early idealism and was now a woman of the world. While she might have relied on her own girlhood memories to understand Sophie, she could not accept such persistent naiveté and absentmindedness in a woman of twenty-seven. In her *Mémoires*, she remarks, "My God! I am impatient to see another ten years on that woman's head."[23] In short, while Sophie's childhood simplicity inspired Rousseau with love, it only made Mme d'Epinay wish she would grow up.

Mme d'Epinay could not contain her knowledge of the Rousseau-Sophie affair for long. Soon she was writing to her lover, Grimm, about Rousseau and Sophie while he was at the front visiting with Saint-Lambert. Grimm was quite distressed that his old friend, Saint-Lambert, was losing his faithful mistress while he was away at war. "What you tell me of Rousseau seems very extraordinary, and these mysterious visits of the countess are even more so," he remarked. And then, in response to another part of her letter, "But why is the countess so gay? Has not Saint-Lambert's departure upset her at all?"[24] Mme d'Epinay defended her sister-in-law to her lover as a woman of naturally ebullient spirits, but she could not quiet her own feelings so easily.

Thérèse, for her part, felt very much alone during the affair. According to Mme d'Epinay's account, Thérèse frequently arrived with fresh bits of gossip and even offered to show the noble lady a letter from Sophie which she had taken from Rousseau's desk. Mme d'Epinay says she instructed Thérèse to throw such letters in the fire when she found them,[25] but perhaps she looked at the letter first and then told Thérèse to throw it in the fire.

Rousseau, meanwhile, continued to enjoy his Sophie, the woman who offered a perfect complement to his every desire. She had mastered to perfection that tender kind of cruelty that he adored. He could have suffered forever at her hands if someone had not thrown the virtuous Sophie into tears by informing Saint-Lambert of the affair. How would Saint-Lambert ever understand? How much had he been told? Would he ever believe there had never been any physical intimacy between them? Rousseau found her in a turmoil over these questions, and she told him he must behave more properly toward her or they would have to break off their relationship altogether. He was suddenly struck with shame over his attempts to seduce her. But at this stage of his life, his response to such situations was almost automatic. Whenever he began to feel guilty, a sense of pity overwhelmed him—pity for himself or for some victim with whom he could identfy. As his pity began to grow, it soon changed to a feeling of self-righteous indignation against the external enemy who had caused this suffering—and he was on the attack. In this case one can almost see the hairy and pointed ears of Mr. Hyde rise out of his skull as he says:

> My tenderness soon changed to anger against the vile informers who had seen only evil in a lamentable but involuntary emotion, without believing, without even imagining the deep sincerity of heart which atoned for it. We did not long remain in doubt as to the hand which had dealt the blow.[26]

Mme d'Epinay was an obvious culprit. Even Sophie suspected her. Thérèse informed him that Mme d'Epinay had been begging her to steal copies of Sophie's letters, or torn scraps that she might piece together. He could not contain his anger and soon his letters to Mme d'Epinay openly accused her of writing directly to Saint-Lambert as part of a deliberate plot to ruin Sophie's reputation or perhaps his own. Mme d'Epinay was deeply hurt by his accusations. In a note to him she both bade him farewell and suggested he visit her. Rousseau, for his part, realized he could hardly remain any longer on the estate of a woman whom he had accused of such villainy. He determined to visit her at once, although he dreaded the scene and feared his own lack of eloquence in an emotional situation in which he could not reveal the basis for his suspicions without compromising either Thérèse or Sophie. However, as he approached her, Mme d'Epinay flung her arms around his neck and burst into tears; Rousseau responded in kind; dinner was served and the accusations were mentioned no further.[27] Mme d'Epinay no doubt felt a certain guilt about the gossip she had been so free in sending to Grimm, and Rousseau took her emotional outburst as a form of penance. The next day he remarked that he could say no more about the basis for his suspicions until he was certain, and Mme d'Epinay showed no urge to press him for details so long as he had dropped the air of the accuser.

Sophie and Rousseau gradually began to see each other more often, and soon the old intimacy between them was reestablished. But such an unstable situation could hardly continue for long. In late July Saint-Lambert returned from the Battle of Hastenbeck full of the knowledge that Sophie had been finding considerable delight in her companionship with Rousseau. He also noticed, as did Mme d'Epinay, that his visit did not inspire Sophie with the kind of extravagant happiness that he had expected. He dined with Sophie and Jean-Jacques at the Hermitage, observed them together, and before his departure cautioned Sophie not to see quite so much of her new friend. He urged these precautions on her primarily, as he said, in order to avoid the gossip which he was receiving at the front; he spoke not a word of reproach to Rousseau. After his departure the dutiful Sophie, distressed by his concern for her reputation, determined to reform and to appear the very spirit of propriety. So proper was she that Rousseau became very upset. The old intimacy seemed to be missing. She was avoiding him.

At this point the *Confessions* and the *Mémoires* diverge sharply concerning the date of a visit from Diderot. In the *Mémoires*,[28] however, are some of the details of what supposedly took place at this encounter. According to this account in the autumn (probably mid-

August to early September) of 1757 Diderot came to the Hermitage to find his friend in despair. Carried away by the drama of the situation, the treachery of Mme d'Epinay in gossiping about her sister-in-law, and his own feeling of injured virtue, Rousseau held forth his case to Diderot. Why was Saint-Lambert torturing poor Sophie with accusations? Was not Rousseau his best friend? How could he suspect anything from such a noble mistress and such a loyal friend? Oh, yes, Rousseau admitted he had fallen in love with the dazzling Sophie. Who could resist her charms? But it was a secret he had revealed to no one, certainly not Sophie, and it would remain locked in his heart forever! Poor Sophie could not understand the accusations of Saint-Lambert because she had no knowledge of his great love for her. (At that time Rousseau had written several letters to Sophie describing all the agonies of his passion.)

To the well-meaning Diderot the situation seemed simple. Rousseau should simply write to Saint-Lambert and tell him the truth, like a man. Certainly, Saint-Lambert would forgive them both and honor Rousseau all the more for his restraint. Rousseau thanked his effusively and swore he would write the letter. Perhaps not until after Diderot left did Rousseau realize that the facts were rather different than he had presented them. He was not sure of the real reason for Sophie's coolness nor was he certain that Saint-Lambert had forbidden her to see him. Perhaps a confession of his love would be premature. On September 5, 1757, he wrote to Saint-Lambert to test his feelings:

> When I began to know you, I wanted to love you. I have seen nothing in you which has not increased this desire. In a time when I was abandoned by all those who were once dear to me, I owed to you a friend who consoled me for everything and to whom I attached myself because of the extent to which she spoke of you. . . . Now everything is changed except my heart. Since your departure she receives me coldly; she scarcely speaks to me, even of you; she finds a hundred pretexts to avoid me; a man with whom one wishes to break off relations would not be treated otherwise than she treats me; at least so far as I can judge since I have never been cast off by anyone. I cannot understand the meaning of this change. If I have deserved it, let me be told and I will consider myself dismissed. If it is fickleness let me be told; I will withdraw today and be consoled tomorrow. . . . Yes, it is from you that I ask an account of her. Is it not from you that she receives all her sentiments? Who knows this better than me? I know it perhaps better than you. . . . Tell me, then, what is the cause of her coolness?

Could you be afraid I would try to injure her opinion of you and that a false conception of virtue could render me disloyal or deceitful? A part of one of your letters, regarding me, has made me suspect this. No, no, Saint-Lambert, the breast of Jean-Jacques Rousseau never held the heart of a traitor! . . . Consult (your heart). It will claim for me the return of the friend I had from you, who has become necessary for me, and whom I have not deserved to lose.[29]

It was clear from Saint-Lambert's reply that he still had no confirmation of the nature of Rousseau's passion for Sophie:

October 11 — Wolfenbuttel

I did not receive until the 10th of this month, my dear friend, your letter of 4 September, and I have the misfortune to have hurt you for much longer than I would have, had I received your letter sooner. Do not accuse our friend of fickleness or coldness. She is capable of neither. . . . It is I alone who must be blamed for her conduct. . . . My own foolishness is the cause of all the evil. I thought I saw a change in her on my last visit. I love her too much not to lose my place in her heart without feeling it cruelly. I admit that I thought you the cause of what I thought I had lost. Do not think, my dear friend, that I believed you disloyal or deceitful, but I know the austerity of your principles. . . . I have made three people unhappy; I am the only one for whom troubles remain, since I am the only one who has cause for remorse. Some time ago I tried to make amends to her; I wish now to repair my injustices to you. Neither of us have ceased to love and respect you. Forgive us and continue to love us.[30]

It seemed for a while that harmony would soon be restored to the romance of Rousseau and Sophie, but the situation was known to too many people, and everyone wanted a part in the drama. Again we must rely on the *Mémoires* for details. The old line of communication from Thérèse to Mme d'Epinay to Grimm to Saint-Lambert was soon reactivated. Diderot, full of his good deed in stimulating Rousseau to write a confession to Saint-Lambert, could not contain the story of his own virtue. He accosted Saint-Lambert one evening at the Baron d'Holbach's. The conversation turned to Rousseau, and Saint-Lambert allegedly showed his contempt quite openly. Diderot could not understand this. Had Saint-Lambert not received Rousseau's letter in which he explained himself? Saint-Lambert supposedly replied that the only letter he received from Rousseau was one which contained a sermon on his immoral relationship with Sophie, a letter "to which one could only reply with a stick."[31]

At this point it is clear that the story as told in the *Mémoires* does not square with the letter from Saint-Lambert, who was apparently on the best of terms with Rousseau. Far from being angry with him, he had apologized to Rousseau for telling Sophie she must not see him. Saint-Lambert's anger clearly came *after* his encounter with Diderot rather than *before*, and this suggests that Diderot revealed the secret of Rousseau's passion for Sophie in his eagerness to tell Saint-Lambert about his own noble suggestion.[32] He probably hinted in order to find out if Saint-Lambert had received Rousseau's confession, and when it was not mentioned he assumed that Saint-Lambert was keeping in back so as not to embarrass Rousseau. But this was no longer necessary! Diderot already knew about it. It was he, the noble soul, who suggested that Jean-Jacques make a clean breast of it all. Out came the whole tale, and Saint-Lambert, furious at his own mildness under Rousseau's criticism, *wished* he had replied with a stick.[33]

After his encounter with Diderot, Saint-Lambert became cold toward Sophie. He chastised her for keeping Rousseau's passion a secret from him and insisted she break with him altogether. Sophie, apparently not wishing to drop her friend abruptly, began to indicate in her letters to Rousseau that her affection had cooled considerably. Rousseau was desperate. He begged for an explanation. Finally, on May 6, 1758, she told him that his indiscretion, "and that of your friends," had revealed his passion to her lover.[34] She pointed out that she would have kept his secret forever so as not to disrupt the friendship between him and Saint-Lambert, but that one of his friends had spoken of it in public and she must break off all relations with him.

Rousseau was filled with grief. The indiscreet friend could have been no one but Diderot, who was the only other one to whom he had confessed his passion for Sophie. It must be this so-called friend who meant to destroy him. Of course, at this point Diderot's revelation was superfluous. The story was all over Paris. Nevertheless, since the *Letter to d'Alembert* was being readied for publication, Rousseau, in the preface, accused Diderot of treachery and of revealing the secrets of a friend.[35] This public announcement served as a final and irreparable break between the two philosophers.

Surprisingly, the relationship between Saint-Lambert and Rousseau suffered least of all by the exposure of the latter's passion for Sophie. Saint-Lambert forgave the virtuous Sophie, and he and Rousseau again regarded themselves as friends, although the friendship was never as close as before. But the experience had been too close for Sophie. She learned, as many women had before her, that virtue is tarnished if one does not also maintain the appearance of virtue. Her attitude to Rousseau gradually became more cool and formal and her correspondence finally ceased. As the romance with Sophie died away, Rousseau's amorous fantasies seem to have died also. *The New Eloise* is his only romantic novel,[36] but it became a model for many others.

The Julie of his novel treats the young hero very much the way Sophie treated Rousseau—with a full assurance of affectionate regard and an insistence that he keep his distance. But Rousseau, with his intuitive understanding of the sense of climax could not merely repeat the story of his own romance. In the novel he could allow himself liberties denied to him in real life. He presented not only the torture of his own courtship, but the long, excruciating, drawn-out agony of Julie's fall from virtue. Yet this very agony of repentance preceded by the long period of languishing, unfulfilled love captivated the ladies of his time and made his novel a success. If the ladies of eighteenth-century France loved to suffer, Rousseau would show them how to suffer with elegance—as he had suffered—at the hands of a loved one. In his novel as in his life he placed the woman in a dominant position, and he portrayed his torments in such graphic detail and with such charm that he inspired several generations of imitators. Once he had enthroned the loved one above him, he approached her with a quivering, masochistic supplication that invited mistreatment, as in this passage from *The New Eloise:*

> Yes, I promise, I swear on my part to make every effort to recover my reason or to contain within the depths of my soul the agitation which I feel growing within me. But in the name of mercy turn from me those tender eyes which hold my very life in their glance, let me not see your face, your expression, your arms, your hands, your blond tresses, your gestures. . . . Even yesterday you almost let me take a kiss as a forfeit: you made only a slight resistance. Fortunately, I took care not to be too persistent. I sensed by my increasing emotion that I would soon be overcome and I held myself back. Ah, if I had taken the slightest taste of such a pleasure, that kiss would have held my last sigh and I would have died the happiest of men. . . . If the compassion which is natural to the well bred can soften your heart toward the troubles of a poor fellow to whom you have shown some regard, a few slight changes in your conduct could render his situation less precarious and make it possible for him to endure more peacefully his silence and his heartache. If his reserve and his

plight do not move you and you wish to make use of your power to ruin him, he will submit without a murmur. He would prefer to perish by your order than displease you by an indiscreet outburst.[37]

Here is a man begging for mistreatment. He projects a certain cruelty on his loved one, but it is always a teasing cruelty—the cruelty of the child who does not know what she is doing; never the cruelty of the deliberate sadist who enjoys watching the victim suffer.

Rousseau's novel also offered him the opportunity of contrasting Julie with the society women of Paris, whom he despised. Their manners and behavior, he said, were studied and false. They were like a group of marionettes.

> It is even worse when they open their mouths. It is not the sweet caressing voice of our Vaudoises. It is a certain hard, sharp, questioning, imperious, and mocking accent and louder than a man's. If any of the grace of their sex remains in their tone, their bold and curious manner of staring at people destroys the effect completely.[38]

In spite of his attack on society women they literally fought each other for copies of his book. Rousseau was the hero of feminine society. "What a soul he must have to write such a book!" cried Mme de Polignac to Mme de Verdelin.[39] Would it be possible to get a picture of Julie? Surely the romantic figure of Saint-Preux could be none other than Rousseau. People crowded the book stores as the editions rapidly sold out, and book dealers retained a few copies to rent by the hour.

Nor did the great ladies easily put aside the romantic image when they finished with the novel. In the "frail, weak girl" and her excitable young tutor, Rousseau had presented a type of love not to be found in the superficial and sophisticated salons of Paris. They thrilled with excitement and identification as Saint-Preux said to Julie:

> But what became of me a moment later when I felt—my hand shook—a gentle quivering—your rose-like lips—the lips of Julie—touch, press on mine and myself held in your arms? No, the fire of heaven is not more swift and sudden than that which swept over me. Every part of me seemed to feel all at once that delicious touch. Our sighs were like breaths of fire from our burning lips and my heart was overcome with delight—when suddenly I saw you grow pale, close your beautiful eyes, you leaned on your cousin and fainted away.[40]

Accustomed to the embraces of some powdered and foppish gentleman who usually followed his kiss with a bored and fashionable yawn and some attempt at a witticism, the ladies of Paris began to yearn for this new love. Rousseau's work had a profound effect on them and on the literature and society of future generations. There were other prominent figures in the romantic movement of the time, but Rousseau presented his readers with more than the excitement of romantic love. In the pastoral ending of his novel he severed the relationship of Saint-Preux and Julie as lovers (when she married Baron Wolmar), but joined them in a new kind of friendship, a *ménage a trois* in which Saint-Preux and Wolmar became firm friends and Julie continued to cherish and respect her former lover. Julie's religious sentiments brought about a spiritualization of love and thus created a kind of intimacy which could be shared by more than two, a society of lovers without jealousy or resentment. Rousseau's followers were captivated by the sweet fantastic world he created in which the good exude an all-pervading love for mankind and only the bad are hostile.

VI

The real world, however, was not destined to fulfill the expectations of Rousseau's novel. At the height of his final argument with Diderot and amid the ruins of his romance with Sophie, he became involved in another costly and heart-rending struggle—a final and dramatic argument with his old friend Mme d'Epinay.

Rousseau's second and final estrangement with Mme d'Epinay began as early as September 1757, when Grimm returned to La Chevrette and Rousseau was moved from the favored room next to the mistress of the house in order to make way for her lover. Another Wintzinried had entered his life. His feeling of being displaced and rejected did not improve when he discovered a secret door from his former room to Mme d'Epinay's which she had not considered necessary to point out to him during the time he occupied it.

Grimm and Rousseau had not been close friends for a long time, but in many respects they had continued to observe the forms of friendship. After Grimm's arrival, however, Rousseau began to notice many things about him which he found intolerable. He was incensed at Grimm's highhanded manner with servants and was outraged at his use of cosmetics. In his *Confessions*, he remarks, "Though he was as conceited as he was vain, with his huge watery eyes and his ungainly figure, he fancied himself with the ladies; and since his farce with Mlle Fels,[41] he passed with several of them for a man of deep feelings. This had made him fashionable and had given him a taste for female toilet-ries."[42] To the Natural Man, this was a sure sign of deceit. If Grimm was any sort of a decent fellow, he would want to show his heart on his face, not hide his character behind cosmetics. He decided, there-fore, that Grimm was not suitable as a friend and announced to Mme d'Epinay his intention to break with him. Ths tactic of calling in some-one to judge his behavior had now become a standard procedure. He had previously asked both Sophie and Mme d'Epinay to arbitrate his earlier quarrel with Diderot, who in turn was asked to judge the ap-proach he should take with Saint-Lambert, and he was later to ask Grimm to decide between himself and Mme d'Epinay. He could not tolerate ambiguity in any situation, and this was his method for getting others to declare themselves for him or against him. It was probably also an indication of his growing uncertainty about the world around him and about the plots he was beginning to see directed against him. He found himself unable to decide what attitude others had toward him, and he needed some help in interpreting reality. Mme d'Epinay, of course, assured him that Grimm was his friend, for she wanted no quarrel between them.

In October Rousseau learned that Mme d'Epinay was ill and that she planned to visit the famous Dr. Tronchin in Geneva. She asked Rousseau to come with her. This request came as a great surprise. He suffered from his old malady of the urethra that made frequent urina-tion a necessity and caused him great pain. Sometimes it was neces-sary for him to use a probe in order to achieve temporary relief. Thus, the idea of a long trip in a carriage with a lady in midwinter was out of the question. However, when he told her he could not accompany her he found that a refusal was not a simple matter. Diderot wrote him from Paris outlining his duties to her and explaining in detail exactly why he was honor-bound to accompany her. He said if Rousseau had ceased to care for her, he was even more obligated to go along in order to pay his debt of gratitude.

Diderot's facility for making moral decisions without having the slightest idea of the considerations involved was typical, but Rousseau, instead of laughing at his pronouncements, trembled with rage and finally sent back a long justification for his refusal. He suspected, he said, that Diderot had written the letter at the instigation of others who wished to embarrass him.

At this period Sophie was becoming concerned for her reputa-tion, and she cautioned Rousseau that if he was too vehement in his refusal to go to Geneva, people might think she was responsible. She urged him not to leave the Hermitage in protest, since this would only serve to advertise his refusal. Rousseau, as usual, was melted into tenderness by Sophie. His fire and his fury left him, and he began to doubt whether he had behaved properly in the affair. He was desperate for a solution to his dilemma, and in the extremity of his desperation he turned to the person least likely to offer him help, his "old friend" Grimm. He recalled that Grimm had appeared to take no side in the decision as to whether or not he should accompany Mme d'Epinay and had professed a certain condescending friendship toward him. Perhaps his coolness would make him a good judge. In any event Jean-Jacques had lost the power to decide. He sent Grimm a long indescreet letter in which he explained that he owed nothing to Mme d'Epinay, that he had already made a sacrifice in coming to live on her estate, but that if Grimm really believed the trip to Geneva was the only proper course to follow, then he would go.[43]

Grimm had very mixed feelings about sending Rousseau to Geneva with his mistress. In all probability he considered himself quite safe in his attitude of cold indifference to Rousseau, never dreaming that this distraught philosopher would call on him at the last moment to decide his fate. Rousseau's turning to him for advice put him in a quandary. In his first note he suggested tentatively that Rousseau might at least offer to go with Mme d'Epinay and that she would probably refuse. But Rousseau did not make the offer. He considered the suggestion a trick, for he believed she was pregnant and that he was being urged to accompany her so the world would think him responsible.[44] Only after Mme d'Epinay had left did Grimm release the full fury of his anger in a letter to Rousseau.

VII

What was, in fact, the cause of Mme d'Epinay's invitation to Rousseau and the apparently unanimous opinion of his friends that he should accompany her to Geneva? It will never be known what suggestions were made by one person to another regarding who should write to Rousseau and what should be said. However, it was apparent to all who were aware of the gossip of Paris during that period that Rousseau's relations with Sophie were damaging to both their reputations. The alert Diderot, with his ears tuned to the opinion of literary salons, may well have decided that Rousseau's reputation was more important than his happiness. Certainly, he needed no encouragement to offer advice.

Sophie, for her part, had reached the point where the excitement of secret meetings with Rousseau was more than offset by the growing suspicions of her lover. If her encounters with Rousseau had begun with a certain delicious anticipation on her part, it was now apparent that her resistance was not going to be overcome with a grand sweep of passion. His attempt to seduce her by preaching of virtue had melted her heart and roused her emotions, but he lacked the final boldness and resolution which might have won his objective. Even the girl who likes to tease and plans to go no further prefers to believe she is in some danger. Rousseau had become altogether too predictable, and the thrill of his presence was wearing away. Sophie told him that he really should go to Geneva with Mme d'Epinay but that she could understand if his health made the trip impossible. However, she added, his refusal would cause her considerable embarrassment. People might think she was urging him to stay.

Here, perhaps, is an answer to the question of why Rousseau was invited on the journey with his benefactress. Mme d'Epinay had long been concerned for Sophie's reputation, and there is reason to believe that this concern was not completely disinterested. While she had no romantic interest in Rousseau, she had enjoyed turning his head, receiving his visits and his attentions, and she was not happy that all Paris knew her position had been usurped by her sister-in-law. If Sophie had confided to Mme d'Epinay her declining interest in Rousseau and her desire to recoup her damaged esteem in the eyes of her lover, Mme d'Epinay might have been only too eager to offer her assistance. She could hardly have anticipated that her invitation to Rousseau would become such an issue with him.

Mme d'Epinay was grievously hurt by Rousseau's letter to Grimm (which Grimm described for her), in which the virtuous citizen of Geneva pointed out that he had really done her a favor by staying on her estate, that he had given up many fine opportunities simply out of friendship for her, that he had ruined his digestion eating her fancy meals, and that his finances had suffered from tipping her servants. If there was a debt on either side, said Rousseau, it was she who should be grateful to him. This letter was the ultimate blow. She had tried for a long time to handle her "bear" carefully, to make him happy without appearing too solicitous, to care for his needs without wounding his pride. Now she was ill and tired. She had lost interest in guarding the sensitivity of this man who was apparently so insensitive to the feelings of others. She sent him a cold letter from Geneva indicating she no longer had any friendship for him. Rousseau replied that friendship between them was dead, but that he still had respect and gratitude toward her for her kindness. He added, "I wanted to leave the Hermitage, and I should have done so. But it is claimed that I must remain here until spring, and since my friends wish it, I will remain if you consent."[45] Rousseau probably referred to Sophie's statement that her reputation would suffer if he left the Hermitage at that time. He was, no doubt, also concerned with his own illness and with the difficulty of moving in winter—it was November 23 at the time of his letter.

On December 10 Rousseau received Mme d'Epinay's reply. It indicated clearly the extent to which their friendship had deteriorated:

> After having given you for several years every possible sign of friendship and interest I have nothing left for you but pity. You are a very unhappy man. I hope your conscience is as clear as mine. That may be necessary for your repose in the future.
>
> Since you wish to leave the Hermitage and should have done so I am astonished that your friends have prevented you. As for myself I do not consult mine as regards my duty, and I have nothing more to say to you about yours.[46]

On receiving her dismissal Rousseau felt it imperative to leave the Hermitage. Fortunately, M. Mathos, prosecuting attorney to the Prince de Condé, offered him a small cottage nearby and thus saved his pride—and possibly his life—for he was determined to move his possessions into the open fields rather than stay another week at the Hermitage. Warmed by the heat of his anger, he moved to his new home and collapsed, weary and discouraged with the long turmoil and the struggle to explain himself to others. What must he have thought when he began to receive the letters from Sophie which indicated that she too had begun to cool in her affection for him. It is well enough to say that Rousseau brought his troubles on himself, but the picture is rather different when the many small weaknesses and the intolerance characterizing the relationship of friend to friend during this tragic period are recognized.

In the eighteenth century there was little understanding of mental illness. People were either mad, with the raving madness of the insane, or they were disagreeable, false, and lacking in virtue. One simply did not expect to find mental illness in one's social equals.[47] But perhaps an even greater problem for the people in this story was the concept of friendship that prevailed. A great emphasis was placed on the beauty of friendship—on being a good friend, a self-sacrificing friend. The primary goal of friendship was to elevate the self and become virtuous by consideration for others. Friends strove to outdo each other in devotion, in sacrifice, and in grief over the absence of a friend. It was a kind of emotional potlatch. The victim of this tender feeling was expected to show due appreciation, or he was unworthy of a beautiful friendship. This was the era of the Golden Rule and before Bernard Shaw's famous maxim: "Do not do unto others as you would have them do unto you—they might not have the same tastes."

Diderot must have seen Rousseau's public accusation about October 1758—a time when the Encyclopedist was more in need of his friends than ever. In January 1757, after an attack on the king, the monarchy and the nobility had been seized with panic. The would-be assassin, Pierre Damiens, had been horribly mutilated by public executioners and finally drawn and quartered, but he had denied having any accomplices. Still the belief persisted in a plot to topple the monarchy, and a reign of terror and censorship was unleashed. Fredrick II was at the height of his success against the French army. The government, previously strong enough to tolerate criticism with amused indifference, was now on the decline. The censorship laws were stiffened, ideas became dangerous, and Diderot's great *Encyclopedia*, the masterwork of his life, came under renewed pressure from the authorities. Many of the most notable contributors, such as Voltaire and Turgot, lost their enthusiasm for the project under the increased political pressure, and Malesherbes, the official censor of Paris who favored the work of Diderot, had to hide the plates of the *Encyclopedia* during a police raid.

Then D'Alembert, Diderot's friend and colleague in his early labors, deserted the project, and his beloved Damon, Grimm, departed for Geneva to be with Mme d'Epinay. It was at this time that Diderot was greeted with Rousseau's final and irreparable rebuke in his *Letter to d'Alembert*. The spectacle of these two great liberal thinkers quarreling over personal trivia while the privileged orders of the old régime began to crumble around them provides a tragic scene.

The Letter to d'Alembert

I

THE REACTION TO ROUSSEAU'S *Letter to d'Alembert on the Theater* is difficult to understand without some knowledge of the historical and political situation at the time. When a great régime begins to totter, it divides into sharply divergent clusters of opinion. Liberalism and conservatism become more marked, and each principal figure is quickly categorized by the multitude. The charge of "traitor to our cause" is common, particularly when a man is in neither of the principal political camps.

Under Louis XIV and his predecessors France had risen to the position of the first nation of Europe. In the fields of science and technology France led the world. The courts of many lands spoke French, and the French way of living, French literature, and French art were copied throughout the Western world. In the field of fashion Paris became the single authority, and the colorful costumes of many countries were swept away in the craze to be like the French. But Louis XV had initiated a reign of irresponsibility, and by 1743 French prestige had already seriously declined. The most prominent voice in the nation was no longer that of the king but of his mistress, Mme de Pompadour. Ministers who wished to strengthen the navy, to propose financial reforms, or to take measures to shore up the declining vitality of the country did not approach the king, for he was bored by matters of state and would yawn in their presence. Instead, they humbly presented themselves to Mme de Pompadour, who examined their proposals and decided whether or not the king should hear them—if indeed she did not decide the issue for him.

In the first stage of the War of the Austrian Succession (1740-43) France had been allied with Prussia, but after Frederick II concluded a separate peace with the Austrians and left France to face the combined wrath of Austria and England there was a coolness between the heads of these two great powers. While some ministers on both sides were attempting to reestablish friendly contacts, Mme de Pompadour, through her relationship with the Empress Maria Theresa of Austria, worked to reverse the traditional alliances of France. Thus, at the beginning of the Seven Years' War in 1756 France found herself on the side of her old enemy, Austria, and challenged by the formidable alliance of Prussia and England. But, after all, the Empress of Austria had been very kind to Mme de Pompadour, and the scorn of Frederick II, who called her Madame Poison,[1] was the gossip of courtly circles! The Prince de Conti, one of the first soldiers of France, might have played a significant role in the coming battles, had he not made the mistake of opposing Madame's wishes regarding the Austrian alliance. Soon this distinguished soldier discovered that he no longer enjoyed the confidence of the king and was forced to give way to Mme le General Pompadour who sent notes of advice to the field commanders on military strategy.[2]

Instead of Conti, the Prince de Soubise was chosen to command the French forces. While no worse than many other aristocratic commanders, he represented the essence of French decadence, bringing with him on the march his actors, his wigmakers, cooks, parrots, and casks of lavender water. Grimm who was at the front with D'Estreés at the Battle of Hastenbeck, was disgusted with the luxury in the army and reported that, despite the heavy equipment having been left behind, it took three hours to get the "indispensable requirements" unpacked. "It is scandalous," he remarked, "and convinces me more than ever that the world is so full of abuses that one would have to be a fool to try to correct them."[3] The cumbersome paraphernalia of luxury may well have been a critical factor in slowing the French advance and hampering effective and orderly retreat. Certainly, no self-respecting general would want to follow up such an impressive victory as Hastenbeck with a hasty advance which might leave his lavender water several days behind.

Splendor, love, and feminine intrigue were everywhere the principal topics of the day. When the king of France let it be known that he would rather visit the theater than attend to affairs of state, one cannot be surprised that the generals regarded warfare as a bore. Mme de Pompadour has often been described as the symbol of this luxury and decay, but her influence was due to her concern for France. She felt that she might make up for the indifference on the part of the king by taking personal command of the situation. She sought to preserve the prestige of Versailles by arranging special theatrical performances and by inviting artists and philosophers to court. The ladies of Paris, however, were not to be outdone by this upstart in the palace. During the reign of Louis XIV a few great houses had reflected with a pale light the radiance of the court of the Sun King. With Versailles on the wane as a cultural center, Mme de Luxembourg, Mme du Deffand, Mlle de Lespinasse, Mme de Boufflers, and other fashionable women of Parisian society sought to create rival courts in their salons. The salon was thus a great flowering of culture and at the same time a symbol of decay of the court of France. The very latest fashions and gossip were paraded for the initiates, bold ideas were discussed, the mistress of each salon sought to present something more novel, more attractive to her guests. To this end the best musicians, playwrights, the brightest wits were sought to entertain the ladies and their friends. This was the atmosphere that Voltaire carried with him to Geneva when he introduced a theater and a taste for French luxury to the austere Genevans.

II

Voltaire is an enigmatic figure in this history. To many he is the symbol of the Enlightenment, the spirit of free inquiry, the champion of liberal ideas. In some respects, however, he was very much a symbol of his times. For the king and his court he served as a kind of jester, poking fun at them, as jesters will, but essentially a believer in the institution of monarchy. He was wise in the ways of courtly etiquette. He lived off the largess of Mme de Pompadour and her arch enemy, Frederick the Great, falling out of favor with both the French and Prussian courts when he went too far. He despised injustice and privilege, but he was inclined to believe that justice might be obtained through the influence of a benevolent despot rather than by the action of the people. Vain, domineering, and completely unscrupulous in money matters, he created his own private empire on the outskirts of Geneva. There he was surrounded by his retinue, who had to appreciate his wit or feel the lash of his tongue. He had the personality of an aristocrat, and it is not surprising that he made his first friendships in Geneva among the wealthy and powerful.

Nevertheless, Voltaire was a much more natural man than was Rousseau, the advocate of naturalism. This was because Voltaire was comfortable with his desire to dominate, with his greed and sexual appetites. Rousseau had to deny his duplicity, Voltaire could laugh at his. He could write pornography and refuse to sign it, without attempting to hide his motives from himself. When he was lacerating Maupertuis with ridicule or torturing a poor Capuchin monk with his demand to be confessed as a good Catholic, he recognized and accepted his own malice. Yet when he was moved by a case of injustice, such as the Calas tragedy, he could persist like an indefatigable bulldog in his defense of the innocent, without thought of time or the sacrifice of funds. He could be petty without being ashamed of his pettiness and noble without being self-righteous. He was, in short, a healthy personality at home with his age. Perhaps for this reason he was not a true revolutionary.

The animosity between Rousseau and Voltaire was, at least in the initial stages, a war of ideas which gained its momentum from the interest of the public in the contrasting views of the two men. Voltaire had initiated the controversy by his letter of August 30, 1755, to Rousseau on his "new book against the human race." He published his letter with Rousseau's reply, with the latter's permission.

On November 1, 1755, in the terrible Lisbon earthquake, fifteen thousand people were killed and at least as many more were maimed. Many perished in the churches of the city, which were filled to capacity on All Saints Day. Voltaire was moved to anguish at the thought of the arbitrary horror measured out to the just and unjust alike. In his poem on the earthquake, written shortly afterward, he departed from his usual satirical style and poured out his feelings of doubt and puzzlement concerning divine justice. It was one of his most sincere and passionate declamations. He asked that a copy be sent to Rousseau in the belief that this man of feeling would surely respond to such a work. By the time Rousseau received this work he was wandering in the woods of Montmorency in an effort to escape the cares of this world. Absorbed in his fantasy of true love and ideal women, he was too far from the agonies of suffering and dying to feel their sting. Voltaire's poem, which might have moved him deeply after his own misfortune, seemed out of place. The thoughts on the Lisbon earthquake were an unwanted interruption, reminding him of a world he wanted to forget.[4] Nevertheless, he was honored by the gift and felt an obligation to reply. He explained to the man of letters that it was not God, or even nature, that had caused the evils of the Lisbon quake, but that man was the culprit. The cause of the tragedy was civilization, which jammed people together into buildings and compact cities where they could not escape disaster. He pointed out that all was really well and, since God is perfect, that everything must happen for the best.[5] When one reflects that Rousseau was living at the time in his own private fairyland, his lack of rapport with Voltaire is not surprising. But Voltaire, who was very much with this world, was annoyed at the superficial optimism. Perhaps he also sensed Rousseau's growing competitive feeling, for his reply was a perfunctory missive which ignored most of the arguments. Meanwhile, he began to prepare a resounding refutation of Rousseau's position in his famous *Candide*, in which the ridiculous philosopher Pangloss proves logically, in the midst of wars, floggings, rapine, and disaster that this is the best of all possible worlds.

Rousseau was given to understand that *Candide* was an answer to his letter, and, although he would not admit to having read the book, he could not avoid becoming aware of its contents. With the publication of *Candide* his indignation began to mount. Later, in 1760, when he discovered that Formey had published his letter to Voltaire on the Lisbon poem without his permission, he raged at Voltaire for releasing a personal letter to a journalist, told him he had ruined the city of Geneva, and announced his enmity with the perplexed and wounded plaint, "I hate you, since you have willed it; but I hate you as a man more worthy of loving you, had you so willed it."[6]

In this final letter Rousseau described his generosity, his friendly overtures, and Voltaire's ingratitude. At the time it was written he had already produced such an uproar in Geneva against Voltaire that the latter was forced to flee from his beloved Les Délices to his estate at Ferney, outside the territory. Yet Rousseau, the professional underdog, was speaking from his heart. He never understood his own competitive feeling toward Voltaire. The thought that he might have a desire to destroy a literary colleague would have been completely unacceptable to him. He persisted in his belief that his *Letter to d'Alembert*, an attack on the theater which dislodged the giant, was part of a simple philosophical disagreement between friends. To the literary world of the time, however, the *Letter to d'Alembert* was the blow of a traitor. To understand the background of these contrasting points of view one must consider the reasons Rousseau gave himself for bringing out this work.

III

In an earlier discussion with Diderot, Rousseau had obtained advance information about an article on Geneva which D'Alembert was preparing for the *Encyclopedia*. Diderot had apparently admitted that this article was part of a plan, backed by "certain Genevese of high rank"[7] to open a theater in Geneva. It was also apparent that D'Alembert had begun his article directly after a visit with that grand lord of the theater, Voltaire, at Les Délices. Voltaire loved to write and act in plays, and he missed the stimulation of a theater. It was clearly as much for Voltaire as for the "Genevese of high rank" that D'Alembert had begun his labors.

When he had lived in Paris, Rousseau had generally attended the theater two to three times a week, and his *Village Soothsayer* had given him a name in the theatrical world. Yet he could not imagine the rustic charm of his native city violated by this Parisian vice. He felt toward Paris and Geneva as he did toward the women he loved. He was always fighting the sensual side of himself, and he required such perpetual virginity in his native city as an accommodation for his own asceticism. Paris was fine for sport, but Geneva was something to believe in. He determined to answer D'Alembert's article with an open letter.

Rousseau prepared his *Letter to d'Alembert* in the spirit of a man defending the honor of his father. He portrayed in all their rude simplicity the hearty amusements and the unspoiled gaiety of the Genevan citizens: their little social clubs, their games, their drunkenness, their occasional profanity, their neighborly friendship and conviviality, their plain, honest unsophisticated sociability. In contrast, he presented the expensive distraction and the ridicule of morality found in the theater, urging his fellow citizens to resist this assault on their virtue.

Since the theater was in a sense an arm of the literary atheists in their battle against the church, many philosophers and writers felt Rousseau had joined entrenched authority in his attack on the theater. In some instances a feeling of personal insult added intensity to the anger. Diderot, who had been accused in the preface, felt the entire book attacked him through the theater. Voltaire, who had already been irritated by Rousseau's reply to his poem on the destruction of Lisbon, felt that Rosseau, in fighting the French theater, was really fighting him, the living embodiment of that institution.

Rousseau was accused of simple jealousy, of taking whatever side would bring him attention. Yet his philosophy of life and his cultural background were so fundamentally different from those of Voltaire and the Encyclopedists that disagreement was inevitable. While motives of which he was unaware contributed to his zeal in dissecting D'Alembert's article, his logic, his intuitive understanding, and his eloquence were never better. The *Letter to d'Alembert* represents the beginning of his most mature and polished writing.

He contended that a republic maintained its freedom only by producing men of virtue, and an institution which failed to contribute to virtue was suspect on this ground alone. He did not deny that a theater might have merit in France, where freedom was out of the question and the populace already corrupt, but he stoutly contended against its establishment in Geneva. It would, he said, break up the many societies of men and women which now occupied the Genevans in more simple amusements. Carried away by his argument, he painted in vivid contrast the "feminine" society of Paris and the "masculine" society of Geneva.

. . . every woman of Paris assembles in her apartment a harem of men. . . . But see these same men, always constrained in their voluntary prisons, get up, sit down again, come and go continually to the fireplace, to the window, pick up and put down a fan a hundred times, leaf through books, glance at pictures, turn and pirouette all around the room, while the idol, lying motionless on a couch, has only her tongue and eyes active.[8]

It would not be difficult to demonstrate that, instead of gaining by these practices, the women lose. They are flattered without being loved; they are served without being honored. . . . As for myself, I can scarcely conceive how they (the men) can honor women so little as to dare to address them continually with these insipid gallantries, these insulting and mocking compliments to which they do not even deign to give an air of good faith.[9]

Even the children were destroyed by the feminine influence.

(Children in my time) had no curls to keep in place; they challenged one another at wrestling, running, and boxing. They battled with a will, hurt one another sometimes, and then embraced in tears. They returned home sweating, breathless, and disheveled: they were scamps, but these scamps made men who have in their hearts a zeal for serving the fatherland and blood to shed for it. Please God that one can say as much for our pretty little dandified gentlemen one day, and that these men at fifteen will not be children at thirty.[10]

In this section of his work we begin to see the source of Rousseau's ambivalence about Paris. To him Paris was, as it has been to many men, a woman. In his vehemence against the sensuality of Parisian life, its display, its luxury, and its finery, he was expressing his resentment at the influence and the power of women in society, the society in which Mme de Pompadour was a more formidable figure than the king himself. The intellectual life, the opinions, and manners of Paris were controlled by a handful of influential women through their salons.

Paris, he said, was already corrupt, but Geneva still had something to lose. In Paris men live too much with women, in a woman's world, and since the women cannot follow the men in the more rugged activities, the men must spend their time catering to the women. In Geneva life was different. Men gathered in their circles and the women in theirs. The women sewed and gossiped, the men argued, boxed, wrestled, and played simple games. He felt that association with a woman weakened a man and sapped his manly vigor. Of course, he was perfectly correct as far as his own experience was concerned, and it was by projecting his own half-recognized feelings onto society as a whole that he reached his conclusions. Rousseau resented the power of women because he felt himself to be weak and lacking in manliness whenever he came under their influence. The women who filled some men with sexual desire and the urge for conquest only made Rousseau tremble and shake with a submissive passion. With him all emotion, even sexual feeling, was soon swept into the vortex of his overwhelming desire for a cuddly kind of puppy love in which he could recapture the imagined childhood with the mother he had never known. Women in whom the impulse to mother was stronger than sexual desire were inevitably drawn to Rousseau. He satisfied their maternal feelings and did not threaten them sexually. For his own part he was both attracted and repelled by these benevolent Circes. He resented them for fostering his dependency needs, but he was unable to resist them. Kindness always inspired him with love, and love brought forth a more urgent need for sympathy and cuddling. Like an alcoholic who knew his poison, Rousseau schooled himself to accept favors from no one—to become completely and totally independent. Yet the cooing voice of a soft female inevitably turned his knees to rubber and he was soon at her feet. This, then, was the basis for his attack on women. For his own personality they were fully as destructive as he believed them to be. His error lay in assuming that they would be equally damaging to all men.

IV

It was not only D'Alembert's suggestion of a theater for Geneva that offended Rousseau. In his article D'Alembert had asserted that the pastors of Geneva were advocates of Socinianism,[11] and Rousseau, who had often attacked religious orthodoxy himself, would not have a Frenchman insulting the pastors of Geneva. Further, he saw that a certain broad-minded attitude might be tolerated by the Genevans, but the suggestion of a specifically named foreign dogma would bring out cries of heresy. With his relentless logic he took D'Alembert's assertion apart.

> According to you, many pastors of Geneva have only a complete Socinianism. That is what you declare openly in the face of Europe. I dare to ask how you learned it: it can only be through your own conjecture, or by the testimony of others or by the avowal of the pastors in question . . . but if this were really their attitude and they had confided it to you, there is no question but that they would have told you in secret, in the free and sincere effusion of philosophical discourse; they would have said it to the philosopher and not to the author. They did nothing of the kind,

and my proof is, without reply; it is that you published it.[12] . . .
I thank you on behalf of my country for the spirit of philosophy
and humanity that you recognize in its clergy and for the justice
which you are pleased to render it. I agree with you on this point.
But for being philosophical and tolerant it does not follow that
they are heretic. In the name of the sect which you give them, in
the dogmas which you say are theirs I can neither approve nor
follow you. Although such a system may perhaps have nothing
but what is honorable to those who adopt it, I will refrain from
attributing it to my pastors, who have not adopted it for fear that
the praises I might give it could furnish others with a subject for
a very grave accusation. . . . Monsieur, let us judge the actions of
men and allow God to judge their faith.[13]

These brave words of defense soon made Rousseau a hero among
the Genevan pastors. Such violent sermons were preached against that
renegade Catholic, Voltaire, with the theater at his home, that the council soon found it necessary to warn him that not even his private little
performances could be tolerated much longer. There was strong class
feeling in Geneva, and to the working man the theater was equated
with luxury, privilege, and the hated aristocracy. Rumblings of anger
and resentment against Voltaire were heard throughout the city, and
he felt it an expedient time to change his residence.

To the Encyclopedists, who were now under severe pressure from
both the clergy and the monarchy in France, Rousseau's words represented more than a mere defense of the pastors of Geneva. In 1752 the
Encyclopedia was formally suppressed, and the clergy began to show
increasing zeal in attacking unorthodox ideas. Sacred burial had long
been refused to both actors and philosophers, and the support of the
infamous editors of the *Encyclopedia*, Diderot and D'Alembert,
brought risk for any man. By attacking Diderot, D'Alembert, and the
French theater, and by defending religious orthodoxy, Rousseau
seemed to be casting his lot with the enemy. Even then the boiling
tumult of revolution was beginning to stir in France. *Ecrasez l'infame!*
was the battle cry of Voltaire at this time—crush the infamous privilege
cloaked in ecclesiastical authority! Almost every letter of his during
this period closed with a declamation against this enemy. The theater,
which he used like a rapier, was his principal weapon, and he regarded
Rousseau's *Letter* as would a fencer who discovered someone loosening
the handle of his foil. Rousseau became, for him, part of *l'infame*, to be
crushed as an enemy of revolt.

The attitude of the literary brethren toward Rousseau was stimulated not only by Voltaire's magnetic leadership but by their reaction to the many desertions from their ranks in this time of crisis. A host of minor writers, sensing the atmosphere of the times, sought to establish themselves with those in power by using the weapons of literature and drama against the Encyclopedists. The philosophers, who were now in fear of their liberty, found it difficult to distinguish honest disagreement from opportunism.

On May 2, 1760, a minor comedy of Charles Palissot, called *The Philosophers*, was presented in the Théâtre-Français. The satire was directed against the Encyclopedists, but few men of letters escaped unscathed. In Scene 9 of Act III, Rousseau was represented coming on the stage on all fours with a lettuce in his pocket, saying he had chosen the position of a beast because of his zeal for philosophy: "Upon these four pillars my body is better sustained and I see fewer fools."[14] Voltaire, who was a powerful, wealthy, and influential bourgeois, was the only philosopher to escape attack in the play—he was extravagantly praised. But support from such a quarter was only an embarrassment to him, and he censured Palissot for the unfairness of his attack.

Another member of the anti-intellectual group of literary critics, however, did not hesitate to attack even Voltaire. This was Jean Fréron, the chief antagonist of the Encyclopedists. He was a wealthy Parisian editor who published *L'Année littéraire*, a weekly journal of criticism supporting the position of the clergy and the monarchy. Voltaire, who despised Fréron as a scheming opportunist, led the counterattack with his play *The Scotch Woman*, in which Fréron was portrayed as Wasp, a literary hack and errand boy for those in power. When a Scotch lass attracts the lover of an English lady, Wasp approaches the lady with an offer to slander her adversary, pointing out that a Scotch woman who goes about unattended in troublesome times is thereby concealing herself and must be an enemy to the state. Some of Voltaire's lines portray clearly the atmosphere of fear and suspicion in the air, the danger of being different, of holding unorthodox ideas, as well as the personal motives and desire for power which he ascribed to witch-hunting.

The opening night of Voltaire's play served as a gathering point for all those in Paris who opposed Fréron and believed in the work of the Encyclopedists. Diderot, D'Argental, and the other philosophers and their friends appeared in force to shake the theater with their applause when the play opened. During this same period Voltaire was involving himself in a series of battles against *l'infâme* as represented by orthodox dogmatism. On October 13, 1761, Marc-Antoine Calas, the eldest son of a small Protestant family in Toulouse, committed suicide. The rumor soon spread throughout this Catholic community that Marc-Antoine had been murdered by his father because he was about to turn Catholic. Several members of the family were arrested. Jean Calas, the father, was tortured and executed for the crime, despite the fact that the old man insisted upon his innocence until the end. Voltaire took up the cause of this unfortunate family. Through appeals to friends, pamphlets, and, finally, through legal action he succeeded in clearing the name of Jean Calas. At the end of this extensive legal and literary battle his name was famous as a fighter against privilege and injustice. Fréron, true to form, used his journal and his literary ability to attack the Calas family and throw doubt on Voltaire's efforts.

This was only the beginning of Voltaire's many struggles on the part of the victims of injustice. His home at Ferney soon became a veritable refuge for the oppressed. The Sirven family sought his help in their flight from an accusation similar to that directed against the Calas family. This was followed by the Espinasse family, the case of General Lally, the Chevalier de la Barre and several others. Under the leadership of Voltaire the opposition to *l'infame* was soon heard throughout France.

V

But oppressors in France were, in reality, quite different from oppressors in Geneva, and liberalism in one place might be reaction in another. The Encyclopedists for all their advanced views were, for the most part, believers in monarchy, as was Voltaire. To them, intolerance and privilege were the great evils, but none of them was prepared to suggest a change in the established order of society. In Geneva the atmosphere was different. Many Genevan pastors were opposed to the aristocracy which dominated the politics of the city. In 1738 pressure from France and from some of the Swiss cantons had resulted in the Act of Mediation, which confirmed the power of the Small Council and the Council of Two Hundred in Geneva. Thus, a de facto aristocracy was established, since the other citizens and burghers could not elect their own people to these councils. The aristocrats of the city, like those of other small principalities, were inclined to mimic the ways of the nobility in powerful nations, and in French-speaking Geneva it was natural for them to turn to Paris for their culture. Thus, they welcomed the suggestion of D'Alembert for a theater at Geneva. It was primarily the members of the "better families" who attended the plays of Voltaire on his estate. Accustomed to power, they chaffed at sumptuary laws and other such restrictions. They longed for the gold lace and finery which distinguished the nobles of Paris.

The Genevan clergy, in support of sumptuary laws, opposition to theaters, and statements of some of its number regarding the older more democratic times in Geneva, was—unlike the clergy in France— a severe critic of the established powers. Rousseau, in his attack on the theater and his defense of the orthodoxy of the pastors, was actually supporting the more democratic elements in Geneva. Such people later formed the party of the Representants, who opposed the burning of the *Social Contract* and *Emile* and demanded a more demo- cratic administration in Geneva.

Thus, while the church was a symbol of reaction and the theater a symbol of liberalism in France, the situation was almost the reverse in Geneva. Rousseau understood this, but he was unable to explain the situation to his fellow intellectuals in Paris. Instead, he began to see that with every step he became more and more isolated from them. He was acutely conscious of the attitude of the literary world toward him. He believed in much of the work of the Encyclopedists and admired their spirit of opposition and defiance; yet he felt that he, too, must speak the truth as he saw it, even if his action placed him in the role of outcast from the very people who counted most with him. In his pref- ace to the *Letter to d'Alembert*, he revealed his sadness and his sense of loneliness and isolation in his new retreat at the cottage of Montmor- ency. Describing the loss of his "severe and judicious Aristarchus,"[15] he concluded the preface with the following paragraph:

If among the essays which have come from my pen this paper is even beneath the others, it is less the fault of circumstances than of myself; I am beneath myself. The disorders of the body exhaust the soul; under the pressure of suffering it loses its flexibility. A passing moment of fermentation produced in me some glimmer of talent. It showed itself late; it extinguished itself early. In return- ing to my natural state, I have gone back to nothingness. I had only a moment; it is passed; I have the shame to outlive myself. Reader, if you receive this last work with indulgence, you will welcome my shadow; for, as for myself, I am no more.[16]

While Voltaire at Ferney and the Encyclopedists in Paris were championing the cause of truth and while the line was being drawn between those who supported Diderot and those who wished to crush him, Rousseau was at his retreat in Montmorency. It was here that Duchesne, the bookseller, sent him a copy of Palissot's *Philosophers*.

Rousseau took no personal offense at it. He even felt that he had been praised by the book, since Palissot quoted some of his own criti- cism of philosophical speculation. But he was deeply offended by the attack on Diderot. He concluded that, as Duchesne was unknown to him, it must have been Palissot who urged Duchesne to send the book. He replied to Duchesne as follows:

Montmorency 21 May 1760

Sir, on glancing through the play you have sent me, I shudder to find myself praised in it. I refuse to accept this horrible present. I am persuaded that, in sending it to me, you did not intend to insult me. But either you do not know or you have forgotten that I once had the honor of being the friend of a respectable man who is unjustly defamed and slandered in this libelous work.[17]

While Rousseau resented any attack on his former friend, he was no longer in a position to take a stand by his side. Having made a public break with Diderot, a defense of him would hardly be welcome. Yet, it is clear that he longed to join the philosophical party, particularly at this moment when he saw his old friend Diderot once again the underdog, fighting against the entrenched authority of church and state. In Paris men were being imprisoned for their support of Diderot, but Rousseau, who had been closer to him than most and who loved him still, in spite of himself, had to watch the struggle from a distance.

VI

In a mood of profound depression Rousseau settled down at Montmorency after his reply to D'Alembert. He had concluded that he would never write again, and he wished only to be alone. However, his fame was such that he was never short of visitors. In spite of his prickly personality he had a capacity for being a charming and spontaneous conversationalist and an agreeable host. When he had attained a measure of peace and security, he could be most cordial, and his informality was always refreshing. Conversation was like a soothing balm to his hurt feelings and, as long as he found no obligation hidden in the folds of friendship, he would relax and enjoy his visitors, chiding them if they became formal and expounding on his belief in the virtue of natural human relationships.

His guests came expecting a "character," and they found what they expected. In his new retreat at Montmorency he was soon as eagerly sought as before—by both the nobility and bourgeoisie. During his stay at the Hermitage he had begun his two greatest works, *Emile* and the *Social Contract*. Now, in new surroundings, stimulated by the conversation of his visitors and his extensive correspondence, he once more resumed work on these books.

The Marshal de Luxembourg and his wife, who had an estate in the vicinity of Montmorency, had already made several overtures to Rousseau through their servants and personal friends, but Rousseau, who seldom visited anyone, declined to stir from his new abode. Finally, however, the marshal himself came to call, and Rousseau felt obligated to return the visit. Soon he was invited to stay in the Little Château on the Luxembourg estate, since the floor of his cottage was rotten and badly in need of repair. Rousseau, after warning the Marshal and Mme de Luxembourg several times that he could not accept their favors without becoming their friend and that with him friendship was an all-or-nothing affair, finally accepted their invitation. It was, of course, Mme de Luxembourg rather than the marshal to whom his warnings were addressed. He was cautioning her as best he could against his possessive nature and the tortures he would put her to in the name of friendship. From his first encounter with her one can see all of Rousseau's masochistic-sensual-hostile-tender feelings toward women blossoming under her influence.

> I was terribly afraid of Mme de Luxembourg. I knew that she was agreeable. I had seen her several times at the theater and at Mme Dupin's ten or twelve years ago, when she was the Duchess de Boufflers and was still in the radiance of her early beauty. But she was said to be spiteful, and this reputation in so great a lady made me tremble. As soon as I saw her I was captivated. I found her charming with that charm which is proof against time and to which my heart is so vulnerable. . . . From the first day my trust in her would have been as complete as it became soon afterwards, had not the Duchess de Montmorency, her daughter-in-law, a foolish and somewhat malicious young woman, and I think a rather quarrelsome one, taken it into her head to draw me out. Thus with all her mama's eulogies and her own sham provocations I was not too sure but that they were toying with me.[18]

Rousseau had long been disturbed by a sense of inability to converse socially, and he determined to improve in this area by reading his yet unprinted *The New Eloise* to Mme de Luxembourg. She was so charmed by the book and by the author that she insisted Rousseau sit beside her at table and would have no one else in his seat. Rousseau, who was aroused by the least mark of affection, soon became devoted to her. However, this new enchantress was to meet in his heart the memory of those who had gone before her. All of his feelings toward Mme de Warens, Mme d'Epinay and Sophie formed a background on which his encounters with Mme de Luxembourg were projected. He was charmed by her, but he was sure she resented him and would expect him to conform to her whims. He loved her as his benefactress and despised her as a member of the deadly female sex. Since he could detect no trace of condescension or animosity on her part, he contented himself with the belief that her preference for him would soon fade, as had that of Mme de Warens. Then, slowly he began to do things, strange things which he knew would offend her; yet he seemed to stumble onto these acts with the best of intentions. Mme de Luxembourg asked him for a manuscript copy of *The New Eloise,* and Rousseau, in order to present her with something not contained in the printed version, included a section from the adventure of Lord Edward, which described a disagreeable Roman marchioness. Even as he prepared the copy he recognized that the marchioness bore an unfortunate resemblance to Mme de Luxembourg.

> I had the stupidity to make this extract with great care and labor and to send this morsel to her as though it were the most beautiful thing in the world, at the same time informing her, which was true, that I had burned the original, that the extract was for her eyes alone and would never be seen by anyone unless she showed it herself. Far from demonstrating my prudence and discretion as I had supposed, this act only revealed to her my opinion of the applicability to herself of those traits which might have offended her. My imbecility was such that I had no doubt that she would be enchanted by what I had done.[19]

Rousseau both loved and hated Mme de Luxembourg, but since he was conscious only of his feelings of love, he could not recognize or control the other side of his feelings. His hostile acts were all inadvertent, the blind workings of fate, as he called them. To some extent his ambivalence toward her spilled over into his relationship with the marshal. The following remark from his *Confessions* illustrates again this mixture of love and hatred.

> It was in one of these transports of tenderness while embracing M. de Luxembourg that I said to him, Ah Marshal, before I knew you I hated the great. Now I hate them even more since you have shown me how easy it would be for them to make themselves adored.[20]

No doubt such remarks were motivated by his desire to express love and yet to show that he had not himself become proud and affected because of his association with the marshal. However, when love becomes so mixed with hatred it becomes difficult to disentangle the two emotions—particularly when loving one of "the great" makes one hate "the great" in general.

It was not long before Rousseau had taken additional steps to his own destruction. He wrote a letter to a political enemy of Mme de

Luxembourg complimenting him on braving the protests of the "money grabbers." Then he showed the letter to Mme de Luxembourg, not being aware, so he says, that she was one of the "money grabbers" interested in the underfarming of taxes. Mme de Luxembourg read the letter without comment and then seemed to forget it. She did not mention it again. But Rousseau could not let the matter drop. He wrote to her accusing her of amusing herself with him and claiming that she would soon lose interest in him.

In spite of his fears, however, he found that when he pleaded for her help in rescuing the Abbé Morellet from prison, she made a special trip to Versailles to secure his release, even cutting short her trip at Montmorency for the purpose. After she gave several more proofs of her friendship, including her offer to look after *Emile* during publication, he finally concluded that "even if she were growing tired of me, she preserved, and always would preserve, the friendship that she had so many times promised would last all her life."[21]

Of course, such a state of affairs could not be allowed to continue. It was immediately followed by Rousseau's confessing all his faults to his friend.

> As soon as I thought I could count on her feelings for me I began to relieve my heart by a confession of all my faults, since it is an inviolable principle with me to reveal myself to my friends exactly as I am, neither better nor worse. I had informed her of my liaison with Thérèse and all of its consequences, not omitting the manner in which I had disposed of my children. She had received my confessions very well, even too well and spared me the censure I deserved.[22]

Rousseau was aware that somehow he was doing the very things which would destroy his relationship with Mme de Luxembourg, but he was unable to recognize that these acts were the product of his own feelings. His *Confessions* are filled with innocent remarks like the following, in conjunction with some obvious piece of provocative behavior.

> There must have been a natural opposition between her mind and my own, since beside the host of blundering remarks which escaped me every moment in conversation, even in my letters and when I was on the best terms with her, there were things which displeased her for reasons which I never understood.[23]

And again,

> It is strange by what fatality all I could say or do seemed des-
> tined to displease Mme de Luxembourg, even when I was the most
> determined to preserve her good will.[24]

Nowhere in his past life had he encountered a benefactress so difficult to provoke as was Mme de Luxembourg. No matter how many
times he placed his head on the chopping block, she refused to strike.
His problem was complicated in that he felt himself rather far removed
from the masochistic little boy who yearned to be chastised and
spanked by his imperious Mlle Goton. These childish impulses had long
ago been repressed and almost completely forgotten, but they had not
been dismissed. They formed a part of his personality of which he was
no longer conscious, a side of himself which moved behind the scenes
arranging events for its own satisfaction. It was important for Rousseau's peace of mind that he remain ignorant of this side of himself. He
knew that he derived a feeling of virtue and happiness from fighting
injustice, but his joy would have been short-lived had he realized that
he himself provoked others to mistreat him. It was much more satisfactory to perceive fate as the assailant. The extravagant nature of his
behavior, he felt, could only be explained by "the blind fatality which
was dragging me to my destruction." "Everything assists the work of
destiny," he said, "when it summons a man to misfortune."[25]

Seeing himself as a helpless pawn in the hands of destiny, he gave
little thought to avoiding these strange and unpredictable incidents in
which he was roasting members of the nobility in the heat of his secret
resentment while all the time smiling at them. Nor were his attacks
confined to the gentle marshal and his wife. His provocative behavior
was exhibited in almost all his contacts.

Rousseau was always setting little traps for people by making them
aware that he was living under difficult circumstances. Then he would
wait for the victim to offer food or financial assistance so that he could
demonstrate his independence by refusing all help. He set similar snares
in conversation. By his own derogatory opinion of himself, he encouraged others to be self-effacing. Finally, when he had drawn them out
into a long sorry tale, he would suddenly turn on the attack, accusing
them of insincerity.

The following excerpt from a letter to Mme de Verdelin displays
Rousseau at the height of his mastery of this technique.[26]

> You tell me, Madame, that you did not express yourself well in
> order to make me understand that I express myself badly. You

speak to me of your pretended stupidity in order to make me aware of mine. You boast of being nothing more than a good woman as if you were afraid of being taken at your word, and you make excuses to me to inform me that I owe them to you. Yes, Madame, I know that very well. It is I who am a blockhead, a "good man," and even worse if that is possible. It is I who do not choose my terms well enough for the taste of a fine French lady who pays so much attention to words and who speaks as well as you. But consider that I take them in their ordinary sense, without knowing or caring about the polite meanings which are attached to them by the virtuous society of Paris.[27]

After having thoroughly mauled Mme de Verdelin in this fashion and noting her "incredible restraint,"[28] Rousseau finally decided to accept her as a friend.

There was, of course, more than mere sado-masochism behind Rousseau's behavior. The strength of his dependency needs made his relationships with the nobility intolerable. He felt a desire to please everyone; yet he hated those who flattered the powerful in order to share their money and influence. Thus, he was always watching his own emotions in the presence of "the great" to make sure he could not be called a flatterer. His frequent episodes of rudeness were simply exhibitions of his own attempt to deny what he felt was a weakness in himself. He was never provocative or rude when certain he was loved, but only with his dog, Turc, could he find such an unambivalent relationship. The death of Turc plunged him into grief, and when Mme de Luxembourg wrote to console him, he replied, "My poor Turc was only a dog, but he loved me."[29]

VII

At the Luxembourg estate Rousseau met another attractive woman who was to have a profound influence on his future: Mme de Boufflers, the "divine countess," one of the most famous and charming women in Europe. She was principal mistress to the Prince de Conti, a powerful figure in the French nobility. With him she maintained a salon at his Temple in Paris, a large fortified enclosure north of the Seine containing its own theater, grand ballroom, spacious grounds, and several houses, among which was one reserved for Mme de Boufflers.

The gathering at the Temple on Mondays was one of the four great salons in Paris. At the Temple a prominent feature was the talk of English freedom and English writers. The Countess de Boufflers was already absorbed with her discovery of a great new philosophical light from Scotland, David Hume.

The Countess de Boufflers, although more sophisticated and poised than the Countess d'Houdetot, had a personality resembling that of Rousseau's beloved Sophie in many respects. She was animated in conversation, affectionate, with an ardor that sometimes produced more effect than she intended, and she had that same peculiar schism in her concept of good and evil previously noted in Sophie. She ceased to be the mistress of the Prince de Conti shortly after their liaison in 1752, but she continued to entertain at the Temple as his friend until his death. She managed to forget she had a husband and a son, and she regarded her attachment to the prince as a "sacred duty." She avoided the double entendre of the salon and was offended by any remark which might imply that her relationship with the prince was in any way improper. In this respect she formed a striking contrast to most of the women of her day. Horace Walpole[30] said of her, "She is two women, the upper and the lower," and Mme du Deffand remarked:

> Her ethics are most austere, always mounted on high principles, which she announces in a firm and decided tone and in the sweetest voice; she seems like a flute which is pronouncing laws and delivering oracles. What is amusing, though a little annoying, is that this lofty morality is not perfectly in accord with her conduct; what is even more amusing is that the contrast does not startle her. She will tell you coldly that it is against good order for a woman to live apart from her husband, that the mistress of a Prince of the Blood is a woman in disgrace; but she says all that so ingenuously, so persuasively, with a voice so pretty and a manner so sweet, that you are not even tempted to find it ridiculous.[31]

With her capacity for self-forgetfulness it was easy for the countess to begin an affair with the philosopher David Hume while still remaining "true" to the Prince de Conti. She wrote le bon David to tell him how his ideas fascinated her. She met him in France, and the two sent many letters of mutual admiration back and forth. But Hume was cautious and reluctant to commit himself. At last she showed her claws, telling him she could be cruel as well as charming. Taking the hint, he decided to succumb to her charms rather than face her wrath. At last he was so thoroughly bewitched that he considered giving up his British citizenship in order to settle in France and be near her always.[32]

The attraction she felt for Rousseau was no doubt based in part on his great reputation as a learned man, but an even more significant psychological bond was their common capacity to disguise their desires under the cloak of virtue. Rousseau, who had desperately wanted an affair with the Countess d'Houdetot, had convinced himself that the whole experience came from his philosophical interest in her and his desire to instruct her in virtue. He saw only her innocence and purity and managed to forget—or almost forget—that she was a woman. Perhaps Mme de Boufflers detected this peculiar quality in him and hoped to exercise a similar charm. More probably she had already heard the story of Rousseau and Sophie. In any event she came to see him frequently and expressed admiration for his virtue and his philosophy. Nor was she merely playing a part, for her letters to others were full of regard for him, and she was quick to defend him against the slightest insult—even against some of the light disparagement of Hume.

But Rousseau had been burned once, very badly, and he did not want to start the whole comedy all over again. The Countess de Boufflers was about twenty-eight when he met her (the same age as Sophie d'Houdetot at their first encounter). She was the intimate confidante of his patroness, Mme de Luxembourg, and while this lady made him no romantic overtures there was a tender relationship between them, similar to the one he had enjoyed with Mme d'Epinay. Would she be inclined to take lightly Rousseau's passionate attachment to her friend? Further, the Prince de Conti had begun to cultivate a friendship for Rousseau and had come to see him on at least two occasions when the Luxembourgs were not at home. Was he now to embark on another affair with the mistress of a friend? The situation was much too similar to the one which had ended in complete personal disruption. Mme de Boufflers visited him several times, made subtle hints, and even brought along a friend, the Chevalier de Lorenzi, to give the hesitant lover some suggestions from the side lines. She expressed enthusiasm for ancient Rome, and Rousseau felt the romantic mood begin to glow within him. But at the last moment he backed away, remaining friendly but aloof. In his *Confessions* he was to remark that this scorned love caused her to join in the plot against his reputation. But in this he was unjust to her.

After reading an account of Rousseau's behavior, one might well wonder how anyone could tolerate this testy hermit and why it was that his small cottage attracted such a stream of visitors. Throughout his *Confessions* he describes his terrible blundering social ineptitude, his frequent withdrawals due to the pain caused by his urethral condition, and the abrupt remarks which punctuated his conversation. Yet the comments of his visitors do not support this picture. Both Hume (during the period before their quarrel) and Boswell describe him as a charming conversationalist, a man made for society. His poor health, although he complained of it in his letters, was seldom evident to others, and while he remarked that he never slept at night he kept his friends awake with his snoring. In his effort to tell the naked truth about himself, he has clearly overdrawn the negative side of his personality.

Another factor which causes undue attention to his negative traits is the extent to which he inadvertently reveals himself in his writings. His rationalizations are so transparent that one forgets he sometimes speaks good sense. Yet he was clearly rational as well as rationalizing. He made an effort always to be direct in his opinions, to say what he thought, and to describe life as he saw it. In the eighteenth-century world of form and politeness, his honesty was often refreshing. Further, he had the capacity for conveying a certain sensitivity, a fearful and somewhat hesitant desire to be loved behind his crisp facade.

VIII

All of Rousseau's efforts to provoke Mme Luxembourg ended in failure. She persisted in her admiration for him and in her eagerness to help in some small way with his work. She was more interested in *The New Eloise* than in *Emile*, but she offered to look after the publication of the latter work, primarily from her conviction that Rousseau himself was a man of genius. She was not aware, nor was Rousseau, of the terrible heresy that would be found in this volume. In Montmorency, those around him found little offense in either *Emile* or the *Social Contract*. It had been a policy for the monarchy that general criticism was always permitted.

But now the monarchy was under attack and the clergy, too, had its back to the wall. Blows that formerly would have glanced off the old régime now shook it to the core. Duclos, fresh from the atmosphere of Paris, gave Rousseau the first hint of the reaction he was to get. "What, citizen," he cried, when Rousseau had finished reading a section from *Emile* on the subject of religion. "Is this part of a book that is being printed in Paris?" "Yes," replied Rousseau, "and it should be printed at the Louvre, by order of the king." "I agree," answered Duclos, "but be so kind as to tell nobody that you read me that piece."[33]

What can one say of Rousseau's motivation in publishing these two books at this time? His urge to identify himself with his former literary friends whom he regarded as underdogs, fighting a great cause has been recognized. He was filled with guilt about remaining in the safety of Montmorency, petted by the Luxembourgs, while Diderot fought for liberty in Paris. Can one say that *Emile* and the *Social Contract* represented another provocation, designed to excite the persecution he required? Somehow such a remark seems trivial when weighed beside such a labor of genius. These two works are clearly products of a provocative personality, but Rousseau had been at work on them for years. They reveal so much more about him and his philosophy than the mere tendency to provoke that they require an examination in depth before one pronounces an opinion on them.

[6]

The Social Contract

I

THE LAW OF SURVIVAL in man's precivilized state was that of tooth and claw, the same law which governed the animals around him. Each man satisfied his desires to the best of his ability and to the limits of his strength by contending against his neighbors and against other animals. Civilizations have arisen and man's desires have changed in content and direction, yet every society contains within itself the elements of this first primitive struggle. Men contend against each other for a variety of reasons, no longer simple survival, and everywhere they struggle against and yet struggle to maintain the shaky structure of the social organization.

At first thought, the maintenance of civil order does not appear difficult. One makes a few simple laws: "Do not kill anyone." "Do not steal anything, including your neighbor's woman." But when we speak of theft we must define possession and when we ask man to refrain from killing we must find some way to avoid those blows which eventually escalate to murder, especially the blow to a man's pride which is so often the first step toward civil violence.

This complex socio-psychological problem was the basic issue of the *Social Contract.*

To find a form of association which defends and protects with all the force of the community the person and property of each member, and where each, while uniting himself with all, nevertheless obeys only himself, and remains as free as before. This is the fundamental problem to which the social contract provides the answer.[1]

In order to find this association Rousseau's first step was to establish the legitimate basis for a society. He began by laying aside previous maxms about the duty of a people to obey the powers that be. If force is the basis of power, he said, then force is a legitimate means of overthrowing it. Any relationship which grants all the advantage to one side and none to the other is against the basic nature of man and, therefore, null and void. One must always return to the idea of a voluntary agreement from which the participating parties have something to gain. Man must have reached, early in his primitive life, a stage at which the pressures of the environment became so overwhelming that he felt it necessary to combine with his fellows in order to survive. By opposing the collective force of the group to the external threat, individual man gained an advantage. But in doing this he had to put his individual will under the direction of the group or general will. Otherwise, the first society would be torn apart by a thousand conflicting desires. This was the essence of the social compact, whether it was written or was merely tacitly understood.[2]

From this point Rousseau proceeded to the definition of terms for the society that emerged from this compact. This is perhaps the most critical part of his book, for the same entity can have different meanings depending on how it is considered.

At once, in place of the particular person of each contracting party, this act of association produces a moral and collective body composed of as many members as there are voices in the assembly, and receiving from this same act its unity, its common self, its life and its will. This public person, thus formed by the union of all the others took formerly the name of *city*, and now takes that of *republic* or *body politic*. It is called by its members *state*, when passive, *sovereign* when active, and *power*, when compared with others of its kind. In regard to the members they take collectively the name *people* and are called *citizens* in particular as participants in the sovereign authority, and *subjects* as they are obliged to obey the laws of the state. But these terms are often confused and taken one for the other; it is enough to know how to distinguish them when they are employed with precision.[3]

In their abstract sense the terms seem quite clear, but in the course of his book Rousseau frequently descended to the practical matters of government in which, while each person is a member of the sovereign, the sovereign can be represented by a single individual. The theory enunciated by Rousseau did not prescribe a specific ideal form of government. Instead, it outlined the basis for the legitimacy of any government, be it a monarchy, an aristocracy, or a democracy, namely, that all authority in the state is derived from the consent of the citizens and that no individual is above the law.[4] In this respect he propounded one of the principles of modern democracy.

The single best guide for the construction of legislation is, according to Rousseau, "the general will." Since each man, as an individual, has inclinations that differ from those he has as a citizen, he may be tempted to respond more to his private wishes than to those of the general will. Rousseau concludes, therefore, that the individual should be "forced to be free" (*Qu'on le forçera d'être libre*), i.e., forced to follow the general will.[5]

At this point there is a peculiar ambivalence toward freedom. Rousseau had a great desire for man to be free, free from tyranny, free to determine for himself what is right and just. But unlike Voltaire and the Encyclopedists, he did not believe in the infinite perfectibility of man through reason, for he did not believe that man, as he existed, was really free to decide what was best for himself. Rousseau, who had reformed his entire character on the basis of a philosophical ideal, was acutely conscious of his own dual nature. He felt that it took all his strength to resist his own base inclinations, and he recognized that his reason had all too frequently been seduced into the service of his desires. This awareness of the corruptibility as well as the perfectibility of man distinguished him from his contemporaries. Like Voltaire and the other liberals of his time, he yearned for a better and more just society, but, unlike his literary colleagues, he did not believe that ignorance alone held man back from virtue and that if man could only be taught to reason his morals would improve. Rousseau saw the civil state as raising man out of his selfishness and forcing him to restrain his particular interest, his passion, his desire for personal pleasure at the expense of others.[6] This was the ideal civil state. But he also recognized that in most real societies men do not lose their personal greed merely because they become members of a community. They know, in one sense, what is good for the community, but they often strive to please only their own whims, or they gather in factions to serve the ends of a small group, thus destroying the very purpose of the civil state and reducing the greater mass of their fellowmen below the state of beasts.

Rousseau was filled with the contradictions of man, his godlike quality and his bestial side. He wanted to convey this complexity in a great rush of words so that his reader would see man all at once, as he is. Whenever he began to develop a single point, he was fearful that he would not be understood, that one side would be taken for the whole truth. Thus, we find him cautioning the reader everywhere with phrases like the following, "All my ideas are consistent, but I cannot explain them all at once."[7]

II

Keeping in mind Rousseau's caveat, it might be profitable to examine in more detail his paradoxical picture of political life and his peculiar remarks about freedom which seem so inconsistent with the generally accepted meaning for the word. Let us return to his statement that man should be "forced to be free." Is not the phrase, in itself, a contradiction? Has Rousseau merely presented an eighteenth-century example of what George Orwell calls *doublethink*? The answer is found in Rousseau's different meanings of the word "liberty," meanings which he did not always distinguish from each other. He pointed out that by a passage from the state of nature to the civil state man exchanged his "natural liberty" for his "civil liberty." Natural liberty, he said, is bounded only by the strength of the individual, but civil liberty is limited by the general will. However, man's greatest acquisition in the civil state is "moral liberty," which is the only liberty that makes him truly master of himself, "because the impulse of appetite alone is slavery, and obedience to a law which we prescribe to ourselves is liberty."[8] It would seem, at first, that we have come full circle from the first *Discourse*, and it is now civil society which is responsible for the moral improvement of man.

But Rousseau was not content to let the matter rest at this point, for the mere existence of a civil state was not sufficient to insure that good laws would be passed and a good government developed. He held that if a state was to be directed toward the general good of all, the only force that could direct it was the general will. The general will was operative when the people were furnished with sufficient information and when they reached a decision independently, without communicating with each other.[9]

Rousseau insisted that the sovereignty of the people as a whole was just as important in monarchy and aristocracy as in democracy. In a monarchy the power of the sovereign is transmitted to a king, but the will—the general will—can be represented by no one except the people as a whole. Any government, whether it be a democracy, an aristocracy, or a monarchy, acts legitimately only when it is in accord with the general will. By acting in accord with the general will Rousseau meant, essentially, governed by laws that the majority would favor in an election in which all votes were counted and in which each man voted his own opinion.[10]

The general will, he said, is always right for a given society, but it does not follow that the deliberations of the people are always the best. Factions, cliques and cabals, and political deals may creep in, votes may be bought and sold, but through it all the general will remains. If people vote for a bad government, they have been deceived, and they only seem to will what is bad. Therefore, if the general will is to manifest itself there can be no partial society within the state, or, if this is impossible, partial societies should be multiplied to the point where the influence of each one is relatively small.[11]

The restrictions which Rousseau introduced were always directed against individual passions and personal gain. He pointed out that the formation of a civil state upsets the natural balance of equality and freedom obtained in a state of nature. Therefore, it is important that society provide man with something better than he left behind, otherwise he will rightfully turn his back on it. The most valuable contribution a society can make to the individual is to force him into an awareness of moral action. As he put it:

> The passage from the state of nature to the civil state, by substituting justice for instinct in his conduct and giving to his actions the morality they had formerly lacked, produces a very remarkable change in man. It is then only that the voice of duty taking the place of physical impulse and right that of appetite—the man who until then has thought only of himself finds that he is forced to act on other principles and to consult his reason before listening to his inclinations. Although in this state he is deprived of many of the advantages which he received from nature, he gains so many in return, his faculties are exercised and developed, his ideas are broadened, his sentiments ennobled, his whole soul elevated to such an extent that, if the abuses of this new condition did not often degrade him below that from which he emerged, he ought to bless continually the happy moment which raised him out of it forever and transformed him from a stupid and limited animal into an intelligent being and a man.[12]

Because of the dual nature of the sovereign, i.e., as the embodiment of the people as a whole and as the executive function in the state, it alone is in a position to decide what the subject must render to the state. However, the sovereign never has a right to demand more of one subject than it does of another, nor does it have a right to demand anything except what is useful to the community. The restraints placed on a man's liberty are thus the very restrictions necessary to make of him a moral being, for the sovereign cannot will anything contrary to its own welfare, i.e., to the general will, and the individual is free to act on his own provided he does not do violence to the general will. Each citizen should render whatever services are necessary to the state, and he should render them whenever the sovereign requires it. Such obligations are binding only because they are mutual. The general will should not only be the sum of all the individual wills of the people, but its consequences should apply to all.[13]

By forcing man to be free Rousseau would then force him to conform to the general will—to what is best for society as a whole.

III

Up to this point in the analysis, Rousseau seems to be saying that the freedom he proposed is a freedom buttressed by self-discipline, a freedom restrained only to the extent that it does not tread on the rights of others. Concern for the fate of individual initiative is almost laid to rest. But other discordant notes to the main theme appear. One finds that the general will can be interpreted and administered by a monarch and that the monarch's commands can pass for the general will so long as the sovereign (i.e., the people) is free to oppose them and offers no opposition.[14] He does not tell how to judge when a people is "free" to oppose the commands of a monarch or whether the opposition, when it comes, is a result of a spontaneous outbreak of the general will or the work of a professional agitator.

The role of the monarch in the interpretation of the general will is only one of the many features of the *Social Contract* which raise, once again, doubts for the safety of individual freedom. A dictatorship is found permissible when the safety of the state is threatened, and the rare situations which call for a dictatorship will be obvious.[15] The sovereign power need give no guarantee to its subjects since, being formed wholly of the individuals who compose it, it cannot have any interest contrary to theirs.[16] This is admirable if one pictures the sovereign as a group of citizens always making decisions, but since the power of the sovereign can be transmitted to an individual such ideas clearly produce a dangerous concentration of power which might be seized by one man to the detriment of all.[17]

It is in Rousseau's discussion of punishment that he seems to deal the most serious blow to individual freedom and to place a frightening power with the state. The individual, he says, becomes a rebel and traitor when he attacks social rights, and, since the preservation of the state is inconsistent with his own preservation, he must be put to death. In such cases frequent pardons are merely a sign of the deterioration of the state, for the right of pardoning belongs to the authority which is superior to both judge and law; i.e., the sovereign.[18] Religion is reduced to the simple forms which might be required to preserve civil society, but Rousseau would punish with banishment anyone who does not accept the civil religion of the state and punish with death those who, after publicly recognizing the dogmas of a civil religion, behave as if they do not believe them.[19]

Just at the point, when one has become convinced this man is a tyrant, one finds a vigorous defense of human liberty or a plea for the rights of man. He would have a man put to death for his failure to live by the civil religion, but one of the key dogmas of this religion is a prohibition against intolerance.[20] In his discussion of the power of the government he recognizes, on the one hand, the need for high councils and privileges belonging exclusively to the prince. He allows dangerous expedients, even a dictatorship, in order to serve the crucial function of preserving the state. On the other hand, he states that things should be arranged so that the government may always be sacrificed to the people, but never the people to the government.[21] He says that the monarch can assume that he represents the general will as long as the people do not oppose him, but he would provide for periodic assemblies of the people, assemblies required by law, where the people are asked if they favor a continuation of the existing government. The prince cannot oppose such assemblies without openly declaring himself a lawbreaker and an enemy of the state.[22] It is not difficult to go from these words of Rousseau to the calling of the Estates-General and to the Oath of the Tennis Court.

Rousseau was himself aware of the striking changes of feeling in the various parts of his book. He frequently warned his readers not to judge him too hastily, and at times it seems that while he was writing he was in conflict with another side of himself. At one point, after cautioning against frequent pardons for criminals he remarked, "But I feel my heart protesting and restraining my pen."[23]

There are many logical explanations for this conflict. Rousseau had taken a vast subject for his field of exposition. He was one of the first to see the kind of state which was evolving for the man of the future and the ambivalence inherent in man's desire to establish his own individuality while preserving his social unity. Having noted the complexity of the problem, one must now ask if there was not something in his own personality which added to his difficulties. There is a peculiar quality of opposition and submission, of command and defiance about many of his utterances which rings a familiar note. At times he seems to be a great liberal and democrat. At other moments he seems blind—blind to the fact that he is betraying the very principles in which he so strongly believes. F. C. Green has expressed this conflict in his comments on the famous passage in the *Social Contract* regarding disobedience to religious dogma and social law:

Quite suddenly, with no perceptible change in the rhythm or quality of his style, Rousseau announces impassively: 'If any one, after having publicly recognized these same dogmas, behaves as if he did not believe them, let him be punished by death: He has committed the greatest of all crimes; he has lied in the face of the laws.' . . . Recklessly, in that fatal article of his civic profession of faith, he conceived the formula for a process of judicial mass murder which, with various refinements, was destined to form the basis of the twentieth-century totalitarian state. That a noble creation like the *Social Contract* should have been disfigured by such a monstrous appendage is one of the most baffling enigmas recorded in literature.[24]

In a sophisticated wit one would not be troubled by contradictions. Many writers seek to charm with a paradox or to present themselves as enigmatic and mysterious personages. But in the case of Jean-Jacques Rousseau one must agree that "there is no possibility of doubt concerning his naked sincerity."[25] Rousseau was always "sincere" and "honest" according to the conventional understanding of these words, just as Sophie was "honest" when she thought she wanted only a platonic relationship with him.

Rousseau was driven by impulses he did not recognize. In his favorite image of himself he was a rebel who despised all authoritarian personalities. He detested those who would force him to conform to social convention or place him under an obligation. He resisted all efforts on the part of his friends to influence his opinion or his actions, and he strongly believed in the right of the individual to think for himself. Yet there was another side to this independent personality, a side that loved not only to dominate others, but to submit to the commands of a great lady, to crawl before power. This sado-masochistic side had formed itself early. It had been of crucial significance in his early sexual development, and it had roots in every corner of his adult personality. It was a side that loved to command ruthlessly and to obey without question. It was a side that he did not like to think about. In fact, its hold over him was like a physical power, an influence which he sought to divorce entirely from his higher, more spiritual side. Since his early days in Paris, when his enthusiasm for self-reform had begun, Rousseau had tried to rid himself of these unpleasant impulses. He succeeded to the extent that he was no longer consciously aware of them, but they had gone underground. They now worked from behind the scenes to guide his pen in subtle ways. The influence of what one might call his "unconscious authoritarian side" caused the blind spots in his writing. It is to this hidden agent that one must ascribe the apparently naive attempt to force man into freedom and the sudden outburst of cruel and repressive measures amid the noblest liberal sentiments. Rousseau was a liberal at war with himself, a man trying to convey a message of freedom to mankind while a dark shadow within him whispered a counsel of submission. His battle was so much greater because he did not see this other side of himself. He fought an unknown antagonist, and he never knew when he had been struck.

Under these conditions one might well wonder how Rousseau the rebel can speak to us at all—if it is not because he derives his energy from the same source as his darker side. One cannot assume that this high-minded rebel and reformer is really an independent entity. He is a part of the same being, and his striving for virtue is the result of his confrontation with the evil in himself. Thus, to say that Rousseau was unaware of his other side is only partly true. His clear memory of the incident of Marion and the ribbon and of his childhood masochistic experiences indicates that he was at least aware of the behavioral results of this side of his personality. In fact, his sado-masochistic tendencies contributed to his positive idealism. Without his direct experience with the corruption inherent in submission, without his knowledge of the subtle forms submission can take, he would be in a poor position to do battle against his enemy. Rousseau's eloquence was derived, in part, from his intimate and detailed knowledge of personal slavery. Without such an experience his arguments would have been dry and academic.

IV

As indicated, there was a serious conflict in Rousseau's mind between his liberal ideals and his sado-masochistic desires. Another trait of his character accounts for his ability to pinpoint the weakness of democracy as a practical form of government. This was his feeling of isolation and aloneness which marked him, in his own conception of himself, as being distinctly different from his fellowman. The sense of aloneness, a trait often associated with negative and antisocial feelings, became in Rousseau a keen tool for examining the defects of a democratic society.

While he accepted the general will as the only legitimate authority in government, he distrusted the easy sociability of the common man, his tendency to abdicate responsibility due to a lack of vigilance for individual liberty, his proclivity for personal gain, and his willingness to unite into small groups in order to have some advantage over his fellowman. He felt that if each individual were to be really free, he must not be subject to the pressure of his social milieu.

Rousseau had himself been the victim of pressure groups. In some instances he exaggerated their threat, but it is clear that there were a number of concerted attempts to urge him into decisions which other people deemed proper. This resistance to propriety formed the basis for his first *Discourse*. Throughout his life he longed to be free of social obligation, but his need to please and to be loved made him acutely sensitive to the demands of others. While he loved freedom, he feared his own tendency to submit. Thus, at Montmorency, only after he had rounded a certain corner on his way to the woods without encountering a visitor, did he feel really free. His dog, his cat, or the birds of the wood were the only creatures who did not interfere with his freedom. To Rousseau the perfect society would be one which allowed everyone a similar freedom from social obligation.

Here one finds the truly original aspect of Rousseau's individualism. He recognized, as did few philosophers of his time, that a man's independence can be found in his freedom from the pressures of his fellow-man as well as his freedom from a tyrannous ruler. A man can pit his individual will against that of a monarch, but he is still vulnerable to those who would form public opinion. In his awareness of this danger Rousseau foresaw a threat to individual freedom which the majority of democratic thinkers were not to recognize until Tocqueville gave them a more concrete example in his *Democracy in America*. Rousseau saw that a democracy would not be, in effect, a true democracy unless the vote of each individual was genuinely independent. A secret ballot is not sufficient. The pressure to conform, to believe as the dominant group believes, constitutes the real threat to independence. However, complete independence in the political sphere would almost require a social isolation similar to Rousseau's conception of that of primitive man. The society which he pictured—capable of having a strong influence over man's moral behavior and no influence on his politics—is difficult to conceive. It is doubtful that Rousseau had a clear idea of what specific social arrangement would produce the effect he desired.[26]

V

It is not difficult to discover a number of separate logical fallacies in Rousseau's arguments, but his method was not that of logical demonstration. He was a master mythmaker, and he came on the scene at a time when the great religious myths of the day were falling into disbelief. The concrete simplicity of the story of Adam and Eve was a tale for primitive peoples which could not survive in the relentless logic and the merciless wit of eighteenth-century France. The miracles and myths of the church were crumbling under the assault of the philosophers. People were beginning to disbelieve, yet they were haunted by a vague sense of guilt, a dread of the unknown, a fear of some devil's intellectual trap against which they had been warned by the most learned theologians of the church. The victory of the philosophers and scientists was one of those many illusions which seem real and permanent at the time of their first occurrence. The power of religion was waning, but scientific superstition was on the rise. Led by a handful of brilliant men, the people had been taught to doubt, but the old credulity had never left them. The skepticism and the worship of originality which characterized eighteenth-century France were a fashionable façade which covered a fervent desire to believe and to follow.

The science of chemistry was growing under the leadership of Lavoisier and Priestley, but so was the legion of alchemists. The idea of what constituted scientific research was very imperfectly conceived. The world of fashion believed, as many still believe today, that "science" was the mere mixing and stirring of chemicals. From such activities immediate miracles were expected, such as the creation of valuable gems and the transformation of base metals into gold. Secret societies were forming everywhere, and many ancient religious texts were revived and restudied with the object of predicting the future. Sir Isaac Newton had wasted the greater portion of his productive years becoming an expert on the interpretation of biblical prophecy. Little groups in Paris and Vienna gathered in private homes to conjure the devil, and a bit of spice was added by the belief that everyone must appear naked before the lord of the underworld or he would not show his face. Charlatans were everywhere commanding the best prices for their amulets and love potions. Louis XV was duped by an Alsatian Jew, Simon Wolff, who posed as Count Saint-Germain and astounded the monarch by making a large diamond out of several smaller ones. Soon Cagliostro was to hold all Paris in his spell.

Herein lies the magic of Rousseau's moment in history. He was a man of his times, imbued with a deep religious conviction. He saw the fall of the old gods, but he was not easily led to follow the fashions of the day. He sensed something false in the excitement over science and learning. He admired Voltaire and the great philosophical leaders of his time, but he saw that they were being mimicked rather than understood. He felt that the new fashions added nothing to the fundamental hypocrisy and insincerity in the world. He wanted people to recognize certain basic human values, values which Christ had taught, but which he found neither in the religion nor the science nor the learning of his day. Somehow people had lost touch with these really important things.

On this basis Rousseau formed a new myth of human society, with the same morphological structure as the ancient archetype of man's creation. It evolved not only from his literary genius, from his close personal contact with the religious myths of his day, but, like many another myth, from a deep personal and psychological truth which he projected on the outer world. The story of the fall of man from his primitive, savage innocence to the onset of civilization and the consciousness of his guilt is the story of the fall of Rousseau after the incident of the broken comb and the discovery that no one can look within us and see the purity of our hearts.[27] Not only is it possible for the innocent to be condemned, but the guilty can learn to simulate an appearance of innocence and to hide the internal knowledge of guilt from others.

Rousseau longed to recapture the lost transparence of his youth; that time when even his wickedness was not evil, for it was betrayed in his countenance and thus transformed into childish mischief. But since he could not recover the transparence and was plagued by the knowledge of his guilt, he sought the *appearance* of innocence. When the thought of the innocent, natural man occurred to him, he became, as he says, "virtuous, or at least intoxicated with virtue"[28] and determined to take on the attributes of the myth he had created, to recapture—if not the genuine transparence—the feeling and appearance of innocence.

There was, as noted, another aspect of Rousseau's idealized childhood which he placed as a mantle over his idealized image of primitive man. This was the absence of any urge for power. Man in his early state, he comments, was capable of struggling for a morsel of food and would fight if threatened, but he had no desire to dominate others for the sheer love of domination. He had no sense of property, no urge to collect subjects, no home; in fact, he did not even know his own children.[29] Modern anthropologists, psychologists, and zoologists have rather thoroughly dispelled this idea, not only with regard to the early state of man, but for animals as well, when they remain in their natural habitat.[30]

But Rousseau was not seeking to establish scientific fact. The mythmaker is a master storyteller. He is not concerned with documentation but with description. Little was known of primitive man at that time, and Rousseau could paint his idealized image without fear of contradiction by the findings of research. Lines of evidence were imperfectly recognized. Learned men were still attempting to prove or disprove the existence of God by the force of ingenious arguments. It is not surprising that he should have attempted to demonstrate his concept of primitive man by the same method. However, the intriguing aspect of this myth of the man of nature who had no urge for

power and no desire for self-aggrandizement is that it apparently released aggressive impulses in Rousseau which had long been held in
abeyance. In the process of describing this innocent creature who had
not yet discovered his own ego, Rousseau was able to create a unique
image for himself, to assert his own individuality. It is as though he
resolved his doubts in this area by projecting the problem onto civilized
man. At least this was the case in the early part of his career. But his
personal doubts later came back upon him with renewed force and drove
him from the field of socio-political conflict.

In his recollection of the innocence of his childhood he saw a
creature who did not struggle for dominance against his father. As
noted, it may well have been his terror following the beatings administered to his older brother, combined with his own success at pacifying
his father by other means, that led him to subdue his aggressive impulses. He convinced himself that he submitted to his father out of
love. His early life, as he saw it, was one in which there was never a
conflict of wills. His own childish ego found itself naturally compatible
with the will of the adult world around him. In those days, before
he was aware of competitive feelings toward others, it seemed that
there was only the will of the family and he did not know what it was
to have a will of his own.[31]

Thus, in the *Social Contract*, even after man has evolved into a
civilized being, it is the individual will which is the primary danger to
society. The very basis of the social contract, then, becomes a voluntary submission of the will of the individual to the general will or the
good of all men.[32] For citizens in the civil state Rousseau recommended
loving submission to a greater will which he recalled from his childhood. The will of his father was replaced by a concept called the "general will" or the will of the citizen taken as a whole, where each man
votes separately and without consultation with his fellows. An important aspect in the functioning of the general will, however, was
that men should follow it spontaneously. Once men became conscious of
their self-interest, they were naturally inclined to look out for it, to
seek private satisfaction at the expense of the general good. Simple men,
by their very simplicity, were not easily lured into ingenious schemes.[33]
Open expressions of disagreement and the tumult of debate were signs
that men no longer listened to the general will and that the decline of
the state had begun.[34] The innocence of a citizen in regard to his own
self-interest was to become, for Rousseau, a critical factor in the development and expression of the general will. Subsequently, he elaborated on the methods for maintaining this innocence of self-interest in
the educational portion of his *Considerations on the Government of
Poland,* discussed in a later chapter.

Thus, even in his concept of the civil state Rousseau held to the notion of natural simplicity. This simplicity, however, seems to reduce itself to the repression of individual self-aggrandizement and of the urge to power. It was not that Rousseau denied the existence of these impulses, but he did believe that they should remain unconscious if society was to survive, just as his own survival as a child depended on his repression of his aggressive and competitive feelings toward his father.

Despite Rousseau's enthusiasm for natural man in his first two discourses and his praise for the arrival of a *civil* society in the *Social Contract*, an important thread of psychological consistency runs through these political works. He hoped to build a society in which men, though living in constant personal association with each other, remained, through a kind of primitive innocence, unaware of their individual egos.

As suggested, it was not simply innocence that restrained Rousseau's aggression as a child, but terror—terror and the discovery that he could gain many of his ends by tears and pathos. Thus, the myth of primitive innocence was based on a false image of primitive man, and the myth of the general will was based on a distorted memory of his own childhood. It was based on a morphological similarity rather than a direct structural analogy with the psychological facts of life. It awakened echos in others who had experienced moments of loving compliance in childhood, and it served as a vehicle for the repression of aggressive and competitive feelings among those who found these feelings uncomfortable.

By his creation of a myth cast in the same general form as the story of Adam and Eve, he presented to the society of his time a tale already familiar—the story of a lost primitive paradise. The substructure for belief was already there. He gave people the substance of an ancient tale without relating it to the moribund religious beliefs of his day. The essence of the similarity lies in the consequences of his theory for society. The social devastation which results from opposing one's individual will to the sacred general will is like the loss of paradise which followed opposition to the will of God.

When speaking of the "truth" of the general will, however, one must consider not only its relationship to individual psychodynamics but the extent to which it corresponded to a broader social need beginning to manifest itself in the people of the eighteenth century—the need for a general consensus, a recognized body of law not subject to individual whim and idiosyncratic interpretation. Rousseau's general will served as a firm basis for the belief that just laws were possible. If there was such a thing as a general will, then the failure to achieve justice must be due to the machinations of individuals. In the *Social Contract* the general will was not the mere whim of a god or a monarch. It was represented by a body of law derived, ideally, from the wisdom of a people. In this respect Rousseau's counsel of loving obedience to a superior power contained a new element in the definition of legitimate authority. The king, too, was subject to the rule of law. He must obey the general will. If he did not, he was not a legitimate monarch.[35]

Despite the English *Magna Carta* and Montesquieu's *Spirit of the Laws*, the idea of a government by law had not really taken hold in France. While the weakness of the French monarchy was evident to many, the idea of government by personal rule was still the chief expectation of the people. Those who anticipated a change visualized an invasion or possibly a great duke rising to challenge the authority of the king. When a man was in trouble, it still seemed that the best way out of it was an appeal to a powerful noble or some other influential personage. Yet the opportunity for such appeals had been diminishing rapidly for almost a century. The nobles had gradually been deprived of their power, and a giant totalitarian state had come into being. Many wealthy bourgeoisie had discovered that money could often speak more eloquently than the voice of a great noble and that the very titles of nobility were for sale. Those who relied on the ancient methods of settling grievances soon discovered that they must appeal, not to the noble, but to the intendant, and often this appeal had to be filtered through a series of clerks and special assistants. Intendants were replaced, and when new ones arrived, they brought new sets of rules. The need was growing for a government based on laws in which a man could place his trust—laws which would be independent of the individual will of the administrator. Rousseau recognized this need. His theory of government was designed to place a damper on personal whim by restricting the range of executive authority. The concept of a general will became, in a sense, a kind of mythology of law, a precursor to later, more rational, legal arguments.

VI

Why does a society require a mythmaker? Could the *Social Contract* have established itself as a great historical document without the myth of the general will? These are questions which cannot be answered by an analysis of Rousseau's theory. A myth represents not a rationale but a justification for belief. Rousseau recognized that it was not sufficient to oppose an old and established myth such as divine right with the frail and delicate tools of reason and law. The idea of the separation of the powers of government was not new. It had been suggested by several writers and reached a certain culmination in Montesquieu. But Rousseau emphasized the psychological basis for this separation and, by tying it to the concept of general and particular wills, indicated its role in the legitimacy of a government.

> . . . If he who has command over men should not have command of the laws it is also true that he who commands the law should no longer have command of men. Otherwise, these laws, ministers of his passions, would often merely serve to perpetuate his injustices; never would he be able to prevent private views from impairing the sanctity of his work.[36]

The law, as he saw it, should take into consideration not only the reasonable and sensible, but, since men do not always follow reason and good sense, it should also take account of human passion and human gullibility. He recognized that a legislator should have superior wisdom, but he was also aware that the wisdom of the legislator may not be appreciated by a people who have experienced nothing but tyranny. How, then, could an enlightened man make laws for a people without some concept of right? Good laws are not immediately apparent to everyone, particularly if they happen to conflict with the individual wills of certain citizens. Great laws make a great people. Could any but a great people accept great laws?

> For a newborn people to be able to appreciate sound political principles and to follow fundamental rules of statecraft, it would be necessary that the effect should become the cause, that the social consciousness which would be created by new institutions should preside over their very formation; and that men should be, before the formation of laws, what these very laws were designed to make them. Since, therefore, the legislator cannot employ either force or reason he must necessarily have recourse to an authority of another order, which can compel without violence and persuade without convincing.[37]

With this consideration in mind Rousseau felt that the legislator may have to make use of some external authority, such as "the voice of God," to establish his laws, since the people may not yet be educated to perceive the general will. But, he added, unless based on reason the laws would crumble through lack of respect.

> Any man can engrave tablets of stone, or bribe an oracle, or feign a secret commerce with some divinity, or train a bird to

speak in his ear. . . . He who knows only such tricks can assemble by chance a crowd of fools, but he will never found an empire, and his extravagant creation will soon perish with himself. Meaningless tricks form a passing bond; only wisdom can make it durable.[38]

In the above quotation Rousseau indicates that he regards reason as the primary basis of law. His acceptance of miracle and myth as a factor in the foundation of government, however, distinguishes him clearly from the humanist tradition of his time, with its faith in man's ability to perfect himself through reason. Despite his statement that man is naturally good, he had a profound distrust in the capability of the average man for self-development and self-realization. He was convinced that the form of government, the political institutions, and the traditions of a society had an all-pervading effect on the character of the people. From this it follows that one must have a good society in order to have a worthy people. Tyrants govern slaves, and slaves do not found great civilizations. Therefore, the only way to build a good society is to work with a people who have never really been civilized or to destroy the existing civilization. Reform is senseless.

Once customs are established and prejudices have taken root it is a dangerous and futile undertaking to attempt their reform; the people cannot stand having its ills touched even with the object of removing them, like the stupid and cowardly patients who tremble at the sight of the doctor. . . . Revolutions do for a people what certain personal crises do for the individual: where horror of the past takes the place of forgetfulness, and where the state, consumed by civil wars, is born again, so to speak, from its own ashes and recovers the vigor of youth as it leaves the arms of death.[39]

Such a political philosophy does not obviate the need for a government which evolves and changes with the times, but it does imply that the government must be in accord with the general will. Otherwise, it cannot evolve further, for the people who have learned to live with injustice will object to any reform which might take privileges from the powerful and level class distinctions. Thus, the process of legislation resolves itself into determining the general will at the very beginning of a society and maintaining the laws in such a state that they always reflect this broad spectrum of public need.

VII

Rousseau's capacity to reify such abstractions as the general will and clothe them in the form of myth accounts for the hold his doctrines have had on many generations of followers. Yet the very process of evolving such an omniscient and perfect force and distinguishing it from crass personal interest created a contradiction in his theory which he was never able to resolve. The general will is always good, but only when everyone votes, when everyone takes the trouble to inform himself on all issues, when no one is influenced by the opinion of anyone else, and when everyone is eternally vigilant against the abuse of power. Each man must be prepared to criticize the administration on his own, without consulting his fellow citizens, whenever he feels his freedom is threatened. As Rousseau remarked, the exercise of the general will by all men demands a race of gods. But since no government can survive unless directed by the general will, the governments of ordinary human beings are doomed to perish. Durkheim has presented Rousseau's dilemma with his usual clarity.

> Given his fundamental principle, Rousseau can accept only a society in which the general will is the absolute master. However, though the government will is individual, it plays an essential role in the state. . . . It is a constant threat and yet it is indispensable. . . . There is clearly no place for an intermediary between two aspects of the same reality (sovereign and people). On the other hand, however, the general will, for want of an intermediary, remains confined within itself, that is, it can move only in a realm of universals and cannot express itself concretely. This conception is itself a consequence of the fact that Rousseau sees only two poles of reality, the abstract, general individual who is the agent and objective of social existence, and the concrete empirical individual who is the antagonist of all collective existence.[40]

The very abstraction which made the general will perfect also made it powerless. Not until Kant was inspired by Rousseau's work to produce his "categorical imperative" did philosophy have a handle to the general will, a way of thinking and behaving which derived from this abstraction. But in the *Social Contract* men were left with no measuring rod for their behavior, no technique for determining how close or how far they were from the ideal, and no way of determining to what extent the laws of a society followed the natural inclinations of a people. If the monarch did not follow the general will, presumably the people would rebel. But how could one determine when a clever agitator was stirring up resentment against a just king?

Despite his lack of faith in the capacity of the common man to change himself and improve his government, Rousseau was apparently willing to let him determine when the time had come to destroy his society. Identifying himself with "the people," he felt them capable of the same indignation against injustice which he had so often experienced. When he became misty-eyed over the virtue of the peasant he expressed his sense of personal outrage at the knavery of the great. The people, by the very fact that they were powerless, seemed to him inherently good. He had no experience of the debates during the French Revolution when howling crowds harassed those speakers in the Tribunal whose opinions they did not approve and wildly cheered a popular figure as soon as he rose to speak. The people in the galleries were the peasants and the so-called "men on the street" suddenly drunk with new-found power. Rousseau, in short, lacked perspective on revolutions —the disillusionment with "little people" which has come about in the last two centuries.

But there was also, in his own personal life, a lack of the kind of experience which might have made him more sensitive to the problem of the administrator with good intentions. He had no political experience. He had held a series of jobs as apprentice engraver, lackey, servant, secretary to the ambassador, and accountant. He had experienced only the demands of an unjust master and those of polite society. He had felt only the pressure from-above, and in his profound identification with the underdog he could not appreciate the threat from below.[41] In his stories the poor people are simple and virtuous. They come by their virtue quite naturally through their poverty. Wealth and power corrupt the soul, and even the best of men can be swept off his feet by their deadly influence. Thus, Rousseau's fear of individual action was directed toward the man in power. Civilizations fall because the individual will of governmental officials must run counter to the general will. This is inevitable.[42]

VIII

While the myth persists in many circles that Rousseau's *ideas* brought about the French Revolution, recent research has tended to discount this notion.[43] His actual political proposals were quite conservative. Yet there is no question regarding his popularity among those who believed in violence, and in many respects his name is associated with the inspiration of revolutionary enthusiasm.

Joan McDonald has described the extent to which Rousseau was literally worshipped by the French revolutionists.[44] She finds his name associated with almost every victory of the revolution; his bust was carried in processions, pilgrimages were made to his tomb by revolutionary leaders, and in emotional scenes his name was invoked amid flowing tears. The concluding chapter of her book leaves no question in the mind of the reader that Rousseau became the symbol of revolt. But why did this happen? Mrs. McDonald demonstrates clearly that his political theory did not support the program of the revolutionists, that he was, in fact, opposed to the principle of representation. The *Social Contract*, hailed with such fervor by later generations, was seldom read or cited prior to the storming of the Bastille. She points out that it was the literary cult of Rousseau which survived into the period of the Revolution and that the political ideas were "grafted onto it." While not saying it directly, she seems to imply that Rousseau was misunderstood by the revolutionists, that they read a meaning into his political statements which he did not intend.

It is true that the political ideas of Rousseau were in many respects contrary to the proposals of the revolutionists, but the spirit of defiance breathes through all his works from the first *Discourse* to the *Considerations*. Rousseau had a way of bursting forth with some dramatic statement, a call to arms against the whole structure of society. He often followed this with a series of caveats and explanations, but it is not the explanations for which his name is famous. He is known for having said, "Man is born free and everywhere he is in chains," not for cautioning against factions and pressure groups within the state.

Perhaps the revolutionists did not really misunderstand him after all. Possibly Rousseau's influence on the development of revolutionary action was more subtle and pervasive than has been recognized by those who examine the history of ideas. While he cautioned his followers to doubt him, he put forth his ideas in a simplistic manner which seemed to imply that they were perfectly obvious and that no serious thought or reflection was necessary in order to understand and act on them. He made frequent pleas for tolerance, but he presented his adversaries (the king and the aristocracy) as such unredeemable scoundrels that one could not conceive of compromise with them. There is a fatality, an inevitability about his description of the decline of the state which seems to outweigh all his constructive proposals and leave no alternative but revolutionary action.

Rousseau, in contrast to Voltaire, was not content to doubt the efficacy of certain social institutions or to ridicule outworn and corrupt government practices. He attacked the basic premises of the social structure. He asserted that the civilization of his time was in need of a complete remaking. His serious and systematic critique of the society as a whole attracted the same type of deadly serious, devoted, and dogmatic follower. Voltaire, like Louis XIV, was a great and powerful personality, but when the Voltaireans faced Saint-Just, Robespierre, and the other disciples of Rousseau over the crumbling ruins of the old order, it was the latter who triumphed in that violent contest of wills.[45] For the Rousseauists were revolutionists, and the world was ripe for revolt. The works of Voltaire inspired skepticism, doubt, curiosity; the works of Rousseau inspired a fanatic kind of devotion.[46]

Just as Rousseau had urged others to read his heart, so his followers sought to catch the feeling behind his books without necessarily reading too carefully what he had to say. His admonition to avoid the formation of powerful subgroups within the state and his insistence that the vote of each man be independent and not subject to pressure from his fellows, were all fine but forgotten ideas. It was his obsessive fear of all authority which drained like a poison into the next generation.

Out of the gutters of Paris and the impoverished and tax-ridden farms of France arose the disenfranchised and disinherited of the nation. They found in Rousseau a man who shared their long grievance, who sympathized with their misery, and whose books breathed an electric spirit of defiance. This man had experienced misery as they had, but had found in his agony a strange pleasure born of suffering. His very wounds proved to him the justice of his cause. He told them that they, in turn, need not feel ashamed of their poverty and nakedness, for they were God's creatures, the offspring of the Supreme Being. The wealthy men, the nobles, the society ladies, the kings of France were not fit to kiss their feet.

As the flood tide of revolution began to mount and the nobility, in their first ecstacy of Voltairean liberalism, renounced their titles and called for a readjustment of the old tax laws, they discovered that the people were not content with mere token concessions. The underdog had suffered too long, and it was too late in the day for a friendly reconciliation. The noble must face the full consequences of his guilt and depravity. The tyrant must bleed and the great must be forced to crawl.

Rousseau did not live to see the revolutionary enthusiasm and its bloody aftermath. If he had, his tender feelings would have been outraged by the grotesque turn given to his ideas. But can he really be absolved from the terrible consequences of his eloquence? If we are to read his heart, as he invites us to do, we must look not only at his tender feeling for mankind, his passion for freedom and justice, but we must also recognize and accept, as an inevitable part of this great man, his deep and unreasoning hatred of all authority and the sado-masochistic substructure on which this hatred was fed.

[7]

Emile

Emile WAS THE SECOND MAJOR WRITING of Rousseau to appear at this critical period of his life. In some respects it was the more provocative of the two works. The idea for a treatise on education had long been fermenting in his mind. His early failures as a tutor and the occasional requests for advice from Mme d'Epinay and from Mme de Chenonceaux, who was upset by her husband's methods with their son, led him to reflect further on this subject. A man who spoke so persuasively of the importance of one's first impulses and the defects of character which were grafted on the original man through the influence of civilization must inevitably turn to the child as the best available example of the precivilized or natural man. Only with a child, a fresh and unformed being, could one hope to avoid the prejudice, the dogmatism, and the rigidity of behavior which had already engulfed the majority of adults. But how could one raise a child to be just himself, to see his own interests clearly, to find his way to the simple satisfactions of life without subjecting him to the omnipresent pressure of society, the conventions and precepts which attack him in his very cradle and form him before he has a chance to choose his own way?

For his vehicle Rousseau invented an imaginary boy, Emile, whose education was to be completely given over to him. From the moment the tutor entered Emile's life, no more was heard of his father. His tutor became a father, mother, educator, and moral mentor for the child. It is possible that Rousseau used Emile to replace in some small way, the loss of his own children, whose abandonment he had now come to regret, for he repeated several times that he would be with Emile all his life and that, as his tutor, he had actually become Emile's real father. It follows, therefore, that in his education of his charge Rousseau would start from birth. He protested against the custom of wrapping children in swaddling clothes, insisting that their little bodies required free and unrestricted movement for proper development. He attacked the custom of farming out children to a wet nurse and demanded that mothers nurse their own babies. These ideas had been proposed before, but Rousseau made them part of a general system of education, a philosophy of life.

The child continually makes useless efforts and exhausts his strength or retards its development. He was less cramped, less hampered, less restrained in the womb than he is in swaddling clothes; I do not see that he has gained anything by birth. . . . Their first feeling is one of pain and discomfort: they find only obstacles to every necessary movement: more unhappy than a criminal in chains, they struggle in vain, they become angry, they cry. Do you not say that their first words are tears? I can well believe it. From birth you are always constraining them. The first gifts they receive from you are their chains. The first treatment they experience is torture. Only their voice is free. Why should it not serve them in protest? They cry because you are hurting them. If you were tied up like that you would cry even louder.[1]

His second major complaint against the child-rearing and educational practices of his day was the custom of teaching children to reason as though they were small adults. Rousseau recognized that the child has a way of thinking and perceiving things characteristic of his age, that he will not absorb abstract ideas but requires concrete examples. In this respect he spoke of imparting physical rather than moral truths, but he was actually proposing merely to teach by example rather than by verbal exposition. He opposed the mechanical stuffing of the child with wise aphorisms and correct statements about the nature of the physical universe. His careful teaching of Emile to think and reason about nature is reminiscent of the role of Socrates in Plato's *Meno*. Emile is to learn the nature of refraction by coming on a stick protruding from the water. When he thinks he sees a "broken stick," his tutor helps him to discover that the stick is not broken but that its image is distorted by the water. Once the child has had his own experience with refraction there is an opportunity to teach him about the abstract concept and the mathematical use of an index of refraction. Other examples of this experiential approach to knowledge had a profound influence on the development of educational methods, particularly laboratory teaching.

As an observer of educational methods, Rousseau had a certain informality which enabled him to brush aside much of the pedantry of his time. He had a gift for displaying the ridiculous aspects of the approved methods and a contempt for the authoritarian approach to which he had been subjected in his brief bout with education at Turin. To Rousseau the teacher was not a god but a friend who helped the child find truth and who inspired him to seek it. He sensed the tremendous importance of *attitude* on the part of the pupil, and all his care and concern were directed at fostering and preserving this attitude.

> A child has no desire to perfect an instrument in order to torture himself, but see to it that this instrument serves his pleasure and soon he will apply himself in spite of anything you do.
> It becomes a great project to find the best method of teaching reading. People invent *bureaux*[2] and cards; they make the child's room into a printing shop. Locke would have him learn to read with dice. Now isn't that clever? And pathetic as well! A more certain method than any of these, and one which is generally overlooked, is to stimulate the desire to learn. Arouse this desire in the child and forget your *bureaux* and your dice. Any method will work.[3]

While Rousseau's "practical" examples, his techniques for creating this desire to learn, suffer from a number of deficiencies, his discovery of the primary problem in education and his effort to solve it was, in itself, a great contribution. His ability to see the educational requirements which had been ignored by so many men of his time was due, in large measure, to his unusual grasp of the nature of the thought processes of children, an ability which he derived from his deep identification with the child. Without a professional background in psychology he presented, in general terms, many of the ideas which Piaget was to develop more explicitly. He sensed the danger of attempting to cram abstract knowledge into the head of a child at a pace determined by the teacher.

> "Reason with children" was the great maxim of Locke; it is all the rage today. However, it appears that the results of its application do not do it much credit. As for myself I know nothing more silly than a child who has been taught by reasoning. Of all the faculties of man, reason, which is, so to speak, the product of all the others, is the last and most difficult to develop and it is this that they wish to use to develop the more primitive faculties! . . . Nature would have children be children before they are men. If we insist on perverting the order of things we will produce early fruit which will be neither ripe nor flavorful and which will decay early. We will have young doctors and old children. Childhood has a manner of seeing, thinking, and feeling which is peculiar to itself; nothing makes less sense than to try to substitute our ways. I would as soon demand that a child be five feet high as to expect judgment from a ten-year-old.[4]

The essence of Rousseau's indictment of formal learning is in the preceding quotation. The early rambling, undisciplined reading with his father, the romantic novels along with the philosophy and theology, prepared Rousseau for a leisurely approach to knowledge. It did not provide him with a balanced educational background, but it gave him the most important ingredient of scholarship—an active curiosity. Despite the acknowledged defects of the older Rousseau, he managed to make reading and learning an exciting experience for his impressionable young son. Rousseau's attack on the educational system of his day was based simply on its failure to provide such an experience. He received just enough indoctrination in the seminary at Turin to teach him to despise doctrine. He was told, all too often, that things were true because the teacher was an authority. He was taught to declaim and prove things by words at a time when his curiosity was leading him to another way of discovering knowledge. He knew that the dogma he absorbed at the seminary was not buttressed by inner conviction, that it did not spring from his own desire to understand. At the same time he recognized that the early education at the hands of his father, while deficient in content, had provided him with something of even greater importance, something which he found difficult to express except by example and story. In the height of the Age of Reason he recognized that education is, above all, an emotional experience, a romance with discovery, and that without romance it is as dry and cold as a marriage of convenience.

Emile was Rousseau's attempt to convey the emotional quality, the motive force which an educational experience should have for the young. But it was also the product of his individuality, of his personal style of writing. Thus, many traits which would appear as detractions in other writers serve to enhance the quality of depth and intimacy to be experienced in Rousseau's work. His naiveté in his earlier writings, particularly the first *Discourse*, has been mentioned. In *Emile* one sees the naiveté, but buttressed now by a style which gives it a special charm. It seems, at times, that the author is merely playing a role to show what fools people are to make the education of children such a complicated matter.

His very naiveté enabled Rousseau to get inside the child, for he never really lost contact with his own childhood. In his identification with the infant and the schoolboy he was able to present a more accurate picture of the child's way of reacting to new experience. He understood the child's limitations in regard to abstract thinking and his impatience with things which have no apparent practical significance. In Rousseau's naiveté there was a freshness, a readiness for the new and untried, a sense of adventure in the simplest pleasures, which is often lacking in adults. He paid a price, in anguish and torment, for his refusal to grow up, but there is no denying that he also purchased something of value. Thus, in saying that he was not "mature" one has not passed the final judgment on his life or his work.

II

Rousseau was never content to confine his observations to one field of interest and *Emile*, which was undertaken as a book on education, branched out into the social, religious, and political spheres. He approached education in the broadest sense of the word, and in his description of the pedagogical and child-rearing practices of his day he characterized the general inadequacy of his society. The farming out of children and the failure of the mother to nurse her own progeny was shown to be an example of the lack of real warmth and human feeling in eighteenth-century France.[5] The child was brought to the mother so that she might cover him with caresses for a few minutes before she returned to the salon, the ball, or the banquet. All was hypocrisy. The method of caring for children was merely a symptom of the general decay. In like manner the educational methods were characterized as a mere show of knowledge, a surface appearance of brilliance, like the wit of society ladies. Students, he said, were taught how to make a show of their erudition, but not how to think for themselves. The educational system was merely a reflection of the superficiality of society as a whole. To reform one was to reform the other.

Between the lines of his educational doctrine he prepared his readers for the upheaval of society. He pointed out that every child, even the son of a noble, should be taught some useful occupation since there was no guarantee that his status would always remain the same.

> You accept the present order of society without dreaming that this order is subject to inevitable upheaval and that it is impossible for you to foresee or prevent those things which may concern your children. The great become small, the rich become poor, the monarch becomes a subject. Are the blows of fate so rare that you can count on immunity? We are approaching a state of crisis and a time of revolutions. . . . Only nature makes characters which are ineffaceable, and nature makes neither princes nor riches nor great noblemen. This satrap that you have schooled for grandeur, what will he do in his degradation? This tax farmer who can only live on gold, what will he do in his poverty? This ostentatious fool who does not know what to do with himself and who takes pride

only in things which are not an integral part of himself, what will he do when he is deprived of everything? At such a time happy will be the man who can give up the station in life to which he is no longer entitled and remain a man in spite of his fate![6]

Rousseau does not show unusual prescience in the above statement. Revolution was in the air, and everyone could feel it. The force of his remark comes, as usual, from his matter-of-fact simplicity. Others predicted the event as though they could scarcely believe it would happen, as though it was a strange and marvelous calamity. Some of the nobility tried to laugh it away, believing somehow that the trouble would vanish if people would only turn the other way and pretend it did not exist. Rousseau spoke of the coming revolution as one would speak of the change of seasons, with a perfect familiarity and a statement that everyone should be prepared for the inevitable. Eighteenth-century France, he said, was a rigid and overspecialized society the elaborate customs of which did not prepare people for the world of the future.

III

At the time *Emile* was published, France was in the most exaggerated stages of the neo-classic era. The Greek ideas of the golden mean, of restraint in all things, the respect for tradition, had passed through the stormy rediscovery of the Renaissance into the severity of the Reformation. The "exuberant humanists," as Crane Brinton[7] has called them, had given way to the "classical humanists," and these at last to the "neo-classical" school of the eighteenth century. Form, which had originally been regarded by the Greeks as a means of discipline and control, had now become a mask for license. It did not seem to matter what was done so long as it was done correctly, so long as the proper social formalities were observed. Rousseau's prescription for the remaking of French society was, therefore, simply the abolition of form. People were to respond to situations from the spontaneity of the heart, and conduct was to be restrained and regulated by reason rather than custom. In his many fulminations against the excesses and overrefinement of civilization, he was protesting always against form, not civilization as such. There is perhaps no better illustration of this conviction than his various attacks on formality, custom, and dogma in *Emile*.

> They (girls) should not be instructed to love their mother. Affection does not come about through duty . . . Fancy dress may attract attention, but it is only the individual who can please us.

Our apparel is not us; its beauty is often spoiled by being too contrived. . . .[8]

Above all avoid giving the child empty formulas of politeness. . . . The fancy education of the rich never fails to make them politely imperious. . . . As for myself I would have less fear of Emile being coarse than arrogant; I would much prefer that he say, as a request, "Do this," then have him say "please" as a command. It is not the word he uses which is important but the meaning he gives it.[9]

But Rousseau's most eloquent thrust was reserved for table manners. In his soliloquy on the misery of wealth and how to overcome it, he sought to teach Emile his own version of good taste. The conventions and amusements of the wealthy were taken apart, one by one, and shown to be empty sham, devoid of enjoyment. Then, with that charm and enthusiasm which marked his greatest passages, he described the life of a truly rich man, a man rich in friendship and the beauty of nature.

There, all the airs of the town would be forgotten, and we would be villagers in a village; we would find a host of varied amusements, and our only problem would be to choose in the evening the sport for the following day. Exercise and an active life would improve our digestion and sharpen our taste. Every meal would be a feast where abundance would please us more than delicacies. Merriment, rude work, and playful games are the best cooks in the world, and fine sauces are quite ridiculous to people who have been rousting about ever since sunrise. The service would be without order or elegance. Our dining room would be—anywhere: in a garden, on a boat, under a tree, sometimes at a distance, near a lively spring, on fresh green grass, under the clusters of alder and hazel. A long procession of jolly guests would carry the preparations for the feast; the turf would be our table and chairs; the edge of the spring our buffet, and our dessert is hanging from the trees. The dishes would be served without regard to their order; appetite can dispense with propriety; each of us would openly serve himself without regard to the others, taking it for granted that everyone will do the same. From this cordial and matter-of-fact familiarity would arise, without coarseness, sham, or constraint, a joking conflict a hundred times more charming than politeness and more conducive to the union of hearts. No annoying lackies listening to our conversation, whispering criticisms of our behavior, counting every morsel with a greedy eye, amusing themselves by making us wait for our wine, and grumbling over the length of our meal. We would be our own servants in order to be our own masters. Time would pass without a reckoning; our meal would be a period of repose and last through the heat of the day. If some peasant comes near us on his way home from work, his tools over his shoulder, I would gladden his heart by some kind words, by a swig or two of good wine, which would help him endure his poverty in a better humor; and I, too, would have the pleasure of a little thrill of satisfaction, and I would say quietly to myself: I, too, am a man.[10]

There is a charm about this informality, but also a certain ringing conviction. The reader might well wonder if he is about to be forced to eat in the bushes, even if he prefers a table. Rousseau would deny this. Before his attack on custom he asserted his own freedom from fixed beliefs and strong opinions. He introduced *Emile* with a modesty that bordered on self-abasement. He denied any special qualification for his task and expressed his willingness to let every man examine the facts and come to his own conclusions.

When one reflects that *Emile* became the educational bible of the French Revolution, that Mirabeau described it as one of the greatest works of the age, that it has inspired many of the tenets of modern education; when we note that it was attacked not only for its influence on education, but for its revolutionary ideas on religion and society as well, one might well smile at the preface in which Rousseau insists that he has no desire to control the opinions of anyone.

> This collection of reflections and observations, without order and almost without continuity, was undertaken to please a good mother who thinks for herself. . . . A man who, from his retreat, casts his work before the public, without anyone to advertise it, without a party to defend it, without even knowing what is thought or said about such things, should not have the fear that, if he is mistaken, people will accept his errors without examining them.[11]

IV

Many of the ideas which stirred a great protest at the time *Emile* was first published—the attitude toward religion (discussed in a later chapter), the demand that children be nursed by their mother and freed from physical restraining devices, the attack on form and propriety, the statement that children do not think as adults and therefore should not be taught as adults—would no longer excite an argument. But the extent to which one person may legitimately control the life of another and the methods that may be used for this control have become the great issue of modern times.

Rousseau's concept of personal control was never intended as a part of his educational doctrine. It is nowhere developed as a proposal and only occasionally referred to directly. It comes mainly through his examples, and in this respect it is everywhere and nowhere. It is a product of his own ambivalent attitude toward authority, that strange mixture of defiance coupled with the thrill he derived from complete and unquestioning obedience. As noted, his desire to suffer and submit was complemented by another desire to command and to be cruel.[12] Yet the sadism of the adult Rousseau manifested itself in an entirely different way from the more overt sadism of another writer of his time, the Marquis de Sade. In the stories of Sade, people are whipped and tortured for the pleasure of watching them suffer. In *Emile* the victim suffers only for his own good. He is never whipped, but he is put through a variety of emotional tortures which surpass the most exquisite refinements of Sade. Further, the victim is taught to love his torturer for the very suffering which he endures.

Rousseau's understanding of the world of children was based, in large measure, on the fact that he still identified with the child in his relationship with most adults.[13] His rebellion constituted not a mere disagreement with the laws and social customs of his time, but a demand for the abolition of authority and social obligation. It was the child's rebellion against the adult, modified and rationalized in accord with his own sado-masochistic needs. In spite of his identification with the child, however, he had a desire to subdue others, to make them submit to his will, and to put them through an excruciating moral torture in the process. But these impulses were so contrary to the dictates of his conscience that he could not accept them. So terrified was he of this side of himself that he leaned over backward to avoid situations which had in them any elements of authority, control, or cruelty.

Since he was unable to examine his sadistic impulses in the light of reason, he was never able to be reasonable about them. The thought of cruel domination filled him with guilt, and this feeling soon generalized to all situations involving authority—even the necessary authority of a teacher fostering learning. The idea of demanding that anyone obey even his most reasonable request was so intimately associated with a secret and shameful pleasure that he could not tolerate it. Yet the urge to dominate was so strong that he could never keep it under control. He stepped gingerly around situations requiring the exercise of authority, but he was imperious in the demands he made in the name of friendship, love, and freedom.

In *Emile*, more than in any other book, one sees the operation of this potent dynamic. Here is a man dedicated to his mission of freeing children from adult authority. By a series of elaborate stratagems he would have the child learn without ever being instructed. Situations are carefully arranged by the tutor so that learning takes place as a consequence of the child's experience. Yet beneath this benevolent desire for a free and "natural" education lies the unconscious wish to completely overpower this helpless creature and seduce him into submission to the will of the "educator." In one of his most revealing passages, Rousseau remarks:

> Take the opposite approach with your pupil; let him always think that he is the master while it is you who are really master. There is no subjection so complete as that which retains the appearance of liberty; in this way the very will is taken captive. This poor child who knows nothing, who understands nothing, and who can do nothing; is he not at your mercy? Do you not control his entire environment, as it relates to him? Can you not influence him as you please?[14] His work, his play, his pleasures, his pain, are they not in your hands without his being aware of it? No doubt he should only do what he wishes, but he should not want to do what you would not have him do. He should not take a step you have not foreseen. He should not open his mouth but that you know what he is going to say.[15]

Here is the heart of that ambivalence about freedom which was at the root of Rousseau's personality. He was sympathetic to the underdog so long as he remained an underdog. He would like to guide children toward a defiance of the adult morality of his day, but defiance of the mentor roused his wrath. In Rousseau's experience as a tutor to the children of M. de Mably he exhibited this attitude quite clearly, as he tells us in his *Confessions:*

> As long as all went well . . . I was an angel. I was a devil when things went wrong. When my pupils did not understand me I raved and when they showed signs of disobedience I could have killed them. . . .[16]

But in *Emile* things were to be different. It was this terrible, aggressive desire for control and authority that had been the cause of his past failures. With his ideal pupil he would be an ideal tutor. He would never thwart the will of his young charge, never make demands on him, but always arrange his life so that he obeyed without command. Emile would be taught to respect private property by having him grow beans. The tutor would excite Emile's interest until he became very fond of his bean patch.

We go every day to water the beans, we watch them grow in transports of happiness. I increase his delight by telling him, "This belongs to you."[17]

Then Rousseau has the gardener destroy the bean patch and point out to Emile that the beans had been planted in the place where he was growing melons, that the property was his and that Emile had no right to trespass.

Rousseau, the arranger, is always present, never lifting a hand to the child himself, never showing anger, yet making sure that the punishment fits the crime. When the child breaks windows he prescribes the following treatment:

He breaks the windows of his room: let the wind blow on him night and day without concerning yourself about his catching cold, because it is better to catch cold than be foolish. Never complain of the inconvenience he causes you, but see that he feels it first. Finally, you have the windows repaired without saying anything at all. He breaks them again? Then change your method: tell him dryly but without anger, "The windows belong to me. I took the trouble to have them put there and I want to protect them." Then you will shut him up in a dark place without windows. At this new approach he starts to cry and rage; no one pays any attention. Soon he gives that up and changes his tone; he groans and complains; a servant comes by; the rebel begs for deliverance. Without finding any pretext for refusing, the servant responds, "I, too, have windows to protect," and goes away. Finally, when the child has remained there several hours, long enough for the experience to worry him and make an impression on his memory, someone suggests to him that he seek an agreement with you by means of which you will set him free if he breaks no more windows. He could not ask for more. He begs to see you; you come; he makes his proposition and you accept it immediately, saying, "That's a good idea. We both gain by it. Why didn't you think of it before?" Then, without asking him to make a vow or confirm his promise, you embrace him with joy and lead him at once to his own room, regarding the agreement as sacred and inviolable as if he had sworn an oath on it. What do you think he will make of all this regarding faith in promises and their utility? If I am not mistaken, there is not a single child on the earth, who is not already spoiled, who could pass through this experience and ever consider deliberately breaking windows again. Follow through the whole train of thought. The little rascal scarcely dreamed that, in making a hole to plant his beans, he was digging a prison in which his knowledge would soon enclose him.[18]

Such a train of thought is indeed very clever, except that the child will not wait for the completion of one lesson before his tutor is required to invent several others. He will break not only windows, but ash trays, chairs, and pictures as well. He will spill ink, smear mud, kick flowers, chase chickens, and tear his clothes. He will, in short, keep well ahead of such carefully contrived lessons and the tutor's ingenuity, as well as his patience, will soon be exhausted. And just as well! For there is in this incident of the broken window a certain emotionless and refined cruelty that chills the blood. One feels that such a methodical tutor, who always presents his discipline "dryly and without anger" and who believes that it is better to catch cold than be foolish, would find it difficult to show any real compassion for the child. Rousseau did well to warn against the infinite perfectibility of man through the exercise of reason. His examples illustrate all too clearly that reason is a very corruptible faculty and that one may satisfy all types of desires in its name.

The incidents of the bean patch and the broken window are not isolated examples. Emile is motivated to learn reading by receiving notes of invitation to little parties with treats, but he cannot read them and there is no one to read them to him. By the time he discovers their meaning, the party is over. Too bad. If only he had known how to read, what an advantage he would have! To teach him the value of finding one's bearing, Emile is taken for a walk in the woods before breakfast and thoroughly lost. Amid his tears of hunger and desperation he is led to solve the puzzle of how to get back to Montmorency.

He is instructed in the dangers of vanity by being thoroughly humiliated by a magician at a fair. After carefully planting the magician and instructing him as to his performance, the tutor takes Emile to the fair, where they watch the amazing performance of a mechanical duck who follows a piece of bread held in the hand of the magician. Whenever the bread is brought near the bird he turns around and directs his beak on the piece of bread. Emile and his tutor return home and discover how they can do the same thing with a magnetized needle buried in the wax beak of the duck and a piece of iron hidden in the bread. The next day Emile goes to the fair and cries out that he can do the trick as well as the magician. At the latter's invitation, he takes his prepared piece of bread from his pocket and offers it to the duck who comes toward him at once. The magician professes amazement and promises to collect an even bigger crowd on the following day if Emile will come to demonstrate his skill.

The child counts the minutes until tomorrow with a laughable anxiety. He invites everyone he meets. He wants the whole human race to witness his glory; he awaits the hour with impatience; he flies to the meeting place; the room is full already. When he enters, his young heart expands. Other tricks precede his; the conjurer surpasses himself and does all sorts of amazing things. The child sees none of them; he twists, he perspires, he scarcely breathes; he passes the time fondling the piece of bread in his pocket, his hand trembling with impatience.[19]

At last Emile has his chance, but today the duck runs away from him. The audience laughs. Emile is chagrined. He tries again. The same result. He cries out that it is all a hoax, that the magician cannot do it either. But the latter performs the trick easily with Emile's own piece of bread. Then he takes out the piece of iron before the audience, humiliating the child still further, and brings the duck to him with only the bread. As a finale he goes to the middle of the room and directs the duck with his voice. The thunderous applause completely defeats Emile. Later, the magician calls at Emile's home to explain that he is only a poor man and that it was unfair for the child to attempt to interfere with his livelihood. He shows his apparatus, which is merely a strong magnet in the hand of a boy under the table. "What mortification attends the first movement toward vanity," cries Rousseau. "Young tutor, watch this first inclination with care. If you know how to make it result in humiliation and disgrace, you can be sure that it will be a long time before it recurs again."[20]

Rousseau contended that the child should never learn that he can influence the tutor's peace of mind by his behavior. Only at the age of puberty does he permit the child to see how eager his tutor is for his success and happiness. At this point, when the awakening sexual impulse begins to stir in the young man, Rousseau takes him aside and describes in vivid colors the dangers of debauchery and the frightening and uncontrollable power of this new passion. The youth is so awed by the dangers that he clings to his tutor for guidance. The tutor now makes it clear to Emile how much his own happiness is dependent on that of his charge. Clasping him in his arms, he points out to him the nobility of virtue and the ultimate value of a good woman. But here love is used much in the same way that logic was formerly employed: to control the child. Emile is reminded of the tutor's love for him and asked to imagine how terribly he would hurt his beloved instructor if he failed to find happiness or a life of virtue.[21] Rousseau, who desperately needed the love of everyone, was acutely conscious that he would be at the mercy of a child who sensed this need. Thus he planned both his love and his anger in the rearing of Emile to condition him as one might manipulate a dog in a laboratory. Every demand on the child was to be a carefully prepared stimulus to which the response was foreordained. But little boys are by no means as predictable as dogs. They absorb and transform the stimulus in the light of a vast ideational network and a host of childhood experiences. The response that finally emerges has a way of confounding the most enlightened and scientific adults. One may seek to teach the danger of vanity and discover that he has implanted a feeling of personal helplessness and a disgust for all knowledge. Further, if the "little rascal" ever discovers he is being educated by such stratagems, he will always be on guard against the crafty tutor. Soon he may come to regard the world of reality as a vast showplace arranged by his mentor to trick him into learning.

v

Having completed both his physical and moral education, the tutor now undertakes to find a wife for Emile. The girl, if she is to be worthy, must have an education comparable to his. The bride-to-be is given parents, a history of her own, and the name "Sophie." She represents an idealized version of his own Sophie as Rousseau might have imagined her at fifteen: burning with a romantic passion for the boy of her dreams, dissatisfied with all the mediocre fops she meets, disgusted with their pretensions at wit, yearning for a sincere, virtuous, and unpretentious young man who will charm her by his very simplicity.

Having introduced Sophie, Rousseau now has an opportunity for a discourse on the education of women and, of course, for another attack on the fashionable society of his day. "Women of Paris and London, forgive me!" he cries, "There may be miracles anywhere, but I know nothing of them; and if there is one among you who is truly sincere, I understand nothing of our institutions."[22] In contrast to these society ladies, Sophie is reared in a quiet country village.

But how will Emile learn to recognize the merit of such a creature? His tutor has seen to this. It is all arranged. Rousseau has encouraged his charge to talk about his ideal girl and has suggested a few ideas himself. Then, just to give this imaginary creature more reality, he suggests a name. Perhaps they should call her "Sophie." Meanwhile, he has arranged with the parents of the real Sophie that he and Emile will go for a long walk, too far to enable them to return home by evening, and they will seek shelter in the home of Sophie's parents. Sophie has been properly prepared for the event by reading Fénelon's *Telemachus*. When Rousseau and his charge arrive the father, always on cue, reminds her of the arrival of Telemachus and Mentor on the island of Calypso, and the girl turns red with emotion. She already adores Telemachus. This, however, is nothing compared to the effect she has on Emile when her mother calls her by name at the dinner table.

> At the name of Sophie you would have seen Emile give a start. Struck by the mention of a name so dear to him, he awakes suddenly and glances eagerly at she who dares to bear it. Sophie! Oh Sophie! Is it you that I love?[23]

The gradual nurturing of this awakened interest into an enduring passion is managed with the greatest care by Rousseau and Sophie's parents. But once Emile is really in love the time has come for another strategem.

> One morning when they have not seen each other for two days I come into Emile's room with a letter in my hand and tell him while looking at him fixedly, "What would you do if someone told you Sophie were dead?" He cries out, jumps up, and strikes his hands together and without saying a single word he looks at me with a distaught expression.[24]

The sadistic aspect of this maneuver is inescapable to the reader, but to Rousseau it is only an educational device. It is a means of focusing Emile's attention on the fact that he is, as yet, too young and inexperienced to marry Sophie. How does Emile know that he can be true to her or that she will not lose interest in him? Besides, Emile has not yet had an opportunity to learn the duties of citizenship, which he will assume when he becomes a husband and father. It is best that he should travel for a few years and learn about the world. He will return experienced and worthy of his stern responsibility. Emile and his tutor depart, and a discourse follows on travel, national character, and the governments of the world, the latter part of which is an abbreviated version of the *Social Contract*. When the tutor finds, on their return, that both Emile and his Sophie are truly worthy of each other, the two are at last permitted to marry—but not to bed! By one last strategem Emile is deprived of the caresses of his bride on the very night of their wedding so that he may learn restraint and respect for the wishes of his spouse.

VI

The curious quality which emerges from *Emile*, and which is evident in Rousseau's entire style of life, is the contrast between his demand for honesty and frankness in all human relationships and his advocacy of extensive deception. It is clear from the incident in the bean patch that Rousseau has at least *implied* to Emile that it is all right to plant beans in a certain spot of ground and that he has ordered the gardener to punish the child by digging up his beans. At the same time, while he is personally responsible for the punishment, he seeks to avoid all responsibility for having administered it. We are reminded, once again, of his remarks at the beginning of his *Confessions:* "If I made myself responsible for the result," he says in describing his character, the reader might feel that he was being deceived. Instead, the reader is asked to "assemble the elements" and determine for himself what manner of being is composed from them.[25] Rousseau presents his refusal to accept responsibility for his own character as though it is a kind of detached and scientific objectivity. There is, however, another side to this detachment. It is as though he is saying he is some kind of natural phenomenon, like a volcano—and, therefore, not personally responsible for his ideas or their effect upon society. If people marvel at the pyrotechnics, they are at liberty to try to understand what is going on inside him. He will even help them get a close look. He will be honest in the sense that he will not attempt to hide anything.

From one moment to the next in the *Confessions*, the *Social Contract*, and *Emile* Rousseau presents strikingly contrasting sides of himself: his demand for freedom and his punitive proposals, his desire for love and his provocative tendency, his anger at the physical restraints placed on children and his naive admission that he believes the child's mind should be completely subject to the will of the teacher, his desire for honesty in human relationships and his advocacy of deception. He presents these contrasts without comment, without any attempt to resolve them, and often without any apparent awareness that they exist. He seems to tell us in his philosophy as well as in his life, "Here I am. If you are dissatisfied with what you see, it is up to you to understand and make some sense out of these discordant elements. I can only present you with the opposition, the conflict, the very irony of life." Yet he proposes to reveal a new morality, as though he were the mere oracle of a new religion, a dumb beast from whose mouth the word of God comes to mankind. The beast cannot interpret the sacred word or resolve the contradictions in God's laws. He is seized by a power greater than himself and can only utter the words of the master. He is not responsible for what he has said.

Of course, Rousseau really does not take such a position. He claims to be inspired but not by any supernatural force. His refusal to accept responsibility for the contradictions in his philosophy represents a refusal to look deeply into his own ideas. As seen in the following chapter, he advocated reason as a means for answering questions of morality, but he was attached to the idea that the good conscience can never go wrong. This tenderness about looking carefully at his own pronouncements may well be related to a fear that he may not have certain evidence of divine grace, the conscience of the righteous.

The Calvinist doctrine of his childhood held that an idea of God is naturally engraved on the hearts of men[26] and that God had sown in the minds of men the seed of religion.[27] While some men suppress this knowledge in their hearts,[28] God has enlightened others with his word through the Scriptures.[29] The true word, however, according to Calvin, can be understood only by a man gifted with the internal testimony of the Holy Spirit without which a mere mental understanding would never redeem him.[30] Thus, the very process of conversion is not a product of our own individual will, but of God's grace. This grace is prior to all human merit, and no propensity of the will to do anything good can be found in anyone but the elect.[31]

For Rousseau to question an idea that "felt" good on its first appearance would be to question the validity of that very conscience which was his true guide. To reflect was to open the door to doubt and to destroy the very faith that was the cornerstone of redemption. He was apparently disturbed by the thought that an idea which came to him spontaneously could be morally wrong. Honesty meant for him, then, not the exploration of an idea and the willinginess to face its consequences, but the mere expression of an idea. To admit that a principle of morality was subject to correction by argument was to admit he had no inviolate and certain source of moral truth within him.

In a later chapter, this tenderness in his thinking will be explored in more detail, for it is also related to his concern with maintaining his innocence, his freedom from deliberate and conscious choice of good and evil.

[8]

The Profession of Faith

I

THE CRITICISM of established social institutions and the revolutionary attitude toward education were responsible for some of the venom directed at Rousseau while he was publishing his most important works. The *Social Contract* was condemned in Geneva and tolerated in France (although sales were clandestine), but in neither country did it excite any great number of public refutations at the time.[1] Instead, a section of *Emile* titled the *Profession of Faith of a Savoyard Priest* was singled out as a terrible religious heresy. Today this brief testimony would probably stand as one of the least controversial of his major works.

The *Profession of Faith* was the section mentioned which had so disturbed Duclos that he had asked Rousseau to forget having read it in his presence. It was a description of Rousseau's doctrine of the natural religion, which was essentially a worship of the Supreme Being without the requirement of intermediaries and formal ceremonies. It contained a critique of the papal policy of celibacy for priests as being against the laws of nature and a general appeal to the use of reason in the understanding of God.

The religious ideas in the *Profession of Faith* were, in many respects, similar to those held by Voltaire, who was no atheist. Although almost every idea it contained had already been expressed by free thinkers, there was in it a quality of reverence and genuine humility completely lacking in the barbed wit of the religious skeptics. It was an attack on religious practices, but it was also an unmistakable defense of religious faith. And while Rousseau preached the exercise of reason in the interpretation of religion, he cautioned against fruitless arguments over points of doctrine.

From Rousseau's point of view, eighteenth-century man had been divided in half. At one moment he was carried away by abstraction, having lost contact with his feelings, and the next moment he was wallowing in the depths of passion and sensuality without any reasonable restraint. He urged the reunion of reason and the passions, with reason in control, but taking as its guide man's intuitive sense of good-

164

ness. Those who have described Rousseau as the apostle of sensuality and self-indulgence have reckoned without the theme of the *Profession of Faith*.

> While meditating on the nature of man I believed I had discovered two distinct principles, one of which raised him to the study of eternal truths, to the love of justice and high morality, to the regions of the intellectual world which wise men contemplate with pleasure. The other led him downward within himself and enslaved him to the empire of the senses, to the passions which are their minister and opposed everything which was inspired by the first sentiment. When I felt myself carried away, pulled apart by these two contrary impulses I said to myself, 'No, man is not one; I will and I will not, I feel myself at the same time a slave and a free man; I see the good, I love it, and I do what is bad; I am active when I listen to my reason, passive when my passions sweep me off my feet; and when I succumb my worst torment is the knowledge that I could have resisted.'[2]

As usual, however, this man who believed so devoutly in simplicity and directness never left his reader with a simple idea. Man was to obey no voice but that of reason; he must resist the passions, but he must also be guided by his conscience. Only his conscience would tell him if the voice he hears is *really* that of reason.

> Conscience is the voice of the soul, the passions are the voice of the body. Is it so astonishing that the two voices often contradict one another? And then to which one should we listen? Too often reason deceives us; we have only too good a basis for challenging her; but conscience never deceives us; she is the true guide of man. She is to the soul what instinct is to the body.[3]

Man requires reason in order to discover the good and conscience in order to love it and follow it.

> To know the good is not to love it; this knowledge is not innate in man, but as soon as his reason discovers it his conscience causes him to love it; it is this feeling which is innate.[4]

As he began to realize the psychological nature of the complex web in which truth may become entangled, he evolved, in his philosophy of religion, three forces, each contending for the soul of man: the primitive animal passions, the more elevated and strictly human capability of reason, and that higher principle of conscience which he believed to be innate in men. While he described these forces in the abstract, he was aware of their constant interaction with one another, and, despite his frequent dogmatic statements on the infallibility of "conscience," even this noble source required prompting by man's sensual cravings to reveal the course of nature and the intentions of the Supreme Being. The Savoyard priest had discovered the false character of that unnatural rule of celibacy when his "conscience" persisted in following the order of nature in making love to a woman.

Throughout *Emile*, Rousseau tried to clarify the three prime facets of man's moral being which he had proposed in the *Profession of Faith:* passion, reason, and conscience. He elaborated on the subtlety of their influence, seeking a way by which man might be led toward truth and justice. After a century of philosophical dispute, Freud has described these forces with greater psychological insight and clarity, calling them the id, the ego, and the superego. But the new labels have not changed the enigmatic nature of the problem. Knowledge has been increased by greater sophistication in regard to the superego and its corruptibility, but the moral triangle posed by Rousseau still functions. The man who would discover ethical truths can find no sure guide.

In his efforts to show his fellowmen the way to virtue, Rousseau succeeded in making them more aware of the problem, but he did not convince himself that he had found the solution. In the role of the Savoyard priest he told his readers:

> . . . give to my discourse only the authority of reason. I do not know if I am mistaken. It is difficult sometimes to avoid taking an affirmative tone when one is expounding an idea, but remember that all my assertions are merely so many reasons to doubt me. Seek the truth yourself; for my part I only promise you sincerity.[5]

With such a remark coming from his imaginary priest, Rousseau called the attention of his readers to the fallibility of all human creatures —even those who spoke as agents of God. In his condemnation of religious ritual and Christian doctrine, he added still other heresies to the long list he was accumulating.

> The worship God asks is that of the heart and that, when it is sincere, is always the same. It is foolish vanity which imagines that God takes such a great interest in the shape of the vestments of the priest, the order of the words he pronounces, or the gestures he makes at the altar and all his genuflections. Ah, my friend, stand up, you will still be near enough to the earth. God wants to be adored in spirit and truth. . . .[6]

While be believed in the virtue of faith, he would not submit his reason to it, as the church demanded.

The one who begins by electing a chosen people and who pro-
scribes the rest of the human race is not the common father of
men. The one who destines for eternal punishment the greater
number of his creatures is not the merciful and loving God that
my reason reveals to me. . . . The God that I adore is not a God
of darkness, he has not given me understanding in order to forbid
me to use it; to tell me to submit my reason is to outrage the creator of that reason. The minister of truth does not tyrannize over
my reason, he enlightens it.[7]

In the zeal of his attack on religious authority, he did not forget his
old friends, the literary atheists of the Holbach salon.

Avoid those who, under the pretext of explaining nature, sow
disheartening doctrines in the hearts of men, those whose skepticism is a hundred times more assertive and dogmatic than the
determined tone of their adversaries . . . overthrowing, destroying,
trampling underfoot all that men respect, they take from the
afflicted the last consolation for their misery, from the rich and
powerful the only curb on their passions. They tear from the
depths of the heart all remorse for crime, all hope of virtue, and
in the face of this they boast of being the benefactors of the human race. They tell us that the truth can do no harm to man. This
I believe and it is, in my opinion, the greatest proof that what
they teach is not the truth. . . . An arrogant philosophy leads to
fanaticism. Avoid these extremes, remain always firmly on the
course of truth, or what appears to be truth in the simplicity of
your heart, and never be diverted from it by vanity or weakness.
Dare to confess God among philosophers; dare to preach humanity
to the intolerant.[8]

In *The Profession of Faith of a Savoyard Priest*, Rousseau had
managed to present his feelings about the atheists without the severity
toward unbelievers found in the *Social Contract*. It was a creed for a
man, not for a state. There was, in this little section, a certain peace
and confidence that seemed to arise from a tranquil soul. Courageous,
but never deliberately defiant, it was free from his malice as well as from
his masochism. Rousseau, always a good critic of his own work, regarded the *Profession of Faith* as his finest piece of writing.

II

Many influences were at work in the development of Rousseau's
ideas on religion. In spite of his rejection of the skepticism of the

philosophic clique, he had been profoundly impressed by the philosopher's use of reason as a means for understanding God. However, in the last analysis the *Profession of Faith* stands as a justification for believing rather than as a logical demonstration of the existence of a Supreme Being. This final position had a long and tortuous evolution from his early Calvinist days in Geneva, through his conversion to Roman Catholicism, the deism of Mme de Warens, and finally his reconfirmation at Geneva into the church of his fathers. The product which emerges from this struggle seems to be a peculiar mixture of religion and patriotism, arising from a desire to be true to the spirit of his church while, at the same time, surpassing it. Rousseau wanted very much to be accepted by the church and the state of Geneva, but not merely as a citizen as virtuous as other Genevans. It was important for him to rise to a higher moral plane, to feel himself "above" the others. The dual advocacy of patriotism and moral reform, so characteristic of his political writings, seems to spring from his peculiar relationship to his family and the city of his birth.

The influence of Geneva on Rousseau is one of the most obvious aspects of his work.[9] His preference for the small democracy as the ideal political unit, his tendency to advise a Genevan austerity (sumptuary laws, etc.) for other emerging political communities such as Corsica and Poland, and the importance which he attached to the personal opinion of one's neighbors and fellow citizens as a force for the development of national virtue are only a few examples of the extent to which his political theories are a reflection of his background. What makes a man so responsive to his native land? All men do not become patriots. What was there about his relationship to Geneva that gave the city such a hold on his political and religious ideas? In his early years, after his voluntary departure from Geneva, he seems to have been much more attached to Savoy than to his homeland. His childhood associations with his mother country were pleasant, but they are not, in themselves, enough to explain his intensely partisan feelings.

Not until his adult years, when he had begun to see in it a reflection of himself, did he begin to "appreciate" Geneva. As a small nation, a bantamweight among the powers, still retaining its strong desire for independence, with a people who took a certain fierce pride in their personal sacrifices and their willingness to do without the luxuries of other nations, the atmosphere of Geneva was particularly congruent with the personality of a professional underdog. His initially favorable reception by the Genevans and the fact that he no longer lived in the city and was not harassed by its laws and restrictions—retaining his distance from the realities of its life—enabled him to become emotionally attached to it.

From a moral point of view, the Genevan tendency to look with disfavor on sensual enjoyment and emotional expression and the ideal of hard work and severe personal deportment were in striking contrast to his languid and sensual temperament. His heart could expand in Paris where "the grand friendship" was all the rage. How was it, then, that he became so receptive to the moral standards of Geneva? Was it merely because the first years of life are so important for moral development, or are there other reasons peculiar to his individual experience?

Regardless of the personal standards of virtue which he came to admire, the desire to be considered "good" was clearly a product of this early environment. The Rousseau family, as noted in the first chapter, was not particularly religious, and there were several instances of rebellion against the accepted standards of church and community by various members of the family. His experience in propitiating his father and his discovery of intense pleasure in connection with a sense of righteousness reinforced his desire to be good—better than anyone else. For the moralist, the very fact that he looked deeply into questions of morality indicates that he was not prepared to accept the conventional virtues of those around him, but sought to raise himself above them. The righteous exhilaration he experienced in the bed with his cousin Abraham attached him passionately to the idea of being—not just good—but better. Rousseau's idea of goodness was not really the cool propriety of the Genevans, but an ecstatic experience with all the overtones of sexual excitement.

In Geneva the standards of the community were congruent with those of the church. The citizens believed in living up to the tenets of their religion. In Paris the religious standards of goodness were not really so different from those of Geneva. The virtues of the Christian martyrs were still admired by the church. Official church morality gave a certain sanction to abstinence and reserve, but official morality was in disrepute and it was fashionable to be wicked. Other moralists and philosophers in Rousseau's own circle had already seemed to raise themselves above their fellowman by pointing to the hypocrisy and pretense dominating social morality. Their answer was to turn from the false religion of the day toward skepticism and to use reason as a guide to virtue. If Rousseau was to surpass them, he must find a concept of virtue beyond mere reason. His emotional attachment to the idea of goodness led him back to the concept of conscience and thence to faith as the dominating feature of the moral life. With the example of Geneva before him, he was not disillusioned with the power of religion as were his Parisian contemporaries. As a result he began to graft onto his own personality many of the attributes of virtue so admired in Geneva. Rude, simple work became his ideal. Honesty and frankness in all personal relationships, even a brutal directness, were far better than the fine polished manners which were only a symptom of moral decay. He would make of himself a new man. As already observed, the graft did not take. The sensual Rousseau was always at war with his severe counterpart. He was always troubled by a sense of not really being the kind of virtuous citizen idolized by his Calvinist culture. Hence, his hero in the *Profession of Faith* was a fallen priest, a man who loved virtue but was haunted by a secret sense of sin.

The war within his own personality might have continued indefinitely, with Rousseau struggling to prove to himself that he was virtuous, mending his doubts from day to day, had not the world passed a judgment on his works and his character. He awoke one morning to find the verdict was "guilty," and he was thrown into a fresh paroxysm of doubt and dismay.

[9]

Flight

THE BUSINESS OF PUBLISHING and selling books in eighteenth-century France was not the respectable enterprise that it is today. Controversial books were published outside the country and smuggled inside the country, usually without the author's name on the title page. This little convention was a kind of gentlemen's agreement between the king and his men of letters. If a book was to be censored, his majesty had no particular desire to lose the talents of one of his literati, provided the man had the decency to deny authorship of the offensive volume. Voltaire smilingly denied most of the books he wrote, though everyone knew the author. Such was not the case with Rousseau. He resolutely signed every one of his books and insisted that he would bear full responsibility for them. He was scrupulously honest with his publishers, refusing opportunities to profit at their expense. Nevertheless, he had encountered a number of dishonest booksellers and publishers. Mme de Luxembourg was incensed at his difficulties. This time, she assured him, she would personally look after the publication of *Emile* and the author would receive his share of the profits. She was a friend of Malesherbes, an enlightened man, who was *directeur de la Librairie* and chief censor of Paris. The two of them assured Rousseau that it would be perfectly safe to have his book published in France. Malesherbes felt that the *Profession of Faith* was so excellent as to win universal acclaim. Since the approval of Malesherbes legalized the book, Rousseau was somewhat reassured. He agreed that the book should be offered for sale in Paris, but he insisted that it be printed in Holland by Néaulme. In this way he felt he would not be breaking the laws of France.

The contract for *Emile* was complicated, and it seemed to take forever to get the book underway. Samples of type were submitted, Rousseau gave his approval, then more samples were sent. Meanwhile, he completed the *Social Contract* and sent it to Rey in Holland, who saw to its publication. Reflecting on the speed with which Rey was progressing, Rousseau became concerned for *Emile*. He had signed an agreement with Duchesne, stipulating that his book should be printed in Holland by Néaulme. But Néaulme did not trust Duchesne and complained to Rousseau that he was not getting the sheets fast enough. Soon it became obvious to Rousseau that an edition of *Emile* was being printed in Paris as well as in Holland. While he did not feel he had given his consent to this printing, he was assured that the Paris edition would carry the notice of Néaulme as printer. In any event he now felt obligated to correct the proofs or see a garbled edition of his work.

Meanwhile, he fell ill with a recurrence of his urethral complaint. This time, however, his difficulties were more severe than any he had previously experienced and, in the fall of 1761, an accident with a probe seemed to aggravate his condition still further. He believed himself close to death and his concern for his still unpublished *Emile* reached a pitch of anxiety. Néaulme had already aroused some suspicion in regard to Duchesne. Now Rousseau began to believe that the Jesuits had gotten hold of the *Profession of Faith* and had arranged to have it held back until after his death, when an altered version would be published.

At this time the Jesuits were themselves suffering from the general unrest in France. This once powerful order had come under the scrutiny of the French Parlement, and a régime which was desperately in need of a scapegoat. The philosophers had stirred up the feelings of the common man against the privileges of the clergy, and Voltaire was soon to make a brilliant defense of the victims of religious persecution throughout the world. Once the giant had begun to weaken, a host of minor writers and politicians began to close in for the kill. The bankruptcy of the Jesuit mission in Martinique served as a pretext. The French Parlement condemned their doctrine and closed their colleges. Already pressure was being exerted on the king to approve the action of Parlement and to suppress the order entirely.

But Rousseau, who had spoken many times of the instability of greatness, could not really perceive the problems of those in power. The strength of the Jesuits seemed monumental and international in its scope. He felt that all rumors of their fall had been circulated by these crafty priests in an effort to take their adversaries off guard. Despite his quarrels with the Encyclopedists, he was still regarded as a member of that philosophical clique by the partisans of the church and the old régime. He had read portions of *Emile* to a number of people. Whenever he heard that a Jesuit had spoken of his forthcoming book he was thrown into a new fit of terror. He believed, with considerable justification, that the *Profession of Faith* was a more serious threat to entrenched orthodoxy than all the ranting of the atheists.

It is typical of Rousseau that during his crisis his fears were always for his book and not for himself. Despising his present life, with his eyes always fixed on the future, he was prepared to undergo any torture if only the world might have his ideas as he had written them.

> I felt I was dying. I can scarcely understand why my extravagant imagination did not kill me, so terrified was I by the thought that my memory would be dishonored after my death in my best and most worthy book. Never have I been so afraid of death and I think if I had died in these circumstances I would have died in despair. Even today when I can see the blackest and most frightfull plot which has ever been hatched against a man's memory advancing without obstacle to its execution, I will die much more peacefully, certain of leaving in my writings a testimony in my favor, which will triumph, sooner or later, over the conspiracies of men.[1]

At last *Emile* was published and Rousseau relaxed. In fact, he relaxed so completely that it was impossible for anyone to rouse him to the real danger which was now threatening him. Moultou, his pastor friend in Geneva, had warned him that his fellow Genevans would not take to the *Profession of Faith* with the same warmth shown to the *Letter to d'Alembert*. Duclos had openly showed his alarm when he heard that the book was being published in Paris. But now that Rousseau had seen his witness in the court of history in its final published form, he developed an attitude of serenity and a conviction that the honest people would see the author's sincerity of heart and would rise in unison to defend him. He had wise and powerful friends in Malesherbes, the Prince de Conti, and the Marshal de Luxembourg, with his charming and influential wife. He was certain these fine people would stand at his side in this final moment of truth, for they had professed their belief in him and his work.

It is impossible, at the present time, to look back and determine what was really responsible for the phenomenal miscalculation of that small group of worldly and sophisticated people who pressed for a Paris edition of *Emile*. Malesherbes, who should have been the most knowledgeable regarding the attitude of court and Parlement, was open and free with his praise and seemed confident the book would offend no one. He even wrote a long letter in his own hand[2] giving the author assurance that the *Profession of Faith* would win wide acceptance. Perhaps Malesherbes and other liberals in his circle visualized themselves as poised on the crest of a new wave of enlightenment that would soon sweep all France before it. True, Rousseau had, in the

Prince de Conti, a powerful protector, and Mme de Boufflers showed a tender solicitude for his welfare. While their relationship had lost some of its intimacy, the "divine countess" was still enthusiastic in her praise of his virtue and his philosophy. At the moment, however, she was deeply involved with a new source of moral stimulation: David Hume. Having introduced herself to him as a woman who loved reading and who admired his work, she invited him to stay with her when he visited France. Hume, shy at first, soon succumbed to her charm. Suddenly, she was struck by the thought that her two philosophers should get to know each other. Always an admirer of England and English freedom, she saw Hume as an ideal protector for the embattled Rousseau. She wrote to him at once, telling him that she was advising Rousseau to seek sanctuary in England.[3]

II

It was not long before Rousseau began to sense a change in the atmosphere around him. The enthusiasm of his friends for the published version of *Emile* seemed rather restrained. Mme de Boufflers was generous with her compliments, but asked Rousseau to return her letter, and he noted that D'Alembert had failed to sign his. But most mysterious of all, M. de Luxembourg asked for the return of all Malesherbes' letters concerning *Emile*. Nevertheless, the book was now a reality, and Rousseau stood ready to face the verdict of his fellowman.

This verdict was not long in coming. On June 3, 1762, *Emile* was confiscated by the police. A few days later, Gervais, a prominent theologian at the Sorbonne, denounced the book and that same afternoon, the Abbé Jean-François Martin sent word to M. de Luxembourg that Rousseau was in serious trouble with Parlement. On June 9 Parlement condemned *Emile* on the grounds that it was an affront to religion and issued an order for Rousseau's arrest. In France it has always been considered unfortunate if a man of prominence has to be apprehended by the police. Every effort is made to induce him to flee the country on his own accord. In the tumultuous times surrounding the publication of *Emile*, the public officials were particularly concerned to silence controversial ideas without, at the same time, rousing the restive citizens. The public trial and punishment of Rousseau would have produced a tempest of such proportions that no one cared to contemplate it. Word was leaked to Malesherbes and the Luxembourgs from a variety of sources. It was expected that Rousseau would be given sufficient warning to avoid the slow machinery of justice. France could ill afford a martyr to truth at this moment in her history.

Rousseau saw things rather differently. The sacrifice of his freedom, even his life, might serve to give his ideas more recognition. He had suffered enough from his acute social sensitivity to feel that the society of man had little more to offer him. He was in constant physical pain. Once his book was published, he refused to take alarm, although he received hints and suggestions from a number of people that his ideas on religion would bring him trouble. One magistrate was reputed to have said that burning such books was not sufficient, that it was the author who should be burned. At first he laughed at these remarks, suspecting the Holbach clique of spreading rumors in order to drive him out of the country. But when M. de Luxembourg began to bring him tales of the controversy he had created and told him that he might be in danger, he took his friend's remarks more seriously.

However, there was still a vast and unrecognized misunderstanding between Rousseau and his friends. To the majority of people in his time friendship meant a liking for someone, a willingness to confide, advise, share a mistress and, perhaps in special cases, loan money without interest. But Rousseau expected his friends to die for him, and in all fairness it should be said that he would have been willing to die for them if they had offered him the opportunity. He remarks in his *Confessions* that while he was upset by the circulating rumors, he felt that he had M. de Malesherbes and Mme de Luxembourg between himself and his enemies and that these good people would defend him. His friends, on the other hand, felt he should recognize the danger in which he placed them by remaining in France. Finally, Mme de Boufflers took him aside to explain that if arrested and interrogated he would be forced to disclose the role of Mme de Luxembourg and Malesherbes in the publication of *Emile* and that if he had any gratitude to his friends he would leave the country. She suggested England and offered him a refuge with Hume. He was impressed by her remarks, but hesitated. He had never cared for the climate of England or its people.

When the letter from Martin arrived, warning of prosecution by Parlement, Rousseau dismissed it as another Holbachian trick. When Guy, the partner of Duchesne, told him that he had personally seen on the desk of the chief prosecutor a rough draft of a summons against *Emile* and its author, he was still skeptical.

> Feeling sure that there was some mystery behind all this that no one would tell me, I quietly awaited the course of events, having confidence in my uprightness and my innocence throughout this affair, and being only too happy, no matter what persecution might await me, to be called to the honor of suffering for truth.[4]

An urge to martyrdom was clearly a factor in this behavior. But there was another reason for this apparent obtuseness on his part. He had long been annoyed by the grand manner of Mme de Luxembourg. She had been attending all her social affairs with her usual assurance and gaiety while he was being warned of impending disaster. Mme de Boufflers had pointed out the danger faced by his benefactress, but he was not one to be convinced by facts. Unless she would humble herself before him with some real show of feeling, he was determined to wait her out. A woman in tears was to him one of the most attractive and charming sights, and he would not miss it for all the police in the kingdom of France.

On June 8, the day before the warrant was issued, Rousseau had a picnic with two Oratorian professors, the three of them sucking wine from a bottle with rye stalks and having a gay time. He retired and was dozing and reading into the morning hours when La Roche burst in on him with a message from Mme de Luxembourg and a letter from the Prince de Conti. The latter gave assurance that he would not be pursued if he made his escape, but warned that if he persisted in courting arrest the police would certainly take him. La Roche told him that Mme de Luxembourg had not gone to bed and was waiting to see him. Rousseau describes their encounter as follows:

> For the first time she appeared to be upset. Her anxiety touched me. In this moment of surprise in the middle of the night I was not free from emotion myself. But when I saw her I forgot myself and thought only of her and the sad part that she would have to play if I let myself be taken. For, while I felt I had enough courage to tell nothing but the truth even if it should injure or ruin me, I did not feel I had enough presence of mind, or shrewdness, nor perhaps even enough firmness to avoid compromising her if I were hard pressed. This decided me to sacrifice my honor to her peace of mind and to do for her, on this occasion, what nothing could have induced me to do for myself.[5]

There she was before him at last, at his mercy, and by a magnanimous sacrifice he would save her. The crucial moment had arrived, the time for the dramatic and tearful farewell. She would be forever grateful, and he would leave, mindful that he had given up his greatest treasure, his chance for martyrdom, to preserve her peace of mind.

But somehow Mme de Luxemburg muffed her lines. She felt that he was only doing what any sensible man would do when faced with arrest. She not only failed to give him his cue for the noble farewell, but she did not seem to appreciate his sacrifice.

The instant I had made up my mind I told her my decision, not wishing to cheapen the value of my sacrifice by making her buy it. I am certain that she could not have mistaken my motive; however, she did not say a word to me to show that she was grateful. I was so shocked at her indifference that I even considered retracting my offer, but the Marshall came in and Mme de Boufflers arrived from Paris a few moments later. They did what Mme de Luxembourg should have done. I allowed myself to be flattered; I was too ashamed to take back what I had said, and it was now only a question of the place of my retreat and the time of my departure.[6]

The aura of a great friendship was now broken, and while the four of them discussed plans for the future safety of Rousseau there was bitterness in his heart. From this moment every gesture of his friends was interpreted in a new light. Did they really care, or were they only anxious to get rid of him? For Rousseau it must be an unreserved love or nothing at all. The thought that their fears for him might be colored by some concern for their own personal safety was intolerable.

Only Thérèse played the role expected of her. She was brought to the Château by La Roche, and she thought that her lover had already departed. When she saw him she uttered a cry and threw herself into his arms. As he embraced her Rousseau felt a premonition of the life which awaited him, and he told her, "My child, you must arm yourself with courage. You have shared the prosperity of my happy days. It now remains for you, since you wish it, to share my miseries. From now on expect nothing but insults and calamity for your loyalty. The fate that begins for me on this sad day will attend me till my last hour."[7] Thérèse remained behind to look after his possessions, and Rousseau, with the Marshal de Luxembourg at his side, prepared to depart. The two men walked across the garden, and Rousseau opened the gate with his key. Then, instead of returning it to his pocket, he handed it to the marshal. The latter took it with a promptness which surprised Rousseau and which he was not able to forget, so sensitive had he become to that haunting question in the back of his mind: were his friends *really* his friends; were they motivated by concern or contempt?

In his rumbling coach between La Barre and Montmorency, with his constricted urethra prodding him with pain, he passed the four officers who were sent to arrest him. They saluted him with smiles and passed on. He reflected on this masquerade, this little ruse that seemed to save his friends from embarrassment while it sent him out into an uncertain world. He reflected also that he had been told the warrant would be issued at seven A.M. and that it was now past noon. Instead of ascribing this discrepancy to administrative delay he began to fit it into the vast and complex picture which was forming in his mind. The world was filled with his enemies, and they had a strange and subtle way of influencing everyone, even his so-called friends, so that they fell in with the plans to ruin him. On this bizarre and tragicomic note Rousseau left the security of the Luxembourg estate to begin the long task of fulfilling the prophecy he made to Thérèse.

[10]

Persecution

I

THE "PLOT" which Rousseau saw forming around him has been the subject of considerable controversy, not only in his own time but long afterward. The Holbachians snickered about it, and many of Rousseau's biographers have described it as nothing more than the morbid supicions of a disturbed mind. On the other hand, Frederika MacDonald,[1] a champion of Rousseau and Rousseauism, has presented supporting evidence to implicate his enemies and many of his friends in a plot to destroy Rousseau's reputation and his sanity as well.

The atmosphere of plot and counterplot which surrounded him is shown in his voluminous correspondence. Many of his friends, out of a mistaken sense of loyalty to him, vied with each other to uncover plotters and bring him every morsel of gossip from Paris and Geneva. While the reports were generally true, there is a flavor, in many of these letters, of a *folie-à-deux*, a certain zeal for the ideas of Rousseau that borders on fanaticism.[2] There is no question that he was a victim of persecution. The question is, to what extent did he stimulate his tormentors and actively seek the role of "victim"? The evidence that he suffered from delusions of persecution is not related to the persecution itself, but to his peculiar interpretation of its cause. To Rousseau these attacks were not merely evidence of the pettiness of mankind, they revealed a dark plot to ruin him which reached international proportions. The usual disagreements and misunderstandings of social living, the reservations on the part of his friends toward the acceptance of his ideas, all these he incorporated into the plot. If he was charged too much for food, this was part of the whole plan. If he was charged too little, this was an effort to humiliate him and to imply that he could not support himself. He was wary of every friendly gift lest it prove a disguised attempt to seduce him from his virtuous austerity. He was, at times, so sensitive to the possible meaning of a gift that he was unable to offer a dignified refusal. It seemed as though he was tortured by a tidbit placed in front of him. D'Ivernois, a Genevan admirer, plagued him beyond endurance with little gifts which he could

179

hardly refuse but which came so frequently that he felt compelled to put a stop to them. On December 29, 1764, he gave vent to a mounting anger that should have discouraged the most stout benefactor.

> The cheese you sent me will be distributed in your name to your family. The case of wine of Lavaux that you announce to me will not be received unless you will accept payment for it. Otherwise it will all remain with M. d'Ivernois. I thought you would pay some attention to what we agreed upon. Since you will not, I must handle the matter myself from now on; and I swear that I commence to fear that your approach to me will produce a rupture between us which will grieve me very much.[3]

But D'Ivernois persisted, limiting his gifts to simple products of his garden and often sending them in the name of his wife. In August 1765 Rousseau complained of a shipment of apricots and again threatened to break with D'Ivernois. In December there is only a curt reference to prunes: "I have other prunes to digest, therefore dispose of yours elsewhere."[4]

In such a manner, Rousseau set the stage on which he was to play the role of a virtuous victim. The plot became an explanation of all his problems, all his personal disagreements. The estrangement of his early friends was now clearly part of a prearranged plan, and he need not concern himself with the thought that he might have offended them or perhaps have been unjust to them.

He had always been sensitive and quick to take offense—socially unsure of himself and fearful that others might be laughing at him. But not until his departure from Montmorency and his period of flight and persecution did he lose his grip on reality and begin to see a phantom army of conspirators plotting to destroy him. In such a state it would be easy to imagine him deteriorating rapidly and ending his life in suicide or in a mental institution. But such was not the case. Rousseau continued to see his friends and entertain them. Letters from such people as Boswell and Hume (before their quarrel) are filled with comments about his sociability and personal charm. He continued to be a salty, testy personality, but he failed to present the classic picture of the "madman" with foaming mouth and wild eyes. Fond of describing his sensitivity and his delicacy, he proved to have sources of strength that few had suspected. Further, he had friends and correspondents who admired his ideas. Social reformers and revolutionists sent him letters of praise and asked his help. Some of his friends, out of the intensity of their devotion, even shared his delusion. Thus, his failing ego received the support he so desperately needed.

II

On June 14, 1762, he arrived in Yverdun in the canton of Bern. His friends welcomed him and urged him to stay. However, Moultou sent word from Geneva that his books had been condemned and burned by order of the city council and a warrant issued for his arrest. This proved a foretaste of what was to follow, for the canton of Bern soon took a similar action, and Rousseau was forced to flee to Motiers in the Val-de-Travers, then part of the domain of Frederick of Prussia. Rousseau was no admirer of Frederick, but he wrote to the monarch with his characteristic boldness.

> . . . I have said much ill of you. Perhaps I shall still say more. Yet, driven from France, from Geneva, from the canton of Bern, I am come to seek refuge in your states. Perhaps I was wrong in not beginning there. This is a eulogy of which you are worthy. Sire, I have deserved no grace from you, and I seek none, but I thought it my duty to inform your majesty that I am in your power, and that I have willed it thus. Your majesty will dispose of me as it pleases you.[5]

Frederick instructed his local governor, George Keith, earl marischal of Scotland, to provide Rousseau with a small hermitage, a garden, firewood, flour, and whatever necessities he required. Rousseau accepted the king's offer of refuge, but declined his gifts on the grounds that, since he was of no use to Frederick, he could not justify accepting support from him.

His relationship with his new protector established, Rousseau settled in a small cottage in Motiers and sent for Thérèse. Milord Marischal soon became his close friend, and the two of them spent many evenings together at Colombier, Keith's summer retreat. This friendship proved to be the precursor of a liaison with another famous Scot—one which was to have disastrous consequences for Rousseau's peace of mind. Milord Marischal frequently wrote to his friend David Hume, describing Rousseau's amiable ways and his gay sociability and suggesting that the three of them could make a great trio if Rousseau could be induced to return with him to Scotland. Hume, who had already heard much of Rousseau through Mme de Boufflers, became interested in providing a refuge for this republican.

But Rousseau, who believed he had found a measure of acceptance at Motiers, was quite content to answer his voluminous mail and botanize in the Val-de-Travers. Since it was the practice, at this time, for the recipient of mail to pay the postage, and since a good portion of his mail was from anonymous cranks who sought to vent their anger at his works, he found correspondence a trying occupation and a considerable financial strain. However, his mail was the one means of contact with his many friends. He learned that Voltaire, who was still smarting from his *Letter to d'Alembert*, had been instrumental in arousing the Genevans against *Emile* and that the firebrand De Luc had taken up the counterattack. He learned, also from Moultou, that the erratic and changeable Voltaire wished to be reconciled with him (but he did not hear it from Voltaire). He felt he had completed his major works and wished to retire from the field of literary controversy. Having consulted with the local pastor, Montmollin, he attended Protestant church services in Motiers. Soon he learned to knit and would sit before his door making laces. His urethral complaint required constant attention and the frequent use of a probe. To facilitate this operation and to ease his own personal comfort, he adopted an Armenian costume with flowing robe and furred hat. Gradually, the townspeople began to take note of this eccentric in their midst who knitted laces like a woman and dressed like an Armenian. They had heard he was an heretic with wild and unorthodox religious views, and several curiosity seekers came to call on him: some to listen politely, others to bait him.

On August 20, 1762, the archbishop of Paris, Christopher de Beaumont, issued a *Mandement* in which he attacked not only the substance of *Emile* but the behavior and morals of its author. Rousseau gathered his forces for a reply. He was truly at his best when he became the victim of a clear and certain injustice. In his *Letter to Christopher de Beaumont*, which he finished in a few months, he picked out the points of his opponent's attack and turned them back against him with a brilliant lucidity and force reminiscent of his *Letter on French Music*.

But Rousseau had started too many conflagrations to be able to relax after he had dispatched the archbishop of Paris. Ever since his *Letter to d'Alembert* he had been the hero of the burghers of Geneva. These people had long been restive under the aristocratic control of the Small Council of Twenty-Five and the Council of Two Hundred, who cooperated with each other in perpetuating the rule of certain select families in Geneva. Rousseau, by his writings on equality and by his condemnation of the proposal for a theater in Geneva, an aristocratic enterprise, had endeared himself to the burghers. After his works were burned and a decree was issued for his arrest, he resigned his Genevan citizenship in a dramatic gesture. When the burghers heard of this they were outraged at the persecution of their hero and demanded action. Finally, De Luc, D'Ivernois, and forty other citizens submitted a "representation," or protest, to the Syndics claiming that the affair of Rousseau should be submitted to a town meeting of burghers and citizens assembled. When this representation was reviewed by the Small Council, they simply declined to pass it on to the General Council, claiming their *droit négatif*—the right to veto any representation sent to them. The whole argument was broadened, and the *droit négatif* became the issue for further representations. The problem passed from injustice done Rousseau to the long-standing injustices suffered by the burghers at the hands of the aristocracy. Eventually, a party called the *Representants* developed, the object of which was to nullify the *droit négatif*. Soon the burghers were talking of revolution.

At this point J. R. Tronchin, procurer-general of Geneva, set forth the aristocratic position in September 1763, in his *Letters from the Country*, a carefully reasoned argument based on the constitution. De Luc and his friends were at a loss as to how to counter Tronchin's erudition. A letter was sent to Rousseau urging him to "avenge these precious virtues so subtly and fraudently attacked."[6] Rousseau protested that he was weary of public controversy, that he longed for a few moments of leisure, that he knew nothing of the constitution or history of Geneva. De Luc replied that he would supply all the factual information required, but that Rousseau's eloquence was absolutely necessary to their cause. Flattered by De Luc's need for him, he began the long and arduous task of preparing his answer to Tronchin.

During the entire period, in which he was arranging his notes and consulting with De Luc and his friends, Rousseau received a stream of visitors and countless letters praising him, asking advice, or attacking him as a menace to organized society. The Prince of Wurtemberg besieged the author of *Emile* for detailed and specific advice on the rearing of his daughter (from the age of four months). He responded to Rousseau's sharp criticism with a patience and mildness unusual for one of his status; however, he also sent a flock of German visitors to add to the growing crowd waiting to see this king of virtue. Rousseau, whose only throne was a chamber pot and who was in almost constant pain, was beginning to grow weary of his title. He was a man who never had much time for casual visitors. He enjoyed his close friends, but had no use for that frequent village occupation of establishing one's position in the community.

With an international reputation as the champion of the underdog, it was not long before another worthy cause was presented before his roving mind. Inspired by the valiant struggle of General Paoli's revolutionary army in Corsica against the rule of Genoa and delighted by their victory in 1755, Rousseau had written in his *Social Contract* that there was still one country in Europe capable of legislation: the island of Corsica.[7] In August 1764, Buttafuoco, a French officer and Corsican by birth, began a correspondence with Rousseau. Buttafuoco, a friend of General Paoli, asked him if he would prepare a plan of political institutions for Corsica.[8] Rousseau was flattered by this request and asked for full information on the history and political situation of Corsica. He determined that as soon as he had finished his reply to Tronchin he would establish a residence on the island for a year or two to investigate its history and its people in detail. Then he would have the first opportunity to put his principles into practice, an opportunity seldom granted to political theorists.

The Holbachians were furious when they heard that the renegade philosopher was involved in the preparation of laws for Corsica—a little country that had become the symbol of liberty for all Europe. In his *Literary Correspondence* Grimm soon spread the rumor that the Corsicans had been writing to all the philosophers of Europe for help in their laws (an assertion that was untrue). He later remarked that the request from Corsica was an attempt to make fun of Rousseau.[9] Needless to say, all of these criticisms reached Rousseau and roused his suspicions regarding the motives behind the Corsican project. The mere suggestion that he might be a source of amusement for some clever fellow was enough to terrify this sensitive philosopher.[10]

In November 1764 Rousseau published his *Letters from the Mountain* in which he defended *Emile* and questioned the authority of the church of Geneva. He described the process by which the Genevans had lost control of their destiny and how the Syndics had risen to such power that they were able to silence all opposition with a veto. It was a lengthy and reasoned defense. He had a brief opportunity to relax before the new storm of protest was generated. His plan for Corsica received some attention, but the greater part of his time was spent with his extensive correspondence and the care of his urethral complaint, which had assumed the proportions of a serious illness.

Despite his condition he still had many callers, so many indeed that the majority had to be turned away without an audience. One of the fortunate few privileged to see him at this time was James Boswell, who had just left his idol, Dr. Johnson, in London, and was out to see the world. With his knack for recording conversations in detail, Boswell has presented one of the most picturesque accounts of Rousseau during this period. Boswell was twenty-four at the time and had wangled a letter of introduction from Rousseau's good friend, George Keith. His infectious, puppy-dog charm made him an agreeable com-

panion to Rousseau, who was threatened only by adults. Boswell left
with an admiration for the natural man which was to withstand even
the mighty assault of Dr. Johnson's withering criticism. After several
visits Boswell composed a story of his life and left it with Rousseau
to read. Then he returned asking for advice. Rousseau told him he
could advise no one, that he, too, had done much evil, but that the
only remedy for evil was to determine to do good to compensate for
it. The following are a few excerpts from Boswell's account of his
visits:

Wednesday, December 5, 1764.

. . . Boswell. "But what do you think of cloisters, penances, and
remedies of that sort?" Rousseau. "Mummeries, all of them, invented by men. Do not be guided by men's judgments or you
will find yourself tossed to and fro perpetually. Do not base your
life on the judgments of others; first, because they are as likely
to be mistaken as you are, and further, because you cannot know
that they are telling you their true thoughts; they may be im-
pelled by motives of interest or convention to talk to you in a
way not corresponding to what they really think." Boswell. "Will
you, Sir, assume direction of me?" Rousseau. "I cannot. I can be
responsible only for myself." Boswell. "But I shall come back."
Rousseau. "I don't promise to see you. I am in pain. I need a
chamber pot every minute." Boswell. "Yes, you will see me."
Rousseau. "Be off; and a good journey to you." (p. 231)

Friday, December 14, 1764.

". . . Come back in the afternoon. Put your watch on the table."
Boswell. "For how long?" Rousseau. "A quarter of an hour, and
no longer." Boswell. "Twenty minutes." Rousseau. "Be off with
you!—Ha! Ha!" Notwithstanding the pain he was in, he was
touched with my singular sally and laughed most really. He had
a gay look immediately. (p. 253)

Saturday, December 15, 1764.

. . . We had red and white wines. It was a simple, good repast.
We were quite at our ease. I sometimes forgot myself and became ceremonious. "May I help you to some of this dish?"
Rousseau. "No, Sir. I can help myself to it." Or, "May I help
myself to some more of that?" Rousseau. "Is your arm long
enough? A man does the honours of his house from a motive of
vanity. He does not want it forgotten who is the master. I should

like every one to be his own master, and no one to play the part of host." (p. 259)

The departure of Boswell.

> . . . Monsieur Rousseau embraced me. He was quite the tender Saint-Preux. He kissed me several times, and held me in his arms with elegant cordiality. Oh I shall never forget that I have been thus. Rousseau. "Good-bye. You are a fine fellow." Boswell. "You have shown me great goodness. But I deserved it." Rousseau. "Yes. You are malicious; but 'tis a pleasant malice, a malice I don't dislike. Write and tell me how you are." . . . Boswell. "Good-bye. If you live for seven years, I shall return to Switzerland from Scotland to see you." Rousseau. "Do so. We shall be old acquaintances." Boswell. "One word more. Can I feel sure that I am held to you by a thread, even if of the finest? By a hair?" (Seizing a hair of my head.) Rousseau. "Yes. Remember always that there are points at which our souls are bound." Boswell. "It is enough. I, with my melancholy, I who often look on myself as a despicable being, as a good-for-nothing creature who should make his exit from life—I shall be upheld for ever by the thought that I am bound to Monsieur Rousseau. Good-bye. Bravo! I shall live to the end of my days." Rousseau. "That is undoubtedly a thing one must do. Good-bye."[11] (pp. 264-65)

III

By the end of November 1764 the interested parties had had an opportunity to digest *The Letters from the Mountain* and the reaction was beginning to grow. Even Rousseau, who had prepared himself for the next move of the hidden army of conspirators, was surprised at its violence and extent. On December 31 he received a pamphlet entitled *The Sentiment of the Citizens*, calling for his punishment by death and describing him as a man who still retained the disfiguring marks of his debaucheries.[12] Rousseau was horrified to read that he had permitted Thérèse's mother to die of neglect while he dragged her from village to village—she was still living—and to discover a host of other crimes of which he was accused, including fomenting sedition and blasphemy against the church.[13] By the style of this pious and rather plodding pamphlet the author clearly identified himself as a citizen of Geneva.[14] Rousseau was convinced that the writer could be none other than Vernes, a pastor of Geneva who had become his enemy. Frustrated by this scandalmonger who refused to identify himself, he had the pamphlet republished with his own point-by-point denials and publicly accused Vernes of being its author. Vernes heatedly denied any knowledge of the work, and his protests were so forceful that Rousseau suppressed a second edition, but he never could bring himself to admit that he had been mistaken.

The true author of the pamphlet was Voltaire, a man Rousseau would never have suspected because of the clumsy style and pious tone of the accusations. This eagle of the literary world had been incensed by Rousseau's casual announcement (in his fifth *Letter*) that Voltaire was the author of the notorious *Sermon of the Fifty*, a fact known by everyone, and which Rousseau, who signed all his works, could not have thought much of a revelation. Voltaire, however, regarded this disclosure as a gross betrayal and a threat to his security.[15] He was determined to hound Rousseau out of society, and he carefully prepared his scurrilous pamphlet in a style which, for once, would not reveal the author's identity. The *Sentiment of the Citizens* was followed by a series of other attacks on Rousseau and his work. The *Letters* were burned at The Hague and condemned by the Council of Geneva. In Paris they were burned with Voltaire's *Philosophical Dictionary*,[16] although the presence of Voltaire's work in the same conflagration with his own did not serve to bring the warring philosophers together.

Rousseau brought a copy of his *Letters from the Mountain* to his pastor, Montmollin, and the latter read it without apparent offense, thanking him for the gift.[17] The relationship between Rousseau and his pastor had been excellent ever since Montmollin had accepted him into his church over the protests of some of the local citizens. After the publication of the *Letters* the public outcry against Rousseau began to mount, and the pastors in Neuchâtel and Geneva began to bring pressure on Montmollin for harboring this heretic in his church. The latter, although a liberal thinker, apparently lacked the fortitude to back up his views, for he soon began to yield to the influence of the *Venerable Class*.[18] Finally, he asked Rousseau to refrain from attending church services. Rousseau insisted on attending on the grounds that only the Consistory could cast him out. Montmollin, now thoroughly incensed at Rousseau's recalcitrance, summoned him to appear before the Consistory to explain why he should not be excommunicated.

Thus, Rousseau found himself at another point in life where the ready wit of Voltaire would have served him well. Conscious of his own inadequacy in verbal exchange, he tried to memorize the points of his defense. On the night before he was to appear he knew them by heart, but by the next morning they had all evaporated and he stumbled over the first sentence. In a fit of anxiety he wrote to the Consistory, summarizing his defense and offering the excuse of his ailments for his failure to attend the hearing. Montmollin had all the weapons in his battle with Rousseau.

Somehow, the excommunication did not quite come off. Rousseau seems to have had sufficient friends among the elders of the church to stay the final order, and Montmollin was reduced to ranting from the pulpit against his rebel parishioner and stirring up feeling against him among the peasants.

IV

In his relationship with the citizens of Motiers Rousseau was placed at a disadvantage by the presence of Thérèse. She had become quarrelsome and raw tempered, given to frequent pulls at the brandy bottle. Rousseau's urethral condition precluded any further sexual intimacy, and the close personal confidence between them had long ago faded to a casual nurse-patient arrangement. In view of the situation it is not surprising that Thérèse could find little significance remaining in her life with Rousseau.[19] She seems to have released much of her pent-up feelings of frustration in trivial quarrels with the peasants in Val-de-Travers. Her disputes with the villagers had already prepared a general atmosphere of animosity toward the Rousseau household, and the citizens did not require much encouragement to increase their displeasure. When their pastor began to tell them that this man with the ill-natured mistress was also a menace to society and a blasphemer against God, they had all the excuse they needed for open and concerted aggression. Soon Rousseau was jeered at and insulted in the street. Stones were thrown at his house. When on a botanizing expedition in the woods he was often pelted with small missiles. The remarks about his blasphemy and his Armenian costume were accompanied by threats against his life, and on one occasion when he passed a house he heard a man say, "Bring me my gun so I can shoot at him."[20] While a frightened and imaginative man can frequently construe threats out of a mere mumble of words, there is no question that the citizens were incensed against him and attacked him on more than one occasion.

Although his relationship wth Thérèse was accompanied by much argument, she never became, in his mind, part of the conspiracy against him. In spite of the disagreeable pettiness she manifested with others, he did not utter a word against her in his *Confessions* or in letters during this period. It may be that the pressures against them both were so severe that they were forced to share each other's problems. Thérèse was never able to determine the point where the persecutors left off their attacks and Rousseau's delusions began. He, for his part, tended to interpret all her quarrels with servants and peasants in her favor. He assumed that the incidents she created were thrust upon her by the conspirators in order to injure him.

He was awakened one night by a hail of pebbles thrown against his window. He was about to enter the kitchen from his room when a large stone smashed the kitchen window and broke open the door of his bedroom. His dog, Sultan, who slept in a room at the back of the house, was so terrified that he ran into a corner and began to claw the wall in an effort to escape. Thérèse, also aroused, ran to him trembling. It was later discovered that someone had tried to force a way into the house that night.[21] Rousseau and Thérèse were profoundly disturbed by this experience, not so much from the physical harm done, which was negligible, but from the awareness of so much hatred directed against them.[22] Despite the offer of protection from the mayor, Rousseau determined to leave. After a hurried consultation it was decided that Thérèse would be safe once the primary object of the conspirators had left Val-de-Travers. Rousseau set out alone for the island of Saint-Pierre, where Thérèse soon joined him with his belongings. He had been charmed by the island on a previous visit and now found that this beautiful memory was illumined with an even more perfect reality. Here was a spot where he could rove about, botanizing at his leisure, and prepare his constitution for Corsica, a project temporarily abandoned under the pressure of the persecution against him in Motiers. For a little more than a month he spent his mornings writing and his afternoons drifting in a boat or wandering in the woods with Sultan. It was a delicious period of tranquility that he was to remember for the rest of his life.

But the island of Saint-Pierre was part of the territory of Bern, the government of which had expelled him three years before. During the fall recess, a meeting was convened to give him notice that he must leave the island. Rousseau was already in a state of agitation, and soon other news arrived to drive him to the edge of despair. He learned that France, a country he loved with an unexplainable passion, had made a treaty with Genoa and was sending troops to Corsica to help the Genoese put down the revolution. His health was failing, he was hounded from place to place, and now the one little nation that had taken pride in his compliments and asked his help was being crushed by insurmountable odds. It seemed that his whole world was dissolving. Suspicions about Buttafuoco's sincerity had already troubled his work. Now, with the intervention of the French, he wondered where this French officer and native Corsican would find his true loyalty.[23] These doubts were too much for his troubled mind, and he gradually abandoned interest in Corsica.

V

Admittedly, the project of a *Constitution for Corsica* was a nebulous and ill-conceived arrangement from the beginning. Rousseau had found it difficult to determine just what was wanted. Buttafuoco had stressed Corsica's need for a "legislator" but asked for a plan of a political system. When Rousseau requested clarification, his correspondent, apparently in a fever to please him, suggested that Rousseau in his infinite wisdom would be able to tell what was needed. Did Buttafuoco want a complete body of legislation, or did the Corsicans already have a body of civil laws? Yes, said Buttafuoco, there was a body of civil laws, but it would be better to rewrite them all in accord with the new system, yet he did not want to be so indiscreet as to demand too much of the sage's good will. Rousseau was cautious; such a task would take time, and he would have to be satisfied with it himself before he turned it over to the Corsicans. He could not send it piecemeal; it must be an integrated system of interdependent laws. But the Corsicans could not continue for two or three years without any permanent legislation. They must have something to guide them. Ah yes, remarked Buttafuoco, Rousseau understood so well how important it was that the constitution be made firm immediately. Of course Rousseau must be content with his own work before it was released, and the Corsican leaders had confidence in his zeal and enthusiasm for the task. However, without meaning to press his legislator, Buttafuoco wondered if he could throw together a few general principles for a starter.

As one reads these letters[24] it becomes apparent that Buttafuoco was impressed by Rousseau's reputation as a man of virtue and political enlightenment; that he hoped to gain stature for the Corsican cause, and perhaps for himself, by associating Rousseau's name with Corsica; that he had no appreciation for the complicated problem of providing a comprehensive system of legislation; that he would be satisfied with almost any morsel of wisdom from the great man provided Rousseau signed his illustrious name to it. Rousseau, for his part, must have reflected that he had had little correspondence with General Paoli, the real authority in Corsica, and that he might spend three years or more providing an elaborate system of legislation which the Corsicans were under no obligation to accept. Harassed by the gibes of Voltaire and the taunts of the Holbachians, chased from one abode to another by hostile governments, exhausted by physical illness, he did not have the strength to continue his task. Further, he was assailed by growing doubts about himself and his reputation for virtue. He needed to turn away from the world and look inward at the problems of personal morality which had begun to haunt him again. The *Sentiment of the Citizens* still disturbed him, and he was determined to tell the truth about himself: a truth so revealing and so completely honest that there would be nothing more to expose. He had already begun his *Confessions* when he wrote to Buttafuoco in May 1765 that he must devote his attention to himself and that, if able, he would use his remaining time in the interests of Corsica. Soon this last fragment of interest was replaced by his involvement in his own life.

VI

During the period of persecution at Motiers and after his departure from Saint-Pierre, he received letters from friends everywhere offering refuge: his pupil, the Prince of Wurtemberg, Mme d'Houdetot, Saint-Lambert, and Rey, his publisher. But his greatest friend George Keith, with whom he had hoped to live, had accepted Frederick's offer of a residence in Berlin. Keith advised him to seek refuge with David Hume in England. The Duchess of Saxe-Gotha invited him to call on her. She received Grimm's *Literary Correspondence*, but she did not easily accept the authority of this self-appointed royal literary critic. She admired Rousseau and wished to entertain him.

Rousseau, after days of consternation and indecision, decided to go to Berlin. He got as far as Strasbourg, where he remained for another month in the adulation of a host of new-found friends and admirers, but at the end of November he felt the icy blast of winter and decided against Berlin. He paused, he hesitated. Mme de Boufflers had left off her pursuit of David Hume to plunge with renewed zeal after the Prince de Conti, whom she hoped to marry now that her husband had died (in 1764). She still retained an affection for *le bon David*, and she urged the two philosophers toward each other. Hume wrote several flattering letters to Rousseau. Mme de Verdelin, who had once opposed the Countess de Boufflers in her enthusiasm for Hume, had now joined those who were praising the Scottish philosopher. She offered to use her influence and that of her friends to obtain a passport to England. The ever-loyal Prince de Conti offered him a sanctuary in the Temple on his way through Paris, Finally, the opinion and the inducements offered by his friends convinced him. He would go to England to find at last the solitude and peace for which he so desperately yearned. Yet England was a strange land with an unknown tongue. He was both attracted and repelled as he set out from Strasbourg. On December 4, 1765, he wrote to Hume that he would leave Strasbourg in four or five days to "throw myself in your arms."[25]

[11]

England

I

THE RAGE FOR ENGLAND, which Rousseau found among his friends, was part of the rising climate of French feeling in the eighteenth century. The corruption and decay of the old régime, subtly apparent to so many for so long, had now been made manifest by the Peace of Paris in 1763. The treaty was a humiliating conclusion to the Seven Years' War in which France had exhausted her strength in a long battle with Prussia, while England routed the French fleet at sea. France came out of the war stripped of almost all her colonies. England had clearly established an empire on which the sun would not set.

Respect for England among the French nobility was one of the more polite forms of defiance of the decadent French king and his mistress whose intrigues were regarded as the source not only of the war but of its tragic outcome. The Prince de Conti, after his defeat at court by Mme de Pompadour, formed the nucleus of one of the principal sources of opposition to Louis among the nobility, causing the king to refer to him as "my cousin the advocate." France was being pulled apart by faction, intrigue, and a growing spirit of unrest among the intellectuals and the nobility. England, on the other hand, was regarded as coming into her granduer. Voltaire's *Philosophical Letters on the English* was enthusiastically received in Paris. The salon of Mme de Boufflers and the Prince de Conti was famous for its English atmosphere—the latest books from across the Channel were served up there with English tea and conversation about the new freedom to be found in that nation. Some were even bold enough to suggest that the rise of England as a world power might be due to the opportunities and the open expression of opinion enjoyed by her citizens.

As an expositor of English thought, Hume had become a popular figure in Paris. A personal representative of the English ambassador from 1763-65, he had been entertained by the first families in France and treated to the compliments of the men and the adulation of the ladies of the French court. A quiet, rather plump, mild-mannered bachelor, Hume, because of his Scottish origin, had never been popular in England, and he enjoyed this public recognition. While he complained of the strain of receiving so many compliments, his letters to his friends indicate that he felt he had, at last, found a nation that showed a proper respect for genius. In the two years before he met Rousseau he made the rounds of the Paris salons and minor literary circles. He became friendly with the Holbach circle. He soaked up the enthusiasms and the gossip of Paris until he was thoroughly and pleasantly fatigued. Now it was time to return and establish himself again in Scotland or England. The initial intensity of his love for the Countess de Boufflers had begun to fade before her ambition to marry the Prince de Conti. With a certain sadness mingled with his customary calm resignation, he was prepared to endure, but not to love England once again.

II

As seen in the preceding chapter Rousseau and Hume were not drawn to one another, but pushed toward one another by the enthusiasm of their mutual friends. Hume was sympathetic to all who were persecuted, but he had no particular interest in meeting Rousseau until the Countess de Boufflers enlisted him in the cause. His sympathy for Rousseau's plight was genuine, and he regarded him as one of the first men of letters in France; however, he felt there was a certain extravagance about Rousseau's style, and his friends in the Holbach circle had warned him about the prickly character of that solitary.

Rousseau, for his part, had read none of Hume's works. His knowledge of his benefactor was limited to the discourse of Mme de Boufflers on the noble character of the man. He was also influenced by the close friendship of Hume with George Keith, whom he revered as a father. As a man of sentiment he intuitively distrusted the reputed coldness of the English character, in spite of that country's reputation as a land of freedom. But he felt pushed into a corner. It was either England or Berlin and, with the approach of winter and the clamor of his friends, England seemed the best alternative.

He set out by coach for Paris and arrived there December 16, 1765, with his dog Sultan. After a brief stay at the home of Mme Duchaine, a bookseller, he moved to the Temple of the Prince de Conti. With men of good will much can be accomplished, and Rousseau and Hume, despite the differences in their character, had determined they would like each other. When at last they met, Hume, still haunted by the warnings of the Holbachians, was greatly relieved to find his reputed hermit to be a friendly and sociable human being. He was charmed by Rousseau's lively conversation, his simplicity, and his surprisingly agreeable temperament. He was profoundly impressed by the crowd of people who flocked to see this fugitive while an order for his arrest still circulated in Paris. Writing to the Reverend Hugh Blair, he remarked:

It is impossible to express or imagine the enthusiasm of this Nation in his favor. As I am supposed to have him in my custody, all the World, especially the great ladies, teaze me to be introduced to him: I have had Rouleaus[1] thrust into my hand, with earnest applications, that I would prevail on him to accept of them. I am persuaded that were I to open here a subscription with his consent, I should receive 50,000 pounds in a fortnight. The second day after his arrival, he slipped out early in the morning to take a walk in the Luxembourg Gardens. The thing was known soon after. I am strongly solicited to prevail on him to take another walk, and then to give warning to my friends: Were the public to be informed, he could not fail to have many thousand spectators. People may talk of ancient Greece as they please; but no nation was ever so fond of genius as this; and no person ever so much engaged their attention as Rousseau. Voltaire and everybody else, are quite eclipsed by him. I am sensible, that my Connexions with him, add to my importance at present.[2]

Continuing in the same letter, Hume gave one of the best portraits of Rousseau at this period, showing both his sociability and his fear of society, his spontaneous gaiety and his sudden changes of mood:

As to my Intercourse with him, I find him mild, and gentle and modest and good humoured; and he has more the Behaviour of a Man of the World than any of the Learned here, except M. de Buffon. . . . His modesty seems not to be good Manners; but ignorance of his own Excellence: As he writes and speaks and acts from the impulse of Genius, more than from the Use of his ordinary Faculties, it is very likely that he forgets its Force, whenever it is laid asleep. . . . I think Rousseau in many things very much resembles Socrates: The Philosopher of Geneva seems only to have more Genius than he of Athens. . . . I hear from all hands that his Judgment and Affections are as strongly byass'd in my favour as mine are in his: I shall much regret the leaving him in England. . . .

When he came to Paris, he seemed resolv'd to stay till the 6t or 7t of next month. But at present the Concourse about him gives him such Uneasiness, that he expresses the utmost Impatience to be gone. Many people here will have it that this solitary Humour is all affectation, in order to be more sought after; but I am sure that it is natural and unsurmountable. I know that two very agreeable Ladies breaking in upon him, discomposed him so much, that he was not able to eat his dinner afterwards. He is short sighted; and I have often observed, that while he was conversing with me in the outmost good humour (for he is naturally gay) if he heard the Door open, the greatest Agony appeared on his Countenance, from the Apprehension of a Visit, and his Distress did not leave him, unless the Person was a particular Friend.[3]

Embarrassment over his urethral complaint caused Rousseau to disguise as much as possible his frequent need for a chamber pot. But the pretense in front of the stream of visitors soon began to wear on him, and he sent an urgent letter to De Luze (who was to accompany the two philosophers to England) in Neuchâtel telling him he was no longer able to endure the spectacle in Paris and asking for an earlier departure date. De Luze consented, and the date was set for January 4, 1766. To throw off the curious and to avoid possible police intervention, an earlier date (January 2) was given out to the public. In two coaches (Rousseau accompanied by his trusty Sultan) the three travelers made a leisurely journey from Paris to Calais in four days. Hume, who had heard much of Rousseau's illness, expected frequent stops, but was surprised to discover that his friend's condition was very little in evidence. Delayed a day because of unfavorable winds, they sailed on the ninth, but experienced a rough crossing. As the boat began to pitch and roll Hume became grievously ill and staggered below deck to seek relief in his cabin, wondering at the same time how the frail health of Rousseau would survive this nightmare voyage. As he prepared to disembark the next morning, pale and shaken, he discovered his charge full of his usual vigor and good cheer. Fascinated by the fury of the elements, Rousseau had stayed on deck all night to enjoy the excitement while the seamen nearly froze to death. In a letter to Mme de Boufflers, Hume expressed his amazement at this sturdy constitution and reflected that he had seen little evidence of the supposed physical suffering of his friend.[4] For this remark he was scolded by the countess, who told him not to judge Rousseau's condition by the fact that he seldom complained.[5]

But the first seeds of suspicion had begun to grow in Hume's mind. He had visited the Baron d'Holbach the night before his departure and had been warned, once more, that Rousseau was a fraud. He reflected on the contrast between the gay, charming, healthy fellow and the picture of the persecuted saint which had been painted for him by the Countess de Boufflers. While still in Paris he had heard Horace Walpole entertain the company at Lord Ossory's table with an imaginary letter from the king of Prussia in which Rousseau's desire to suffer was held up to ridicule. Now he was somewhat unsettled. Like Rousseau, Hume was a man who did not really feel secure among the sophisticates of society. With his great bulk, his awkward French, and his direct and literal manner, he had frequently been the butt of jokes and clever little witticisms, the meaning of which often escaped him. He dreaded having someone make a fool of him. Perhaps he pictured the Holbachians back in Paris repeating his words of admiration for Rousseau and roaring with laughter over his naiveté.

Before crossing the Channel he had suggested to Rousseau the possibility of a pension from the king of England. Rousseau was not nearly so opposed to such an idea as he had been told. If his physical illness was a façade, perhaps he also feigned poverty in order to secure public sympathy and protection. Could he possibly have a great wad of funds in Paris or Geneva? If so, Hume's efforts to secure a pension made him look like a dupe. It was not too late, however, to salvage his reputation. The literary crowd in Paris would not think him such a fool if he were the first to expose the secret cache of this prince of virtue. While still professing a high regard for his friend, and continuing his efforts to obtain the pension, he began an investigation of Rousseau's financial condition.[6]

III

On arrival in London, Rousseau was immediately unsettled by the crowds and the many people who wished to talk with him, paint him, intercede with him, bait him, or just stare at him. He would have scorned them all for the quiet companionship of his dog, Sultan, but George III, who had already been approached on the matter of a pension, was one of those who wanted to have a look at this famous recluse. Mrs. Garrick of the Drury Lane Theatre proposed to seat Rousseau in her box so the king and queen might observe him during one of the performances, arranging with Hume to have his protégé at the theater at the appropriate time. But they had reckoned without the whim of Sultan, who almost became the first dog in history to deprive a king of his evening's entertainment. We had best let Hume tell this story himself:

> When the hour came, he (Rousseau) told me, that he had changed his resolution, and would not go: For—what shall I do with Sultan? That is the name of his dog. You must leave him behind, said I. But the first person, replied he, who opens the door,

Sultan will run into the streets in search of me, and will be lost. You must then, said I, lock him up in your room, and put the key in your pocket. This was accordingly done: But as we went downstairs, the dog howled and made a noise; his master turned back, and said he had not resolution to leave him in that condition; but I caught him in my arms and told him, that Mrs. Garrick had dismissed another company in order to make room for him; that the King and Queen were expecting to see him; and without a better reason than Sultan's impatience, it would be ridiculous to disappoint them. Partly by these reasons and partly by force, I engaged him to proceed. The King and Queen looked more at him than at the players.[7]

Soon Rousseau expressed a desire to get away from London—the more remote the location the better. His protector was at first reluctant and wished to settle him a few miles from the city, but Rousseau put so many conditions in the way of this prospect that it became impossible. Still Hume was cheerful. To Mme de Boufflers (January 19, 1766) he wrote, "My companion is very amiable, always polite, gay often, commonly sociable. He does not know himself when he thinks he is meant for solitude."[8] Gradually however, with Rousseau persisting in his desire for southern Wales or some place equally remote, Hume began to realize that his friend, in spite of his apparent amiability, had very definite ideas on where he wanted to live. He learned that Thérèse would soon arrive in London to complicate the problems of residence, and when he heard that her escort across the Channel was James Boswell he remarked to Mme de Boufflers, "I dread some event fatal to our friend's honour."[9] In this matter his fears were fully justified, but fortunately Boswell managed to keep quiet about this escapade until the publication of his *Journal*, a difficult task for a man who so loved to make known his intimate connections with famous people.

Hume had heard from De Luze that Thérèse was "wicked and quarrelsome, and tattling,"[10] that she was so dull she could not tell time nor reckon money, and that she governed Rousseau like a nurse with a patient. With her approach he became more concerned to settle his "pupil" as soon as possible. Several suggestions were made, but Rousseau, after accepting, frequently changed his mind. On February 12 Thérèse arrived. She was announced as his housekeeper, for it would not do that this man of virtue acknowledge a mistress. However, Rousseau would not have her treated as a housekeeper and insisted that all invitations issued to him should include her on an equal basis. This added a further complication to Hume's social plans for his friend. On February 16 he was still mentioning Rousseau's "singularities" as though they were marks of virtue, but in his letter to the Marquise de Barbentane he had settled on his opinion that Rousseau's physical illness was imaginary. Rousseau was "not insincere, but fanciful in that particular."[11]

During this period of growing doubt Hume, of course, kept his feelings to himself in the presence of Rousseau. But with someone so sensitive to the regard of others it was difficult to avoid the escape of some expression, some gesture or mark of indifference which might display his diminishing respect. Hume began to ask many detailed questions, particularly in regard to Rousseau's correspondence, probably in connection with his investigation of his friend's finances. He was unaware that his curiosity had begun to unnerve Rousseau. Finally, after having arranged to settle him at Wooton, an estate of Mr. Davenport in the north of England, he invited Rousseau and Thérèse to his lodgings on Lisle Street for dinner on March 18. Before the meal Hume expressed his curiosity about a letter Rousseau was writing and during the meal he noted that his friend was sulking and suspicious. Rousseau had interpreted Hume's remarks as a maneuver to gain possession of the letter. Sitting before the fire, Rousseau glanced in Hume's direction and noticed what he felt was a look of mockery. Hume, who had often been told he had a disconcerting stare and that he should try not to look so directly at people, was completely unaware of the havoc his gaze had provoked. He continued looking at Rousseau. The latter was filled with horror and felt a cold shudder run through him. He was forced to lower his gaze before that penetrating regard. Then, bursting into tears at the thought that Hume might be innocent, he rushed toward him and, throwing his arms around him, cried out, "No, David Hume is not a traitor; that is not possible. If he is not the best of men he must be the blackest." One can imagine the surprise and puzzlement of Hume in this situation. Calm and reserved by nature, completely unaware of the dark suspicions his questions had aroused, he could do no more than pat Rousseau gently on the back saying, "My dear Sir! What troubles you, my dear Sir"?[12] For a man of sentiment, such a bland response was far from satisfactory.[13] Why had Hume expressed no desire to know the reason for the accusation? Was it because he had no defense against the charge that he was a traitor? These were the thoughts which took root in Rousseau's mind as he settled in his solitary retreat at Wooton.

IV

Rousseau's outburst on Lisle Street was not a mere product of the events of the evening. Fearful and disturbed by years of persecution, possessive of his few remaining friends, he had become wary of defection and quick to observe any sign that a friend had grown weary of him. In the early months of his arrival he was full of gratitude to Hume and delighted with the English, whom he felt knew how to indicate their esteem without flattery. While he was fatigued by visits he was pleased to discover the high regard that seemed to exist for him throughout England. On January 18, in a letter to Mme de Boufflers, he mentioned having heard of a pretended letter from the king of Prussia, making sport of him. He was mildly disturbed by it, but decided not to inquire further.[14] However, on January 27, Du Peyrou wrote to him that the Prussian letter was making the rounds of Paris and that Horace Walpole was its author.[15] Walpole was a good friend of Hume, and Rousseau, knowing the letter to be a forgery, could not believe that someone so close to Hume could be part of the plot against him. He steadfastly refused to believe that Walpole had anything to do with it. On January 28, when Hume placed him temporarily at Chiswick, Rousseau began to brood on his friend's behavior. Already, Hume's interest in his mail was very much in evidence. He seemed insistent that Rousseau remain near London. Why? Was it not obvious that he desired only peace and solitude? Why had Hume so many friends who were his avowed enemies? The Holbachians, the son of Tronchin who was now in London, and, yes, even perhaps Horace Walpole.

On March 9 Du Peyrou enclosed a copy of the Prussian letter which, as he had already mentioned, was receiving wide circulation.[16] With his acid wit Walpole had etched a portrait of the masochistic and exhibitionistic side of Rousseau, a side which Rousseau had never really acknowledged to himself, but which was, unfortunately, altogether true to life. For Walpole this bit of wit made him the talk of the Paris salons for a few days. To Rousseau it may well have been one of the factors which contributed to a psychotic episode.

My Dear Jean-Jacques:
  You have renounced Geneva, your native land. You have brought about your expulsion from Switzerland, a country so much praised in your writings: France has issued a warrant against you; come therefore to me. I admire your talents; I am amused by your reveries which (be it said in passing) occupy you too much and too long. You must at last be sensible and happy; you have caused enough talk about yourself by singularities which are unsuitable to a truly great man: show your enemies that you can sometimes have common sense: that will annoy them without

doing harm to yourself. My states offer you a peaceful retreat: I wish you well and will treat you well if you can accept it. But if you persist in rejecting my help do not expect me to tell anyone about it. If you are determined to torment your spirit in order to find new misfortune, choose whatever you wish. I am a King, I can procure the very things you desire; and, that which will surely not happen in the case of your enemies, I will cease to persecute you when you cease to take pride in being persecuted.

Your good friend
Frederick[17]

Walpole, in Paris at the time, was thoroughly chastised by Mme de Boufflers for his cruel joke. He had carried off his act of contrition when the Prince de Conti arrived on the scene and gave him another dressing down, at which point he nearly lost his temper.[18] Mme de Boufflers was so incensed by the whole affair that, on hearing that Hume had laughed at the letter and perhaps supplied a line or two, she wrote to him to get the full particulars. Hume denied any involvement, but admitted that he was present when the letter was described at Lord Ossory's table. He seemed embarrassed by the affair, assuring her that Walpole was a worthy man, that he really admired Rousseau[19] (Walpole despised Rousseau),[20] and that the whole matter was only a piece of levity. When Rousseau asked Hume if Walpole was really the author of the letter, he uttered something vague and dropped the matter.[21]

By the time of the evening on Lisle Street Hume's evasive answers, his questions about the correspondence of his friend, and the mysterious appearance of the Prussian letter had perplexed Rousseau. He had begun to wonder if another Motiers was on the way. Who would betray him this time? He must be ready for attack. He must be prepared to learn who in England was in league with his enemies.

Hume, who had hoped to be a friend to all men, was gradually discovering that one cannot be neutral in the quarrels of Jean-Jacques Rousseau. Seeing himself as an objective philosopher, he had hoped to arbitrate for Rousseau, to explain him to others, to play the role of the grand international observer who saw all men's faults but quarreled with none. But, somehow, people were turning angry faces to him. His failure to cut Walpole was being taken as a hostile act against Rousseau. Insensibly, without plan or awareness, he had slipped from the position of spectator to become one of the participants. Events unfolded like the scenes in a nightmare, and the more he struggled to avoid offending, to avoid being noticed, the more he was pushed into the front ranks of battle. Soon he was to find himself the principal combatant against a mad and implacable enemy. The incident on Lisle Street was merely the climax of the first engagement.

v

When Rousseau was finally settled at Wooton, Hume was greatly relieved. His letters read as though a great burden had been lifted from him. "This man," he wrote to the Reverend Hugh Blair, "the most singular of all human Beings, has at last left me. . . ."[22] Much of the anger that had been welling up inside him while Rousseau was evaluating and rejecting one residence after another, could now come forth. In the same letter he remarked:

> He was desperately resolved to rush into this solitude, notwithstanding all my Remonstrances; and I foresee, that he will be unhappy in that situation, as he has indeed been always, in all situations.[23]

He was obviously remembering the prophecy of the Holbachians, and particularly of Diderot, who prided himself on having warned Rousseau against the dangers of solitude on the D'Epinay estate. Hume had already begun to regret having told everyone what a splendid fellow he had found in Rousseau, and was preparing to find what others had discovered in him.

On April 3 he was announcing to Mme de Boufflers that he had discovered Rousseau had a secret source of funds which he had not mentioned to Malesherbes or himself. He did not describe the nature of his evidence or the person who supplied it,[24] but merely added, "It is one of his weaknesses that he likes to complain. The truth is, he is unhappy, and he is better pleased to throw the reason on his health, the circumstances and misfortune, than on his melancholy humour and disposition."[25]

On May 2 Hume was again spreading word of Rousseau's secret funds and again without evidence. To Malesherbes he remarked that he had discovered these secret monies "by chance."[26] In both these letters Hume was still casting himself in the role of the beneficent protector who was merely amused by the "singularity" of his charge. He was still exerting his efforts to secure a pension for Rousseau, still concerned for his welfare. However, in his letter to Mme de Boufflers he seemed perturbed by her great sympathy and partiality for Rousseau. After describing the comfortable surroundings of Wooton and mentioning that Mr. Davenport had granted Rousseau a life rent in his will, he told her, "You see, then, that in point of circumstances he is not to be pitied. . . ."[27] Perhaps he had already begun to wonder which of her two philosophers she would choose if a battle should break out between them.

On May 3 he was able to inform Rousseau that the king had granted him a pension and he asked him to express his acceptance through General Conway, who had been the one to apply to the king on his behalf. On May 15 General Conway presented Hume with a letter from Rousseau in which he refused the pension on a temporary basis, i.e., he "suspended his resolution" to accept it,[28] and gave as his reason some vague new misfortune which had befallen him.

Hume was furious. He wrote immediately to Mme de Boufflers, enclosing a copy of Rousseau's letter, saying he would tell Rousseau that, "he had already taken his resolution, when he allowed me to apply to the minister; and again when he allowed the minister to apply to the King; and again, when he wrote to Lord Marischal; and again, when he allowed me to notify Lord Marischal's answer to the minister. . . ."[29] Before his letter to Rousseau on May 17, however, he had apparently controlled his mounting anger. He urged his friend to explain himself on the matter of the pension and expressed his concern over the new calamity which had apparently befallen him. Rousseau answered not a line either to Hume or to General Conway. Hume next wrote to Davenport to see if his letters had miscarried, then again to Rousseau, this time in a more distant and cold manner. Hume told him he was assuming that the principal objection to the pension was its private nature and he would try to arrange to have it granted publicly.[30] Still no answer from Rousseau.

Hume was grievously perplexed. He could not believe that Rousseau was angry with him. True, there was that peculiar incident on Lisle Street the night before Rousseau's journey to Wooton, but they had parted friends and Rousseau had since written him a letter full of friendship and expressions of high regard. Why, then, the long silence and the refusal to answer such a reasonable request? He urged Davenport to visit Rousseau and attempt to find the cause.

Finally, on June 23, Hume received his answer. It was a letter filled with vague accusations delivered in a tone of absolute certainty. "I know you, Monsieur," said Rousseau, "and you know that I do." He continued by accusing Hume of having brought him to England with the intention of dishonoring him. Then, reminding Hume of the evening on Lisle Street when his suspicions had first been aroused, he asserted that his heart had repulsed these evil thoughts and he had flung himself into his friend's arms. Hume had deceived him, and he would be able to deceive the public of England since Rousseau had no contact with them. "I know however, one man you did not deceive, and that is yourself."[31]

Hume was aghast. What could have produced such an outburst? He could recall no action of his which could possibly cast suspicion on his intentions. We shall try to follow the devious and tangled course of Rousseau's thoughts during this period and discover why, in his own mind, he felt justified in attacking his benefactor.

VI

On the evening of his arrival at Lisle Street, Rousseau had carried with him many hazy ideas about the role of Hume and his friends in soiling his reputation. He had made a violent effort to overcome his doubts in his emotional encounter with Hume, but, unlike Mme d'Epinay in the tearful scene Rousseau had experienced with her years ago, Hume did not throw himself into the situation with the enthusiasm expected of him. His quiet, phlegmatic nature left a pall over the evening. There was no cleansing of the soul, no orgiastic scene of forgiveness, only a calm and stolid pat on the back. Without such an emotional resolution Rousseau still felt suspended and hesitating in his attitude toward Hume as he departed the following day.

On arrival at Wooton, he was delighted with his new surroundings. For the moment, at least, he began to believe that Hume had merely made some innocent mistakes in dealing with him. In a letter of gratitude and friendship on March 22 he included a note of caution. On a previous occasion Hume and Davenport had attempted to save him money by pretending they had found a *retour chaise* to Derby at a cheaper price, Davenport secretly paying the cost of the coach. Rousseau, irked by this secrecy, insisted on the need for complete honesty in their relationship. Then he closed with a statement of his high regard and his cordial feeling toward his benefactor.[32]

By the end of March, however, he had already begun to find stories in the newspapers which he felt presented a distorted version of his past troubles. As a celebrity he received a great deal of mail from cranks and some from well-meaning friends who sent him newspaper clippings to let him know what the English press was doing to him. Voltaire was still pursuing him with his vindictive thrusts, and the press was eager to publish any charming libel from that master craftsman. In the spring Voltaire's *Letter to Pansophe* appeared and in the fall some notes on one of his letters to Hume, both ridiculing Rousseau. Rousseau was acutely sensitive to his reputation, and every hint of public criticism disturbed him terribly. He imagined the press as an evil instrument which could work up the entire English nation into a fury against him.[33] His memory of the Motiers incident was still vivid.

Soon he began to wonder if someone was tampering with his mail and feeding information to his enemies. In a letter to D'Ivernois he remarked that Hume was a friend of some of his most dangerous enemies and that, while he owed him recognition for all the material help he had given, "my reputation has not gained from it, and I do not know how it happens that the newspapers which spoke so much of me, and always with honor, before our arrival are now silent or unfavorable."[34] At the same time he felt guilty about his suspicions, longed for a true friend to advise him whether he was right or wrong, and commented that he would have to make peace with his own conscience if Hume turned out to be innocent.

On April 3 the notorious Prussian letter finally made its appearance in the *St. James Chronicle*. There it was, in black and white, in the original French with an English translation. Somehow the printing of this letter in a public paper seemed to cap the matter for Rousseau. He wrote to Stafford, the publisher, insisting that the letter was part of a plot to ruin him, that it must be exposed as a forgery, and that the author, though French, had accomplices in England.[35] Now things were becoming clear for Rousseau. Little incidents, seemingly insignificant by themselves, began to fall into place when one saw the whole picture.[36] He had commissioned the firm of Becket and De Hondt to publish Du Peyrou's letters to him on the Swiss affairs. For a long time he had wondered why they delayed the execution of this work. Suddenly, it became obvious that they, too, were part of the plot against him. Immediately, he wrote to Messieurs Becket and De Hondt to tell them he was on to them; the Prussian letter had given them away.[37]

Then he turned to Mme de Verdelin. Perhaps this poor woman was innocent, even though she had delivered him into the hands of his enemies. In that case she must know the truth about David Hume. All France must know. He was trapped in England, surrounded by his enemies, unable to communicate with anyone. They had planned it all very well, but he would get help before it was too late. In a letter to Mme de Verdelin he carefully outlined the "evidence" he had collected: his persecutions in Switzerland had been concealed, his welcome in Paris had been falsified, Hume had taken public credit in the newspapers for having arranged for his passport (which Mme de Verdelin had actually obtained for him), the Prussian letter was translated and printed and, as though on signal, the newspapers changed from praise of him to a tone of contempt.[38]

If this evidence was not sufficiently overwhelming, two more incidents seemed to Rousseau conclusive. On the first evening of their departure from Paris when the three men slept in the same room, he heard Hume call out in his sleep several times in a loud voice, "Je tiens J.-J. Rousseau"[39] (I've got J.-J. Rousseau). At the time he had interpreted it favorably—even though there was something frightening and sinister in Hume's voice—but now the meaning of that dreadful cry in the night was all too clear.

The second item was the evening at Hume's quarters before his departure for Wooton. In meticulous detail he reported Hume's attempt to get hold of a letter he was writing by offering to mail it, his fears that Hume would stop at nothing to gain information about him, his remorse at "judging such a great man" and the tearful scene that followed. But the thing which troubled him the most about the whole experience was Hume's chilling caress and his calm reception of such an unburdening of the soul.[40]

Mme de Verdelin was completely undone by this outburst. If word of Rousseau's feelings leaked out it would set tongues wagging from one end of Paris to the other. The Holbachians would be gleeful, and Mme du Deffand, whose salon formed the locus of all the principal opponents of Rousseau, would be provided with a month's entertainment. In a hurried reply she told the lonely recluse that people would judge him by his life and not by the newspapers. She reported Hume's high regard for him and tried to explain how illogical it would be for such a man to dishonor someone whom he had sought to protect.[41] However, she felt the futility of all her efforts. Rousseau's letter was full of detail about inconclusive events, and yet he sounded thoroughly convinced. There was perhaps only one person, she remarked to Coindet,[42] who could step into this growing quarrel and soothe the egos of the two philosophers. This was Mme de Boufflers, the "Divine Countess," who was still, for Hume, the brightest star in France, the woman whom he felt had saved him from a life of boredom and complacency. Rousseau, too, was stirred by her electric presence and had nearly lost his heart to her. Could she be induced to go to England as a mediator? Mme de Verdelin determined to seek her aid.

Meanwhile, Rousseau had received and rejected the offer of a pension from the king of England (presented by General Conway), and Hume immediately communicated this news to Mme de Boufflers. Unaware of the dark suspicions brewing in Rousseau's mind, she determined to get at the bottom of this perplexing behavior. Hume had kept her informed of his troubles in settling her fugitive philosopher, and she was thoroughly annoyed that Rousseau was becoming such a source of embarrassment to everyone. She sent him a letter in which her annoyance was only slightly veiled by compliments and concern for his welfare. What was it that distressed him? Why did he not write to Hume? Why had he refused the pension after all Hume had done for him? She closed by reminding him that his friendship for the Chevalier d'Eon,[43] a disgraced French nobleman living in England, might only involve him in an association of bitterness. "Remember," she said, "that individual misfortunes, merited or not, do not occupy or interest the public beyond the moment, and when they have ceased to be interested, one offends if one continues to complain."[44] The mediatrix had clearly become a partisan and, to a man who had already begun to weave his own delusional system, she was now in the camp of the enemy. Later, after she had chastised him for his open break with Hume,[45] Rousseau concluded that she, too, was part of the "plot," that she had been extolling the liberty of England and the virtue of Hume only that she might more effectively deliver him into the hands of his enemies.

The lines of battle were being drawn, and Rousseau, who could converse with none of his friends, occupied himself with writing letter after furious letter. Du Peyrou was the next to hear the story of the conspiracy, then Malesherbes in a lengthy communication in which the cry in the night and the evening on Lisle Street were repeated in all their dramatic detail. In this letter Rousseau rose to the height of eloquence. If he had found a cause more worthy of his efforts the French Revolution might well have begun twenty years in advance of its time.

> Alone in a country which is unknown to me, among a people lacking in warmth, where I do not know the language, where they are incited to hate me, without support, without friends, without any way of avoiding the slurs which are cast on me, I could, for this reason alone, be worthy of pity. I protest to you, however, that I am sensitive neither to the unpleasantness which I suffer nor to the dangers which come upon me: I have become so resigned to my reputation that I no longer think of defending it; I abandon it without difficulty, at least during my life, to my indefatigable enemies. But to think that a man with whom I have never quarreled, a man of merit, estimable for his talents, esteemed for his character, opens his arms to me in my dis-

tress and suffocates me when I throw myself into them. That Monsieur, is a thought which overwhelms me![46]

With such thoughts in mind the offer of a pension, brought about by the offices of Hume, could bring nothing but further disgrace. The very offer of the pension was, no doubt, a part of the attempt to dishonor him. He determined, therefore, that he could not accept such a gift.

In spite of his vehement declaration to Malesherbes, Rousseau had not expressed any of his sentiments to Hume. He was conscious that the "evidence" of Hume's treachery was very flimsy. He knew in his heart that Hume was guilty, but he was aware that the evidence of the heart would not stand up in the court of public opinion. As long as he was not forced to declare himself he could retain a slender contact with reality in the hope that David Hume might yet prove his innocence. Then he would throw himself at the feet of his beloved friend and gladly suffer the agony of remorse for his terrible thoughts. As late as May 25 he could still write to Mme de Verdelin, "such is the deplorable state of my soul that without being absolutely convinced, I am every day more persuaded. In this horrible perplexity what can I do except to say nothing and wait."[47] And wait he did. He might never have spoken of his feelings had Hume not forced the issue. But the patience of the sweetest natures has its limits. General Conway was waiting for a reply; so was the king. After Rousseau's failure to answer several of his letters, Hume became more distant and formal, reminding Rousseau of his impending departure for Scotland and the need for some resolution to the issue of the pension. On June 23 he received the "I know you" letter.

Now it was Hume's turn to suspect a secret plot. What earthly reason could Rousseau have for this fiendish accusation? None, other than "a cool plan to stab me," he concluded.[48] Baron d'Holbach and the philosophic clique in Paris were immediately informed of this monstrous treachery, this deliberate plan to induce Hume to arrange for a pension from the king so that this Prince of Virtue might ostentatiously give his refusal. The Holbachians were in a frenzy of delight. Another piece of ammunition had come their way in the battle against Rousseau. The news spread like a fire through Paris, so rapidly that by the time Hume had written to Mme de Boufflers in Pogues on July 15, his letter found her fuming because Baron d'Holbach had been the first to hear of his open break with Rousseau. As a result she must obtain the news second hand from such a source, and her letters to Paris had reflected her ignorance of the affair while the Holbachians were broadcasting the important information through every fashionable salon in the city.[49] Such is the frailty of the human ego.

Hume asked her advice in the affair, frankly confessing that he feared Rousseau's skill in literary combat. He had seen Rousseau's power over the multitude in Paris. He knew this famous martyr was preparing his memoirs, and he did not wish to find himself the villain in a best seller. Perhaps he should prepare his arguments and present his case to the public. What did she think?

Seeing herself as the principal figure in bringing these two philosophers together, Mme de Boufflers was now rather disgusted with them both. She had counted on Hume's "divine impartiality" to raise him above all trivial argument. Instead, she found the two men whose wisdom she had so much admired had been making hideous and frightening faces at each other like two children, and her noble Hume was quivering in fear of his reputation. He was rushing to prepare his story of the quarrel lest Rousseau turn loose his terrible eloquence and destroy his good name. She told her noble philosopher that his reputation was secure for the ages, and that he was invulnerable to such petty assaults. She pointed out that his hot letter to Baron d'Holbach, a man eager to exploit any rupture with Rousseau, had not served to perpetuate that image of him as *le bon David*, the great mediator. While she admitted Rousseau's letter was atrocious, she insisted that it was not part of a plot to ruin him, that Rousseau was genuinely upset and incapable of such artifice. She warned him that his own fears might cause him to do more harm to his reputation than Rousseau could ever accomplish.

But Hume had other counsel. Holbach and D'Alembert advised him to publish his story and offered him aid in bringing out a French version of the quarrel. Hume yielded to their entreaties, although he tried to avoid any personal responsibility for the French publication of his *Concise Account*. Rousseau, however, always the unpredictable, never published a line about the affair,[50] and, to some of his public, Hume's haste to present his case appeared to be that of one protesting too much.

The evidence was, of course, all on Hume's side. After the first accusation and Hume's demand to know the specific charges against him Rousseau sent him a letter of eighteen folio pages[51] in which he gave vent to all the ruminations of his paranoid ideation and exposed in full the circumstantiality of his thought. He described the way Hume's landlady looked at him as evidence of the evil remarks which she had heard about him. He commented at length that London newspapers had turned against him after Hume brought him to London and that a picture that Hume had induced him to pose for had turned out badly. This letter alone, without any supporting testimony, clearly indicates that Rousseau was mentally ill.[52]

Once the letter was out of him, Rousseau seems to have relaxed for a while. When Hume's *Concise Account* appeared he made no reply. His own letters remained calm, and he settled himself at Wooton to write his *Confessions*. But his solitude was often disturbed by the thought of the many friends he had lost in his latest quarrel, the dearest of whom was his beloved George Keith, who loved repose as much as did Rousseau. Keith had indicated that their correspondence would have to be less frequent, since he did not wish to involve himself in the Rousseau-Hume debate and since, if he continued to write, he must also continue to point out to Rousseau how grievously he had wronged Hume.

From April 1766 to May 1767 Rousseau alternated between periods of contentment and despair. In one letter he speaks of his pleasure in botanizing at Wooton; in another, to Keith, he rends his heart in an ecstacy of torment, beseeching his friend for news of himself. "My protector, my benefactor, my friend, my father, can none of these titles move you? I prostrate myself at your feet to demand only a word from you," and at last a dramatic closing "the pen falls from my hands."[53]

Meanwhile he continued an amiable correspondence with his host, Davenport, who busied himself sending to Rousseau the trunks, packages, and letters which were still arriving from Paris. Davenport managed to have the expense of customs rescinded, repacked damaged cartons, and served his guest in a hundred other ways. He also suggested, with much hesitation, that the king was still interested in offering Rousseau the pension and that it need not come through the offices of Hume.[54] Rousseau was at first suspicious. He refused to make inquiries. It was up to the king to act, he remarked. On February 9, 1767, he agreed on certain conditions, "I do not wish to owe this gift to anyone but the King alone and to his ministers. If the pension is offered at the suggestion of the King himself I would accept it with the suitable recognition and respect, but if I owe it to the solicitations of anyone else, I do not want it. That is my resolution, Monsieur, and you may be sure it is unbreakable."[55] By March 19 Davenport was able to inform Rousseau that the pension of 100 pounds had been granted[56] and by March 21 Rousseau was informing his host that he was preparing to quit the premises and go to London. Thérèse's health, he said, had been deteriorating at Wooton and perhaps the change would do her good.[57]

From the moment he realized negotiations were underway for the pension, his anxiety began to mount once more. This time, however, Thérèse had been agitating the situation in her own manner. Gone was the bashful maid whose eyes had sought Rousseau's in a silent plea for help. She was now a quarrelsome middle-aged woman, jealous of her position as the mistress of a great man, and, conscious of her lower-class origin, always fearful that the servants at Wooton might fail to treat her with the proper respect or try to cheat her in some way. Her arguments formed a constant source of tension in the household, and it was not difficult for her to convince Rousseau that she had been deliberately insulted and that their presence at Wooton was resented by the entire household staff.[58]

The *folie à deux* had begun once more. Thérèse had her imaginary enemies, Rousseau had his, and each fed his private suspicions into the common delusion. Davenport's servants were in the plot and had decided to attack Rousseau through Thérèse. None of this information went to Davenport, but it was bounced about and magnified between them until even their genial host was not free from suspicion. He had promised to visit them at the end of April when he had recovered from his gout. Very well, they would give him a chance and await his arrival. Meanwhile, packages, trunks, and letters continued to pour in, and Davenport, despite his illness, continued to see to their safe arrival at Wooton. He was somewhat concerned about Rousseau's proposal to visit London and made several inquiries after Thérèse's health, offering his house in Cheshire where the air was better.[59] Rousseau answered with wishes for the good health of the Davenport family and an anticipation of the April visit, but said no more about his own plans. While his letters to Davenport were filled with pleasantries and solicitations, the histrionic note had already crept into his letters to Du Peyrou and the Marquis de Mirabeau. To Du Peyrou he remarked that he was being carefully watched and that he might not be able to reach London.[60] To Mirabeau he sent an even more dramatic farewell.[61]

Toward the end of April, Davenport had a serious attack of gout and could not stir. On May 4 he sent Rousseau a letter telling of his illness and inability to travel and offered to send a coach for his guest so that they might visit.[62] But the letter was already too late. On April 30, when Davenport had failed to arrive, Rousseau sent him a letter telling him that as master of Wooton he should know what was going on in the place and that if he did know, he was even more seriously in the wrong. Further, he had broken his promise to visit, and this was unkind. He abruptly informed his host that he was leaving and that his baggage would remain as security against the expenses he had incurred. (It was actually too much to carry on such a sudden journey.)

"I am ignorant neither of the ambushes which await me nor of my own impotence to overcome them, but Monsieur, I have lived, it remains for me only to finish with courage a career passed with honor. It is easy to oppress me but difficult to degrade me. It is that which fortifies me against the dangers which I am going to encounter."[63] Then, instead of going to London, he made a mad dash for the Channel with Thérèse in tow. After reversing his direction several times, he wrote to Davenport from Spalding asking to be taken back.[64] Seeing a paragraph in a newspaper which described his departure from Wooton, he assumed that it had been placed by Davenport and that this kindly gentleman was also his enemy. He was blown by this wind once again toward Dover, and on May 18 he wrote a pitiful letter to General Conway describing the plot to destroy him and asking to be allowed to depart for France. He explained that his reputation in England was destroyed, but that he was being prevented from leaving the island for fear he would publish abroad the insults he had received there.[65] On May 21, 1767, he crossed the Channel and was once again in France. With the sound of the French tongue again in his ears he seems to have recovered his reason. During the months of his arrival and establishment we hear no more of Hume or the plot against him. His letters to his friends were, relatively speaking, calm and rational, filled with his plans for a pleasant and quiet retreat.

From the great melee of wounded egos and shattered friendships that constitutes Rousseau's adventure in England, the name of Richard Davenport emerges untarnished by the hail of insults and suspicions. In his complaints about the conduct of the Davenport servants, his flurry over the *retour chaise*, his sudden departure, and his accusation that Davenport had inserted an item in the newspaper against him, Rousseau had been as unjust to his host as to anyone in England. But Davenport, sensing at once the acute emotional disturbance of his guest, treated him always with patience and consideration. He was content that he was at least able to be helpful in arranging the pension for his unfortunate recluse. But Rousseau, after he had accepted the king's beneficence for about a year, suddenly declined further installments and once again asserted his right to live on the edge of poverty.

VII

In examining the psychological factors behind Rousseau's psychotic episode in England, the matter of the pension assumes paramount importance. The *meaning* this gift came to acquire in the eyes of both Hume and Rousseau made it a *cause célèbre* between them.

Very little is known about the personality of David Hume. His own epilogue,[66] written at the close of his life, is a masterpiece of understatement. He presents himself as a man of mild disposition on whom disappointments made little or no impression, whose character was never attacked, and who never had cause to defend himself. Many of his contemporaries regarded him as phlegmatic and stolid, but the Countess de Boufflers might have told a different story. His letters to her show him as a man capable of strong passion when sufficiently aroused. For the most part, however, his correspondence tells very little about him. Only once, in the early years, was he strongly motivated to reveal himself completely to another person. Taxed by the intensity of his first literary effort, he was then suffering from a condition which he (probably correctly) diagnosed as psychosomatic. In a letter to a Scottish physician he described his desire to write and his inability to drive himself at the pace he wanted to go.[67] The resulting conflict finally made him physically ill. Perhaps the most significant revelation from this early letter is the intensity of Hume's urge toward greatness. It is a desire which strikes many men of ability, but only in the rare individual does it develop into such a compelling and dominating drive that it absorbs the entire personality. Hume's first book, the *Treatise on Human Nature*,[68] is filled with this sense of mission. In a later edition he managed to reduce the egotistical tone of his first effort, but even there one is sensible that the author feels he has brought a new revelation for mankind. To Rousseau, who brought his own discoveries to the world, the aura of divine destiny which surrounded Hume must have been very apparent. When a man is full of himself, it is difficult for another, similarly inclined, to abide him for long. Hume for his part, may well have been both impressed and perturbed by the tumultuous demonstration Rousseau received in Paris, a welcome that eclipsed his own.

But a deeper and more important issue divided these two men: Rousseau's tormenting need to be taken care of, while at the same time remaining completely independent and free from all sense of obligation. Hume had some awareness of this conflict in his friend, but he did not really understand his ambivalence. He felt that if he could arrange a privately granted pension from the king, without any public show, Rousseau need not be offended by such an honor. He was naturally somewhat pleased by the success of his efforts, and he wrote to several of his friends about his fine work. In contrast to the discreet old soldier, George Keith, who had offered Rousseau a pension for the care of Thérèse and who deemed himself honored when the great philosopher actually accepted his gift, Hume seemed to feel he was doing Rousseau a favor, and it is very likely that he conveyed his feeling to Rousseau.

As previously noted Rousseau showed a mounting concern about the most trivial gift, and his chastisement of D'Ivernois, during the Motiers period, for presents of prunes, apricots, and other edibles was so severe as to suggest a loss of perspective. At that time another more formless element flitted through his anger and only momentarily raised itself into a distinct shape. In a letter to D'Ivernois on December 29, 1764, complaining of gifts of cream cheese and wine, Rousseau remarked:

> One thing sure is that in no one would I take badly a wish to force presents upon me. Yours, sir, are so frequent and, I dare say, so obstinately continued, that from another man with whose frankness I was less familiar, I would think they contained some secret purpose, to be discovered in proper time and place.[69]

The desire to be taken in, to experience a passive-receptive kind of love, was so strong in Rousseau, and yet so unacceptable to his concept of himself that he could not acknowledge the feelings that tormented him. Instead, he imagined that someone else, an enemy from the outside, was deliberately attempting to seduce him, to implant feelings in him which were not really a part of himself.

The public stir surrounding his departure from the Hermitage and the fruitless question so indecently argued, as to whether he owed Mme d'Epinay more gratitude than she owed him, had served to heighten his concern about receiving gifts from anyone. He felt that all such material things were traps by which people could boast of what they had done for him, whereas he could put no label on the gifts of his heart, which he gave so freely.

It was, of course, the very intensity of his desire to be taken care of that caused Rousseau to lean over backward in the other direction. His puritanical attitude toward gifts, like other forms of prudery, was based on his despising his own desires. The slightest gratification of his urge to receive aroused in him the strange, tender, trembly quality that he had come to regard as a disgusting weakness. He had become so disturbed by this side of himself that he could no longer face its existence. Thus, if a proffered gift upset him, he did not ask himself why he was annoyed. Instead, he turned his tension outward in the form of an angry attack on the giver. Since he had barely enough to sustain himself, his difficulty and his need were intensified. He was always torn between desire and refusal, painting his situation in pitiful colors and ranting at those who sought to alleviate it. At times he recognized he had been rash and ridiculous in his pride. After accepting two hampers of game from the Prince de Conti, he had sent a note to say he would receive no more. Then he blushed at the thought of what he had done and chastised himself for his stupid sensitivity. However, since he could not understand why he behaved in this way, he could not control his outbursts. He could only confess them later when the heat of his feelings had subsided and the injustice of his position was apparent.

His contact with Hume, like that with Mme d'Epinay and Mme de Luxembourg, brought back all the old longings he had experienced with Mme de Warens. But in this case the benefactor was a man and, as such, probably reactivated many of his childhood feelings toward his father as well. Rousseau had obtained the indulgence of his father by his sweetness and femininity. He had performed for him and read to him. Hume was another powerful figure who took an interest in him. They had only recently met, and yet Hume's enthusiasm for Rousseau was the talk of the literary world. Why? What did he want? What did he expect of Rousseau? Mme de Warens had not only taken charge of his intellectual life but had insisted on dominating and directing his sensuality as well. How, then, must he repay Hume?

It is clear that Rousseau never allowed himself to think directly about such things. The very idea of a homosexual encounter filled him with disgust. It was associated with the vile sense of nausea and perversion which he had felt on his first experience at the hospice of Turin. Yet the awareness of his early feminine identification and his desire for a passive role in his sexual experiences must have remained a haunting shadow over most of his relationships with men. With George Keith there is little evidence of this fear, but with others there is a possessive clutching and a sudden pushing away that suggests a man terribly mixed up in his feelings. In this connection his frantic desire to get out of Paris, the abode of Diderot, and his urge to get far away from London, and Hume, as soon as possible, may have represented more than a mere revulsion from the evils of city life.

However, one must be cautious at this point. The expression "latent homosexuality" has too often been applied in a mechanical fashion to all cases exhibiting paranoid symptoms ever since Freud discovered the relationship between the fear of persecution and the homosexual wish.[70] One must look more deeply into Rousseau's feelings about Hume before being content with a mere label for his behavior. Rousseau obviously wanted a close personal relationship with his newfound mentor. He wanted the kind of emotional scene he had experienced with Mme d'Epinay, Mme de Luxembourg, Diderot, and Grimm, a mutual passion, an unburdening of the soul. He had attempted this once on that evening on Lisle Street when he confessed the injustice of his suspicions about his friend. But Hume had failed to fling himself into the situation with the appropriate enthusiasm. Rousseau was left hanging in the air, his desires unfulfilled, and his need, instead of subsiding, began to mount to an even greater intensity.

That he was prepared to confess his unjust suspicions, to humiliate himself, so to speak, suggests that the primary satisfaction he sought with Hume was a masochistic one. He wanted to throw himself at his friend's feet as he had done with the ladies of his past. It was the erotic element of this masochistic urge that was particularly disturbing to him. In his letter to Hume of July 10 this element is unmistakable.

> I am the unhappiest of men if you are guilty; I am the most unworthy if you are innocent. You make me desire to be this despicable object. Yes, the state in which you would see me, prostrate, trampled under your feet, crying for mercy and doing everything to obtain it, loudly proclaiming my indignity and rendering the most glittering homage to your virtue, would be for my heart a state of full-blown joy, after the breathless and deathlike state in which you have put me.[71]

The situation with Hume was further aggravated in that by accepting the pension he would become obligated to his benefactor as he had been to Mme d'Epinay. Before he could accept such an obligation there must be a complete union of souls. Rousseau, who wanted so desperately to be taken care of by someone who loved him, was in mortal fear of becoming dependent on a man who might not care for him and who could withdraw his affection at any moment. In the case of Hume, as seen, his fears were partly justified. Hume was beginning to cool toward him. But Rousseau had no evidence other than a vague sense that all was not well between them. The very lack of justifiable grounds increased his anxiety and his fear of dependency and obligation.

Rousseau loved to loaf in the sun, to lie quietly and let the thoughts and fantasies run through him, to indulge his imagination and his whims. Only his poverty kept him at work copying music and maintaining an austere and frugal existence: the very model of Swiss virtues. An extra hundred pounds a year would certainly arouse his voluptuous side and bring forth desires which he would have to gratify. Once he accepted the pension, he would soon need it in order to live. He would become its slave and the slave of those who controlled it. Thus it was that he bit with such ferocity the hand that fed him.

He had learned to live with persecution and to derive a certain masochistic satisfaction from his role as the martyr to truth. But temptation was something he could not tolerate, and his flight from England was clearly a retreat from this danger to his emotional stability. The extent of his fear of temptation is manifested in that he could not even acknowledge its existence, but must project the cause of his anxiety on the crafty plans of his enemies. In his quarrel with Hume he reached, perhaps for the first time, the extremity of psychosis.

His delusional system became the only exit from an otherwise impossible situation. It served in a devious way his peculiar needs in relating to others, and it also buttressed his growing doubts about his virtue. When he was a little boy the persecution to which he and his cousin were subjected served as a proof of their virtue. It was not the knowledge of their innocence alone which gave them such a sense of being in the right as they clasped each other in their bed, it was the sense of being unjustly treated. Persecution made them feel even more virtuous. Further, it completely masked and justified the pleasure they obtained from each other. Thus, Rousseau's delusional system became a guarantee of his own innocence, of his right to Paradise. Why would those others exert such an effort to malign him? Why would the plot reach international proportions? Would they waste such time with a man who was really evil? And if he was haunted from time to time with thoughts of Marion, his desertion of Le Maistre, and other fleeting qualms which he found it difficult to identify, had he not atoned for these errors here on earth by all the suffering he had endured? Surely, there could be no more of hell waiting for Jean-Jacques Rousseau!

His persecutors became an absolute necessity to him. The suffering he experienced because of their fantasied existence was his only means of bribing that overpowering Genevan conscience which haunted his every pleasure.

[12]

Last Performance

I

AT THE HEIGHT OF HIS QUARREL with Hume, Rousseau had received a
letter from the Marquis de Mirabeau, the notorious iconoclast, professional "friend of man," and father of the more famous Mirabeau. Filled
as it was with the author's own egotism, it was nevertheless one of the
most original and outspoken letters that came to Rousseau in those
hectic days. Expressing his admiration for Rousseau's work, Mirabeau
also showed himself capable of understanding the agony inherent in such
a great sensitivity. Then, with disarming frankness, he put himself
in Hume's place and imagined what should have been said to Rousseau.
First, he would admit that they were both fools, Rousseau for his
suspicions, Hume for taking him seriously. Then he would say:

> Believe, therefore, that it is only your imagination overheated
> by an inextinguishable fire which has produced all the beautiful
> tales of the machinations of which you accuse me and do me too
> much honor because I have never been clever enough to invent
> such a scheme that only you could unravel.[1]

Finally, he would invite Rousseau to laugh at the whole ridiculous
situation including his long letter to Hume, a masterwork of prolonged
reverie, eloquence, and sentiment, "for which I thank you." He concluded the letter with a lengthy description of his various estates and
invited the harassed philosopher to stay at any of them when he returned to France.

Rousseau's first reaction to this letter is not known, for his reply
is dated three months later. However, he does not appear to have been
offended by it, and his warm response suggests, as do some of his other
remarks to his friends, that he had moments in which he, too, doubted
the validity of his delusional system. He accepted Mirabeau's effort
and the generous spirit of consolation in which it was offered, but
he warned his new friend that if he came to one of his properties he
would want complete privacy and would entertain no one with his conversation. The letters between the two continued, and their friendship
increased. Rousseau admired Mirabeau's directness and good sense, but

he was wary when the marquis chided him for his life of idleness, for he was determined that he would no longer involve himself in political controversy. In the frantic period at Wooten, when first thinking of flight, he gave Mirabeau one of his dramatic farewells. Telling him that he was about to depart for London and would write if he arrived, he announced with a roll of drums:

> Adieu Monsieur. I will never see the Château de Brie, and, what afflicts me still more, it does not appear that I will ever see the lord of the estate, but I will honor and cherish him all my life: I will remember always that it was at the time of my deepest miseries that his noble heart made me advances of friendship; and mine, unworthy as it is, will be devoted to him until my last breath.[2]

Unabashed by his safe voyage, he contacted Mirabeau again as soon as he arrived in Calais and arranged to receive his correspondence in Amiens. From there he accepted Mirabeau's offer of refuge at Fleury-sous-Meudon, telling him at the same time it had been impossible to keep his identity a secret. This was certainly an understatement, for he had received a public welcome at Amiens, and the Prince de Conti was writing to warn him that the news of his arrival was everywhere in Paris. Conti offered him refuge and urged him to change his name and depart in secret, since the warrant for his arrest was still in force. But Rousseau, who was only willing to engage in the minor subterfuge of calling himself M. Jaques, continued to wander about in public places even after he was settled on Mirabeau's estate. Surrounded as he was by the silent army of phantom conspirators and terrified by the slightest sign or word of disapproval, he was blind to the real dangers threatening him. Conti warned him again that he had been seen in the park of Meudon and that he was in constant danger of arrest. Flattered by Conti's concern, Rousseau decided to change his residence once more and accepted the prince's estate at Tyre. Here he assumed the name Renou and Thérèse was represented as his sister.

He was troubled by his separation from Sultan and was delighted to hear from Coindet that the dog was alive and well. Coindet made arrangements to send Sultan to him by coach, but when Rousseau arrived to pick him up, the driver could recall no dog as passenger. At last he remembered that there had been such a creature but that he had been forgotten at Pontoise.[3] Rousseau was plunged into despair, only to have Sultan arrive the following day. Coindet had taken the precaution of engraving the name of the chateau on Sultan's collar.[4]

Under the protection of the powerful Prince de Conti and with Thérèse and Sultan once more beside him, it appeared that he could settle down and enjoy his last years. But immediately he noted that the attention of Manoury, the hunting steward of Tyre, was almost excessive.[5] Soon the dark clouds of suspicion gathered once again, and Manoury became an agent of the grand conspiracy, receiving his orders directly from Hume. On June 23 a new concierge (Deschamps) was appointed, and this man also came under suspicion.[6] Coindet attempted to settle this rising storm, but received a sharp reprimand for his pains, and even Mme de Verdelin, who had the discretion to remain silent, was caught in the cannonade. Remarking that he had heard nothing from her, Rousseau told Coindet:

> I do not doubt that she thinks as you on this subject (the new persecutors). Since it is established that I am mad it is obvious that the misfortunes that happen to me are no more than visions.[7]

Soon he began to detect in the looks and behavior of everyone signs of evil intent:

> . . . they have raised all the village and the neighboring villages against me; the priest is part of it; I cannot take a step in the Château or outside without receiving a sign of disdain and malevolence. . . .[8]

Whenever Rousseau was under attack it was always difficult for his friends to determine whether the enemies were real or imaginary. The village of Motiers had certainly been raised against him. The servants of Tyre, not knowing that they had to deal with a famous writer, may have been lacking in respect. Coindet visited the Prince de Conti to present Rousseau's complaints. The prince was distressed by the situation and determined to come in person to set matters straight. But in order to punish the guilty he must have the facts. What acts, what insults had been dealt his illustrious guest? Coindet conveyed this request for specifics as tactfully as possible to Rousseau,[9] but the latter had been trapped in that net before. The prince, from his exalted position, could not possibly see the little details of his troubles, he replied, and he would not explain everything, but Coindet would see for himself when he arrived.[10] He requested permission of the prince to leave Tyre.[11] Mirabeau also came in for his share of vagaries. In answer to his request for details of the new troubles, Rousseau replied that he would not burden the noble heart of a friend with such a dreary tale.[12] With Coindet he was more voluble but no more specific. In a letter dated August 25, 1767, he gave the following information:

> There is a continual subterranean going and coming of which the effect appears only in the countenance of the inhabitants, but

there is no mistaking it, and through it one can guess what is said in the cavernous councils of these moles. Further, the whole country is on the knee of M. le Concierge (Deschamps). . . . Persuaded that he has the complete confidence of the Prince each villager hurries to put himself under his protection, and to merit it, does me some new affront, which turns out admirably. I cannot conceive what hand directs this man, but he has been very well chosen. He moves with assurance and without compromising himself. It is too bad he missed his calling as an actor, for he has all the attributes of a true chief of conspirators.[13]

The prince issued orders that Rousseau be treated with respect and offered to dismiss those servants whom his guest suspected, but the victim was determined to flee. He again requested permission to depart; Conti then expressed the hope that his guest would remain long enough to receive a visit from him, when he might straighten out the situation.[14] However, when the prince came, on October 6, 1767, the results were inconclusive and his guest was still determined to leave.[15]

In the course of this discussion, Rousseau received a visit from Du Peyrou, who might have helped to sooth the turbulent feelings of the inhabitants of Tyre had he not fallen ill shortly after his arrival. In his fever he apparently cried out that he had been poisoned and thus plunged the wary recluse into a new fit of terror. It was, concluded Rousseau, the crafty domestic of Du Peyrou, who had been intercepting all their letters (on the instructions of the conspirators), who had at last devised this scheme for turning the head of his master against his trusted friend.[16] Even after Du Peyrou was restored to himself and had left his fears of poisoning far behind, Rousseau was still distrustful of him. He canceled the plans by which Du Peyrou would have become trustee of his manuscripts. When his friend protested, he remarked that such terrible ideas would never enter the mind of an honest man even when it was in a state of disorder.[17] At last his feelings were assuaged, and Du Peyrou was partly restored to the ever-shrinking list of the friends of Jean-Jacques. Soon Rousseau was to break with Coindet, following the latter's decision not to relay one of his letters on the politics of Geneva to his friend Moultou. But we will not trace details of his suspicions regarding Coindet's membership in the conspiracy and his letters to Du Peyrou and Moultou regarding this newly discovered betrayal. Coindet's many pathetic attempts to restore himself ended by Rousseau permitting him to execute a few minor commissions, but never really taking him into his confidence again.

In the summer of 1768, he left Tyre for Lyons and from there wandered over the towns of his youth—Chambéry, Grenoble—and on August 11 he and Thérèse went through a marriage ceremony in Bourgoin. But he was a constant prey to his delusion, and the slightest incident sufficed to reactivate the entire "conspiracy" in his mind. A leatherworker who claimed that Rousseau owed him nine francs immediately fell into the plot. The investigation cleared Rousseau of the debt, but he persisted in his belief that this new accuser was merely a tool of the conspirators.

During the following months Rousseau changed his residence several times, often on the basis of what he suspected were the secret plans of the conspirators. If they were making plans to attack him in France, he must go to England. If they alerted their agents in England, he would fool them and remain in France. By the summer of 1769 he was in Monquin. His relationship with Thérèse had seriously deteriorated since their marriage, and they were on the verge of a separation. At the end of the year he was considering a return to Paris, but he was unable to get any clear indication that his presence there would not arouse the ire of the authorities. Conti strongly urged against such a venture. By the winter of 1769-70 Rousseau had become very disgruntled, for the sedentary indoor life, the cold weather, and the rheumatism of Thérèse all combined to make his life miserable. He had many hours in which to think about the conspiracy and to examine the behavior of all his old friends. One by one he began to drop them into the great steaming cauldron of his fantasies. Each one was assigned a place, and behind the whole operation emerged a new, sinister mastermind, the Duke de Choiseul, foreign minister of France.

II

The duke climbed slowly to his position of prominence in Rousseau's delusional system. In those anxious months of 1762, when the rumors began to circulate that the *Social Contract* was to be condemned and its author arrested, the Marshal de Luxembourg asked Rousseau if he had criticised Choiseul in his work. He answered that he had praised Choiseul's administration. He sensed, however, a certain hesitation in the marshal, as though this nobleman would like to mention things which propriety would not allow.[18] The thought that he might have offended Choiseul began to fester and ferment within him from this moment. Perhaps, he thought, his eulogy of Choiseul was taken as a sarcasm. In 1764-65 the French sent troops to help the Genoese put down the Corsicans, and a long series of negotiations was undertaken which ended in the sale of Corsica to France on May 15, 1768. Significantly, less than two months before this event Rousseau sent a letter to Choiseul explaining that he had nothing but praise for that minister. He expressed his hope that Choiseul would believe him, that he would not read anything sinister into Rousseau's passage in the *Social Contract*.[19] He received a polite, but apparently unsatisfactory reply a few days later.[20] Why did he write to Choiseul after a delay of nearly six years and just before the final negotiations for the sale of Corsica? Did he already suspect that Choiseul (and hence France) was crushing the freedom of Corsica just to thwart Jean-Jacques Rousseau? If he did, he told no one about it, but it was his custom to keep his suspicions to himself until they had had a chance to fructify.

In the summer of 1768, Rousseau requested a passport from Choiseul. When he received no answer he turned to Mme de Luxembourg for help. Impatient to depart while the weather was still favorable, he became agitated when he did not hear from her. Writing two years after the event, he remarked, "This silence, under such circumstances, appeared to me decisive." He concluded that she, if not actually a member of the conspiracy, knew of its existence and did not wish to help him.[21] It is unlikely, however, that his ideas crystalized so soon, for the passport did arrive, after a delay of six weeks,[22] and Rousseau, who then found the season unfavorable for travel, was concerned lest he offended Choiseul by not making use of the document.

Again, on May 31, 1769, in a letter to Conti, he expressed his concern lest he offend Choiseul by not making use of the passport.[23] In the summer of 1769 French troops proceeded to wipe out the last vestige of Corsican resistance, and on June 16 General Paoli, with his brother and their few remaining followers, was forced to flee Corsica on a British ship bound for Leghorn. Choiseul, who had engineered the enslavement of Corsica, and who had used as his agent that same Buttafuoco who had once sought a legislator for free people, now became for Rousseau the ringleader of all the fiends and plotters who surrounded him. On February 26, 1770, he reviewed the entire conspiracy. In a long letter to his friend Saint-Germain[24] he examined all the old wounds, one by one: Diderot's betrayal, the estrangement of the Countess de Boufflers and Mme de Luxembourg, etc., etc. But now it appeared that Choiseul had been in on it from the very beginning. Rousseau had praised him in his work, and Choiseul, knowing that he did not merit such praise, had taken it as an insult. The extent of Choiseul's hatred was unbelievable, he said, but some day the whole world would realize that poor Corsica was only a tool by means of which this schemer hoped to get at him. Delusions of persecution, when pushed to such an extreme, become delusions of grandeur.

With minute detail, he described the vast superstructure of the conspiracy, the extent of the plot, the monumental organization that was necessary to destroy one virtuous man.

> . . . the floors on which I stand have eyes, the walls which surround me have ears. . . . I cannot take a step without being observed, not a movement of the finger which is not noted. . . .
> Nothing has been omitted in the execution of this noble enterprise: the power of the great, the resourcefulness of the women, the ruses of their satellites, all the vigilance of spies, the pen of authors, the voices of scandalmongers, the seduction of my friends, the encouragement of my enemies, the malicious investigations into my life in order to soil it, into my writings in order to falsify them; the art of corrupting everything, so easy for the powerful, that of rendering me odious to all classes, of defaming me in every country. . . .
> [From the addition to Rousseau's letter.] Add to all that the expedition to Corsica, that iniquitous and ridiculous expedition which outrages all justice, humanity, politics and reason; an expedition the success of which renders it still more ignominious in that, not being able to conquer the people by iron, it was necessary to vanquish them with gold. . . . It is thus that man finally betrays himself in catering so much to his animosity. M. de Choiseul well knew the most cruel wound with which he could rend my heart, and he has not spared me; but he has not seen how this barbarous vengeance has unmasked him and revealed his conspiracy. I defy him to ever soften this expedition with any reason or pretext which can satisfy a man of sense. It will be recognized that I was the first to see a people free and capable of discipline at a time when all Europe saw only a mass of rebels and bandits; that I saw palms[25] sprouting in this new-born nation, that it had selected me to water them, that this choice brought about their misfortune and mine. . . .[26]

The small, tight, delusional system began to expand as one personality was linked with another. So powerful was the eloquence of one man that it became necessary for world leaders to hire an army of spies and slanderers to libel this Prince of Virtue, lest his brilliance overturn empires. In the end even the political machinations of courtiers and the fall of nations were mere by-products of the anger directed at Jean-Jacques Rousseau.

But in the spring the weather improved and so did Rousseau's disposition. He traveled to Lyons, visited Mme Boy de la Tour and her family and botanized for two months. Finally, Paris, the city of his greatest triumph and his first inspiration, asserted its hold on him once more. He had been longing to return to Paris ever since his "escape" from England, but the warnings of the Prince de Conti and his other friends had dissuaded him. In June 1770 he made a triumphal entry, welcomed by Robinet and hosted and dined by a variety of prominent people in the city. Everyone wanted to meet him, and he had more invitations than he could accept. In Paris, amid the adulation of the multitude, he found the therapy his starved soul required. He discovered at last that the whole world did not despise him. There were still a few intelligent beings who could appreciate him after all. Gradually, a note of calm appeared in his life, and the intensity of his delusional ideas began to subside. He settled in the Hôtel du Saint-Esprit in the rue Plâtrière and began, once again, his occupation of copying music.

In 1771 he completed his last political work as a response to the appeal of Count Wielhorski of Poland, who had asked his aid in devising a constitution for that strife-torn nation. Rousseau, who had long ago taken a resolution against political writing, was at first inclined to provide a few general principles and words of encouragement. But soon, his inspiration fired by the magnitude and the importance of the task, he worked with furious haste—for a full six months[27]—to complete his *Considerations on the Government of Poland*. More than any of his other works, this document reveals the dangers as well as the merits of Rousseau's political philosophy. He illustrates both the difficulty and the necessity of maintaining the active interest of the citizen in his government. Laws cannot force such participation, he says, but only a glowing patriotism, which must be constantly tended and fired anew.

The *Considerations* cost Rousseau many precious hours of privacy, hours which he had to steal from the crowd of visitors who importuned him for an audience. He needed time not only for his private ventures but for music copying, which was his only source of income, since he had abandoned once again the pension from King George. He avoided writing letters except to special friends and often left home early in the morning for a walk in the *bois*, thus avoiding the press of visitors who still longed to see the famous recluse.

Had he contented himself with this quiet life his last eight years might have been filled with the peace for which he ostensibly yearned. Perhaps it was the discovery of the many partisans he had in that great city which fixed his determination to vindicate his reputation by giving public readings of his *Confessions* and by writing his *Dialogues*, a lengthy justificaton for his life and works. The readings of the *Confessions*, which contained many unsavory stories about well-known persons still living in Paris, produced such a stir that the police (promoted by Mme d'Epinay) intervened, and he was forced to discontinue them. He attempted to present his *Dialogues* to the world by another dramatic device: depositing them on the altar of Notre Dame. But he was foiled in this attempt by an iron screen which happened to be in front of the altar on the day of his visit. Taking this as a sign from heaven he returned home, confused and beaten, eventually giving copies of his book to various friends who, he hoped, would justify him to posterity.

In 1776 he began his last work, *The Reveries of a Solitary Wanderer*, in which he described his means of seeking consolation, in the quiet contemplation of nature, from the cruelties inflicted on him. This work, like the *Dialogues*, is marred by an excessive preoccupation with the personal suffering occasioned by the international plot against him. It was never completed. On July 2, 1778, he died suddenly at Ermenonville with Thérèse at his side, following a brief illness in which he was apparently aware that his end was near. Modern authorities give no credence to the theory that he committed suicide. He apparently died peacefully, except for the last few moments, when he tried to get out of bed and struck his head on the floor.

III

In references to the life and writings of Rousseau the term "insanity" has more often been an accusation than a diagnostic opinion. The charge that he was mad or a "moral cretin" has, at times, become the basis for dismissing his work as well as the significance of his life. As a means of defending him, his friends and admirers too often tried to prove that he was not mentally ill—as if this would somehow vindicate his work. Even generations after his death a writer can translate in full his pathological letter to David Hume, present it to the reading public, and announce that Rousseau was simply the victim of persecution.[28]

Generally, when a person is mentally ill, his friends are willing to concede the point, but continue to protect him and to seek some refuge for him. Rousseau's friends, however, did not react to his psychosis, but to his symptoms. When he broke with Du Peyrou, Coindet, and others there was often a desperate pleading, an employment of reason to explain the case. Mme de Boufflers scolded him for his behavior toward Hume, and Mme de Verdelin reasoned with him to show that he had made a mistake in suspecting *le bon David*. The Prince de Conti, although obviously distressed by Rousseau's mysterious accusations, offered to dismiss those servants of whom Rousseau disapproved.

The difficulty in reaching an objective view of Rousseau seems to lie, in part, in the nature of his illness. The typical psychotic individual deteriorates rapidly. He becomes withdrawn, often incoherent, and can no longer carry on a rational conversation or write sensible letters. He hears "voices" and talks to imaginary persons. Rousseau did none of these things. His *Considerations on the Government of Poland*, written in 1771-72, shows him capable of the same eloquence and style which characterized his earlier writings. One can read it without the slightest suspicion that in his waking moments the author is surrounded by a fantastic web of plot and counterplot.

Another aspect of Rousseau's mental illness was its intermittent character. As Heidenhain[29] has pointed out, it does not follow the classical format of a disease process with a clear onset and definite course. Heidenhain discards various diagnoses from schizophrenia to involutional paranoia, primarily on this basis. He has suggested that Rousseau's inability to assimilate or work through his homosexual impulses produced a "wave-like" recurrence of his symptoms throughout his life.[30] Even in this respect Rousseau differed markedly from the typical person struggling with a latent homosexual conflict. It is true that he suspected men toward whom he was attracted (Diderot, Grimm, Hume) of seeking to dishonor him in some mysterious way. However, in place of the usual suspicion that people were accusing him of perversion, he managed to avoid the directly homosexual aspect of his problem. For him the key issue was always that of dependency. On this level he fought his major battles. Thus, he could sit before his door in the long flowing robes of his Armenian costume, knitting laces for the young ladies of Motiers. He was apparently untroubled by this feminine appearance and feminine behavior. But let someone offer him a gift for which he felt he could not make repayment, and he was at war. He recognized that his behavior in this respect was irrational, but such moments of insight came after the event.

Both Proal[31] and Grimsley[32] have examined and commented on the variety of diagnoses which have been applied to Rousseau. It is sufficient to say that from the taxonomic point of view he had symptoms from most of the major diagnostic categories, from the older "psychaesthenia" and "hysteria" to the still surviving "paranoia." While the majority seem to favor the idea that he suffered from a functional psychosis, some authorities have justifiably emphasized the role of physical illness in his total problem.

Physiology is not to be discounted in the case of Rousseau. It may be that some persons are constitutionally predisposed toward sexual displacement and that circumstances merely determine the direction. Heidenhain has mentioned the possibility of physiological factors, particularly an endocrine disturbance which may have contributed to Rousseau's condition,[33] and Green[34] has pointed out that the ups and downs of his emotional life, as revealed in his letters, followed the crises of his urethral condition. However, such a parallel does not really follow throughout his life. Starobinski remarks that "from the very moment conspiracy becomes obsessive, less is to be heard of difficult micturition and repeated soundings."[35] The faculty of judgment or interpretation was the critical one in the life of Rousseau, and it is possible that both physiological and psychological disturbances impaired this faculty. It would appear, therefore, that Heidenhain's[36] diagnosis of paranoia[37] is the most meaningful. This is a condition in which a failure of judgment is the principle feature, and signs of deterioration appear late in life, if at all. In his "good periods" Rousseau was capable of being a charming and sociable companion until almost the end of his life, but the failure of judgment and the paranoid ideation appear as early as the quarrels prior to his departure from the Hermitage, if not before.

In the last analysis, the determination of a diagnostic category for a writer does not answer either of the two major questions about his work: what were the sources of his genius, and where and how did he fail to achieve his fullest capability? *The discovery that Rousseau had a deficiency in judgment does not, in itself, invalidate any of his works, nor does it explain the origin of his insight into the problems of domination and submission as they appeared in the society of his time.*

Rousseau's deficiency in judgment was complemented by an unusual acuteness of perception in human relationships. His works present a rare mixture of basic psychological insights and the misapplication of many of these insights. Unlike the other political thinkers of his time, he searched behind the façade of the institutional and rational basis for authority and emphasized the emotional factor—the pleasure that the ruler derives from his position of power.

The study of his diagnosis will not lead to an understanding of the psychological factors which influenced his political works. One must look, instead, at the interplay of drives that formed the background of his life experience. Rousseau understood the totalitarian mind because he partook of its very substance. It is my conviction that, just as self-doubt, self-questioning, and self-abnegation, in their extremes, are forms of moral masochism, so the unquestioning belief in one's self, the single-minded insistence on one's own point of view, the urge to accumulate greater power and influence (in their extremes) are forms of "moral sadism." Rousseau's social behavior was primarily masochistic, but sadism and masochism are two aspects of the same drive, and Rousseau's political writing bears out the truth of this statement. Particularly in *Emile*, and to some extent in his other political writings, the urge to dominate, which he reacted against in his social behavior, became manifest both in the style and the substance of his writing.

Corsica and Poland: War and Peace

I

ROUSSEAU MADE TWO ATTEMPTS to apply the principles of his *Social Contract* to specific states which were in a process of reformation. The first, a *Constitutional Project for Corsica*, was never finished, and only the first part was put together in any kind of final form. The second, *Considerations on the Government of Poland*, was prepared at the request of Count Wielhorski, a representative of the Confederation of Bar, the last bastion of Polish independence before it was parceled out as spoils in the series of partitions which were to follow. The *Considerations* was completed in 1772 and sent to Count Wielhorski as a private document, not for publication.

In these final political works, particularly in the *Considerations*, from which most of my observations will be drawn, Rousseau reached the climax of a tendency which first began to show itself in the *Discourse on Political Economy*. While he made occasional references to the virtues of "natural man" in his later writings, and spoke often of liberty and freedom, there is no mistaking a decided shift in his political philosophy from what Vaughan has called "individualism to collectivism."[1] In looking at these final writings one can note some of their salient characteristics.

First, it is clear that Rousseau continued to favor a democratic form of government to the very end. In the *Social Contract* he referred to an "elective aristocracy" as the best aristocracy,[2] but he meant by this that the people elect their own rulers and representatives as is done in the democracies of today. His reluctance to advocate democracy openly may have been occasioned by his hope that his work might be allowed to pass unmolested if it were not too controversial. However, in his *Constitutional Project for Corsica*, he directly recommended democratic government by name[3] and urged the complete abolition of hereditary nobility.[4] He referred to elected leaders as the "political nobility" (*noblesse politique*), but here, again, he was probably reluctant to give up a term which still had such strong emotional connotations for the majority of his readers. Rousseau believed in change, but he was acutely aware of the danger of cutting a nation free, in one stroke, from all the institutions in its past. With both the Corsicans and the Poles his advice was to learn to appreciate the value of the present institutions and to change them only with the greatest reluctance. There was, of course, much practical politics in this advice. In the *Social Contract* he had already warned that men will clutch desperately at old institutions. Comparing men accustomed to a bad government with the cowardly invalid who trembles at the sight of the physician, he cautioned all revolutionary reformers to be guided by the flexibility of a people. His boldness in suggesting the abolition of the Corsican nobility arose from the fact that Genoa had already undertaken this task for selfish reasons of its own, and he was faced with the prospect of reestablishing the old nobility or giving it a final *coup de grâce*. He told the Corsicans not to protest to the Genoese for the favor they had received and pointed out that to identify the dignity of the state with the titles of some of its members was to confuse shadow with substance.[5]

In Poland he also recognized the old feudal nobility as an evil, and he provided a system for the gradual enfranchisement of the common people. Here, however, he was facing not only an entrenched nobility but a mass of restive serfs who had no experience in responsibility. Thus, he advised the continuation of the old system until the people were prepared for responsibility.

> Liberty is an appetizing food but it is difficult to digest. It takes a healthy stomach to support it. I laugh at those degraded people who, allowing themselves to be organized by agitators, dare to speak of liberty without having any idea of what it means and, their hearts full of all the vices of slaves, imagine that in order to be free it is enough to be mutinous. Proud and sacred liberty! If these poor people could only know thee, if they realized at what a price thou art won and preserved, if they sensed how much more is demanded by the austerity of the laws than by the weight of the tyrant's yoke: their feeble souls, enslaved by passions which they would have to stifle, would fear thee a hundred times more than servitude; they would flee from thee in terror, as from a burden which was about to crush them.
>
> To liberate the people of Poland is a great and worthy undertaking; but bold, perilous, and not to be attempted without careful consideration. Among the precautions to be taken, there is one which is indispensable and which takes time; that is, before everything else, to make the serfs that one wishes to free worthy of liberty and able to sustain it.[6]

There is a basic psychological truth in this statement which has only recently begun to be recognized. Man will learn to adapt to any environment, and when he has forgotten his liberty he will sing in his chains. The sudden shock of freedom under such conditions is analogous to turning a child loose in the world without any preparation for adulthood. The leaders of the more turbulent phases of the French Revolution, whose eyes would water at the sound of Rousseau's name, were obviously unfamiliar with this aspect of his philosophy.

The real test of a man's belief in democracy is a concrete statement of how he would put his ideas into action. One can make the statement that slaves are not yet ready for freedom and let the matter go at that. Having accepted the facts as they are, it is possible to defer indefinitely any changes to the existing order. Rousseau would not leave things on such a general level. He provided for a censorial or benevolent committee (*un comité censorial ou de bienfaisance*) which would meet regularly to draw up a roster of serfs worthy of manumission and which would compensate the master for the loss of their labor.[7]

In contrast to the abolition of the nobility, which he recommended for Corsica, he proposed that Poland develop a graded system of civil service, in which a man advances from one rank to the next on the basis of merit. With the various honors, insignia of office, and influence which he assigned to the members of this system, it was obviously his intention that it should come to replace the hereditary nobility as a source of prestige and power in Poland.[8] Rousseau would compose the Polish diet only of deputies who have been elected from the lower orders of his system, and senators (formerly appointed by the king) would now be elected by the chamber of deputies. In order to find a place in the first order of the system called "servants of the state," a man would be required to give evidence before his local dietine that he had performed with merit in some local function (such as lawyer, assessor, judge) for three years. The insignia of the orders would consist of plaques of various metals which must be worn by the members at all times. The plaque of the lower order would be gold, the next, silver, and the highest of blue steel. "The orders of knighthood, which formerly were proofs of virtue, are now no more than signs of royal favor."[9] Thus, the old Polish nobility would be abolished not by fiat, but by a gradual process of transferring prestige and power to the "elective nobility." The king would be reduced in power by taking from him many of his former capabilities for appointing officers of the court and by making the crown itself elective.[10]

II

A democracy, however, soon loses all meaning if that dangerous menace, the individual or private will, is allowed to assert itself and upset the balance of equality once it has been established. The clever man will soon discover a means of acquiring a disproportionate share of the wealth, and with this he will purchase his own power. To prevent this evil Rousseau was prepared to make great sacrifices in the efficiency of the state. Because it can be easily hidden, transported, and used in secrecy without leaving a trace, he regarded money as the prime agent of corruption.[11] Some of the personal factors behind this feeling about money have already been observed in his struggle with the proffered pension of George III. He would slow down the circulation of money in both Corsica and Poland by allowing tax payments in kind and by encouraging a primitive system of barter to replace money whenever possible.[12] But more important than any overt measure, he planned a campaign of psychological warfare against money and all other symbols of worldly wealth. The device of making the higher ranking official wear a plaque of the baser metal was only one aspect of his campaign. "Financial systems make venal souls," he said in the *Considerations*, "and if a man only wants to make money, he can always make more as a rogue than as an honest man."[13] The solution is to "make money contemptible, if possible, useless."[14] He acknowledged the loss, the waste, and the storage problems involved in payments in kind, but he brushed these problems aside with the remark that the decrease in efficiency would be compensated by the elevation of the souls of men. He would discourage the use of items of luxury in Corsica, such as gold plate and fine silks, but he would direct sumptuary laws primarily at the leaders of the state so they would serve as an example to others. Likewise, he would substitute honor for luxury in Poland, making all ranks and awards from the state matters of public virtue, distinguished by external insignia, and letting no citizen go abroad without them. In this way

> . . . a man who was rich and nothing more would be constantly overshadowed by poor and titled citizens, finding neither esteem nor pleasure in his own country; this would force him to serve his country in order to gain recognition. . . . That is how to deplete the power of wealth and create men who are not for sale.[15]

These three principles, the substitution of honor for wealth, the prohibition of luxuries, and the replacement of money exchange by an actual transfer of goods and commodities whenever possible, formed the cornerstone of his economic program. He would further diminish private property as much as possible by reserving large portions of land for the public domain. These could be worked by corvees, and a similar form of labor would be used for the construction of roads and other public works. In this manner he hoped to diminish public taxes to the point where they were no longer burdensome. If taxes were still necessary, he warned against the use of a professional tax farmer and insisted that collecting should be done by those being initiated into public service as a stepping stone for further advancement. If the young and inexperienced would be less efficient in this task, he was convinced they would be more humane.

One cannot but be impressed by Rousseau's democratic ideals and his zeal for honest government. But, already noted, is a rather disquieting tendency to sacrifice individual aspirations which are not in accord with the goals of the state. Public approval and the virtue of public service appear to be the only paths to glory in the societies he was striving to create. One does not mourn the loss of the professional tax collector until it is recognized that his demise was to be followed by that of the other professions as well. Rousseau was an opponent of professionalism in any form, and his plans for Corsica and Poland involved the gradual absorption of lawyers, teachers, minor administrators, and many other professional groups into the machinery of government, their rank depending on the merit they demonstrated in their previous assignments.[16] He felt that once a man had settled in a profession for life he was inclined to restrict himself to his professional role and fail to see his larger role as citizen. The teacher became a dusty academician who made parrots of his students; the lawyer became interested in the intricacies of the law, as it served his interest to multiply laws and needlessly increase the complexity of the legal system; the minor administrator came to regard graft as a special privilege of his office and was soon an expert in covering the traces of his petty thefts. All professionals were subject to seduction by certain personal advantages of their occupation, a danger which could be minimized if each man saw his position as temporary and recognized that the eyes of his fellow citizens were upon him, evaluating him for the next step in public advancement. Only by making public service the highest possible goal for every citizen could the state attract the highest type of men to positions of public responsibility. This was Rousseau's answer to the corruption he witnessed everywhere in the political life of his times. The individual or private will should not and could not be eradicated, it should merely be surmounted by the general will, an enthusiasm for the good of society as a whole.[17]

The general will, which remained at an abstract level in the *Social Contract*, now bears a suspicious resemblance to the mass opinion of one's neighbors and associates. The individual will, the very foundation of the independent man in a state of nature, has become a menace to society, an evil which, though it can never be completely suppressed, must be forever held in check. Man's natural goodness seems to apply only to man in a state of nature. Thus, the advantages of professionalism in the development of the knowledge, self-respect, and personal integrity of the individual are ignored on the grounds that such specialization isolates a man from the thinking and the moral standards of his fellow citizens.

III

With Rousseau's confidence in the efficacy of the general or national will and his insistence on the participation of the citizen in government, it is not surprising that patriotism became an important aspect of his political philosophy. A man will not allow the general will to triumph over his own self-interest, nor will he sacrifice his private advantage to the public good unless he is motivated by an intense love of his country, an earnest desire for the happiness and well-being of his fellow citizens. The extent to which he was willing to sacrifice the personal privacy and freedom of the individual for this objective is seen with a frightening clarity in his advice to Poland on the development of education and the preservation of institutions. One finds, in his remarks on this subject, a decided lack of faith in the capability of the average man to work out his own destiny. He was convinced that, unless goaded from the outside, the natural passivity of the individual would cause him to abdicate his responsibility, to seek repose and private amusement in preference to active public service.

He felt that the institutions and educational environment of the citizen should be arranged in such a way that he was constantly preoccupied with his country. He advised the Poles to develop exclusive and individual customs which differentiated them so markedly from other nations that no Pole could ever find anything in common with a foreigner.[18] He would have them incline the passions of the Poles in a way that would "prevent them from blending, from enjoying the company (of other peoples), from allying themselves with them. . . ."[19] Further, he would fill the mind of the Pole so completely with patriotism that he would have time for no other interest.

I would wish that, by honors, by public rewards, one could give a sense of brilliance to the patriotic virtues, citizens would be kept constantly occupied with their fatherland, that it would be their primary business, that they would have it always before their eyes. . . .[20] An infant, on opening his eyes, should see his fatherland and until his death he should see nothing else . . . when he is alone he is nothing; when he no longer has a fatherland he has ceased to exist; and if he is not dead he is worse than dead. . . .[21] You can judge from this that it is not the ordinary studies, directed by foreigners and priests, that I would prescribe for children. The law should regulate the content, the sequence and the form of their studies. . . . They should not be allowed to play alone according to their fancy but all together and in public in a manner that will give them a common goal toward which all aspire . . . their games should always be public and common to all; because it is not only a question of keeping them occupied, of forming a robust constitution, of making them agile and muscular, but of accustoming them at an early age to rules, equality, fraternity, competition, *to living under the eyes of their fellow citizens and to the desire for public approval* [italics mine]. For this reason the prizes and rewards of the victors should not be distributed arbitrarily by the games masters or school officials, but by acclamation and the judgment of the spectators; and you can count on these judgments being just, particularly if care is taken to make the games attractive to the public, by presenting them in a spectacular manner with some show of pomp. Then it can be presumed that all respectable people and all good patriots will consider it a duty and a pleasure to attend them.[22]

The above series of quotations will awaken many conflicting echoes in the modern reader.[23] The specter of nationalism, which it raises, recalls the countless abuses of the totalitarian state. The suppression of individuality reminds one of the future forecast by *Brave New World* and *1984*. But it was Geneva that Rousseau had in mind when he presented his advice to the Poles, and the chapters of his *Considerations* are filled with examples taken from the government and customs of Geneva. It was, in short, the small democracy and not the vast empire that he would stimulate with patriotism. If we must find a modern fantasy which represents a logical fulfillment of Rousseau's dream we are more likely to find it in the *Exodus* of Leon Uris than in the totalitarian model. Here the intense nationalism, the reversion to ancient customs and an ancient language, the sacrifice of individual ambition to the spirit of group unity, all those aspects which might be called "reactionary" in a large and well-established state, take on a different aspect because of the size and formative stage of the nation, the lack of expansionist ambitions, and the democratic character of its government.

However, it was not by accident that Rousseau allied his idea of militant nationalism with a tiny republic. Nor was the small size of Geneva the only determining factor in this concept. It is clear from his works on both Corsica and Poland that the more deeply he became involved in forming their institutions the more he came to think of them as a reflection of himself. The extent to which he regarded the subjugation of Corsica as a personal attack on himself is a good illustration of this point (see chapter 12). Rousseau had always cast himself in the role of the underdog and gained much of his sense of virtue from his feeling of being alone, small, weak, but defiant in the face of the more powerful and influential figures of the world. He offered Poland the alternatives of being wealthy and powerful, and therefore evil, or creating a free, wise, and peaceful nation, with simple customs and no ambitions for expansion.[24] He would, in fact, advise Poland to contract her borders.[25] As a small nation struggling among the corrupt giants she would attain a prosperity and virtue by her very size. He hoped to infuse into the Poles not power, but defiance; not a large standing army but "a warlike spirit without ambition."[26]

What Rousseau had in mind was a spirit of patriotism which was always struggling but never victorious, a kind of tiny, provocative, nationalistic state ennobled by its high social aspirations. The day of Scaevola was fading, and martyrdom had lost much of its appeal for the general public. Recognizing this, Rousseau was still tempted by any device which would inspire the Poles to personal sacrifice. There are examples of this in the economic, military, and administrative sections of his documents, but perhaps the most striking illustration is to be found in his handling of the *liberum veto*, a procedure in the ancient government of Poland by which any member of the diet, acting alone, could veto any legislative and most administrative proposals. Rousseau recognized that the *liberum veto* had to be reformed, and he presented the very sensible proposal of limiting its use to the formation of fundamental laws. But he added that it might have been possible to preserve the *liberum veto* in its original form if its use had been made dangerous. It was altogether too easy for a man to obstruct legislative action with the veto and then go home to enjoy the havoc he had wrought. If, however, he were tried by a special court six months after his veto and either condemned to death or given public honors, depending on the court's opinion of the value of his action, the *liberum veto* might be a more useful instrument of government. Rousseau would have no equivocation in such a court.

. . . this court could not simply absolve him of guilt, but would be obliged either to condemn him to death without mercy or award him compensation and public honors for life without ever being permitted any middle course between these two alternatives. Institutions of this kind, although favorable to the stimulation of courage and love of liberty, are too far removed from the modern spirit for us to hope that they would be adopted or become fashionable. But they were not unknown to the ancients, and it is by such means that the founders of their institutions knew how to elevate their souls and, when necessary, enflame them with a truly heroic zeal. We have seen, in republics where even more severe laws were in force, that unselfish citizens would dedicate themselves to death when the fatherland was in peril in order to offer advice which might save it. A *veto* which involved the same danger could save the state when the opportunity presented itself, and would never give it cause for anxiety.[27]

With such an important device in his hands, the man who cared not a whit for his own life would soon dominate the diet, or, if he finally exasperated his colleagues to the point where they were willing to destroy him, he would go to his grave unjustly treated for his well-meaning opposition to some minor matter. Here was an institution truly made for a Jean-Jacques Rousseau. The very manner in which he recommends and yet does not recommend this particular variety of the *liberum veto* is an indication that, while he recognized its impracticability, he found it irresistibly attractive.

From his first liaison with Thérèse down to his last romance with Poland, Rousseau was always attracted by littleness surrounded by bigness, virtue overshadowed by vice, the contrast of the powerful and the powerless. Thus, the idea of the single honest and courageous statesman amid a pack of scheming politicians and of the small but virtuous nation in a world of corrupt and powerful empires was a basic theme in his writing. Likewise, in his private life he saw himself as the last feeble defender of liberty, hemmed in by a vast army of conspirators who sought to crush his spirit and destroy his reputation so the world would never know the truth.

IV

Rousseau has often been criticized for turning his back on the large and powerful state and for his refusal to accept the fact that such states represented the future of Europe, for good or evil. It has also been remarked that his attachment to the early formative stages of a nation and his conviction that all states eventually become corrupt and expire after they depart from the spirit of primitive simplicity were so directly opposed to the trend of the times as to leave no really constructive course open to the modern state. As an indication of the limitations of his political philosophy, such criticism is legitimate. Since it was not his object to prepare constitutional theory for the giant empire one must look elsewhere to discover his merit.

Because of his particular bias and his deep intuitive understanding of the subtleties of man's interaction with his society, he has cast into relief a special aspect of the problem of individual freedom within the law. He recognized that it is only when a man is an active organic part of a community that his membership in and his relationship to that community has some meaning. When he ceases to concern himself with the selection of representatives, when he ceases to study the laws and plan for their modification, when he directs his attention to private success—or even to private creative work—he forfeits a certain measure of influence in the community. The more the libido of the individual is directed away from the state and toward his private life, the more the state will fall into the hands of the few and the government will cease to represent the will of all of the people.

Rousseau has shown that an idea or a way of life can only have significance when it involves some risk and some sacrifice for each individual participant, that one must be suspicious of a world that is too comfortable or ideas that are too convenient and easy to accept. In our society where we believe that one's "standard of living" is all important, that the better state is one which makes its citizens secure and affluent, it requires a man with a personal predilection for suffering to recognize the importance of continuous struggle and sacrifice in the preservation of a democratic way of life. Ideas which arrive without cost to the individual are held without conviction. This is why a placid democracy may be more vulnerable to despotism than a monarchy in which the people have always had to struggle for their rights against a king—or against more powerful neighbors. When the individual loses that intense personal concern for his country and his fellow citizen the whole nation is in danger.

Rousseau would counter this problem of social indifference by making every man a vigilante, always concerned about the abolition of obsolete laws, always on the watch for a lack of civic spirit or an excessive love of personal luxury in himself or his neighbor, always informed on the merit of his representatives, always eager to demonstrate his love of country in public ceremony or give his time and labor to the improvement of public roads. One does not obtain this type of public responsibility without great sacrifices in personal privacy and individual freedom. The paradox of liberty is that one must sacrifice some of it in order to preserve the remainder. The threat to freedom is always with us, and it comes from within ourselves as well as from foreign princes. Rousseau saw this danger with a greater clarity than most of his contemporaries because of his own internal struggle. But this same struggle brought about his excessive wariness of any threat to freedom—to the extent that he regarded any private interest such as business activity, pleasure, or even the cultivation of one's individual creative talents and the private pursuit of knowledge as a threat to one's communal feeling, one's absorption in the general will. His devices to preserve freedom became, in the end, as burdensome as despotism.

Why did his concern for liberty reach such fantastic proportions? His personal history shows that he was always afraid his own freedom of action was being threatened. To a large extent his fear was based not on the threat from without but on his own secret desire to submit to the rule of another—the thrill of being someone's slave. He despised this side of himself and fought against it. He placed himself on a war-time footing and impoverished his entire personality to save his soul. It is not surprising to find him making similar demands of his ideal society.

The problem of social indifference on the part of the specialist was very real, and it remains. It is certainly conceivable that the development of a money economy and the expansion of the arts and sciences could be a means of distracting men from the great social issues of the day. But regardless of the state of culture and finance there will always be men more interested in removing the crab grass from their front lawn than in the problems of government, the rights of the poor, and the threat to freedom. If experience has taught anything in this regard it is that participation of the citizen in his government must be voluntary and that the pressure of one's fellow citizens can be as tyrannical as that of a king. We cannot avoid specialization, and when we demand that the specialist demonstrate some kind of social consciousness, when we organize the government and citizenry in such a way that the specialist feels obliged to participate, we have already created a mechanism to direct the nature of his participation. Soon the government is demanding that the artist paint pictures of tractor farmers instead of pretty girls and that every novel demonstrate its social message. When too much social prestige is attached to virtue and patriotism, men will begin to strive for the appearance of these traits rather than their actuality. Whenever an idea achieves wide popularity, it is easily cheapened by a host of superficial followers who seek recognition by associating themselves with it.

V

It is not merely his opposition to professionalism, specialization, and private interest which strikes the authoritarian note in Rousseau's philosophy. It is, more precisely, his discontent with man as he is, his desire to build a world in which there will no longer be community strife. In short, it is the utopian quality of his thinking that is likely to rouse the greatest resistance in the modern reader. When he speaks of remaking the human personality by remolding the form of government, of ceremonies and games, of plaques and insignia to impress the people, one is reminded of a clever god who manipulates men for their own good because they are too ignorant and helpless to direct themselves.[28] In Rousseau's society the direction of the people would have to come from a master planner, a great legislator, or leader who recognized their problems and pointed toward their goal. Not for him was a society of different political parties in which men struggle against each other to control the drift of social forces. His objection to specialization was based on its creation of out-groups, minorities essentially antagonistic to the main stream of political life, in conflict with the general will.

Rousseau's principal value to his society was in his role as critic, the outsider who looked at the institutions of his day and found them wanting. In his ideal state he made no provision for men like himself. His desire that every man find a place in the community was so intense that he was prepared to make great infringements on personal privacy. Private property, private religion, private amusements, such as the theater, private parties, and balls, even the pleasures of private and casual sexual affairs came under his censure for such "secret liaisons . . . do more to separate, to isolate men, and to quiet their hearts."[29] Every citizen must become so much a part of the community that he scarcely has a private will. He must not be allowed to play alone, but must be forced to find his happiness in public games and other amusements which involve the active participation of his fellow citizens. How can one account for such an attitude in a man who was devoted to privacy in his personal life, who devised secret passages and trap doors through which he could escape with his dog when he saw visitors approaching his retreat?

Paradoxically, Rousseau longed for privacy, but suffered from a sense of loneliness. Having lost his mother at birth, he thought he had found another, only to be abruptly deprived of her in a fashion that left a lasting scar on his personality. Deserted by his father, he had been a wanderer most of his life. His one lasting sense of identity and belonging came from his native city, and his great pride was to sign his name with the title, *Citizen of Geneva*. Finally this, too, was lost when his books were burned by the Genevans and he abandoned his citizenship. He avoided the Parisians and most of the nobility because he did not feel that he knew how to act in their presence, and he never felt really at home with them. He longed for a country and a people he could call his own, a citizenry with whom he could feel compatible in morals and manners. Thus, he provided, for the citizens of his ideal Poland, a direct, obligatory, and continuous participation in the customs and activities of the community. In such an environment the future citizen would develop a strong sense of group identification. He would come to know his place. He would not be as Rousseau had been, always wavering between arrogance and servility. He would wear his status on his sleeve, and every day would find him deeply involved in some activity which reaffirmed his place in his society. This communal life became Rousseau's substitute for the acceptance and stability of the family, a security which had been, for him, altogether too precarious.

VI

If Rousseau had occasion to examine the world situation in which he had placed his small, independent states, he might well have paused to wonder how long they could continue among the larger powers. It is clear that the spirit of defiance and national individuality which he would infuse into the little warrior state of Poland would prove an aggravating thorn in the side of the Russian giant and a great temptation to Prussia. How could the little provocateur be protected? How else than by an international federation of states, a natural and important link in his political ideas. Some evidence suggests that Rousseau had prepared a rather extensive work on this subject,[30] but no fragment of it has survived. Favorable references to this idea appear in *Emile*,[31] and he remarked that the subject of world federation was *part* of his grand project on political institutions,[32] the greater part of which he destroyed. Aside from this, one must turn to his *Extract of 'Perpetual Peace'* and his *Judgment* of this work by the Abbé de Saint-Pierre.

It is curious, but by no means incongruous, that the man who devoted so much attention to the development of a ferocious, independent, and almost militaristic provincialism in his plan for the small states of his choice should be attached to the idea of world peace. His conviction that war was the very origin of man's slavery placed him in the position of supporting both extreme national independence and national subordination to the power of a world community. Again, it seems important to point to a significant difference between Rousseau and the typical authoritarian personality who regards a love of peace as a sign of weakness and warfare as a great stimulating and strengthening experience for a people. Rousseau demonstrated clearly in his many references to this subject that armed conflict was justified, in his mind, only in cases in which a nation was defending its liberty and that wars of ambition served only the ruler who wished to distract his people from their misery and increase his personal power.

But a proud little nation with a heightened sense of national honor and a firm attachment to its independence cannot survive alone among the giants. Not only does it require powerful allies, but allies who will not use it as an item of barter as Corsica was used by France and Genoa. Only a world federation with a single centralized authority and an international army could insure the kind of security which would protect the little nation against its neighbor.

Rousseau's interest in world peace predated his works on Corsica and Poland by at least a decade. In 1754 he undertook to make an extract of the works of the Abbé de Saint-Pierre at the request of Mably and Mme Dupin and had finished two of these, the *Extract of Perpetual Peace* and the *Extract of the Polysynody* (or council of ministers) by 1756. That he selected *Perpetual Peace* as the first of the abbé's works to extract is a clear indication of his own interest in this subject. Another is the fact that he used *Perpetual Peace* with great freedom, injecting many of his own ideas into the extract and introduction while presenting a fairly direct rendering of the concept of the Polysynody.[33] In both works, however, the ironic style of Rousseau is very much in evidence, and the ideas had clearly been absorbed as a part of his philosophy at the time the extracts were written.[34]

The bulk of the abbé's work proved too immense for Rousseau's capability and his fading motivation. Further, after a thorough examination of the voluminous writings he discovered what he felt to be Saint-Pierre's fatal error: his belief that men are motivated by reason rather than passion.[35] This appears many times in his *Judgments* of the two documents. Both of the *Judgments* end on a strong note of pessimism, a feeling that the ideas themselves are very sensible and very worthy, but that man was much too occupied with his private interests to consider world order and that no prince would participate in such a venture unless he could find a means of subverting it to some secret end which would prove profitable to himself alone. However, in his sarcasm Rousseau indicates all too clearly his own bitterness and his sense of frustration that such a thing as world peace is not possible in his time. In the very force of his pessimism he reveals his yearning for the dream of Saint-Pierre:

. . . you would take from the sovereign the right of creating their own justice, that is to say the precious right of being unjust when it pleases them; you would take from them the power of aggrandizing themselves at the expense of their neighbors . . . that magnificence of power and terror with which they love to frighten everyone, that glory of conquest from which they derive their honor; and finally, in short, you would force them to be equitable and peaceful. What would be the compensation for such cruel privations?[36]

Because of the tone of this remark, which appears in the *Extract*, and other similar comments in the *Judgment*, I am inclined to disagree with Vaughan's statement that Rousseau preferred a loose confederation of nations to a firmly knit centralized federation.[37] His intensely practical mind and his suspicion of the motives of men made it imperative that his world organization should have teeth in it. It should have the power to interfere, with its own army, whenever one large power tried to use one of the smaller states as a pawn or to sell it into slavery to another power for an appropriate consideration. Further, he makes it clear that he would give the world organization the right and the duty to interfere in the internal affairs of its member nations. He had already indicated in the *Extract* that the federated power would compensate the sacrifices of the prince by helping him to suppress an uprising in his own territory which threatened his power. But he added in the *Judgment:*

. . . you cannot guarantee princes against the revolution of subjects unless you guarantee subjects against the tyranny of princes. . . . Now I ask you if there is in all the world a single sovereign who, thus limited forever in his most cherished projects, would endure without indignation the very idea of seeing himself forced to be just, not only with strangers but even with his own subjects.[38]

With his intuitive understanding of the pleasure which can be derived from injustice, Rousseau grasped a certain aspect of the psychology of power politics at a much deeper level than many of his contemporaries. While he was genuinely attached to the value of local customs and would encourage local peculiarities in dress, in manners, and in law, he would not favor local autonomy in regard to the administration of justice. He was much too aware of the corrupting influence of power to permit a petty despot to have his way with his own people under the aegis of his membership in a world federation. While he does not indicate this in his own *Judgments* it would seem that the Polysynody or council of ministers would have to be in existence before the world power could become a practical reality. Further, the monarch would have to be not merely subject to the advice of his council but obliged to follow its decision. In short, eighteenth-century monarchy would have to be abolished to create a stable world government. The two ideas are actually interdependent.

Clearly, Rousseau had not completely reconciled his ideas on the sovereignty of the small state with his concept of a world government, at least not in any of his works which have survived. However, the apparent inconsistency of his attitude is due as much to the complexity of the situation itself (the dual need of mankind for both independence and security) as it is to the internal conflict arising out of the author's psychodynamics. The right of the individual states to self-determination, versus their responsibility to their people and to the larger body of whch they are a part, is still one of the critical problems in national politics today.

[14]

The Fall of Jean-Jacques Rousseau

IN SUMMING UP THE LIFE of Jean-Jacques Rousseau one must return again to his original intention, his discovery of the meaning of evil in falsehood and his determination to strip the hypocrisy from his society and reveal man in his true nature. Throughout his life Rousseau persisted, or claimed to be persisting, in that first goal. In following the tortuous path to truth he somehow lost sight of his original objective. In the course of his desire to lay the groundwork for an honest society he came to advocate subterfuge and deception.

The first indication of this tendency is in *Emile*, where he pointed out that children are not motivated to learn by perceiving the beauty of logic but by the discovery that reason can aid them in solving some of the practical problems of their lives. Fine, but how are children to be led to such a discovery? Rousseau felt that the influence of the instructor should not be visible to the student or he would resist. Somehow the teacher must arrange the life of his pupil so that he learns without formal lectures. The pupil must be cleverly stimulated by situations which present problems for him. To this end Rousseau began by feigning an emotion which he did not feel and passed to the elaborate falsification of events. Before he was finished he was manipulating not only the desire of his charge to learn, but his social and sexual tastes, his choice of a mate, the time of his marriage and the experiences on his wedding night—all with the best intentions in the world, to be sure. When this line of thinking was carried to the political scene, he approved the use of tricks on the part of the legislator, such as the pretense of receiving his laws from God, in order to present sound laws to an ignorant people who were not yet ready to appreciate them on the basis of logic and wisdom.[1] He advocated the use of public games and rituals to foster a particular brand of national consciousness in a people, and he warned of the danger of permitting children to develop private tastes and ideas on their own apart from the educational system of the state. Denying the legitimacy of force but not the legitimacy of subterfuge, he became an advocate of the very hypocrisy he so despised as a young man and that he regarded as the very genesis of evil.[2]

It seems that the disgust Rousseau expressed for his own works in the latter part of his career arose from a partial awareness that, despite the skillful and eloquent writing and the profound political insights of his more famous works, he had failed himself in some important way. He discovered, not only that he had been false to his original intentions, but that there was a secret and unsavory gratification connected with his political writings which he regarded as somehow unclean.[3] To Rousseau the liberal, the thrill of moral reform was based on his naive faith that he was utterly incorruptible. The discovery that pure virtue was not really his primary motivation was a shattering experience for his ego. The romance had gone out of it all. Soon he began to shrink back in horror when he took pen in hand to write about social reform. The full extent of these feelings is not revealed in his *Confessions*. It is, however, most striking in some of his letters to the Marquis de Mirabeau who encouraged him to continue his political writings. In this struggle with the temptation to write, Rousseau reminds one of a small boy who refuses to look at dirty pictures.

June 9, 1767
I repeat and declare to you that I will never again take up my pen for the public on any subject whatever; that I will neither produce nor permit anything of mine to be printed during my lifetime, not even what I still have in manuscript; moreover that I neither can nor will in future read anything which might awaken my dormant ideas, not even your own writings . . .[4]

August 12, 1767
I am sorry, Monsieur, that you make it necessary for me to refuse you anything, but that which you ask is contrary to my most unbreakable resolution . . . to remove once and for all every temptation of that kind, I declare to you that from this moment I renounce every kind of reading except books on plants, and I will avoid even those parts of your letters which might awaken in me ideas which I wish to and should stifle.[5]

August 22, 1767
I was wrong in saying nothing for the abbé. . . . The reason which prevented me from even responding to his politeness is flattering for him, since it was the fear of being drawn into discussions that I have forbidden myself and in which I fear I would not be the strongest. I will tell you quite frankly that I glanced through, at your home, a few pages of his work which you had carelessly left on the desk of M. Garcon and sensing I was about

to become hooked (que je mordois un peu à l'hameçon) I hastily shut the book before I was completely taken. . . . I promise you that I will never again open it, nor yours, nor any other like it.[6]

Like the hero of a romantic novel who resolves never to touch his sweetheart again when he discovers within himself an ugly and disquieting lust for her body, Rousseau turned away from political writing rather than come face to face with his own loss of innocence.

He could derive no satisfaction from impulses within himself which were not congruent with the general will. Nor would he recognize that such impulses could make any positive contribution to civilization. As a result, there is a cloying sweetness about his picture of himself which is infused into his idea of the perfect primitive society. His man of nature shed blood only to appease his hunger for food and even then he was moved by pity. He never dreamed of destruction on a grand scale, nor did he seek power. Only by taking thought did he lose his primitive innocence and raise the terrible juggernaut of civilization on which he rode to power over his fellowman.

II

The fall of Jean-Jacques Rousseau, like that of other rebels who attempt to set new directions for society, raises the disturbing question of the morality of revolt. Are his works the product of a sincere desire to discover moral truths, or are they a mere façade to cover his urge for personal aggrandizement? The reader will recognize that this question cannot be answered by a mere selection of one of the two alternatives. It is the interplay of motives which is critical in shaping the "truth" which follows. Rousseau's political writings, like his personal *Confessions*, were the product of many forces at work in his personality.

The act of confession, which feels like a wholesome impulse to the penitent, can have a variety of meanings. On the surface there are noble thoughts, as in the case of the legend of George Washington who "could not tell a lie" because he had such a manly respect for honesty. From another point of view confession can actually be an act of ingratiation. The man who maintains his façade is telling us that he will not yield. To deny one's guilt with a smile is a way of saying, "prove it, if you think you can." Confession can mean, "I will cast aside all my defenses. I will lay myself helpless before you, if you will only forgive me and love me." A child who is often rewarded for confessing can come to enjoy the act since it is followed by a demonstration of love from his parents. Eventually, as he grows older, he learns to be naughty. Not really wicked, for this might be unforgivable. Just naughty enough to confess, since he has discovered that his pathetic and tearful defenselessness can move the heart of an otherwise obdurate parent. At such a point the original admonition to "stand up and tell the truth like a man" has been twisted by the mind of the child to his own needs. Courage has been transformed into masochism.

Did Rousseau discover as a small child that a full confession, in which he threw himself tearfully at the feet of his father and declared his helpless dependency, reduced this fearful figure to remorse and brought forth the demonstration of love he so ardently desired? It is clear from the incidents which he does reveal about his childhood (particularly the one in which he said goodnight to the roast) that he often got his way with his father by his pathetic appearance, by his capacity to inspire pity. There is no mistaking this same tendency in his writing. But the person who calls on us to pity him is playing a delicate game. He must appear to be completely unselfconscious, unaware of his own hardship. He must not "call on us" for pity, but merely allow us to become aware of his pathetic condition. If he fails in this play, if he appears to pity himself, he only inspires contempt. The game is suddenly lost. After ascending to the heights of a sense of virtue, a virtue dependent on a look of pity which emanates from the other, the look suddenly changes to contempt and its object is transformed from hero to buffoon. Characteristically, there was nothing Rousseau feared more than ridicule.

For a man who seeks both truth and innocence, he was caught in a difficult situation. As a child, he had learned to play a game in which a confession of "the truth" brought forth a sense of virtue, a sense of being loved. In that tender age, sincerity was the primary virtue. It was, as Starobinski[7] has remarked, an unreflective sincerity. One did not ask one's self any questions, one simply told all. As an adult it was not always possible to retain the innocence of childhood, the lack of the sense of self which makes spontaneity natural and easy. Yet his particular game depended on his remaining unaware of what he was trying to do. Unlike the physical masochist who knowingly courts punishment, who even pays money to be punished, Rousseau, the moral masochist, could not obtain his sense of virtue unless he remained unaware of his urge to suffer. As a child when he was being sent to bed without his supper and he paused sadly in front of the roast to bid it goodnight, he melted the heart of his father. But he was successful in his performance precisely because his act was completely spontaneous and naive. As an adult, reflecting on this scene, he was seeking to understand the truth about himself. At the same time he wanted to reach the hearts of others with the touching image of his own innocence.

But the adult cannot really become as a little child. To present a genuine picture of innocence he must not only deceive others, he must deceive himself. Thus, the very mechanism of Rousseau's psychodynamics was such as to prevent the discovery of truth. He forgot that for an adult there is a basic incompatibility between innocence and truth. Unlike the child, the adult is responsible for his own decisions. A young man has reached maturity when he stops attributing his bad behavior to his unhappy childhood or his cruel parents. When he reaches maturity it is no longer enough for him to have good intentions. He must be judged by his acts. Innocence has become a barrier to truth.[8] Innocence is ignorance of self. The very trait associated with virtue in a child—the innocence that we affect to find so charming in children— becomes a dangerous pitfall for the adult. Unless a man is prepared to face the full enormity of his evil intent, the intensity of his urge for self-aggrandizement, the road to self-discovery will be filled with barricades and his capacity to prepare the good life for others will be hampered by self-interest. When a sense of virtue is tied to innocence, a loss of innocence will plunge the individual into a sense of absolute evil. Yet the great discoveries of truth about society, and about men, take place through a progressive loss of innocence. This was the problem faced by Rousseau. He wanted to know the truth, but he also wanted to maintain his innocence of evil.

He wanted to be honest, but he also wanted the world to *know* he was honest and, more important, innocent of all subterfuge and hypocrisy. That "Rousseau the actor," whom we observed as a child, the little performer who was the idol of his family, was still on the scene. The desire to be the center of attention, to humiliate himself by exposure, but at the same time to present such a pathetic and moving scene that he roused the compassion of his readers, the desire to be naughty and to be loved in spite of his naughtiness—all of these impulses struggled with the single conscious desire to uncover the truth. Here is the source of that seemingly incredible blindness in his works, the sudden flashes of revelation followed by an innocent naiveté which seems to ignore all that has gone before.

In his inability to recognize his own dual nature he projected this duality onto society. He identified his own femininity with everything female in the external world, and since femininity was a frightening and evil thing to his own ego he regarded it as the source of evil in society. It became his purpose to abolish the dual nature of man, to unify him into a single principle of goodness. Such a society would have no need for a loyal opposition, since it would be set right from the beginning. It would be masculine, i.e., simple and not complicated like the female. In eliminating the nobility, he noted that the "ribbons and jewels which distinguish them have the air of baubles and feminine adornment.... "[9] He would discourage luxury and other such feminine vices. The drama was also feminine for one pays money to see ". . . effeminate and dissolute theaters, where they speak of nothing but love, where actors declaim and prostitutes smirk. . . ."[10] Physical exercise, the amusement of men, would come to replace the social graces: ". . . a taste for physical exercise discourages dangerous idleness, effeminate pleasure, and superfluous wit. . . ."[11] The arbitrary power of slave nations was associated with "caprice and whim" and "luxurious decorations," whereas the festivals of a free people were characterized by the more masculine traits of gravity and propriety.[12] Thus, the very essence of freedom was masculine, and slavery was feminine.[13]

For Rousseau the devil was a woman, a malevolent empress who demanded unquestioning obedience; languid and voluptuous, yet capable of a terrible energy of will; surrounded by every luxury and pleasure, yet eternally greedy; a slave of her own desire, yet exuding a charisma powerful enough to enslave all mankind. This was the danger he feared would deprive young republics of their freedom as she had deprived France. This was the enemy he found so difficult to fight, because she was a secret side of himself. He could pull aside the veil for others, but he could not look upon the thing he had revealed.

Thus, he could not relate to a woman as a man who might see her as a sexual object. The aura of the female exerted such a magnetism upon his own identity that he was afraid of being completely consumed by her. He was afraid and at the same time he was drawn toward her. In spite of his efforts to remain free and independent he found himself gradually enslaved by a strange mixture of filial devotion, gratitude, and love. He found himself being sweeter than he really wanted to be, and he hated himself for it. He longed to break loose, to tell her off and be done with all pretense. Yet, imperceptibly, he became more deeply enmeshed until he felt his very soul was no longer his own.

In the early years of his manhood in Paris he was conscious of his terrible vulnerability, both despising and cherishing his secret desires. But under the tree on his way to the keep, in the throes of ecstasy, a vision of independence came to him. He would harden himself like a Roman. He would call out against submission, and effeminacy. He reformed his habits and his way of life. His new personality was a denial of the sweetness that had characterized his childhood. He found, however, that he could not grasp his entire being and rivet it into a new mold merely by taking thought. The old tender feelings swelled within him, in spite of his protest, and the mystic woman of his dreams returned to haunt him with her dark caress.

It is conceivable that this fear of femininity is the primary factor that shaped what we have called the "authoritarian element" in his philosophy. His first essays were praised for their boldness and masculinity, but the kind of masculinity which he exhibits is a certain impatience with sustained thought, a fear of weighing alternatives, as though some weakness, some "feminine" hesitation might overtake him if he allowed himself to reflect on a point. It is the masculinity of the hunter who must guard against any squeamishness as he closes on the kill. It is not the masculinity of the philosopher, of the man of reason. In his mind anything fancy became associated with the hated feminity. In thought, as in dress and manners, he was always on his guard against any temptation which might lead him from the most direct and simple ideas. The result was a conflict between his desires for simplicity and the inherent complexity which he began to see was an inescapable part of man in society.

The struggle with his hidden enemy eventually drove Rousseau from the scene of political combat, but not before he had laid the foundations for human liberty on which others were to build. Tolstoi, one of the great independent forces against tyranny in Russia, reports that from the age of fifteen Rousseau was one of the two beneficent influences in his life, the other being the Gospel.[14] Kant, who formerly had a contempt for the masses, records that Rousseau converted him to a respect for the individual and a recognition of the role of philosophical inquiry in establishing human rights.[15] Emerson was one of Rousseau's great admirers, and through him Thoreau came to know some of the basic ideas of Rousseau, which may well have been influential in his famous essay on *Civil Disobedience*.[16]

Rousseau has also had a negative influence on society. Babbitt[17] holds him responsible for all the excesses of romanticism. Talmon[18] says that Rousseau gave rise to "totalitarian democracy." Countless writers find in him the spirit of the revolutionary Terror in France and the living animus of Robespierre and Saint-Just. It is futile to argue such questions at length. Certainly, quotations could be selected from his works which would support all of the views. The secret of understanding Rousseau is not in the discovery of his "real" or conscious attitudes, but in the recognition of his conflict of values.[19]

The proud republican, the advocate of individual freedom, represented the more acceptable and conscious aspect of Rousseau's personality. This was the Rousseau who inspired Tolstoi and Kant, the man who sought to bring fundamental honesty back to the world. Today, those who like to think of themselves as liberals can identify with this image.

But then there are the inexplicable statements that seem to issue from a shadowy figure behind the scenes. Many partisans of Rousseau have tried to rationalize away these strange remarks, but there are too many of them. These remarks reveal something significant not only about Rousseau, but in regard to the general process of social reform. In an attempt to examine his own motives Rousseau has taken us closer to an understanding of the meaning of revolt, a goal quite beyond his original intention.

The Urge to Suffer for Truth

I

THE IDEA THAT A MAN'S POLITICAL and moral attitudes are a product of his early childhood experiences is popular among modern novelists. So clear is the picture conveyed by the deft writer that one observes the rise of the authoritarian personality from the roots of weakness and effeminacy without a ripple of doubt. Alberto Moravia's *Conformist* and Jean Paul Sartre's *Childhood of a Leader* present articulate and convincing pictures of the fascist whose political life serves as a defense against his deeply repressed latent homosexual impulses, who strikes out at the Jew as a means of stifling his own sensuality, and who finds an outlet for his sadistic impulses in the group-sanctioned cruelty of the party. The danger of such stereotypes is not that they are untrue but that they are liable to become too pat. It is reassuring to find support in psychoanalytic theory for the belief that our opponent's ideas are not only politically reprehensible but the product of a weak and nasty personality, stewing in the juice of perverse sexual fantasies.

While busy congratulating ourselves on our clean minds we are likely to overlook a certain uncomfortable resemblance between the acts of great liberal reformers and the dynamics of masochism, as well as the extent to which masochism and sadism partake of each other. If one examines the literature on the intellectual, it is not difficult to find references to illustrate this point. The term "intellectual," when it is used in the political sense, generally refers to the liberal reformer, the conscience of his times, as Brombert[1] describes him. While many intellectual workers ignore the field of politics, it seems that, in the political field, the liberal reformers have received the general designation of "the intellectuals." As Benda[2] has pointed out, this appellation is probably justified only when it is applied in such a sense. Those who use their intellectual tools in support of the powers that be, are not really intellectuals by profession but servants of the state. Brombert[3] remarks that masochism, in the sense of public confession and sacrifice, is one of the traits of the French intellectual. Simone de Beauvoir speaks of this characteristic both explicitly and implicitly through the self-questioning and self-accusation of some of her characters in *The*

Mandarins.[4] Clearly, the term "masochism" does not mean the same thing in all these discussions. Riesman describes it as a tendency to return to the fold, a final desire to submit to the experience that everyone else has had, to end the struggle of dissent. Thus, a man will search the philosophical systems of the world to find Jesus at last, or he will discover, as did Rousseau, virtue in the humble attitude of the poor and helpless, and insist that simple, honest labor is superior to the finest philosophical speculations.

But just as we have become convinced that we are speaking of masochism, the hero struggles to take the whip in his hand after he has received the final lash. As Riesman remarks:

> Coupled . . . with the masochism of pain and of rejection of the person's own talents and values, there is an even more concealed desire for domination, in which great claims are covertly staked out for leadership in the day-to-day social scene. Such a person privately feels that he has his finger in the dike against fascism, or whatever other evils threaten, and that if this finger were removed, but only then, the flood would overwhelm us.[5]

In such cases there seems to be an actual transformation within the personality, a change from liberalism to authoritarianism. This transformation raises some of the deepest questions concerning the morality of revolt. Psychologically, the impulses of sado-masochism are closely connected with the desire to dominate, to rule, on the one hand, and the desire to submit, to follow a leader, on the other.[6] Further, the provocative aspects of masochism are related to the emotions of the rebel against authority. Some conclude from this that the rebel, the dissenter in modern politics, is merely provoking abuse in order to feel the thrill of his own virtue—or he attacks the status quo so that he may, himself, take command. However, while there is no absolute truth in regard to questions of social justice, in specific cases truth can become an issue of importance. It is possible for governments or parents to be in error and for that error to be corrected through the medium of dissent and protest. To say that masochistic and sadistic impulses can influence the nature of protest and can even affect a man's perception of truth is only to say that dissent and, if necessary, revolution must be thoughtful and not hysterical processes. It is to say that we must always stand ready to question our motives, that we must not delude ourselves with the false idea of the sacrifice of the self for the sake of mankind.

Man will have his pleasures, be they sex or social work. The picture of the saint who gives up everything of value in his desire to serve others is not consistent with what we know of human nature. The pleasure in suffering is often most attractive to those individuals who, as a result of certain repressive experiences, have come to feel an intense guilt about their desire to dominate or to be cruel to others. However, a crisis in the life of the social reformer may bring this repressed urge close to the surface. Sometimes it actually breaks through to become a principal trait of the personality, as in the case of the little old lady from the antivivisectionist society who wanted to "mow down with a machine gun those cruel doctors who torture helpless little puppy dogs."

The pleasure in suffering has many forms, but its most exquisite and at the same time its most dangerous manifestation is the thrill of personal righteousness. For righteous ecstasy is only one step removed from the surge of moral indignation toward "those others." With the arrival of this moralistic orgasm the intellect has surrendered, and the drive for sadistic satisfaction is exposed in all its naked reality. The little old lady with the machine gun is one with the young Jean-Jacques who chased the miserable cock down the street, pelting it with stones because it "felt itself stronger" than others. Power corrupts, not because power, in itself, is inherently evil, but because it can release latent sadistic forces in the most kindly and self-sacrificing social reformer.

On the surface, the personality of the fascist appears to be completely different from that of the liberal humanitarian: the one cruel, the other kindly; the first determined to dominate at all costs, the second devoted to freedom and civil rights. But "freedom" is a philosophical concept, and governments are acts of men. Between the two lies a long train of events in which the human personality—that strange and variable mechanism—must come into play. Justice which appears so pure, so pristine, and so simple in the morning of our political thought, becomes clouded and confused in the oppressive heat of political action; and the underdog, whose wants appeared so reasonable when he was weak, is soon clamoring at the gates of power.

If we believe that a democratic society will grow and flourish in an atmosphere of just and reasonable dissent, the critical question is whether or not a specific case of dissent is just or reasonable. To answer this question we must look deeply into the motive of dissent, for here alone lies the morality of revolt. The satisfaction of a man's personal instinctual cravings is a legitimate personal goal, but when this goal becomes confused with the urge for social reform, society is in danger. Not only do we risk losing the fruits of a great revolution, but the very act of revolt is brought to trial and the meaning of dissent is lost.

Freedom, which begins as a democratic ideal, can become nothing but a dirty word if it means the freedom to exploit others. The desire to find "the truth" about the relationship between man and his society and to discover the principles of social justice must inevitably fail if we cannot face our own private desires and achieve a certain comfort with our impulses. The inability to know ourselves will cause us to turn away in disgust when we confront some of the difficult truths about mankind. If we succumb to the impulse to cover our motives with the "witchery and sugar"[7] of high-minded public interest, we inevitably find it difficult to face the elemental and animalistic qualities of mankind. If we are unwilling to face the truth about man and his nature, we will not build a beautiful society merely because we can create a beautiful and charming falsehood.

II

The life of Jean-Jacques Rousseau is a story of great significance for the modern political theoretician. His ideas, if one examines them carefully, with their reservations and caveats, had much to offer the society of his time. But the feeling-tone—the emotional content of his political writings—is decidedly destructive and denunciatory. Nowhere more than in the writings of Rousseau is one aware that the rebel has within him many of the attributes of the tyrant. How can we guard against such tendencies in the political world of today? How can we make constructive use of the contribution which our rebels can make to society while insuring, at the same time, that a movement which sets out to correct abuses will not degenerate into tyranny? This question follows naturally from the previous discussion, but our knowledge of man and his society has not yet provided an answer. The theoretician interested in social reform has the responsibility to look carefully at his own motives, but we have no assurance that he can ever achieve a perfect personal honesty. The desire for personal honesty, when carried to an extreme, brings us close to the same trap which we saw closing upon the altruist in the previous section. It is all too reminiscent of the urge to eliminate the animal in man and make him into a god.

In the early days of this century, when both psychoanalysis and Marxism were in their youth, many enthusiasts decided that the problem of human frailty in thinking might be solved if educators and politicians would all be psychoanalyzed. The Marxists believed that such a process would lead to Marxism. We were in the grip of something like a new Age of Enlightenment, and it was felt that only some misunderstanding (perhaps this time a psychological misunderstanding) held people back from a great step forward into a new and better world. In his *The Intellectuals and the Wage Workers: A Study in Educational Psychoanalysis*, H. E. Corey explained that

> . . . recent behavioristic and psychoanalytic investigations restore a good portion of the utopist's belief that the most fundamental feature of man's original nature is his wish to love his fellows, that fear, hate, and the possessive impulses are vicarious, and that therefore the fundamental forces in a successful revolution must always be the love of our fellows and a sense of growing freedom. . . . General strikes abound in sublime instances of the release of love and magnanimity. . . . Every teacher should be psychoanalyzed, for psychoanalysis is the science par excellence which gives content to the sublime doctrine of the autonomy of the individual.[8]

In recent years, the Marxists have tended to oppose psychoanalysis.[9] It has become, for them, a tool of the reactionaries who want to make people adjust to a capitalist society. Nevertheless, there is still a prevalent suspicion that educators, politicians, and others who hold positions of responsibility should submit to a good cleansing of the psyche before they report for work.

It would be pleasant to believe that we have at last discovered an answer to the dilemma which impaled Rousseau in his construction of an ideal political system: the problem of personal bias, the setting of the individual tastes and desires against the general good, the emotional impairment of intellectual functioning. If this were true we need only insist that every politician and political theorist place himself in the hands of a good psychoanalyst and all would be right with the world. Unfortunately, no real evidence supports this belief. Aside from the fact that the social reformer must recognize that he has a problem before he can get help toward solving it, one suspects that psychoanalysis is as dangerous as any other doctrine when it becomes a refuge from responsibility. When a man recognizes he has a personality problem, he can seek treatment, but a requirement that he accept psychological guidance before he is ready may do him a decided injury. *Further, there is no assurance that a well-adjusted Rousseau would have seen the problem faced by the hero of our story.* His ideas on the defects of society were created from the depths of his own misery as well as from his genius. The struggle to understand and to cope with the problem of liberty versus slavery received its very energy from sources deep within his psyche. When one asks what led Rousseau to his particular insights in the psychology of submission, it seems clear that his personal combat with this phenomenon in his life focused his attention on the problem and helped him to understand the role of sensuality and private satisfaction in the loss of freedom for a people.[10]

We understand, as yet, almost nothing about the essential features of motivation, the fires that drive intellectual effort. We know little about the subtle factors having to do with the structuring of a problem—that all important first step toward solution. The role of suffering in creativity is still a mystery. We are not yet in a position, from the standpoint of either psychological knowledge or political sophistication, to prescribe the conditions for the fulfillment of genius. It seems that the answer to the problem of personal bias lies, not in the creation of an unbiased (i.e., perfect) individual, but in the creation of a society which allows a maximum potential for individual variation. The nectar of self-righteousness, which produces an intoxication with virtue, is not so potent when we do not all quaff from the same goblet. The danger faced, then, from all great political reformers, is not personal bias, but the silencing of dissent. It is not the thinker, but the thinker turned hero who threatens the freedom of thought.

The hero is a dangerous man, not only because of his urge for glory, but because of the responsive society in which he lives. During the revolution, Paris, the city which had once mocked him, turned the eyes of its multitudes upon Rousseau's image and followed, like a great hypnotized brute, the emotional content of his doctrine. No man named unfavorably in the *Confessions* was safe in the city. *Emile* became the bible of the Revolutionary Tribunal, and educational reforms gathered their authority from the name of Rousseau. Ignoring all the traditions of the past, the natural boundaries and regional customs, France was parceled into a series of minor states in a blind attempt to achieve the ideals of the *Social Contract*. Robespierre raised "virtue" to a national requirement and searched, with a truly Rousseauist suspicion, to uncover the enemies of virtue. The watchful attitude of the Parisian citizen toward his neighbor became a kind of caricature of the inquisitive Genevan. In Paris, however, the charge was not "levity" but "treason," and the sentence was death. Rousseau had let it be known that there was a higher voice than reason in the affairs of men and that words were poor means of communication between one heart and another. The sensitive soul clasped the hand of another and looked deep into his eyes. Here he found either complete trust or total betrayal; there was no middle ground. A look, a gesture, an association, a habit of dress; each of these could become a sign which gave meaning to one's whole life. Thus was the emotional froth skimmed off Rousseau's ideas in revolutionary France.

Ideas which become doctrine, and which are used to organize mass movements, soon lose their function as stimulators of thought. They become rallying points for emotion. This is not really as strange as it appears, for countless great intellectual ideas have been accompanied by a strong component of personal feeling. A thrill of pleasure is important to the process of thought. It is the thinker's only immediate reward. But when ideas become doctrine they capture the emotion of the masses without necessarily involving their intellects. The mass ecstasy of popular enthusiasm is quite distinct from the personal excitement induced by thinking; just as the urge to be a hero is different from the need to worship a hero. Even if it were desirable we could not prevent the emergence of the hero-saint who strives for perfection, but we must build a society which is proof against his excesses. Faith in heroes is not our salvation but our greatest danger, for it absolves us from the responsibility of personal judgment. We are in a world without certainty where our "true feelings" and "the worth of the inner man" can never be communicated to another by any absolute means. The thoughts of lovers, like the plans of politicians, cannot be read in their eyes. We must rely on words, deeds, and other forms of expression, and we must distrust the evidence. We will never be in possession of all the elements needed to sound the utmost depths of another being.

The hero is dangerous only to the extent that he charms us into casting aside caution so that we fail in our responsibility to guide him in his own darkness. Those of us who are not heroes can make mistakes. We can exhibit malice or self-interest. We can admit being sometimes more concerned about our own welfare than that of others. But the hero must be a god or a devil, and often, in striving for the godhead, he falls into the pit of his own unsuspected evil.

Notes and Sources

For ease of reference I have included both specific citations and notes together in the sequence in which they appear in the book. Abbreviations for the principal sources are as follows:

Annales — *Annales de la Société Jean-Jacques Rousseau.*

E. — J.-J. Rousseau, *Emile ou de l'éducation.* Paris: Garnier, 1961.

C. G. — J.-J. Rousseau, *Correspondance générale de Jean-Jacques Rousseau,* ed. Dufour & Plan. Paris: Colin, 1924-34.

C. S. — J.-J. Rousseau, *Du Contrat social* (an edition which includes the *Lettre à M. d'Alembert, Lettre à Mgr. de Beaumont,* and other works). Paris: Garnier, 1962.

H. — D. Hume, *The Letters of David Hume,* ed. J. Y. T. Grieg. Oxford: Clarendon, 1932.

M. — Mme d'Epinay, *Les Pseudo-mémoires de Madame d'Epinay: Histoire de Madame de Montbrillant,* ed. Georges Roth. Paris: Gallimard, 1951.

O. C. — J.-J. Rousseau, *Les Oeuvres complètes de Jean-Jacques Rousseau.* Paris: Gallimard, Bibliothèque de la Pléiade, 1959-64.

V. — J.-J. Rousseau, *The Political Writings of Jean-Jacques Rousseau,* ed. C. E. Vaughan. Oxford: Blackwell, 1962.

Titles of other sources are occasionally abbreviated in the notes. The complete titles can be found in the References, which are arranged alphabetically. Notes in which a page is not specified have reference to the book or article as a whole.

PREFACE

1. O. C., III, p. 8.
2. A. Camus, *The Myth of Sisyphus,* p. 15.
3. L. Proal, *La Psychologie de J.-J. Rousseau.*
4. A. Heidenhain, *J.-J. Rousseau: Persönlichkeit, Philosophe, und Psychose.*
5. J. Starobinski, *La Transparence et l'obstacle.*
6. J. Guehenno, *Jean-Jacques.*
7. C. E. Vaughan (Ed.), *The Political Writings of J.-J. Rousseau.*
8. *Emile* is discussed by Vaughan only to the extent that it relates to the *Social Contract.*
9. E. Cassirer, *The Question of Jean-Jacques Rousseau.*
10. A. Choulguine, *Annales,* 1937.
11. A. Cobban, *Rousseau and the Modern State.*
12. R. Derathé, *Jean-Jacques Rousseau et la science politique de son temps.*
13. E. Durkheim, *Montesquieu and Rousseau: Forerunners of Sociology.*
14. C. W. Hendel, *Jean-Jacques Rousseau, Moralist.*

CHAPTER ONE

1. See J. Parton, *Life of Voltaire*, p. 187, for a similar observation.
2. E. Ritter, *Annales*, 1924-25, XVI, pp. 47-50. Ritter is one of the great Rousseau scholars of another generation.
3. *Ibid.*, p. 60.
4. *Ibid.*, p. 81.
5. *Lettre à M. d'Alembert*, pp. 232-33, found in C. S.
6. Ritter, p. 79.
7. *Ibid.*, pp. 81-82.
8. *Ibid.*, pp. 82-83.
9. O. C., I, p. 6
10. Ritter, p. 99.
11. *Ibid.*, p. 111-12.
12. O. C., I, p. 7.
13. O. C., I, p. 7.
14. O. C., I, p. 7.
15. See R. Laforgue, *La Psychopathologie de l'échec*, p. 23.
16. O. C., I, p. 7.
17. O. C., I, p. 9.
18. C. Klingerman, *Psychoanalytic Quarterly*, 1951, XX, pp. 237-52.
19. O. C., I, p. 10. This childhood memory is interesting in many respects. It indicates Rousseau's denial of competitive and hostile feelings toward his brother, but also illustrates his feeling of guilt about his favored position. Even as a child he felt uneasy about the frequency with which his father took his side in arguments with his brother, and he sensed that he could only achieve some feeling of closeness with François by suffering with him. In this connection see Freud's paper "A Child Is Being Beaten," *Collected Papers*.
20. O. C., I, p. 8.
21. O. C., I, p. 9.
22. O. C., I, p. 32.
23. O. C., I, p. 12.
24. In one of the Neuchâtel manuscripts, which was obviously a preparatory note for the *Confessions*, Rousseau describes this same incident. Here he says: "I dreaded this punishment more than death before I received it" (O. C., I, p. 1155). This is typical of him. All pleasures and pains which he had not yet experienced were magnified by his imagination. With such an intense fear it is not surprising that he received the actual punishment with, at the very least, genuine relief. In this same connection Reik (*Masochism in Modern Man*, p. 11) has pointed out that threat is a critical factor in the genesis of masochistic fantasies and of the sexual sensations accompanying them. Of the well-remembered and unusual incidents of punishment in childhood of the type which Rousseau describes, he remarks: "I have well-founded reasons for surmising that in these exceptional cases the punishment was already unconsciously wanted and striven for, and intentionally provoked by

naughtiness. In other words the punishment was not the cause of the instinctual development, but its effect, invited by the child" (*ibid.*, pp. 11-12). The dynamic development of this desire for punishment is understandable if we recognize that Rousseau had learned to bargain for love by his pathetic and tearful appearance and that punishment made him appear pathetic and tearful.

25. She was forty at the time. Rousseau was eleven.

26. O. C., I, pp. 15-16.

27. In commenting on this incident in the life of Rousseau, Freud (*Complete Works*, VII, p. 193) said that "the painful stimulation of the skin of the buttocks is one of the erotogenic roots of the passive instinct of cruelty (masochism)." He remarks that educators have rightly concluded that such spankings "should not be inflicted upon any children whose libido is liable to be forced into collateral channels by the later demands of cultural education." It would seem that Freud places undue emphasis on the effect of the physical spanking on later cultural education, just as the patient himself is liable to place a great deal of emphasis on certain childhood memories, certain formative incidents. Freud later became more suspicious of the "critical incident" as the formative factor in character and neurosis.

28. Rousseau's masochistic development follows in detail the model proposed by Freud (*Collected Papers*, II, pp. 172-201, 266) and elaborated by Reik (*Masochism in Modern Man*, pp. 16-21) that the dominating woman in the fantasies of the masochist is the representative of the father, whereas the victim identifies himself with the mother. The reversal of sexual roles in the fantasy is necessary to disguise its homosexual content and avoid arousing castration fears.

29. O. C., I, p. 19.

30. Torturer.

31. O. C., I, p. 20.

32. O. C., I, p. 20.

33. See S. Freud, *Basic Writings*. Krafft-Ebing, Ellis, and others have also pointed out that cases of sadism show masochistic impulses and vice versa. It is usual, however, for one trait to be dominant in the personality while the other is repressed. The repressed impulses can find expression only in unguarded moments, at times of crisis, or in the more subtle and pervasive aspects of the person's life experiences.

However, in the sadism of Rousseau we are dealing with something quite different from the torture of people or animals for sexual purposes. Just as his masochistic desires had been desexualized and transformed into a pleasure in suffering morally, his sadistic impulses were represented by his urge to dominate and destroy for high moral purposes. It might be difficult to distinguish his aggression from normal aggressive impulses if it were not for two important factors: (1) a thrill of righteousness which accompanied his acts and (2), often preceding them, a feeling of identification with some persecuted and innocent creature. Rousseau could never push people aside in order to get his way. He could never admit to himself that he had any desire for power. Instead, he must first imagine himself as utterly powerless, humiliated, mistreated by those who tortured him and who knew what they were doing. Then, after he had pumped himself up with a certain ecstasy of suffering, he could give vent to a full-throated roar of rage. His rage was not an automatic response to a frustrating situation. It was a primitive urge, the very pleasure of which was derived from its uncontrollable nature. If he had to control it, he could not enjoy it. This quality of being without limits suggests the primitive erotic sadism of infancy (see O. Fenichel, *The Psychoanalytic Theory of Neurosis*, p. 73).

34. O. C., I, p. 28.
35. O. C., I, p. 27-28.
36. O. C., I, p. 28.
37. O. C., I, p. 17.
38. O. C., I, p. 28.
39. There are many reasons why Rousseau preferred to keep his relationships with women at a playful level. He was frightened of becoming too deeply involved, too dependent. He was not prepared to accept the responsibility for his actions. But a critical factor was his desire to protect his own innocence. A playful relationship was an innocent relationship and Rousseau felt unconsciously that he could not be condemned for anything which emerged from it.

CHAPTER TWO

1. O. C., I, p. 58.
2. In his play *Narcissus* (O. C., II, p. 957) the hero falls in love with a modified portrait of himself.
3. O. C., I, p. 50.
4. O. C., I, p. 51.
5. O. C., I, p. 197.
6. A. de Montet, *Madame de Warens et le Pays de Vaud*, pp. 47-48, 203-41.
7. *Ibid.*, pp. 56-82.
8. *Ibid.*, pp. 165-70.
9. *Ibid.*, p. 22.
10. P. M. Masson, *La Religion de J.-J. Rousseau*.
11. F. Mugnier, *Mme. de Warens et J.-J. Rousseau*.
12. H. Ellis, *From Rousseau to Proust*, p. 24.
13. Claude Anet was the nephew of Mme de Warens' gardener in Vevey, and she and Anet left Pays de Vaud for Annecy on nearly the same day. It has been conjectured that he was her lover before she left Pays de Vaud. Mugnier, pp. 118-19.
14. O. C., I, p. 77.
15. The same priest who directed Jean-Jacques to Mme de Warens.

16. O. C., I, p. 85.
17. O. C., I, p. 84.
18. O. C., I, p. 86.
19. J. Lemaître, *Jean-Jacques Rousseau*, p. 20.
20. See also Starobinski, *La Transparence et l'obstacle*, p. 213. This incident is not really as inconsistent with Rousseau's masochistic character as it may seem at first glance. In his masochistic role Rousseau is the accused, and his one great desire is to throw himself at the feet of a beautiful woman and beg forgiveness. In his sadistic role he is the accuser, the prosecuting attorney, a role which he assumes in magnificent posture in the first and second discourses, a role which he will frequently assume with his friends, particularly Hume, to whom he developed an intense sado-masochistic attachment.
21. O. C., I, p. 104.
22. The chronology of this illness is difficult to establish, and the symptoms are varied. However, they are not the simple fatigue symptoms of "neurasthenia." The roaring in the ears, the pounding of the heart, and the constriction of the chest suggest intense suppressed rage, fear, or perhaps both feelings. Some of his symptoms occurred about the time he discovered the relationship between Claude Anet and Mme de Warens. There was another flare up on the arrival of Wintzinried. At this time Rousseau was so ill he decided to leave "mama" and take a cure at Montpellier. His departure may have been occasioned, in part, by a desire to arouse Mme de Waren's interest in him, but its primary impetus probably came from Rousseau's inability to tolerate the ambivalent situation with his rival and his own intense rage.
23. Le Maistre.
24. O. C., I, p. 136.
25. O. C., I, p. 137.
26. See T. Reik, *Masochism in Modern Man*, pp. 59-71, 97-105, 113-28, where the masochistic suspense is discussed in detail.
27. O. C., I, pp. 137-39.
28. O. C., I, p. 125.
29. O. C., I, p. 149.
   See also J. Starobinski, *La Transparence et l'obstacle*, pp. 71-73. Starobinski, in commenting on this Lausanne performance, is struck by the profound psychological difference between Rousseau's behavior and that of an impostor. Unlike the impostor who fears a test of his identity, Rousseau welcomed a chance to demonstrate his ability. His role playing was almost as complete as in hypnosis, and, as in hypnosis, he could not break the spell until it was broken for him. Also, unlike the impostor, he could not escape from his new identity when it was no longer useful but had to live it through to the final denouement. We are reminded of certain actors who report that their off-stage personality often becomes similar to their stage role when they are playing a particularly powerful part. It seems that Rousseau, while attempting to remain un-

defined, was drawn like a feather into the vortex of any powerful personality which appealed to him. This phenomenon will be observable again when he is cast under the spell of his own myth and becomes "natural man."

30. Rousseau does not know where to place this episode chronologically. It may be from an earlier period. See O. C., I, p. 165.

31. O. C., I, p. 197.

32. As with his stay at Les Charmettes, later students of the *Confessions* have discovered discrepancies in Rousseau's facts at this point. He reports that Anet died after becoming overheated searching for genipi in the upper reaches of the Alps. Mugnier, who established the date of Anet's death as March 13, 1734, points out that one does not go into the Alps to collect aromatic plants at that season. See F. Mugnier, *Mme de Warens and J.-J. R*, p. 120. There is some suspicion that Anet may have committed suicide because of Rousseau's relationship with his mistress. Such a distortion would, however, take Rousseau's *Confessions* out of the realm of error and into that of deliberate falsification. This does not seem consistent with his character.

33. O. C., I, p. 206.

34. O. C., I, p. 224.

35. See F. Mugnier, *Mme de Warens et J.-J. Rousseau*, p. 160-61. The entire question of the date of habitation and the significance of the valley of Charmettes is discussed in detail in O. C., I, p. 1338, n. 1. See also A. Schinz, and I. Lawrence, *Revue d'histoire littéraire de la France*, 1928, XXXV, pp. 85-91.

36. L. Aurenche, *Annales*, 1907, III, p. 74.

37. O. C., I, p. 253.

38. O. C., I, p. 254.

39. O. C., I, p. 254.

40. O. C., I, p. 254.

41. Olive oil.

42. C. G., I, pp. 60-64.

43. C. G., I, p. 73.

44. O. C., I, p. 263.

45. O. C., I, p. 262.

46. C. G., I, p. 102.

47. In French such a slip is more difficult to ascribe to purely mechanical causes such as haste. Rousseau wrote *avec* instead of *sans*. It should be noted, however, that the original of this letter is not available. Dufour used the De Boubers edition of Rousseau's letters.

48. O. C., I, p. 263.

CHAPTER THREE

1. A. Toynbee, *A Study of History*.

2. W. H. Lewis, *The Splendid Century*, pp. 39-43.

3. Louis XIV was not so clever as to "create" a society which would

destroy the country noble. The society evolved slowly, and he gave encouragement to forces which flattered his own tastes and ideas. It is difficult to say just how consciously he set about molding his society and how much of it was done for him by his predecessors.

4. A procedure which originated with Henry IV.

5. A. de Tocqueville, *The Old Régime and the French Revolution*, pp. 22-77. Modern authorities do not support Tocqueville's condemnation of the role of the intendant. See L. Gershoy, *From Despotism to Revolution*, p. 22, who regards the intendant as an enlightened public servant.

6. For a psychological discussion of this phenomenon see E. Fromm, *Escape from Freedom.*

7. O. C., I, p. 164.

8. O. C., II, pp. 231-32.

9. C. G., I, pp. 184-88.

10. C. E. Vulliamy, *Rousseau*, p. 88.

11. O. C., I, p. 136.

12. O. C., I, p. 330.

13. O. C., I, p. 331.

14. O. C., I, p. 1135-36.

15. Diderot's claim, repeated by his daughter, was that he gave Rousseau the idea for the first *Discourse* (Diderot, D., *Mémoires*, I, p. 62). While Diderot may have offered suggestions, the style as well as the content is unmistakably Rousseau. Hendel (*J.-J. Rousseau, Moralist*, p. 25-26) makes a similar point.

16. O. C., I, p. 350.

17. The expression of tenderness between members of the same sex was characteristic of eighteenth-century French culture, as shown by the quotation from one of Diderot's letters describing his emotion after Grimm returned from a journey:

> With what ardor we clasped each other. My heart was swimming. I could not speak, nor could he. We embraced without saying a word and I wept. We were not expecting him. We were all at dessert when he was announced, "It's M. Grimm. It's M. Grimm." I took it up with a cry and sprang up, I ran to him and flung myself on his neck. He sat down and ate very little, I believe. As for me, I could not open my mouth either to eat or to speak. He was beside me, I pressed his hand and looked at him. (D. Diderot, *Mémoires*, I, p. 148.)

Possessiveness and lavish affection toward a friend of the same sex was not only acceptable but expected in a man of feeling. The same was true for French women of the times. In their description of the woman of the eighteenth century the Goncourt brothers report:

> Encouraged by the taste and example of the age, she flung herself on the friendship of some brilliant woman of fashion, and embraced it with all the frenzy, the ardor, the excessive enthusiasm of her sex

. . . She would pledge her companion a life long devotion, and prove it with sighs and embraces, whispered effusions and tiny transports! There was no leaving her, no living without her; every morning she must write her a letter. *My heart, my love, my queen:* thus if at all, must you name her with inclined head in a voice limpid and languid. You wore her colors, nursed her nerves, weighed her worries, whispered a thousand secrets in her ear; you went only to suppers where both were bidden, and to invite you meant to have her. . . . All your talk was of the charms of friendship: you took pride in advertising your *sentimental intimacy,* and the portrait of your bewitching friend must always be dangling from your wrist band. (E. and J. de Goncourt, *The Woman of the Eighteenth Century,* pp. 91-92.)

18. O. C., III, p. 5.
19. O. C., III, p. 7.
20. *Social Contract and Discourses,* ed. G. D. H. Cole, p. 144.
21. *Ibid.,* p. 150.
22. V. Brombert, *Partisan Review,* 1960, XXVII, pp. 480-502.
23. His *Discourse* was apparently only one of his provocations against established authority at the time of Diderot's arrest. Francis Winwar (*Conscience of an Era,* p. 195) makes the interesting statement that Rousseau did everything he could to get himself arrested at that time, including writing a letter to Mme de Pompadour asking to be put in the keep with Diderot. I have not been able to locate this letter.
24. O. C., III, p. 3.
25. R. M. Bucke, *Cosmic Consciousness.*
26. F. C. Green, *J.-J. R: A Critical Study of His Life and Writings,* pp. 101-2.
27. G. Gran, *Annales* 1911, VI, p. 11.
28. J. Starobinski, *La Transparence et l'obstacle,* pp. 1-14.
29. O. C., III, pp. 7-8.
30. O. C., III, p. 7.
31. O. C., III, p. 8. What deformity would fancy dress conceal? Perhaps his emasculated condition.
32. O. C., III, p. 14.
33. O. C., III, p. 21.
34. O. C., III, p. 22.
35. M. Grimm, *Correspondance littéraire,* III, p. 53.
36. O. C., I, p. 352.
37. O. C., III, pp. 7-8.
38. O. C., III, p. 7.
39. O. C., I, p. 384.
40. Grimm, II, p. 307.
41. O. C., I, p. 182-83.
42. O. C., I, p. 371.
43. O. C., I, p. 368.
44. O. C., I, pp. 377-78.
45. O. C., I, p. 380.

46. I am inclined to discount Mrs. MacDonald's opinion that the children never existed, i.e., that they were a hoax on the part of Thérèse to bind Rousseau to her by making him feel guilty. While Mrs. MacDonald presents abundant circumstantial evidence (*J.-J. R., A New Criticism*, I, pp. 144-81), it is difficult to credit Thérèse with the cunning to simulate five pregnancies. And why five? Having carried off the act once, why would five simulated children bind him closer than one? Clearly, the risk of detection would increase. For a man as suspicious as Rousseau it would be remarkable indeed if he did not suspect her of faking. Yet he showed no sign of suspicion. One can only assume that Thérèse bore unmistakable evidence of her pregnancy.

From a psychological point of view it is irrelevant whether or not the children were really Rousseau's. The point is that he thought they were. We have already noted his strong need to play the role of the child in his relationship with others. His pet names for Thérèse were "aunt" and "boss." His abandonment of his children probably represents a panic reaction caused by the arrival of creatures who had a more legitimate claim than his own to a position of emotional dependency. Rousseau loved children because he could identify with them, but he loved them as fellow-sufferers, not as one who could accept responsibility for them.

47. V., I, p. 146.
48. O. C., I, pp. 392-93.
49. V., I, p. 169.
50. V., I, p. 259.
51. V., I, pp. 243-44.
52. V., I, pp. 256-57.
53. V., I, p. 245.
54. V., I, p. 249.
55. V., I, p. 249.
56. V., I, pp. 266, 272. Here, again, the influence of his early years in Geneva is evident.
57. V., I, p. 269.
58. V., I, p. 273.
59. V., I, p. 265.
60. V., I, p. 267.
61. V., I, p. 192.
62. O. C., I, pp. 416-17.
63. O. C., I, p. 369.
64. There was actually considerable ambivalence about this new role, an ambivalence which he retained while writing the *Confessions* and *Dialogues*. In the *Confessions* he speaks of his enthusiasm for justice as "my foolish pride" (O. C., I, p. 416). But, like an old reprobate remembering the follies of his youth, he seems to lick his lips as he recalls once more those grand feelings of defiance.

The same feeling is evident in the *Dialogues*, in which he refers to the "unfortunate question" of the Academy which came before his eyes. But, speaking in the third person, he remarks that this same question unraveled "the chaos in his head, opening up to him another universe, a veritable golden age, of societies of simple, wise, happy men." Yet, says he, it was this very dream of man's grandeur which unsettled his mind (O. C., I, pp. 828-29).

65. O. C., I, p. 424.

66. O. C., I, pp. 426-27.

67. C. G., II, pp. 203-5.

68. C. G., II, pp. 206-9.

69. O. C., I, p. 397. Voltaire was now in the city of Rousseau's father, taking a place which Rousseau coveted. This seems to have aroused his repressed competitive feelings.

70. E. Ritter, *Annales*, 1916-17, XI, p. 112.

71. M., I, pp. 1-352. F. MacDonald, *Studies in the France of Voltaire and Rousseau.*

72. O. C., I, p. 396.

73. O. C., I, p. 396.

74. O. C., I, p. 412.

75. O. C., I, p. 414.

76. O. C., I, pp. 414-21.

CHAPTER FOUR

1. F. MacDonald, *J.-J. R., a New Criticism.*

2. O. C., I, p. 1450.

3. M., III, p. 169. Despite its frequent repetition, this incident has never been substantiated. We have only Diderot's account.

4. D. Diderot, *Mémoires*, I, p. 63.

5. D. Diderot, *Le Fils naturel*, in his *Collection complète*, V, p. 63.

6. Rousseau's conscience was capable of a peculiar moral twist when he was the aggressor in a literary insult. In his *New Eloise*, the heroine remarks that she would rather be the wife of a coalheaver than the mistress of a king. This statement was extremely offensive to Mme de Pompadour, but Rousseau felt, as he says in the *Confessions*, "This phrase had come to me in the heat of composition, and I swear that no personal allusion had been intended" (O. C., I, p. 512). When he read over the work later he saw the meaning that could be read into it, but since his conscience assured him that he had not intended this meaning when he wrote the phrase, he let it stand, contenting himself with substituting the word *prince* for *king*. In his characteristic attitude he took it for granted that Mme de Pompadour, if she was a woman of true virtue, must read his heart and not his mere words.

7. O. C., I, p. 456.

8. C. G., III, pp. 49-50.

9. O. C., I, pp. 403-4.

10. O. C., I, p. 437.

11. O. C., I, p. 427.

12. O. C., I, p. 427.
13. O. C., I, p. 434.
14. O. C., I, p. 432.
15. This may have greatly increased her attractiveness for Rousseau. For a discussion of his latent homosexual impulses, see Chapter 12.
16. J. Morley, *Rousseau*, pp. 263-64.
17. O. C., I, p. 439.
18. O. C., I, p. 439.
19. O. C., I, p. 426.
20. O. C., I, p. 442.
21. O. C., I, p. 443.
22. O. C., I, p. 444.
23. M., III, p. 108.
24. M., III, p. 124.
25. M., III, p. 147.
26. O. C., I, p. 448.
27. O. C., I, p. 454.
28. M., III, pp. 252-53. There is no independent account of this incident. Rousseau mentions only that he told Diderot of his passion for Sophie.
29. C. G., III, pp. 118-21.
30. C. G., III, pp. 143-45.
31. M., III, pp. 253-54.
32. Mrs. MacDonald (*J.-J. R., a New Criticism*, II, pp. 27-45) makes a similar point, but she doubts that Rousseau's confession of his love for Sophie (to Diderot) occurred prior to his letter to Saint-Lambert. N. L. Torrey ("Rousseau's Quarrel with Grimm and Diderot") supports the same chronology as mine.
33. As to the date of Diderot's visit, there is no clear evidence to support either the *Mémoires* which place it in the autumn of 1757, the *Confessions*, which mark it a few days after November 23, or the Courtois *Chronology*, which puts it some time in December of that year. As to the encounter between Diderot and Saint-Lambert, which the *Mémoires* place a few days after Mme d'Epinay's departure (October 30, 1757), we are again in doubt. If there was a clear break in the relationship between Saint-Lambert and Rousseau it might be used as a more reliable indication, but Saint-Lambert apparently took his anger out on Sophie, and she did not convey exactly when her more serious troubles with her lover began. We have only the long pause in her correspondence with Rousseau for a clue (a six-week period before the final break in May 1758). It seems unlikely, however, that Diderot could have contained his secret so long if he really learned it toward the end of 1757.

I have used the earlier date for the visit because it comes at a time of turmoil for Rousseau, when he was uncertain of Saint-Lambert and highly motivated to unburden his soul to a friend. It also comes before Diderot's advice that Rousseau accompany Mme d'Epinay to Geneva, a suggestion which did much to rupture their friendship.

Rousseau's version of the visit from Diderot differs only in what is not mentioned. He admits that he presented his passion for Sophie as one of silent longing, without telling Diderot that he had openly declared his love to her. He does not, however, mention any promise to make a full confession to Saint-Lambert. Diderot's three conflicting versions of this story (as described by Guillemin, *Annales*, 1941-42, XXIX, pp. 65-258) were written after the death of Rousseau.

34. C. G., III, p. 320.
35. The break was announced by reference to a passage from Ecclesiasticus (xxii. 21, 22) with the text in Latin so as not to cause a public scandal.
36. Aside from the romantic tales in *Emile*.
37. O. C., II, pp. 33-34.
38. O. C., II, p. 268.
39. C. G., V, p. 356.
40. O. C., II, p. 64.
41. The actress who threw Grimm into a spell of depression when she scorned his love.
42. O. C., I, p. 467.
43. C. G., III, pp. 136-43.
44. In this he was mistaken.
45. C. G., III, p. 211.
46. C. G., III, p. 227.
47. In this respect D'Alembert was an exception. He seems to have taken the attitude that Rousseau was mentally ill and not responsible for his behavior. When Voltaire, in the heat of his fury, was attempting to crush Rousseau, it was D'Alembert who asked him to show some forebearance (R. Grimsley, *J.-J. R., a Study in Self-Awareness*, pp. 195-99). When the literary world was subscribing a statue for Voltaire and Rousseau sought to add his name to the list of subscribers, it was D'Alembert again who interceded with Voltaire urging him not to return the money (J. Parton, *Life of Voltaire*, II, pp. 504-5).

CHAPTER FIVE

1. She was born Jeanne-Antoine Poisson.
2. Mme de Pompadour was more a symptom than a cause of the decline of France. She was a product of the economic and social changes of her time. She could not have achieved her position of influence had not the king ignored his responsibility.
3. M., III, p. 120.
4. O. C., I, p. 429.
5. C. G., II, pp. 303-24.
6. C. G., V, p. 135.
7. O. C., I, p. 494.
8. C. S., p. 205.
9. C. S., p. 207.
10. C. S., p. 214.

11. A belief similar to Unitarianism.
12. C. S., pp. 128-29.
13. C. S., p. 131.
14. *Oeuvres de Palissot*, II, pp. 102-3.
15. Diderot.
16. C. S., p. 127.
17. O. C., I, pp. 536-37.
18. O. C., I, p. 519.
19. O. C., I, p. 525.
20. O. C., I, p. 527.
21. O. C., I, p. 557.
22. O. C., I, p. 557.
23. O. C., I, p. 523.
24. O. C., I, p. 551.
25. O. C., I, p. 525. For the relationship between fate and masochism see T. Reik, *Masochism in Modern Man*, pp. 10-11. After the masochistic impulse has become unconscious it becomes necessary for the person to project all his injuries on the action of "fate." When a man has lost touch with the springs of his own motivation, fate (or God) will indeed work in mysterious ways.
26. This same letter also contains a condemnation of her numerous presents and the subterfuges and pretexts that she used in order to give him food.
27. C. G., V, p. 243.
28. O. C., I, p. 530.
29. C. G., VI, p. 169.
30. Quoted from E. C. Mossner, *The Life of David Hume*, p. 456 (*Walpole Letters*).
31. *Ibid.*, p. 457. (*Walpole Correspondence.*)
32. See *The Letters of David Hume* for the correspondence between Hume and Mme de Boufflers.
33. O. C., I, p. 564.

CHAPTER SIX

1. V., II, p. 32. It would seem that Rousseau means, here, the *concept* of a social contract and not his book which bears that title.
2. V., II, pp. 26-33.
3. V., II, pp. 33-34.
4. V., II, pp. 32-33, 49-50.
5. V., II, p. 36.
6. See J. W. Chapman, *Rousseau, Totalitarian or Liberal*, p. 39, for another interpretation of this point.
7. V., II, p. 47.
8. V., II, pp. 36-37.
9. V., II, p. 42.
10. V., II, p. 49-50.

11. V., II, pp. 42-43.
12. V., II, p. 36.
13. V., II, pp. 43-46.
14. V., II, p. 40.
15. V., II, p. 120.
16. V., II, p. 35.
17. Rousseau recognized this danger, but he saw it as in inevitable consequence of government.
18. V., II, pp. 46-48.
19. V., II, p. 132.
20. V., II, p. 133. While Rousseau's type of civil religion was unique to him, it was Calvin who first proposed the idea of a civil religion (see M. Walzer, *The Revolution of the Saints*, p. 55).
21. V., II, p. 68.
22. V., II, pp. 101-2.
23. V., II, p. 48.
24. F. C. Green, *J.-J.R: A Critical Study of His Life and Writings*, p. 304.
25. H. Ellis, *From Rousseau to Proust*, p. 130.
26. As an example of his conflicting attitude toward independence of the individual, there are sections in his *Considerations on the Government of Poland*, particularly in the area of education, which place the individual at the mercy of his neighbors.
27. J. Starobinski, *La Transparence et l'obstacle*, pp. 1-14.
28. O. C., I, p. 416.
29. V., I, p. 166. From the second discourse.
30. An urge to acquire territory appears extensively in mammals, and a "pecking order" or rank in the scale of dominance is quickly established in many species (Carthy and Ebling, *The Natural History of Aggression*, pp. 7-14, 23-38). As to the generalized and universal nature of aggression, in a recent symposium on that subject, which included representatives from all the sciences of man, the editors concluded:

> The current psychiatric evidence seems almost unequivocal . . . aggression is not merely a response to frustration, it is a deep seated, universal drive. (Carthy and Ebling, p. 3.)

And Lorenz remarked:

> There cannot be any doubt in the opinion of any biologically minded scientist that intraspecific aggression is, in Man, just as much of a spontaneous instinctive drive as in most other higher vertebrates. The beginning synthesis between the findings of ethology and psychoanalysis does not leave any doubt either that what Sigmund Freud has called the "death drive," is nothing but the miscarrying of this instinct which, in itself, is as indispensable for survival as any other. In this symposium there has been a most satisfying agreement, on this point, between psychiatrists, psychoanalysts, and ethologists. (Carthy and Ebling, p. 49.)

31. O. C., I, p. 10.
32. V., II, p. 33.
33. V., II, p. 102.
34. V., II, p. 104.
35. V., II, pp. 49-50.
36. V., II, p. 52.
37. V., II, p. 53.
38. V., II, p. 54.
39. V., II, p. 55.
40. E. Durkheim, *Montesquieu and Rousseau, Forerunners of Sociology,* pp. 128-29.
41. As J. R. Tronchin remarked in his refutation of the *Social Contract*, Rousseau could not see any reciprocal relationship between those who govern and those who are governed. The former appear to be but instruments of the latter and can be changed with a change in taste (R. Derathé, *Annales*, 1950-52, XXXII, p. 18). Apparently, the dictatorship of the masses was to be as complete as was formerly the domination of "the great" over the little people with whom Rousseau identified.
42. V., II, pp. 88-92.
43. Joan McDonald, *Rousseau and the French Revolution, 1762-1791.*
44. *Ibid.*, pp. 155-73.
45. Proal (*La Psychologie de J.-J. R.*, pp. 204-6) and Choulguine (*Annales*, 1937, XXVI, pp. 233-34) have noted the extent to which both the actions and ideas of Robespierre came directly from Rousseau. In his own works he frequently cited Rousseau. His insistence that the National Convention pass a decree recognizing the existence of God and immortality of the soul comes from Rousseau's idea on civil religion. His festival of the Supreme Being follows Rousseau's recommendation for public festivities in which the people affirm their faith in God and country. Choulguine's chapter on the secret of Rousseau's influence is filled with examples which indicate his popularity, not only with the leaders of the Revolution, but with followers as well. The newspapers of the time contained frequent quotations from his *Social Contract.*
46. As Choulguine (p. 229) has indicated, the revolutionists were not the only ones to make use of Rousseau's ideas in order to strengthen their position. Calonne wrote a pamphlet in 1790 pointing out that the deputies, as mere representatives, did not express the will of the people, and Malouet attacked the revolutionary clubs on the ground that private organizations within the state were contrary to the principles of liberty.

CHAPTER SEVEN

1. E., pp. 14-15.
2. An eighteenth-century version of the teaching machine consisting of a frame with letters to be arranged to form words.
3. E., p. 116.
4. E., pp. 76-78.

5. Rousseau's special attention to this period of the child's life is probably a reflection of his own motherless childhood and the strong sense of deprivation which resulted from this experience.

6. E., pp. 224-25.

7. C. Brinton, *The Shaping of the Modern Mind*, pp. 31-35.

8. E., pp. 462-65.

9. E., p. 72.

10. E., pp. 439-40.

11. E., p. 1.

12. With Rousseau the desire to suffer was often conscious and quite congruent with his concept of himself. However, it was not perceived as a desire but rather a "willingness" to suffer for a noble cause. The desire to be cruel, on the other hand, was completely unacceptable. It could not be rationalized into his concept of himself, and therefore it had to be repressed, that is, forgotten.

13. This identification is evident from the first quotation in this chapter (E., pp. 14-15). The first few chapters of *Emile* add additional evidence that Rousseau regarded the child as a special kind of underdog who, like himself, had been mistreated by society.

14. This notion of the susceptibility of the child to external influence was derived from the notion of the *tabula rasa*, which was the starting point for all of Locke's psychology. Rousseau, despite the statement above, did not really believe that the mind of the child was blank at birth. He felt, instead, that it had certain capacities which develop according to "natural" stages and that this natural development of the mind must be respected by the teacher. His departure from his own principles in this instance is all the more striking.

15. E., p. 121.

16. O. C., I, p. 267.

17. E., p. 90.

18. E., pp. 92-93.

19. E., p. 194.

20. E., pp. 196-97.

21. This is the only method of direct personal control which the tutor may exercise. It is a control which is congruent with the dynamics of masochism. "Look at what you have done to me!" is what the tutor seems to be saying. It is this expression which is designed to arouse a restraining guilt in his charge.

22. E., p. 492.

23. E., p. 526.

24. E., p. 564.

25. O. C., I, p. 175.

26. Calvin, J. *Institutes*, I, iv, 4.

27. *Ibid.*, I, iv, 1.

28. *Ibid.*, I, v, 4.

29. *Ibid.*, I, vi, 1.

30. *Ibid.*, I, vii, 5.
31. *Ibid.*, II, iii, 6-8.

CHAPTER EIGHT

1. See Fabre, *Annales*, 1933, XXII, p. 9. Derathé (*Annales*, 1950-52, XXXII, p. 11) mentions four refutations from 1762 to 1766. This does not mean that it was received without interest. It was not an easy book to read. Filled with eloquence and contradictions, it served to raise doubts about the existing state of things, but the steps to be taken for reform were not clear. Not until 1789, when the revolutionary fever was reaching a climax, did the *Social Contract* receive a stream of public eulogies (Derathé, pp. 7-12).
2. E., p. 337.
3. E., p. 348.
4. E., p. 354.
5. E., pp. 360-61.
6. E., p. 362.
7. E., pp. 367-68.
8. E., pp. 385-86.
9. Choulguine (*Annales*, 1937, XXVI, pp. 7-283) has investigated this matter at length, particularly in regard to the spirit of patriotism.

CHAPTER NINE

1. O. C., I, p. 568.
2. O. C., I, p. 534.
3. H., II, p. 368.
4. O. C., I, p. 579.
5. O. C., I, p. 580.
6. O. C., I, p. 581.
7. O. C., I, p. 583. It is very likely that this prophecy was an afterthought which Rousseau inserted in his *Confessions* when he began to think about what had happened to him. In later years he was inclined to make dramatic separations between the "good" and "bad" periods of his life.

CHAPTER TEN

1. F. MacDonald, *J.-J.R., a New Criticism*. Mrs. MacDonald has unearthed many facts which indicate that the conspiracy was, in some cases, more than a series of independent attacks by those who disliked Rousseau or disagreed with his work. The Holbachian clique was relentless in its rumormongering and gossip. Grimm and Diderot, who had developed a passionate fondness for each other, found themselves drawn even closer by their mutual hatred of Rousseau. Mme d'Epinay and Diderot, who, at first, disliked each other, were finally reconciled by their mutual friend, Grimm, and by the happy discovery that Rousseau had treated them both unjustly. Mme d'Epinay had been collecting her letters and those of her friends to write a novel. Grimm and Diderot, on

examining these documents, decided that they presented an account of Rousseau that was much too favorable. They offered their long experience in the literary world to help her revise her memoirs in such a way that Rousseau would appear as the kind of villain that the three friends knew him to be. The alteration was by no means a clever piece of work, for in many instances Mme d'Epinay had rewritten her new manuscript directly over the faded (but still visible) ink of her earlier work. Further, Mrs. MacDonald found notes in the manuscript, in Diderot's handwriting, giving instructions to Mme d'Epinay on the technique for changing her description of Rousseau's character. This alteration had been suspected by many authorities for a long time. Almost fifty years before Mrs. MacDonald's discovery, J. Morley remarked of the *Mémoires*, "We cannot be sure that Grimm did not manipulate these letters long after the event" (Morley, *Rousseau*, I, p. 283). But writers in French literature continued to use the *Mémoires* as an authentic source until Mrs. MacDonald uncovered the forgery.

In her eagerness to defend Rousseau, Mrs. MacDonald ignored the fact that many of the most damaging letters in the *Mémoires* were repeated in the *Confessions* and others appeared in the *General Correspondence*. It is primarily Mme d'Epinay's letters to Rousseau and the reports of Grimm and Diderot regarding their encounters with him which are suspect.

Mrs. MacDonald has done much to unearth the collusion on Mme d'Epinay's *Mémoires* and to expose Grimm's attempt to assail Rousseau's reputation in his *Literary Correspondence*. Grimm's task was made easier by the fact that Rousseau's books were generally proscribed and thus difficult to obtain. This enabled him to generalize at length, with little fear of contradiction, to accuse Rousseau of having lent cruel arms to fanaticism, and of having justified the persecution of Protestants (MacDonald, II, p. 126; M. Grimm, *Correspondance littéraire* III, p. 375). If one recalls that it was about this time that Voltaire was conducting his celebrated defense of the Calas family and entering the lists against religious persecution everywhere, it is not difficult to imagine how Grimm's remarks inflamed all those who stood with Voltaire.

In her zeal for discovery, Mrs. MacDonald lost sight of the balance and objectivity essential to scholarly research. Rousseau became for her all innocence and virtue, and she sought to justify his accusations against his enemies, even those against Hume. The *Literary Correspondence* which Smiley describes as a journal for royalty "discreetly circulated" became for her a "secret" journal through which Grimm exercised a "hidden control" over opinions at court in order to ruin Rousseau's reputation and deny him any refuge among the European nobility (J. R. Smiley, *Diderot's Relations with Grimm*, p. 1; MacDonald, I, pp. 39-42). In this and other interpretations she gave an unfortunate twist to the very significant and meaningful data which she unearthed.

However, she has presented extensive and valuable documentation along with her own opinions, thus enabling the reader to select those portions of her research which have lasting value.

2. The following letter from Rousseau's Genevan pastor friend, Paul Moultou, reprinted in the *Annales*, was written not to Rousseau but to Solomon Reverdil in the Canton of Vaud in late 1763. It illustrates the intensity of feeling on both sides of the Rousseau controversy in Geneva, as well as the extent to which the "plot against Rousseau" had become an accepted idea among his supporters:

It was not, my friend, the religion of Rousseau that brought about the decree of Geneva. Those who persecuted him were not Christians, but they made use of the imbecile credulity of Christians in order to ruin him. These are the times when they supported Voltaire with one hand while they crushed Rousseau with the other; and the profession of faith of the priest was only the torch with which a free people burned the social contract. I saw this cabal forming over a long period of time, I foresaw its designs and warned Rousseau of it. I knew they were disturbed by his friendship with De Luc, that they were wary of his republican principles, that they feared his powerful genius; in a word that these men who were not able to tolerate equals, were preparing to exile a citizen who would have no master. But Rousseau, since his dedication to the Republic [in his *Discourse* on inequality] and his book on the drama [his *Letter to d'Alembert*], which preserved our morals and postponed our ruin at least a hundred years, had become the idol of our bourgeoisie. It would be an attack on this very bourgeoisie to attack a citizen to whom it owed so much. His enemies sensed it, but this obstacle did not stop them. They concluded only that it was necessary to conduct their plot more slowly and with more skill. They began by spreading false rumors concerning his habits; they searched his works for anything that would cast doubt on his religious beliefs. *Eloise* appeared, and you can judge for yourself how they abused this book in order to give some credence to their vague insinuations. A blow was about to be struck, the consistory was already won over, but the praise which Catholic Paris had given to a work in which only the Protestants were spared caused the Protestant Council to hesitate and to fear the ridicule it would incur in prosecuting such a book.

Meanwhile, *Emile* advanced and Rousseau, who had a higher opinion of my feeble talents than he should have, sent me the manuscript of the profession of faith of the priest. I saw at once that it would ruin him if he published it: that the Jansenists who were very powerful in Paris and who were mistreated in *Julie* would not fail to seize this occasion for vengeance, and that his enemies in Geneva, leaning on the authority of the Parlement of Paris, would imitate its conduct in all aspects. I wrote to Rousseau, almost in the same terms, and never was a prophecy so literally fulfilled. Rousseau disdained my fears. He assured me that by wise precautions he had taken care of all risk. I saw these dangers more clearly than he did himself.

The book appeared; you know its lot in Paris. The news of it spread immediately to Geneva. I will not tell you the sensation it caused there, you would think I was embellishing or exaggerating it. In fact it caused a public scandal, a lightning stroke for the bourgeois, a triumph for the others. The charge of Omer de Fleury in hand, they went to spread the alarm everywhere: Rousseau was no more than a man of bad faith, a hypocrite, an impious one; he had finally cast aside the mask which he had been wearing; he had come to Geneva to make sport of the religion of his country by pretending to return to it. There was not enough executioners, chains, and burning faggots to destroy this monster who should never have existed. . . . (G. Vallette, *Annales*, 1907, III, p. 375.)

3. C. G., XII, p. 172.
4. C. G., XIV, p. 308.
5. C. G., VIII, p. 7.
6. C. G., X, p. 143.
7. V., II, p. 61.
8. C. G., XI, p. 246.
9. Grimm, IV, pp. 247, 315.
10. MacDonald, II, pp. 133-34.
11. J. Boswell, *Boswell on the Grand Tour: Germany and Switzerland 1764*, ed. F. A. Pottle, pp. 231-65.
12. F.-M. A. de Voltaire, "Sentiment des citoyens" in *Oeuvres de Voltaire*, ed. M. Beuchot, XLII, p. 81.
13. *Ibid.*, pp. 75-84.
14. The style was deliberately disguised.
15. Voltaire, *Les Oeuvres complètes de Voltaire*, LIX, pp. 5, 500. MacDonald, II, pp. 334-83.
16. G. Lanson, *Annales*, I, p. 115.
17. O. C., I, p. 624.
18. It should be mentioned that the pressure on Montmollin was more than that of a few casual remarks. His relatives, friends, colleagues, and the leaders in the church seem to have joined in an effort to influence his opinion. The evidence presented by Berthoud (*J.-J.R. au Val de Travers* and *J.-J.R. et le pasteur de Montmollin 1762-1765*) in this regard, would move the reader toward some sympathy for this distraught cleric.
19. It is not known what effect the enforced abandonment of her children may have had on the attitude of Thérèse and to what extent this served as a lingering source of friction between them.
20. O. C., I, p. 628.
21. O. C., I, pp. 634-35.
22. Berthoud (*J.-J.R. au Val de Travers*, pp. 301-2) reports D'Escherny's contention that the attack on Rousseau was a product of his own desire

for a dramatic departure from Motiers, in short, that it was a deliberate hoax. Grimm (*Correspondance littéraire*, V, pp. 60–61) tells his readers that Rousseau's lively imagination transformed a few pebbles thrown by a drunk into great stones. As a speculation this is better work than D'Escherny's, since Rousseau did not falsify events in order to gain public attention, but he often exaggerated the dangers facing him. Grimm goes further and reports his opinion as fact, allegedly supported by a judicial inquiry. The documents collected by Dufour (C. G., XIV, pp. 362-70) concerning the inquiry tend to confirm Rousseau's description of the events. The malice of the citizens is unmistakable. That the house was not seriously damaged tells little about the psychological threat Rousseau experienced, surrounded by the open hostility of his neighbors and subject to constant harassment whenever he went into town or walking in the woods.

Thérèse was evidently responsible for a great deal of the animosity directed against Rousseau (O. C., I, p. 1598, n. 1). She was bored at Motiers and may have exaggerated the severity of the situation in order to frighten Rousseau into leaving the town. Margaret Peoples (*Annales*, 1927-28, XVIII, pp. 75-79) in her story of the later quarrel between Rousseau and Hume, makes the point that Thérèse was a strong factor in embroiling Rousseau with his neighbors in Motiers as well as with his friends in England.

23. Rousseau's doubts about Buttafuoco were justified. This officer became the agent of Choiseul, minister of Foreign Affairs, in a nefarious deal with the Genoese through which Corsica was literally sold to France in 1768 with all her people as chattels. Corsica, however, had the last word in this bargain, for she contained within her bowels a poisonous gift in the person of Napoleon Bonaparte, who was to place his foot on the neck of France and leave a mark that two centuries have not erased (see J. Morley, *Rousseau*, II, p. 99).

24. The correspondence between Rousseau and Buttafuoco can be found in C. G., XI, pp. 246-351.

25. C. G., XIV, p. 315.

CHAPTER ELEVEN

1. A roll of money.
2. H., I, p. 529.
3. H., I, pp. 530-31.
4. H., II, p. 2.
5. H., II, p. 2, n. 1.
6. Mrs. MacDonald makes the point, and with good evidence, that Hume opened and read Rousseau's letters in the course of this investigation. See MacDonald (*J.-J.R., a New Criticism*, II, pp. 177-82).
7. H., II, pp. 14-15.
8. H., II, p. 1.
9. H., II, p. 11.

10. H., II, p. 3.
11. H., II, p. 16.
12. C. G., XV, pp. 156-57.
13. Hume, in his letters to Mme de Boufflers, gives a different account of the events of this evening. He reports that Rousseau was upset over an attempt (on the part of Davenport and Hume) to pay for his coach on the pretext that it was a *retour chaise* and could be had for a cheaper price. Green favors Rousseau's story, remarking that Hume's letter to the Countess de Boufflers was two weeks after the event, and "it is evident from the *Correspondance* that Jean-Jacques did not find out about this kindly plot until after he left London" (*J.-J.R., a Critical Study of His Life and Writings*, p. 335).

Actually, the *Correspondance* supports but does not confirm this interpretation. On March 22 Rousseau speaks of the incident of the *retour chaise* as though for the first time (C. G., XV, pp. 117-18), chastising Hume for his part in the affair. But it is quite possible that Rousseau simply could not leave the subject alone and was reiterating a point he had made much earlier. Further, on March 25, only three days after Rousseau's letter was written (and quite possibly before Hume had even received it), Hume was describing his version of the evening on Lisle Street to the Reverend Hugh Blair in almost the same words he used with the Countess de Boufflers (H., II, pp. 313-14). To believe that Hume predated their discussion of the *retour chaise* incident one would have to assume that he was telling a deliberate falsehood. For a man of Hume's integrity this is unlikely, even, as Green has suggested, in order to inflate his virtue and innocence in the eyes of the Countess de Boufflers (see Green, pp. 335-36). What happened, in all probability, is that Hume was simply mistaken about the reason for Rousseau's agitation.

There are two other points of difference in Rousseau's and Hume's versions of the evening. Hume reports a rather elaborate apology by Rousseau for his behavior and also mentions that he embraced Rousseau with a "plentiful effusion of tears" (H., II, p. 30). In regard to the apology I am most inclined to credit Rousseau's version, since he was the speaker whose conversation was reported and since his own version is more congruent with his manner of expression (Hume's Rousseau sounds more like Hume than Rousseau). As to the embrace and the tears, quite possibly a pat on the back was to Hume an "embrace," and if he had been weeping on this occasion Rousseau, with both arms around him, was probably not looking at his face.

I emphasize these different accounts because the two men were later to accuse each other of being liars, primarily due to their differing reports of this evening.
14. C. G., XV, p. 20.
15. C. G., XV, p. 36.
16. C. G., XV, p. 93.

17. C. G., XV, p. 367.
18. H., II, p. 10, n. 2.
19. H., II, p. 10.
20. H., II, p. 4, n. 2.
21. C. G., XV, p. 99.
22. H, II, p. 28.
23. H., II, p. 29.
24. There are no letters in Greig's collection which support Hume's claim. A letter from Baron d'Holbach, written *after* Hume's remark, quoted above, speaks of the transfer of some funds from Rougemont, Rousseau's banker, but there are no dates and no indications of what the money was for, or if it was returned. In general, the evidence is inconclusive. The letter seems to reveal more about Hume (i.e., that he had asked the aid of his friends in investigating Rousseau's finances) than it does about Rousseau (H., II, pp. 37-39, 410-11).

Mrs. MacDonald (*J.-J. R., a New Criticism*, II, pp. 177-82) stresses Hume's use of the term "by accident" to describe his discovery of the financial status of his friend. She points out that Hume could not be more explicit because he had found small undisclosed amounts of Rousseau's money by reading the latter's mail.

25. H., II, pp. 37-38.
26. H., II, p. 39.
27. H., II, p. 37.
28. C. G., XV, p. 233.
29. H., II, pp. 45-46.
30. H., II, pp. 51-52.
31. C. G., XV, p. 275.
32. C. G., XV, pp. 117-18.
33. He made several requests to Davenport for information on newspaper articles hostile to him. Davenport's letters show, at first, his perplexity; second, his attempt to avoid involvement by suggesting that Rousseau clip the articles himself, and finally, under Rousseau's continued questioning, his statement that articles were appearing "for you or against you, Hume, and Voltaire in every St. James Chronicle" (*Annales*, 1910, VI, p. 179).
34. C. G., XV, p. 134.
35. C. G., XV, p. 153.
36. Margaret Peoples (*Annales*, 1927-29, XVIII, pp. 307-20) has reproduced a series of letters and articles appearing in the *St. James Chronicle* concerning the Rousseau-Hume quarrel and Voltaire's *Lettre au Docteur Pansophe* (a ridicule of Rousseau). The commentary, in general, shows the sympathy of the English people for Rousseau, whom they regarded as an unfortunate and tormented creature.
37. C. G., XV, pp. 153-54.
38. While some of the articles and letters to the *St. Jame's Chronicle* were mocking and unfavorable, directly after Rousseau's letter to the pub-

lisher (printed in April) complaining of the Prussian letter, there was a gradual change toward December, at which time letters of criticism toward Hume and encouragement of Rousseau were in the majority. However, Rousseau had probably discontinued his reading by this time. (See Peoples, pp. 307-20).

39. Hume remarked in his own defense that he was not in the habit of dreaming in French. However, it scarcely seems necessary to defend one's self against such an accusation. As Rousseau reported this incident several months after the event, it is not clear whether he misinterpreted one of Hume's mumbles, dreamed the whole experience himself, or suffered a genuine hallucination. The first explanation appears the most likely.

40. C. G., XV, pp. 154-57.

41. C. G., XV, pp. 184-88.

42. C. G., XV, pp. 237-38.

43. A notorious transvestite.

44. C. G., XV, p. 202.

45. H., II, p. 419.

46. C. G., XV, p. 228.

47. C. G., XV, p. 241.

48. H., II, p. 61.

49. H., II, pp. 415-19.

50. Rousseau's *Confessions* ends with his journey toward Berlin.

51. C. G., XV, pp. 299-324.

52. This letter, printed in full in Hume's *Concise Account,* did not diminish the enthusiasm of Rousseau's English admirers. One of them, in a letter to the *St. Jame's Chronicle,* remarked that the letter, by its very openness, portrayed Rousseau's honesty, his lack of guile, his willingness to expose all the terrors of his heart to Hume. The writer also took note of Hume's insensitivity in publishing this confidential letter from a friend (Peoples, p. 316).

53. C. G., XVI, p. 276.

54. C. G., XVI, p. 227.

55. C. G., XVI, pp. 276-77.

56. C. G., XVI, p. 361.

57. C. G., XVI, p. 366.

58. Margaret Peoples (pp. 75-82) cites letters from the Countess de Boufflers, De Luze, and others to support the view that Thérèse was the cause of Rousseau's troubles in England. She presents the assertion of Kirwan, a local chemist and acquaintance of Hume, that the agitations of Thérèse produced the quarrel between Rousseau and Hume and that without her Rousseau would have been happy at Wooton. However, while Thérèse stoked the fires of Rousseau's imagination for her own purposes, there is no doubt that the major conflagration was his own.

59. C. G., XVI, p. 368-69.

60. C. G., XVII, pp. 14-18.

61. C. G., XVII, p. 28.
62. C. G., XVII, p. 43.
63. C. G., XVII, pp. 41-42.
64. C. G., XVII, p. 49.
65. C. G., XVII, pp. 57-62.
66. H., I, pp. 1-7.
67. H., I, pp. 12-18. This letter may never have been sent.
68. D. Hume, *The Philosophical Works of David Hume.*
69. C. G., II, pp. 172-73.
70. S. Freud, *Collected Papers*, II, pp. 152-53; III, pp. 426-27.
71. C. G., XV, p. 324. This same fragment was quoted by Ronald Grimsley (*J.-J. R., a Study in Self-Awareness*) to illustrate a somewhat different point of view.

CHAPTER TWELVE

1. C. G., XVI, p. 236.
2. C. G., XVII, p. 28.
3. C. G., XVII, p. 111.
4. C. G., XVII, pp. 111-12.
5. C. G., XVII, p. 108.
6. Cortois, *Annales*, 1923, XV, p. 194.
7. C. G., XVII, p. 122.
8. C. G., XVII, p. 147.
9. C. G., XVII, pp. 201-3.
10. C. G., XVII, pp. 205-8.
11. C. G., XVII, p. 204.
12. C. G., XVII, p. 205.
13. C. G., XVII, p. 224.
14. C. G., XVII, pp. 290-91.
15. C. G., XVII, pp. 300-301.
16. C. G., XVII, p. 333.
17. C. G., XVIII, p. 1.
18. O. C., I, pp. 576-77.
19. C. G., XVIII, pp. 179-82.
20. C. G., XVIII, p. 179, n. 1.
21. C. G., XX, p. 18.
22. C. G., XVIII, p. 365.
23. C. G., XIX, pp. 115-16.
24. C. G., XIX, pp. 233-62.
25. A symbol of honor.
26. C. G., XIX, pp. 235, 255, 257.
27. C. G., XX, p. 292.
28. F. MacDonald, *J.-J.R., a New Criticism*, II, pp. 183-210.
29. A. Heidenhain, *J.-J.R., Persönlichkeit, Philosophie, und Psychose.*
30. *Ibid.*, p. 83.
31. L. Proal, *La Psychologie de J.-J.R.*, pp. 308-59.

32. R. Grimsley, *J.-J.R., a Study in Self-Awareness*, pp. 188-94.
33. Heidenhain, p. 82.
34. F. C. Green, *J.-J.R., a Critical Study of His Life and Writings*, p. 330.
35. J. Starobinski, *Yale French Studies*, 1962, No. 28, p. 69.
36. Heidenhain, p. 82.
37. This diagnosis was first proposed by Möbius in 1889. See Starobinski, p. 69.

CHAPTER THIRTEEN

1. V., I, pp. 1-117.
2. V., I, pp. 36, 75.
3. V., II, pp. 310-313.
4. V., II, p. 314.
5. V., II, p. 314.
6. V., II, p. 445.
7. V., II, pp. 499-500.
8. V., II, pp. 492-97.
9. V., II, pp. 492-93.
10. V., II, pp. 502-9.
11. V., II, pp. 476-79.
12. V., II, pp. 478-85.
13. V., II, p. 477.
14. V., II, p. 476.
15. V., II, pp. 479-80.
16. V., II, pp. 438-39.
17. V., II, pp. 491-92.
18. V., II, p. 434.
19. V., II, p. 432.
20. V., II, p. 433.
21. V., II, p. 437.
22. V., II, pp. 438-40.
23. See M. Walzer, *The Revolution of the Saints.* p. 47. Calvin originated the idea that social control by the state would be more effective if the individual could be made to will that control himself.
24. V., II, pp. 475-76.
25. V., II, p. 442. In this he was probably influenced by Montesquieu's view that the survival of a republican form of government depends on the state being small.
26. V., II, p. 476.
27. V., II, p. 470.
28. Chapman (*Rousseau, Totalitarian or Liberal*, p. 61) has remarked that Rousseau would build a society designed to manipulate men toward its objectives by appeal to their pride and vanity. Here again Rousseau projected his own personal attributes on mankind as a whole. It was his pride that made him most vulnerable to manipulation.
29. V., II, p. 430.

30. V., I, p. 95.
31. E., p. 596.
32. V., II, p. 134.
33. V., I, p. 360.
34. The abbé's plan for a council of ministers was reflected in Rousseau's scheme for a promotional civil service system for Poland.
35. O. C., I, p. 422
36. V., I, pp. 379-80.
37. V., I, pp. 98-101.
38. V., I, pp. 389-90.

CHAPTER FOURTEEN

1. Rousseau takes this from a similar theme in the *Republic* of Plato.
2. In the fourth *Promenade* of the *Reveries* (O. C., I, pp. 1024-39) Rousseau discourses at length on "what is truth?" He points out that a work of fiction is not true, but we do not condemn the writer for his falsehood. Casting aside the fact that the writer of fiction indicates by his approach and style that his work is not intended as an accurate record of events, Rousseau insists that it is an untruth. However, he adds, fiction is not really a lie if it has a high moral purpose, because it is telling a moral truth. To the real man of truth the words "justice" and "truth" are synonyms, and it is a matter of indifference which one is used (O. C., I, p. 1032).

   Here the real meaning of truth has become blurred. The requirement that a fictional tale be "true to life" is replaced by the insistence that it have an uplifting message. By such standards hard and brutal truths might be judged "false" because in the eye of the critic they tended to corrupt the reader. Likewise, the most tawdry sentimentality could be "true" if it semed to have a high moral object. This idea was to have a profound influence on the literature of future generations.
3. Fenichel (*Psychoanalytic Theory of Neurosis*, pp. 138-39) has pointed out the relation between shame and exhibitionism. While a "return of the repressed" was responsible for Rousseau's disgust, one might well question whether this repressed material represented the sadistic-authoritarian content of his works or their exhibitionistic character. There is ample evidence of the strong exhibitionistic element in Rousseau's moral masochism. However, I have emphasized the sadistic-authoritarian element for two reasons: (1) this side of his personality was constantly pressing toward consciousness and involving him in direct conflict with society from the standpoint of his provocation and his demands upon others; and (2) in a very realistic sense this side of his personality most seriously marred his works. His exhibitionism produced a certain flamboyance in his writing, but it also contributed to his eloquence by a profusion of examples and expressive detail. The sadistic-authoritarian drive invaded the very core of his political thought.
4. C. G., XVII, p. 80.

5. C. G., XVII, pp. 204-5.
6. C. G., XVII, p. 219.
7. J. Starobinski, *La Transparence et l'obstacle*, p. 248.
8. Starobinski (*ibid.*, pp. 1-14) has presented convincing evidence that Rousseau's memory of his childhood punishment for the broken comb represents a justification for his later attempt to deceive the world as to his own innocence (which was obviously overdrawn in the *Confessions*, *Dialogues*, and *Reveries*) and his partially successful effort to deceive himself in the same regard. After the beating at the hands of his uncle, Rousseau reports that he and his cousin recognized that their guardians could not read the truth by looking into their hearts. They had been condemned by appearances when they were really innocent. Thus, from that time onward they became more concerned with appearances than with actual wrongdoing. They began to be secretive, to rebel, and to lie. Since appearances had condemned them, they would learn to live in the world and concentrate on presenting an appearance of virtue. To a phenomenon that the psychoanalyst would call a "screen memory," which, in this case, represented an unconscious justification for falsehood, Starobinski has given a somewhat more deliberate significance in keeping with existential philosophy. Rousseau, he says, has made a choice. Unable to achieve the lost transparence, he has learned to derive satisfaction from the very obstacle to this transparence, the veil of appearance. Since the real truth cannot be known, since his beautiful soul cannot really be seen by others, he will concentrate his efforts on the appearance of virtue.
9. V., II, p. 493.
10. V., II, p. 430.
11. V., II, p. 435.
12. V., II, p. 436.
13. When one looks at this characteristic picture of femininity as it occurs in all of Rousseau's writings there appears to be something inconsistent about it. Luxury is feminine and enslaving. Women are seen as striving to dominate men when they should obey. The person who loves repose and who develops a need for the luxuries of life soon becomes a slave. Yet it is women, the masters, who are seen to have such a greedy appetite for luxury and display. One is reminded of the legend of Samson and Delilah. The object of the woman was to deprive the man of his power and make him like herself. In this way he became helpless, enslaved. The danger Rousseau felt from women was not that of being sexually attracted to them, but the dread of being turned into a woman—of releasing the female within himself.
14. L. Tolstoi, *Annales*, 1905, I, p. 7.
15. I. Kant, *Kant's gesammelte Schriften*, XX, p. 44. Cassirer also mentions Kant's high regard for Rousseau in his *The Question of Jean-Jacques Rousseau*.
16. In this connection see M. J. Temmer, *Yale French Studies*, 1962, 28, pp. 118-19.

17. I. Babbitt, *Rousseau and Romanticism*.
18. J. L. Talmon, *The Origins of Totalitarian Democracy*, p. 43.
19. Since the discoveries of psychoanalysis, it has often been implied that a person's unconscious attitudes are the only ones that are important, i.e., the ones which influence his behavior. Rousseau's life and writings present a graphic example of the fact that a man's behavior is a product of both conscious and unconscious forces.

CHAPTER FIFTEEN

1. V. Brombert, *Partisan Review*, 1960, XXVII, pp. 495-96.
2. J. Benda, *The Betrayal of the Intellectuals*, pp. 56-57, 127-28.
3. Brombert, pp. 480-82, 497-98.
4. S. de Beauvoir, *The Mandarins*.
5. D. Riesman, *Selected Essays from Individualism Reconsidered*, p. 43.
6. Philip Rieff (*Freud: The Mind of the Moralist*, pp. 255-60) has established this idea as an integral aspect of the Freudian approach to politics, but he makes the point that all political activities are not Freudian. "It does not illuminate the emotions behind hard bargaining and counter-bargaining. . . ."
7. F. Nietzsche, *Beyond Good and Evil*.
8. H. E. Corey, *The Intellectual and the Wage Workers: A Study in Educational Psychoanalysis*, pp. 240-43.
9. J. Wortis, *American Journal of Psychiatry*. 1945, CI, pp. 814-20. J. T. Stone, "The Theory and Practice of Psychoanalysis" (unpublished paper).
10. There is some evidence to suggest that Rousseau's creative struggle may be more than just an isolated experience. It may be that the great moralists of our civilization have been motivated to combat what they perceive as evil because of a partial awareness of this trait within themselves, that the detailed knowledge of the adversary and the very impetus of the urge toward virtue spring from the, often unacknowledged and unrecognized, shadowy side of our character, that one is, in short, the mirror image of the other. Tucker has pointed to this phenomenon in his study of Karl Marx. Marx portrayed the diabolical aspects of money-worship and its tendency to absorb all of man's energies, leaving him a self-alienated being, divorced from the source of his productivity. In commenting on Marx's graphic imagery, Tucker remarks:

> It goes without saying that Marx drew inspiration from the inner depths of his own being in portraying the 'inhuman force.' A person who has not experienced this urge to self-aggrandizement within himself, in one or another of its many expressions, could never have produced such powerful images of it as Marx did in his manuscripts and his later writings (R. Tucker, *Philosophy and Myth in Karl Marx*, pp. 140-41).

While he gives psychology its due in the field of inspiration, Tucker points out that the "conceptual source" of Marx's idea was the Hegelian philosophy. However, if one looks at Tucker's own material from a psychological point of view, attention is immediately focused upon Marx's early paper, "On the Jewish Question," in which Judaism or "commerce" is described as a religion in which money is the god. "Money is the jealous one God of Israel, beside which no other God may stand" (*ibid.*, p. 111). One might well raise the question as to what extent Marx regarded the urge to accumulate capital as a negative aspect of himself and of Jewishness in general; whether his attack upon the capitalist philosophy was not an attempt to destroy a side of his own Jewishness which he regarded as repugnant and basically evil. One sees here a peculiar inversion in which the Jew learns to feel guilty about his desire to accumulate capital because the larger Gentile community has condemned it as a "Jewish vice." This hatred of one's self is both repressed and turned outward again toward the larger community. Greed now becomes, not a despised aspect of the self, but the very embodiment of evil in society. Such a view does not really conflict with Tucker's theory regarding the "conceptual source" of Marx's ideas. It does imply, however, that Marx would have evolved an anticapitalist philosophy with or without his Hegelian background.

We are dealing here with a fluid situation in which there is an interplay between the major events in a man's life, his resulting psychodynamics, and his intellectual experiences. As indicated, Rousseau evolved many of his ideas from reading the prominent political writers of his time. He frequently acknowledged his own debt to Montesquieu. However, a certain fever drives a man to search for moral truth, a conviction that he is somehow uniquely suited for the particular quest on which he embarks.

As Edmund Wilson has pointed out in *The Wound and the Bow*, the very product of this quest, the work of genius which results, may be due to the personal conflict—even the weakness—of its creator, as well as his particular intellectual gifts.

PRIMARY SOURCES FOR THIS STUDY

The three chief works I have consulted in this study have been (1) the *Correspondance générale*, (2) *The Political Writings of Jean-Jacques Rousseau*, and (3) the *Oeuvres complètes* in the Pléiade edition of Rousseau, published by Gallimard. The *Correspondance* was first undertaken in 1864 by Theophile Dufour, who collected thousands of Rousseau's letters, but who died in 1922 before his work was complete. It remained for Pierre-Paul Plan to finish this task. These two scholars have given us the first reasonably complete collection of Rousseau's correspondence. Leigh (*Annales*, 1959-62, XXXV, pp. 263-80) has recently pointed out a number of defects in this edition. It is, however, the most complete published edition of Rousseau's correspondence available at present. Leigh is now working on a new edition from the original Neuchâtel manuscripts.

No one has done more than C. E. Vaughan, the editor of the *Political Writings*, to define the place of Rousseau in the history of political thought

—and this was one of the avowed objectives of his study. Vaughan worked from Rousseau's original manuscripts, comparing various drafts of his political works and preparing an authentic text of each of his major political writings (in addition to many of his minor political essays). Having spent several weeks at the Bibliothèque de Neuchâtel studying the Rousseau manuscripts, I have some appreciation for the difficult task which faced Vaughan. Rousseau scribbled on everything from playing cards to wallpaper. He inevitably prepared more than one copy of his major works, since he was afraid that they would be stolen, and two versions were never the same. He directed arrows from one paragraph to another and had the habit of crossing out the title (or sometimes a page) when it had been transcribed. Therefore, one is often in doubt as to whether he intended to discard an idea or had merely transcribed it.

Vaughan's work gives some idea of the extent to which Rousseau had to struggle with his ideas and to work over an expression before it seemed right to him. While Vaughan records, as footnotes, many of the changes in Rousseau's sentences, there are numerous instances in which paragraphs were shifted from one place to another. These and other changes are not noted in Vaughan's work. Only the original manuscripts convey the painful process of Rousseau's composition.

The Pléiade edition of Rousseau's complete works, published by Gallimard, is remarkable not only for the care and attention to detail on the part of the editors but for the wealth of historical information regarding the writing and the subsequent history of Rousseau's various works. Here one finds the story of that vast network of events which finally persuaded Rousseau that he should write his *Confessions*. Here one can review the agonizing doubts about his own salvation which form the basis for the *Dialogues*. Here also are the thousands of notes which bring together the many different versions of Rousseau's works and the corrections and changes made by various editors. Altogether these introductory essays and notes represent a story of great depth, a journey into the mind of a great writer as fascinating as a detective novel.

There is one more important work on Rousseau which I have used, in part as a reference, but primarily as a source of inspiration. This is Jean Starobinski's incomparable *La Transparence et l'obstacle*. Starobinski has taken a single idea and followed it, with its various ramifications, through the entire range of Rousseau's writings. With this tool he has created a broad and unified concept of Rousseau's ideation which exposes the many facets of his shifting intellect. However, the most remarkable thing about Starobinski's work is its lucidity. Starobinski has taken a very complex idea and elaborated it in a variety of contexts so that a new facet is exposed with every turn of thought. It is unfortunate that there is, as yet, no English translation of his work.

The following References list other works consulted either for their direct bearing on Rousseau or for historical and political background. I have tried to restrict my references to works quoted in the text or forming the basis for some of my conclusions.

References

1. Aurenche, L. "J.-J. Rousseau et Madame de Larnage." *Annales*, 1907, III, pp. 69-81.
2. Babbitt, I. *Rousseau and Romanticism*. New York: Meridian, 1957.
3. Beauvoir, Simone de. *The Mandarins*. New York: Meridian, 1960.
4. Benda, J. *The Betrayal of the Intellectuals*. Boston: Beacon Press, 1955.
5. Berthoud, F. *J.-J. Rousseau au Val de Travers*. Paris: Fishbacher, 1881.
6. Berthoud, F. *J.-J. Rousseau et le pasteur de Montmollin 1762-1765.* Paris: Fleurier, 1884.
7. Binswanger, L. "Studien zum schisophrenie Problem." *Schweizer Archiv fur Neurologie und Psychiatrie*, 1952, LXX, pp. 1-32.
8. Boswell, J. *Boswell on the Grand Tour: Germany and Switzerland 1764.* Ed. F. A. Pottle. New York: McGraw-Hill, 1955.
9. Brinton, C. C. *The Anatomy of Revolution*. New York: Prentice-Hall, 1952.
10. Brinton, C. C. *The Shaping of the Modern Mind*. New York: New American, 1953.
11. Brombert, V. "Toward a Portrait of the French Intellectual." *Partisan Review*, 1960, XXVII, pp. 480-502.
12. Bucke, R. M. *Cosmic Consciousness*. New York: Dutton, 1959.
13. Burton, J. H. *Life and Correspondence of David Hume*. Edinburgh: William Tait, 1846.
14. Calvin, J. *A Compend of the Institutes of the Christian Religion*. Ed. H. T. Kerr. Philadelphia: Presbyterian Board of Christian Education, 1939.
15. Camus, A. *The Myth of Sisyphus*. New York: Random House, Vintage, 1955.
16. Camus, A. *The Rebel*. New York: Alfred A. Knopf, 1956.
17. Carthy, J. D., and Ebling, F. J. (Eds.). *The Natural History of Aggression*. London & New York: Academic Press, 1964.
18. Cassirer, E. *The Question of Jean-Jacques Rousseau*. New York: Columbia University Press, 1954.
19. Chapman, J. W. *Rousseau, Totalitarian or Liberal?* New Yolk: Columbia University Press, 1956.
20. Choulguine, A. "Les Origines de l'esprit national moderne et Jean-Jacques Rousseau." *Annales*, 1937, XXVI, p. 7-283.
21. Cobban, A. *Rousseau and the Modern State*. London: G. Allen and Unwin, 1934.
22. Corey, H. E. *The Intellectual and the Wage Workers: a Study in Educational Psychoanalysis*. New York: The Sunwise Turn, 1919.
23. Courtois, L. J. *"Le Sejour de Jean-Jacques Rousseau en Angleterre* (1766-1767)." *Annales*, 1910, VI, pp. 1-305.
24. Courtois, J. L. "Chronologie critique de la vie et des oeuveres de Jean-Jacques Rousseau." *Annales*, 1923, XV, pp. 1-240.

25. Derathé, R. *Jean-Jacques Rousseau et la science politique de son temps.* Paris: Presses Universitaires de France, 1950.

26. Derathé, R. "Les Réfutations du "contrat social" au XVIIIᵉ siècle." *Annales,* 1950-52, XXXII, pp. 7-54.

27. Diderot, D. "Le Fils naturel ou les épreuves de la vertu" in *Collection complète des oeuvres philosophiques, littéraires et dramatiques de M. Diderot.* London, 1773.

28. Diderot, D. *Mémoirs, correspondance et ouvrages inédits de Diderot.* Paris: Paulin, 1834.

29. Durkheim, Émile. *Montesquieu and Rousseau: Forerunners of Sociology.* Tr. by Ralph Manheim. Ann Arbor: University of Michigan Press, 1960.

30. Ellis, H. *From Rousseau to Proust.* New York: Houghton Mifflin, 1935.

31. d'Épinay, Mme. *Les Pseudo Memoires de Madame d'Épinay: Histoire de Madame de Montbrillant.* Ed. Georges Roth. Paris: Gallimard.

32. Erikson, E. H. *Young Man Luther.* New York: W. W. Norton, 1962.

33. Fabre, J. "Examen du Contrat Social de J.-J. Rousseau avec des remarques pour servir d'antidote à quelques principes: Introduction." *Annales,* 1933, XXII, pp. 9-53.

34. Fenichel, O. *The Psychoanalytic Theory of Neurosis.* New York: W. W. Norton, 1945.

35. Franklin, B. *Autobiography.* Cambridge: Houghton Mifflin, 1956.

36. Freud, S. *Collected Papers.* Ed. E. Jones. London: Hogarth, 1953.

37. Freud, S. *The Basic Writings of Sigmund Freud.* Ed. A. A. Brill. New York: Modern Library, Random House, 1938.

38. Freud, S. *The Standard Edition of the Complete Psychological Works of Sigmund Freud.* Ed. J. Strachey. London: Hogarth, 1953.

39. Fromm, E. *Escape from Freedom.* New York: Rinehart, 1941.

40. Gershoy, L. *From Despotism to Revolution: 1763-1789.* New York: Harper and Row, Torchbook, 1963.

41. Goncourt, E. and J. de *The Woman of the Eighteenth Century.* London: George Allen & Unwin, 1928.

42. Gran, G. "La Crise de Vincennes." *Annales,* 1911, VII, pp. 1-17.

43. Green, F. C. *Jean-Jacques Rousseau, a Critical Study of His Life and Writings.* Cambridge: Cambridge University Press, 1955.

44. Green, F. C. *Rousseau and the Idea of Progress.* Oxford: Clarendon Press, 1950.

45. Gribble, F. *Rousseau and the Women He Loved.* New York: Scribners, 1908.

46. Grimm, F. M. f. von. *Correspondance littéraire philosophique et critique.* Paris: Longchamps, F. Buisson, 1812-29.

47. Grimm, F. M. f. von. *Correspondance littéraire philosophique et critique.* Paris: Garnier, 1877.

48. Grimsley, R. *Jean-Jacques Rousseau, a Study in Self-Awareness.* Cardiff: University of Wales Press, 1961.

49. Guéhenno, Jean. *Jean-Jacques.* Paris: B. Grasset, 1948-52.

50. Guillemin, H. "Les Affaires de l'Hermitage." *Annales*, 1941-42, XXIX, pp. 65-258.
51. Heidenhain, A. *Jean-Jacques Rousseau Persönlichkeit, Philosophie, und Psychose.* Munich: Bergmann, 1924.
52. Hendel, C. W. *Jean-Jacques Rousseau, Moralist.* London: Oxford University Press, 1934.
53. Hume, D. *Enquiries Concerning the Human Understanding and Concerning the Principles of Morals.* Oxford: Clarendon Press, 1961.
54. Hume, D. *The Letters of David Hume.* Ed. J.Y.T. Greig. Oxford: Clarendon Press, 1932.
55. Hume, D. *The Philosophical Works of David Hume.* Eds. T. H. Green and T. H. Grosse. London, 1874-75.
56. Kant, I. *Kant's gesammelte Schriften.* Berlin: Walter de Gruyter, 1942.
57. Kligerman, C. "The Character of Jean-Jacques Rousseau." *Psychoanalytic Quarterly*, 1951, XX, pp. 237-52.
58. Laforgue, R. *La Psychopathologie de l'échec.* Revised ed. Paris: 1950.
59. Lanson, G. "Quelques documents inédite sur la condamnation et la censure de *l'Emile* et sur la condamnation des *Lettres écrites de la Montagne.*" *Annales*, 1905, I, pp. 95-136.
60. Lefebvre, G. *The Coming of the French Revolution*, 1789. Tr. by R. R. Palmer. Princeton: Princeton University Press, 1947.
61. Leigh, R. A. "Vers une nouvelle édition de la correspondance de Jean-Jacques Rousseau." *Annales*, 1959-62, XXXV, pp. 263-80.
62. Lemaître, J. *Jean-Jacques Rousseau.* London: Heinemann, 1908.
63. Lewis, W. H. *The Splendid Century: Life in the France of Louis XIV.* New York: Doubleday, 1957.
64. MacDonald, Frederika. *Studies in the France of Voltaire and Rousseau.* London: T. Fisher Unwin, 1895.
65. MacDonald, Frederika. *Jean-Jacques Rousseau, a New Criticism.* London: Chapman and Hall, 1906.
66. McDonald, Joan. *Rousseau and the French Revolution.* London: Athlone, 1965.
67. Masson, P.-M. "Mme.d'Épinay, Jean-Jacques . . . et Diderot chez Mlle. Quinault." *Annales*, 1913, IX, pp. 1-28.
68. Masson, P.-M. *La Religion de J.-J. Rousseau.* Paris: Hachette, 1916.
69. Maurois, A. *A History of France.* New York: Grove Press, 1960.
70. McGovern, W. M. *From Luther to Hitler.* New York: Houghton Mifflin, 1941.
71. Montet, A. de. *Madame de Warens et le pays de Vaud.* Lausanne: Georges Bridel, 1891.
72. Morley, J. *Rousseau.* London: Chapman and Hall, 1873.
73. Mossner, E. C. *The Life of David Hume.* London: Nelson, 1954.
74. Mugnier, F. *Mme. de Warens et J. J. Rousseau.* Paris: Calmann Levy, 1895.
75. Murray, G. *Five Stages of Greek Religion.* Oxford: Clarendon Press, 1925.

76. Palissot de Montenoy, C. *Oeuvres de M. Palissot*. Paris: Libraire de la Reine, 1788.
77. Parton, J. *Life of Voltaire*. Boston: Houghton Mifflin, 1884.
78. Peoples, Margaret. "La Querelle Rousseau-Hume." *Annales*, 1927-28, XVIII, pp. 1-322.
79. Polanyi, M. *Personal Knowledge*. Chicago: University of Chicago Press, 1958.
80. Pottle, F. A. "Appendice à "La querelle Rousseau-Hume" par Albert Schinz." *Annales*, 1926, XVII, pp. 13-51.
81. Proal, L. *La Psychologie de Jean-Jacques Rousseau*. Paris: Alcan, 1930.
82. Raymond, M. "Deux aspects de la vie interieure de J.-J. Rousseau." *Annales*, 1941-42, XXIX, pp. 7-57.
83. Reik, T. *Masochism in Modern Man*. New York: Grove Press, 1941.
84. Rieff, P. *Freud: the Mind of the Moralist*. New York: Doubleday Anchor, 1961.
85. Riesman, D. *Selected Essays from Individualism Reconsidered*. Garden City: Doubleday Anchor, 1954.
86. Ritter, E. "La Famille et la jeunesse de Jean-Jacques Rousseau." *Annales*, 1924-25, XVI, pp. 5-250.
87. Ritter, E. "Jean-Jacques Rousseau, notes et recherches." *Annales*, 1916-17, pp. 1-235.
88. Ritter, E. *Magny et le Piétisme romand*. Lausanne: *Société d'Histoire de la Suiss Romande*. Second Series, III, 1891.
89. Rokeach, M. *The Open and Closed Mind*. New York: Basic Books, 1960.
90. Rousseau, J.-J. *Correspondance générale de Jean-Jacques Rousseau*, Ed. Dufour & Plan. Paris: Armand Colin, 1924-34.
91. Rousseau, J.-J. *Les Oeuvres complètes de Jean-Jacques Rousseau*. Paris: Gallimard, Bibliothèque de la Pléiade, 1959-64.
92. Rousseau, J.-J. *Émile ou de l'éducation*. Paris: Garnier, 1961.
93. Rousseau, J.-J. *Du contrat social*. Paris: Garnier, 1962. (Includes the Lettre à M. d'Alembert, Lettre à Mgr. de Beaumont and other works.)
94. Rousseau, J.-J. *Social Contract and Discourses*. New York: E. P. Dutton, Everyman, 1950.
95. Rousseau, J.-J. "Lettre sur la musique française." *Les Oeuvres complètes de J.-J. Rousseau*, VI, pp. 168-98. Paris: Hachette, 1891.
96. Rousseau, J.-J. *The Political Writings of Jean-Jacques Rousseau*, Ed. C. E. Vaughan. Oxford: Basil Blackwell, 1962.
97. Saint-Pierre, J. H. B. de. *Paul and Virginia*. London: Orr, 1839.
98. Schinz, A. "La Querelle Rousseau-Hume." *Annales*, 1926, XVII, pp. 13-51.
99. Schinz, A., and Lawrence, I. "Le Problèm de la date du premier séjour de Madame de Warens aux Charmettes." *Revue d'histoire littéraire de la France*, 1928, XXXV, pp. 85-91.
100. Sells, A. L. *The Early Life and Adventures of Jean-Jacques Rousseau, 1712-1740*. Cambridge: W. Heffer & Sons, 1929.

101. Simmons, E. J. *Leo Tolstoy*. New York: Vintage, 1960.
102. Smiley, J. R. *Diderot's Relations with Grimm*. Urbana, Ill.: University of Illinois Press, 1950.
103. Spitz, D. *Patterns of Anti-Democratic Thought*. New York: Macmillan, 1949.
104. Starobinski, J. *Jean-Jacques Rousseau, la transparence et l'obstacle*. Paris: Plon, 1957.
105. Starobinski, J. "The Illness of Rousseau." *Yale French Studies*, 1962, XXVIII, pp. 64-74.
106. Stone, J. T. (pseudonym) "The Theory and Practice of Psychoanalysis." (Unpublished paper.)
107. Talmon, J. L. *The Origins of Totalitarian Democracy*. London: Secker & Warburg, 1952.
108. Temmer, M. J. "Rousseau and Thoreau." *Yale French Studies*, 1962, XXVIII, pp. 112-20.
109. Tocqueville, A. de. *The Old Régime and the French Revolution*. Garden City: Doubleday, 1955.
110. Tocqueville, A. de. *Democracy in America*. Tr. Henry Reeve. London: Oxford University Press, 1946.
111. Tolstoi, L. (A letter written to the Société Jean-Jacques Rousseau), *Annales*, 1905, I, p. 7.
112. Torrey, N. L. "Rousseau's Quarrel with Grimm and Diderot," from *Essays in Honor of Albert Feuillerat*. New Haven: Yale University Press, 1943.
113. Toynbee, A. *A Study of History*. London: Oxford University, 1934-39.
114. Tucker, R. *Philosophy and Myth in Karl Marx*. Cambridge: Cambridge University Press, 1964.
115. Vallette, G. "La Condamnation de Rousseau à Genève." *Annales*, 1907, III, pp. 225-42.
116. Voltaire, F.-M. A. de. *Les Oeuvres complètes de Voltaire*. Société Littéraire, Typographique, 1785.
117. Voltaire, F.-M. A. de. "Sentiment des citoyens," in *Les Oeuvres de Voltaire* by M. Beuchot, XLII, pp. 75-84. Paris: Chez Lefèvre, 1831.
118. Vulliamy, C. E. *Rousseau*. London: G. Bles, 1931.
119. Walzer, M. *The Revolution of the Saints*. Cambridge: Harvard University Press, 1965.
120. Wilson, E. *The Wound and the Bow*. New York: Oxford University Press, 1965.
121. Winwar, Francis. *Jean-Jacques Rousseau, Conscience of an Era*. New York: Random House, 1961.
122. Wortis, J. "Freudianism and the Psychoanalytic Tradition." *American Journal of Psychiatry*, 1945, CI, pp. 814-20.

Index